Integrating the Rorschach and the MMPI-2 in Personality Assessment

The LEA Series in
Personality and Clinical Psychology
Irving B. Weiner, Editor

Integrating the Rorschach and the MMPI-2 in Personality Assessment

Ronald J. Ganellen
Michael Reese Hospital and Medical Center
and
University of Illinois at Chicago

LEA   LAWRENCE ERLBAUM ASSOCIATES, PUBLISHERS
1996   Mahwah, New Jersey

Lawrence Erlbaum Associates, Inc., Publishers
10 Industrial Avenue
Mahwah, New Jersey 07430-2262

Library of Congress Cataloging-in-Publication Data

Ganellen, Ronald J.
   Integrating the Rorschach and the MMPI-2 in personality assessment
 / Ronald J. Ganellen.
      p.   cm.
   Includes bibliographical references and index.
   ISBN 0-8058-1617-8 (c : alk. paper)
      1. Rorschach Test.   2. Minnesota Multiphasic Personality Inventory.
   3. Personality assessment.   I. Title.
   BF698.8.8.R5G36   1996
   155.2'83 – dc20   96–2583
                                                         CIP

Books published by Lawrence Erlbaum Associates are printed
on acid-free paper, and their bindings are chosen for strength
and durability.

Printed in the United States of America
10 9 8 7 6 5 4 3 2 1

Contents

Preface

The impetus for writing this book came from my experience at Michael Reese Hospital and Medical Center where I have participated in a training program for psychology interns and externs as a clinical supervisor, teacher, and staff psychologist. Most graduate students enter this program having been exposed in classes and in their clinical training to both the Rorschach and the MMPI-2, the most widely used projective and objective instruments for personality assessment. Over the years I have observed that many trainees believe strongly in *either* the MMPI-2 or the Rorschach and therefore emphasize the findings from one test when conducting a personality assessment, showing relatively less interest in the other test. It is rarely the case that trainees have learned to integrate the results from the Rorschach and MMPI-2, nor have they learned to consider the clinical implications when test findings converge, diverge, or complement one another.

The tendency to rely primarily on either the MMPI-2 or the Rorschach and to assume that that instrument consistently provides the most meaningful data whereas the other consistently yields relatively little of value reflects a schism within the community of psychologists actively involved in clinical personality assessment. This division is evident in the large body of literature concerning the MMPI-2 and Rorschach that treats these different approaches to personality assessment independently, often without reference to the other approach, and provides little guidance on using these two powerful assessment techniques conjointly to develop meaningful inferences about an individual's psychological makeup, symptoms, and the reasons for their behavior. Although much has been written about each test individually, little has been written about how to use the two tests together, even though many psychologists use a battery of psychological tests when conducting personality assessments in clinical practice.

The basic premise of this book is that the psychologist's armamentarium of assessment techniques can be strengthened by using the Rorschach and MMPI-2 together in a complementary fashion, and that essential information may be lost if one test is used to the exclusion of the other. A framework for integrating Rorschach and MMPI-2 findings in a complementary fashion based on existing research findings and clinical theory is presented.

Interest in using the MMPI-2 and Rorschach may be influenced by psychologists' impressions and beliefs about these tests. Experience suggests that some widely held assumptions about these tests are either outdated or unfounded. The first chapter, therefore, identifies and critically examines common stereotypes and prejudices concerning the MMPI-2 and Rorschach. The fact that the MMPI-2 and Rorschach have comparable reliability and validity may come as a surprise to those psychologists who dismissed the Rorschach because of the questionable psychometric properties of Rorschach systems that existed prior to the development of the Exner Comprehensive System and who are unaware that the Rorschach has been shown to have respectable reliability and validity when the procedures and principles of the Comprehensive System are followed.

A relatively small number of empirical studies have examined interrelationships among the MMPI and Rorschach. In general, the two have low levels of correlation, if any correlation is found at all. Methodological issues limiting the conclusions that can be drawn from these studies are discussed in chapter 2. These issues include changes over time in the method of administering, scoring, and interpreting the Rorschach; criteria used to include or exclude subjects based on the validity of their test protocols; ambiguity concerning definition of the constructs being measured; and application of inappropriate statistical methods, among others. In addition, questions are raised concerning the situations in which the Rorschach and MMPI-2 should and should not be expected to correlate given differences in the approach to assessing psychological functioning each employs.

Although personality assessment frequently involves administration of a battery of tests, relatively little has been written about how to integrate the results from one test with results from other tests. A conceptual framework for integrating the diverse data from the Rorschach and MMPI-2 is presented in chapters 3 through 5, which explain how the interpretive process proceeds when test findings converge, when they diverge, and when they complement one another. One central point in this discussion involves the recognition that findings may be related at different levels, the level of specific test scores or the level of specific psychological constructs. Issues to consider when test findings appear discrepant are outlined systematically, including weighing how robust each measure is, the strength of association each has with a criterion variable, and the possibility that discrepancies among test findings highlight a psychological conflict or occur because objective and projective tests may be differentially sensitive to those psychological characteristics patients acknowledge as opposed to those characteristics about which they have limited awareness. Ways in which relationships among the measures can be used to modify, accentuate, or tone down interpretations are discussed in chapter 5. Although the framework presented focuses specifically on conjoint use of the MMPI and Rorschach, the general principles apply to integration of findings from any measures of personality functioning, such as the conjoint use of the Rorschach, MMPI-2, MCMI, TAT, or PAI.

The historical association between specific theoretical positions, the MMPI, and the Rorschach also influences clinician's choice of assessment instruments. Naturally, psychologists select the tests they believe are most compatible with the theoretical orientation to which they adhere. Rather than assuming that a test is allied with a particular theoretical position, this book advocates that clinical interpretation of test data will be most valuable when the clinician uses both the empirical and theoretical literatures. The important ways in which theories of personality, psychological development, and psychopathology enrich conceptualizations of individual cases are discussed in chapters 3 through 5.

This approach to developing an integrated interpretation of MMPI-2 and Rorschach findings is illustrated in a series of in-depth case presentations in chapters 6 through 15. In each case, historical information, diagnostic issues, and relevant research findings are discussed before MMPI-2 and Rorschach data are considered. A balance is maintained between the foundation provided by research and by clinical theory for conceptualizing and understanding patients with a variety of psychological disorders. The discussion of the test data in these case examples assumes that the reader is familiar with current approaches to interpretation of the MMPI-2 (Butcher & Williams, 1992; Friedman, Webb, & Lewak, 1989; Graham, 1993; Greene, 1991) and the Rorschach Comprehensive System, including the search strategy Exner developed specifying the order in which Rorschach variables are considered during the interpretive process (Exner, 1991, 1993).

The cases presented in chapters 6 through 15 reflect one reality of clinical practice, namely that for some patients MMPI-2 and Rorschach data converge neatly, for others the results diverge, and for still others the findings can guide the clinician to highlight or modify a specific conclusion. An attempt is also made to illustrate how MMPI-2 and Rorschach results can be translated from the jargon associated with each test into clinically meaningful conceptualizations of an individual patient's psychological organization, emotional adaptation, and patterns of interpersonal functioning.

Practical applications of integrated MMPI-2–Rorschach findings are discussed in the case presentations, including the implications of these findings for differential diagnosis and for treatment planning. Although no one-to-one correspondence exists between the criteria needed to make a *DSM–IV* diagnosis and MMPI-2 or Rorschach variables, psychological tests are not irrelevant when a referral involves questions of differential diagnosis. The ways in which historical information, clinical data, and MMPI-2 and Rorschach findings contribute to the process of differential diagnosis are considered. The implications of test findings for selecting specific therapeutic modalities, anticipating difficulties in the course of treatment, and anticipating issues likely to arise in the therapeutic relationship are reviewed in each case presentation.

As powerful as the MMPI-2 and the Rorschach are in terms of the information each provides concerning an individual's psychological makeup, neither test is infallible and neither test provides "all" the answers in all cases. The strengths and weaknesses of each test are considered carefully for specific clinical issues, such as identifying a potential for substance abuse or the ability to regulate expression of emotions. In addition, the unique contribution each makes to an understanding of individual patients is weighed in the case examples. It is my hope that the guidelines presented in this volume for integrating Rorschach and MMPI-2 data will be of value for advanced graduate students who are learning the fundamentals of test administration, scoring, and interpretation; for practicing clinicians who use the MMPI-2 and Rorschach in their clinical practice; and, ultimately, for the patients we serve.

ACKNOWLEDGMENTS

As I have grown older, I have learned that many sayings that sound like empty clichés when first heard often contain a kernel of truth, and sometimes several kernels of truth. One such cliché is that a teacher often learns more from teaching than the students who are taking the class. At the risk of sounding as though I were spouting platitudes, it is certainly true that I have benefitted enormously from working with the interns and externs at Michael Reese Hospital in individual supervision and in the seminars I teach. I am grateful to them for what they have taught me and for their influences in developing many of the ideas expressed in this book.

There are at least three major influences on my development as a psychologist and clinician. During graduate school I was fortunate to establish a productive collaboration with Paul Blaney, PhD, who was an excellent role model as a scientist-practitioner. His encouragement, patience, and sound, critical feedback were essential to my intellectual development. Chuck Carver, PhD, was also a significant influence whose intellectual rigor, clear thinking, methodological sophistication, skill at writing, and sharp wit are ideals to which I aspire.

While a postdoctoral fellow at the University of Chicago, I became involved in a supervision group led by Merton Gill, MD, an experience that has profoundly shaped the ways in which I conceptualize psychotherapy, dynamics, psychological problems, and theory. Merton's passion for ideas, love of a good argument, sensitivity to the core issues expressed by patients, impatience with dogma, and intolerance for intellectual sloppiness were always provocative, invigorating, and insightful—although being at the receiving end when he let loose was not always comfortable! My appreciation for the painful internal conflicts, emotional difficulties, and interpersonal problems with which patients struggle was deepened by Merton's compassion and by the sophisticated and empathic input of the other members of the group, from whom I benefitted greatly.

It has been my good fortune over the past 10 years to have found a comfortable and stimulating professional home at Michael Reese. Martin Harrow, PhD, David Hawkins, MD, and Harry Soloway, MD, played important roles in creating an environment that promoted my professional and intellectual development and provided the freedom to pursue this and other projects. My colleagues in psychology, Floyd Irvin, PhD, Vita Krall, PhD, Neal Rubin, PhD, Peter Shabad, PhD, Billie Strauss, PhD, and Debbie Zimmerman, PhD, have also taught me much about clinical issues and challenged me to critically examine and, as needed, modify my beliefs, assumptions, and values concerning a variety of professional issues.

My interest in the Rorschach was sparked to a large extent by Phil Erdberg, PhD, who made the Structural Summary come alive for me, as he has for many others. His talent for explaining how those numbers, ratios, and indices say something not only statistically meaningful, but also psychologically meaningful and vivid about a living, breathing person's life situation is astonishing. Phil's encouragement when I considered whether or not to write this book and his helpful feedback along the way are deeply appreciated.

One impetus for this book was a series of lively and, at times, heated discussions about a variety of issues related to clinical uses of the MMPI-2 and Rorschach with Peter Newman, PhD. His grasp of these tests, awareness of their shortcomings, and skeptical view of the research relating to them was challenging and thought provoking.

Irv Weiner's wise counsel as this book was being written was invaluable.

His grasp of the literature; ability to convey complicated and subtle issues clearly, succinctly, and elegantly; and careful attention to detail improved the quality of this work greatly.

A number of colleagues made helpful comments about early drafts of the material contained in this book. I am particularly thankful for the time and energy spent in this regard by Seth Warschausky, PhD, and Alfred Sporn, MD.

Finally, I am deeply indebted to my wife, Natalia, for her constant encouragement, understanding, and tolerance while this book was being written — as well as for agreeing not only to read and comment on drafts of each chapter, but also for her perseverance and willingness to listen patiently as I described the progress of the book and the thoughts, ideas, and issues I was grappling with, even when she was sleep deprived after our third child was born. This book would never have been completed had it not been for her love and support.

1 Introduction

The Minnesota Multiphasic Personality Inventory (MMPI, MMPI-2, and MMPI-A) and the Rorschach are the two tests used most widely in clinical personality assessment to evaluate personality functioning, current emotional state, and the presence, nature, and severity of psychopathology, as well as to formulate treatment interventions (Archer, Maruish, Imhof, & Piotrowski, 1991; Lubin, Larsen, & Matarazzo, 1984; Lubin, Larsen, Matarazzo, & Seever, 1985; Piotrowski, Sherry, & Keller, 1985; Watkins, 1991; Watkins, Campbell, Nieberding, & Hallmark, 1995). Psychologists' vigorous interest in and intense loyalty to the Rorschach and MMPI are reflected in the large and still growing theoretical and empirical literature concerning these tests. Butcher (1987), for instance, reported that more than 10,000 books and articles on the MMPI had been published between 1943 and 1986, whereas Exner (1986) reported that more than 4,000 books and articles on the Rorschach had been published by 1970. Butcher and Rouse (in press) tallied the number of research articles concerning psychological assessment methods in adults and found that the most frequently researched tests were the MMPI/MMPI-2 and Rorschach, with 4,542 and 1,969 articles published between 1974 and 1994, respectively.

Given the enduring popularity of these two tests, it is an unexpected surprise to find that only a small percentage of these numerous studies have examined the relationships between the Rorschach and MMPI (Archer & Krishnamurthy, 1993a, 1993b). For instance, Archer and Krishnamurthy's comprehensive literature reviews of MMPI–Rorschach interrelationships

1

identified fewer than 50 studies examining this issue among adults and adolescents. In other words, less than 1% of the more than 16,000 publications pertaining to the MMPI and Rorschach have directly addressed the relationship between these widely used personality tests. The reasons that this topic has been virtually ignored deserves consideration.

One might speculate that the lack of attention to how these tests relate to one another and to clinical phenomena reflects a tendency for practitioners to use only one personality test instrument when performing a psychological evaluation. Thus, some clinicians might give a Rorschach and not a MMPI-2, whereas others might give an MMPI-2 and not a Rorschach. However, in clinical practice, it is quite common for a psychologist to administer a battery of tests rather than relying exclusively on one test alone. The use of a test battery was initially described by Rapaport, Gill, and Schafer (1945), who illustrated how the clinician could combine data from different sources of information to create a fuller, richer, more accurate, and more complete description of an individual than could be reached from the results of one test in isolation. Graham (1993) endorsed a similar approach to psychological assessment in a discussion of strategies for interpreting the MMPI-2 when he stated that "the inferences generated from an individual's MMPI-2 protocol should thus be validated against other test and nontest information. . . .The MMPI-2 will be most valuable as an assessment tool when it is used in conjunction with other psychological tests, interview and observational data, and appropriate background information" (p. 200).

The fact that so little attention has been given to the conjoint use of the MMPI-2 and Rorschach reflects the existence of two distinct camps within psychology that developed soon after each test was developed and introduced into clinical practice. Historically, these camps have differed in terms of their philosophy about personality assessment, their theoretical orientation, and, as a result, their loyalty to one test or the other. Although open hostilities have never broken out between these two groups, members of each camp have tended to view the methods of psychological assessment and test interpretation practiced by the other with considerable skepticism and active distrust.

Historically, the MMPI-2 and Rorschach have been associated with very different traditions and theoretical orientations. The Rorschach was initially developed using an empirical, atheoretical approach (Rorschach, 1921/1942), and this tradition was further advanced by others (Beck, Beck, Levitt, & Molish, 1961; Klopfer & Kelley, 1942; Piotrowski, 1957). Since the pioneering work of Rapaport et al. (1945), however, the Rorschach has been associated with the psychodynamic tradition. Lerner (1991), for instance, described Rapaport's integration of psychoanalytic thinking and

Rorschach methodology in the following manner: "Rorschach did not wed his procedure to a specific theory of personality — Rapaport did. The marriage forged by Rapaport between the Rorschach and psychoanalysis was a perfect one of technique and theory" (p. vii).

In contrast, the MMPI-2 has been associated with the tradition of "dust bowl empiricism" that aimed to base interpretation of personality test data entirely on empirically identified behavioral, psychological, and diagnostic correlates of test data independent of a particular theory of personality and psychopathology. In this tradition, interpretation of personality test data ideally would be generated by actuarial formulas or interpretive "cookbooks" rather than by a psychologist relying on clinical judgment and familiarity with theory. This philosophy was articulated by Meehl (1954) when he argued that actuarial predictions are more reliable and more cost effective than clinical prediction:

> Putting it bluntly, it suggests that for a rather wide range of clinical problems involving personality description from tests, the clinical interpreter is a costly middleman who might better be eliminated. An initial outlay of research time could result in a cookbook whose recipes would encompass the great majority of psychometric configurations seen in daily clinical work. . . . I invite you to consider the possibility that the emotional block we all experience in connection with the cookbook approach could be dissolved simply by trying it out until our daily successes finally get us accustomed to the idea. (p. 271)

It is easy to imagine how these two very different philosophies concerning personality assessment contributed to a division among psychologists actively involved in clinical personality assessment. As a result, many practitioners seem to have developed a strong allegiance to one test, the MMPI or the Rorschach, and to rely on that test when performing psychological assessments. The other test was then viewed, at best, with great skepticism and considered to have marginal relevance to the clinical issues at hand or, at worst, dismissed as being useless.

These attitudes and allegiances have been transmitted directly and indirectly to successive cohorts of psychologists by instructors teaching courses on personality assessment and by clinical supervisors in a variety of ways, such as their discussions of the merits and shortcomings of each test, judgments about the value each test has, and by example during supervision of trainee's cases or presentation of their own clinical work. Of course, many clinicians do use both tests when performing psychological assessments, although a large proportion of these clinicians seem to favor either the MMPI or Rorschach and to rely primarily on that favored test. Other clinicians earnestly try to use both tests but have had little training or guidance on how to combine the results from both of these powerful tests to develop meaningful inferences about the patient's psychological make-up, symptoms, and the reasons for their behavior.

Stereotypes concerning the strengths and weaknesses of the Rorschach and MMPI that reflect the biases and beliefs of the two camps are heard frequently and fairly consistently. The next section presents and then discusses the accuracy and fairness of the stereotypes expressed by members of the psychology community, including supervisors, instructors of assessment courses, colleagues, graduate students, and trainees, as well as those attitudes expressed explicitly and implicitly in the literature.

Proponents of the Rorschach historically have talked about the MMPI-2 as though it provides information about patients' symptoms but is otherwise superficial because they believe it provides only limited data about patients' personality characteristics and the dynamics of their behavior. The MMPI-2 is a self-report instrument, thus the information provided by the MMPI-2 is thought to be limited to what persons want to say about themselves. Furthermore, many Rorschachers think of MMPI-2 interpretations as involving a rote recitation of a series of prefabricated, probabilistic statements, most of which are not relevant to the individual patient. In contrast, the proponents of the Rorschach view the Rorschach as a rich source of information about each individual's affective life, defensive operations, wishes, drives, conflicts, and interpersonal functioning, information they believe cannot be provided by the MMPI-2. Furthermore, they extol the virtues of the Rorschach as a psychodynamic instrument that allows "deep" interpretations in contrast to the superficial listing of symptoms obtained from the MMPI-2.

Proponents of the MMPI-2, on the other hand, proudly refer to the extensive research that has demonstrated convincingly the test's validity, reliability, and usefulness in clinical practice. They emphasize the fact that reliable descriptions of an individual's symptomatology, interpersonal functioning, self-perception, and behavior can be reported after the clinician identifies the extra-test correlates of clinical scales and high-point codetypes. Interpretations of the MMPI-2 profile can be trusted because they are based on a solid empirical foundation. In contrast, the MMPIer traditionally distrusts the Rorschach because of its reliance on the "projective hypothesis," questionable psychometric properties, and connection with a psychodynamic orientation. From this perspective, results of the Rorschach have historically been considered to be completely subjective, unlike the objective results of the MMPI-2, and were therefore viewed with considerable skepticism as having about the same reliability as reading tea leaves and as reflecting the examiner's gut impressions, intuition, and personal preoccupations rather than reliably saying anything tangible and substantial about a particular patient.

These stereotypes about each test are examined critically here.

LIMITS DUE TO THE SELF-REPORT FORMAT

Obviously, one way in which the MMPI and Rorschach differ involves the method for obtaining information about the testee. The MMPI uses a self-report format in which individuals completing the test decide whether or not a series of statements are accurate descriptions of their mood, behavior, and attitudes, whereas during the Rorschach the individual is asked to describe what a series of inkblots might be.

The format of the MMPI has been viewed by some as limiting the data to the conception subjects have of themselves as well as their concerns about self-presentation. For instance, Acklin (1993) stated that:

> The MMPI is a self-report instrument. The broad range of the item pool provides the opportunity for the test taker to create a sort of psychological self-report within the parameters of the test's fixed response format. Despite the K correction and validity scales, the test must inevitably be seen in light of the way the person sees himself or herself or wishes to be seen by others. . . .we could say that the MMPI assesses the domain of self-report of problems, symptoms, and behaviors in which the view that the person has of himself or herself or the way that he or she wishes to be seen by others emerges. (p. 127)

A similar point was made by Meyer (1994), who contrasted self-report and projective methods of personality assessment. Meyer characterized self-report methods, such as the MMPI-2, as tapping patients' "conscious self-awareness and verbally-mediated self-representations, while the other (projective) method of assessment, such as the Rorschach, yields data about tacit representations of self and others, un-reflected upon modes of perceiving the world, and underlying feelings, conflicts, and dynamics" (p. 5). In other words, one might conclude that because of its self-report format, information obtained from the MMPI-2 is limited to what patients know about themselves and what they want the clinician to know about them.

Although it is true that the MMPI-2 is a self-report instrument, there are several reasons why results from the MMPI-2 are not limited simply to what persons say about themselves. First, the MMPI-2 clinical scales were constructed using an empirical criterion approach, rather than being constructed on the basis of item content and face validity. Items were included on each scale only because a group of patients who met diagnostic criteria for a particular disorder responded differently to that item than did the normative group. Items were organized into scales without regard for the content of the items and without regard for whether the items accurately described the criterion group. Greene (1991), for example, discussed how psychopaths responded differently than would be expected to the item, "I have been quite independent and free from family rule." Although one might expect psychopaths to say this was true of them on the basis of an expected history of disregard for rules, psychopaths in fact said this item was false more often than the normative group. This does not mean that psychopaths have actually been constricted and constrained by family rule. From an empirical perspective, it is not as important whether subjects accurately describe themselves as that there is an empirically demonstrated association between a particular response and a given scale. Thus, subjects' knowledge about themselves or their willingness to acknowledge certain information about themselves is not the issue; the issue is whether subjects respond to items in a manner similar to a group of patients with specific psychological characteristics.

Second, the view articulated by Acklin and Meyer may be true for an instrument that is face valid, such as a depression checklist containing a number of items addressing specific symptoms of depression and no more. As discussed previously, however, MMPI-2 interpretation does not rely on the face validity of items endorsed by patients but involves identifying psychological characteristics found to be empirically associated with elevations on a particular scale or with a defined codetype. These correlates go beyond a simple checklist of symptoms, problems, or diagnosis to discuss characteristic behaviors, patterns of interpersonal functioning, self-perception, dynamics, defenses, and, in some instances, family background (e.g., Gilberstadt & Duker, 1965). Thus, an MMPI-2 profile may reveal information about an individual's psychological makeup that was not addressed directly, overtly, or explicitly in the content of any of the 567 items to which they responded. As a result, subjects are not likely to be aware of all the information they have revealed about themselves, information they may not have wanted to expose as well as information about which they may have little or no conscious awareness. In other words, the psychological characteristics, mood states, defenses, concerns, and dynamics associated with each MMPI-2 codetype often go beyond what individuals consciously "know" and are willing to say about themselves to identify aspects of their psychological functioning they may not acknowledge or recognize. This is important as it is generally accepted that clinical disorders frequently involve defensive efforts to deny, repress, disavow, project, or split off from conscious awareness painful, shameful, or unacceptable emotions and negative self-perceptions.

For instance, a 45-year-old woman, Mrs. N, was referred for a psychological evaluation by the court during a bitter divorce proceeding with a central dispute involving custody of her three children. Mrs. N claimed that the father had proven himself to be an irresponsible, unfit parent when he moved out of the house, initiated divorce proceedings, and did not provide financial support for the family for several months. She insisted he had forfeited his right to have a say about any decisions regarding the children in the future as a result of these actions. The father expressed concern to the court about his wife's capacity to parent because of incidents when she allegedly lost control, angrily hit, kicked, and pushed the children, and broke furniture. He claimed he had to restrain her during these outbursts. He also claimed that Mrs. N abused alcohol, marijuana, and cocaine. She adamantly denied all of these allegations. The judge ordered both parents to complete psychological evaluations to assess their psychological functioning, capacity to parent, and potential for aggressive, violent behavior.

In this context, only Mrs. N's MMPI-2 profile is presented (see profile at end of this chapter). These results are directly relevant to the issues discussed previously concerning individuals' control over what they reveal about their psychological functioning in a self-report format. The validity scale configuration indicates Mrs. N's responses to the MMPI-2 were skewed by a naive attempt to create a picture of robust psychological health. She described herself as being morally virtuous and emotionally stable, while denying and minimizing problems. This configuration is quite common when someone knows that a decision about an important outcome will be based in large part on the results of a psychological evaluation. In this situation, Mrs. N had a considerable incentive to emphasize positive features about herself and to minimize and deny emotional and behavioral difficulties.

This defensive response set has the effect of lowering scores on the MMPI-2 clinical scales. This suggests that Mrs. N's scores on the clinical scales might have been higher had she responded openly and honestly to the MMPI-2. In spite of her efforts to deny psychological problems, however, she produced elevations on scales *4* (Psychopathic Deviate) and *9* (Mania). The *49/94* two-point codetype describes this woman as having a marked disregard for social standards and commonly held values. Behavioral correlates of this codetype include a tendency to act impulsively, poor judgment, limited frustration tolerance, and intense feelings of anger and hostility. She has a poorly developed conscience and may have a history of current or past antisocial behavior. Based on these behavioral correlates, one can infer that this profile indicates a high potential for poorly controlled, angry outbursts, particularly when she is frustrated. Furthermore, the *49/94* codetype is commonly produced by people who abuse alcohol and/or other substances, although this does not definitively identify current substance abuse.

Although this capsule summary does not do justice to all that can learned about Mrs. N from the MMPI-2, this example illustrates the point that the MMPI-2 often provides information above and beyond both what persons say about themselves and what they want others to know about their psychological characteristics. Given the context of this evaluation, it is understandable that Mrs. N tried to avoid admitting any personal problems, particularly in the areas of self-control, management of anger, impulsivity, and alcohol abuse. In spite of the efforts at impression management identified by the validity scale configuration, the profile of clinical scales revealed information that could potentially be quite damaging to Mrs. N's position in the divorce proceedings. This example indicates that information obtained from the MMPI-2, particularly the behavioral correlates associated with particular codetypes, frequently reveals information about individuals' psychological functioning that goes beyond persons' self-image or the image they would like to project to others. Furthermore, the clinical correlates of MMPI-2 codetypes can provide valuable insights into aspects of psychological functioning outside of individuals' conscious awareness. The contributions of the MMPI-2 and the Rorschach to identifying and accurately describing psychological characteristics that have been minimized or concealed for conscious or unconscious reasons are discussed further in chapter 5.

SYMPTOMS VERSUS DYNAMICS

One stereotype held by Rorschachers concerning the MMPI-2 involves the perception that the MMPI-2 data is used to describe the symptoms and overt behaviors reported by the subjects and little else. In its most extreme form, this stereotype includes the belief that MMPI-2 test results are used simply to string together a set of symptoms and behaviors in an overly general way without reference to the individual patient. Furthermore, the MMPI-2 data are viewed as being incapable of identifying and describing persons' issues, conflicts, and defenses. In contrast, individuals' responses to the Rorschach are thought to directly represent their inner world and psychic reality. This attitude is captured in the following comments:

> The MMPI provides a picture of manifest problems, symptoms, and personality characteristics. . . .The rationale for the Rorschach's inclusion in the test battery [is that it] provides a less structured task than the MMPI, allowing more leeway of response and consequently richer clinical material. . . .The Rorschach is best suited to elucidating personality organization and dynamics in contrast to the MMPI's focus on manifest symptoms and problems. (Acklin, 1993, p. 128)

This attitude may be broken down into two subgroups, one relating to the clinician's theoretical affiliation and the other to the clinician's comfort with these tests.

Theoretical Loyalty

The belief that the MMPI-2 picks up information only at the level of external reality, manifest behavior, and symptoms whereas the Rorschach picks up information at the level of internal reality including subjects' dynamics, conflicts, and defenses is a direct reflection of the view that the Rorschach "belongs" to the psychodynamically oriented practitioner, whereas the MMPI-2 "belongs" to practitioners with an empirical orientation. One should not automatically assume that these tests are associated with one school of thought and none another. It is not the test itself that makes it a dynamic or an empirical instrument, it is how the practitioner uses the test that makes the difference. In other words, the practitioner's philosophy determines how the test data are interpreted.

For instance, the Wechsler Adult Intelligence Scale–Revised (WAIS–R) and Wechsler Intelligence Scale for Children–III (WISC–III) (Wechsler, 1981, 1991) are widely regarded as objective assessment instruments used to identify mental retardation, classify level of intellectual ability, measure areas of cognitive strengths and weaknesses, and identify deterioration in intellectual functioning as a result of neuropsychological insult or psychiatric disturbance. The development and construction of the WAIS–R and WISC–III have been commended for the size and representativeness of the standardization samples and attention to issues of reliability, as well as attempts to establish their concurrent validity, construct validity, and criterion-related validity (Anastasi, 1988). For these reasons, the Wechsler scales are generally viewed as paragons of objective psychological tests that set the standard for subsequent test development.

Although the Wechsler scales are objective psychological test instruments, some psychologists interpret the Wechsler tests using both objective and projective approaches (Allison, Blatt, & Zimet, 1988; Rapaport et al., 1945). Allison et al. (1988), for instance, proposed that an individual's ego functioning can be understood by analyzing the patterns of scatter among WAIS subtests. For example, they suggested that significant discrepancies between scores on the Information and Vocabulary subtests reflect specific defenses or personality styles. When Information is significantly lower than Vocabulary, the following possibility should be considered: One of the individual's primary defenses is repression that interferes with his or her ability to acquire general knowledge or to retrieve material from memory storage. These blocks in memory functioning caused by repression are often associated with an hysterical personality organization. When Vocabulary is significantly lower than Information, in contrast, another possibility should be considered: This individual has a high investment in intellectual pursuits and shows a careful, if not excessive attention to detail, characteristics that are often associated with an obsessive–compulsive personality organization.

It should be noted, however, that the interpretations suggested by Allison et al. are largely conceptual in nature, have not been well supported by empirical research, and may not be representative of the approach used by most psychologists.

This discussion of different approaches to interpreting the WAIS–R and WISC–III points out that although the Wechsler scales are clearly objective measures, they are used as projective measures by some clinicians, whether or not that was the purpose originally intended by the test developer. This underscores the point that no test instrument is intrinsically allied with a particular theoretical orientation but that tests are used by a clinician informed by a specific theoretical framework who makes sense out of the test data in a manner consistent with that framework.

Although the Rorschach has commonly been thought of as allied with the psychodynamic tradition, some Rorschach systematizers have explicitly stated that the Rorschach can be interpreted without reference to psycho-analytic theory (Rorschach, 1921/1942). Piotrowski (1957), for instance, took the position that the clinician need not hold a particular theoretical framework in order to interpret the Rorschach. Similarly, whereas the MMPI has traditionally been thought of as atheoretical, some psychologists have interpreted MMPI data from a psychodynamic perspective (e.g., Trimboli & Kilgore, 1983). In other words, it is not the test itself that determines how data obtained from that test are interpreted, it is the psychologist doing the interpretation who operates within the framework of a particular theory of personality functioning and psychopathology. This point was expressed somewhat differently by Schafer (1954) when he stated that, "no matter how helpful a clinical tool it may be, the psychological test cannot do its own thinking. What it accomplishes depends upon the thinking that guides its application. The guiding thought is psychological theory, whether explicit and systematized or implicit and unsystematized" (p. xi).

Comfort

The second issue related to the belief that the MMPI-2 is limited to overt behavior and self-reported symptoms is a reflection of many clinicians' discomfort with the MMPI-2. Based on an informal survey of trainees over several years at Michael Reese Hospital, it is my impression that some clinicians are turned off by the MMPI-2 because they think it is to be used in the following fashion; by looking up interpretations in the existing interpretive manuals and cookbooks and then simply copying down the descriptors associated with a particular scale elevation and/or codetype. That is, psychologists often feel constrained that they must say only, no more and no less, what is contained in the cookbook, rather than using that information as the starting point for developing hypotheses about a particular patient. Put differently, some clinicians see the MMPI as yielding global, general statements obtained from cookbooks at which point no further interpretation is permitted or tolerated. They believe they are not allowed to use the MMPI-2 data as the basis for generating additional inferences. Furthermore, the clinicians' hesitation to think through the various findings, decide which apply to the particular patient being evaluated, and to then attempt to integrate the findings in order to explain that patients' dynamics may be compounded if they use computer generated reports, because such reports ostensibly reflect the accumulated knowledge and wisdom of the MMPI-2 expert who wrote the interpretation.

Of course, the previous is a caricature of how the MMPI can be used to develop a description of patients based on the MMPI data to be fleshed out with historical data, the results of other test data, and inferences generated by psychologists based on their knowledge of clinical theory. Graham (1993), for instance, described in detail an approach to interpreting the MMPI-2 data that addresses the test subjects' symptoms, traits, major needs, coping strategies, self-concept, and interpersonal relationships. The dynamics and etiology of these behaviors and problems are also addressed during the interpretive process, either by reference to information contained in the relevant codetype itself or by formulating inferences about etiology and dynamics based on "the clinician's basic understanding of behavior, personality, and psychopathology" (p. 207). Graham, for instance, gave an example of an MMPI-2 profile suggesting that an individual fears being hurt or exploited by others and so avoids emotional involvement. He described how the clinician might speculate that these fearful, distrustful attitudes developed as the result of earlier experiences in which the person had been harmed, used, manipulated, or taken advantage of.

Although Graham's interpretive strategy was presented in reference to the MMPI-2, similar approaches have been advocated in discussions of interpretation of the Rorschach. Lerner (1991), for instance, proposed that interpretation of Rorschach data begins by first noting what individual test responses and test scores suggest and then integrating these findings to arrive at higher order inferences and theoretical formulations. Although couched in different terms, Exner (1993) also described how the interpretive process proceeds by first examining the test data, formulating hypotheses based on these data, and then integrating these findings into a "clinical conceptualization of the psychology of the person . . . [in which] clinicians go beyond specific data, using their propositional statements as a base and adding to that base their own deductive logic and knowledge of human behavior and psychopathology" (pp. 325–326).

This indicates that the process of clinical interpretation is similar regardless of the psychological test instrument being used. The clinician first identifies which test data and specific test scores are significant and interpretable and then identifies the correlates of that data (e.g., an elevation on the MMPI-2 scale *4* suggests difficulties with authority figures, poorly developed conscience, impulsivity, and interpersonal manipulation; a positive Rorschach Depression Index (*DEPI*), $C = 4$, and $V = 3$ suggests the presence of clinically significant depression, a negative, pessimistic view of events, self-critical attitudes, and feelings of guilt). The clinician then attempts to organize and integrate the diverse information produced during the initial step of the interpretive process. Hypotheses about these findings can then be generated, either on the basis of a set of related findings or on the basis of the clinician's knowledge about personality functioning, behavior, and psychopathology. These hypotheses allow the psychologist to extend interpretation beyond what is contained in the data itself.

As indicated previously, however, many clinicians seem to feel they are not permitted to make these higher order inferences when they use the MMPI-2 but instead feel constrained to reporting only the "facts" as determined by the cookbooks and computer generated interpretations. In contrast, many clinicians appear much more comfortable making these kinds of inferences based on clinical theory when using the Rorschach as though the subjective, "ambiguous" nature of the Rorschach gives permission to be creative, whereas the objective nature of the MMPI-2 denies permission to think for themselves and to use their clinical knowledge and theory.

A number of Rorschachers have expressed similar feelings of being constrained by the explicit guidelines for scoring and interpretation of the Comprehensive System (Aronow, Reznikoff, & Moreland, 1995; Sugarman, 1991). In spite of the hard-earned advances made by the Comprehensive System in establishing the psychometric respectability of the Rorschach, these clinicians are turned off by the Comprehensive System because they do not see how the language, the "jargon," translates into the constructs and relates to the issues they grapple with daily in clinical settings (Kleiger, 1992). Perhaps this is because Exner's approach, unlike psychodynamic approaches to the Rorschach, is determinedly atheoretical and was not intended to be directly linked to the constructs and terminology of a particular theory.

Neither the MMPI-2 nor the Comprehensive System preclude clinicians from integrating test data, clinical theory, and knowledge about behavior and psychopathology to formulate higher order inferences about an individual's psychological makeup, defenses, dynamics, and the development, meaning, and consequences of maladaptive patterns of behavior. This is consistent with the position described previously concerning the psychologists' role in test interpretation. To paraphrase Schafer (1954), the MMPI-2 and Rorschach do not do their own thinking; clinicians think, organize, integrate, and speculate about the data provided by these tests. It must be emphasized, however, that the usefulness and accuracy of clinicians' conclusions about what the MMPI-2 and Rorschach data say can only be enhanced if their inferences are firmly rooted in assessment methods and interpretive strategies that are empirically supported.

OBJECTIVITY VERSUS SUBJECTIVITY

Historically, the MMPI-2 and Rorschach have been described not only as objective and projective personality tests, respectively but also as exemplifying objective and projective methods of personality assessment. One implication of the distinction between objective and projective approaches is that objective tests provide information that is real and factual, whereas projective tests provide information that is subjective. Before accepting that the Rorschach provides subjective data whereas MMPI-2 data is factual, one must consider how objective or subjective each test is. The objective/subjective nature of several dimensions of each test are discussed here, including the format and stimuli and the scoring and interpretation of each test.

Test Stimuli

Obviously, the stimuli of the MMPI-2 and Rorschach are quite different. Subjects are asked to read and respond to a series of statements on the MMPI-2 that seem quite straightforward and clear, such as "I like mechanics magazines." In contrast, the Rorschach inkblots are generally considered to be relatively ambiguous, which allows if not demands that subjects interpret them in a highly personalized, subjective manner.

Although many MMPI-2 items are straightforward and clear, it would be a mistake to assume that individuals do not interpret the items at all as they respond to the MMPI-2. Greene (1991), for instance, discussed how test items have different meanings for different subjects and how much room there is for a subjective, highly personal reading of many MMPI-2 test items:

> For example, for a test item such as "I have headaches frequently," persons may interpret "frequently" to mean once a day, once a week, or once a month and respond "true" or "false" accordingly. One client might endorse this item as being "true" since he has headaches once a month; another might endorse this item as being "false" since she has headaches only once a week. The ambiguity inherent in any test item makes it extremely difficult to obtain a veridical self-description since the person answering a specific test item and an

observer rating the person on that item's content may each interpret the item somewhat differently. (p. 9)

A similar point was made by Weiner (1993) as he discussed the room for subjective interpretation when responding to items on self-report measures, such as "I often lose my temper." Weiner pointed out that people differ in terms of their conception of what it means to lose one's temper. A meek, inhibited, unassertive person might view raising his or her voice as an instance of losing their temper, whereas another person might view shouting with rage and pounding on the table as being appropriately assertive, but not aggressive. Furthermore, Weiner noted that no benchmark is provided to help the subject decide whether instances of loss of temper, no matter how this is defined, occur frequently or infrequently. Subjects may vary considerably in their view of how "often" is often. The MMPI does not define whether "often" means an event occurs more than once a week, weekly, or monthly. The examples given by Greene and Weiner illustrate not only that individuals interpret MMPI-2 items in a subjective manner but also that their subjective, personal understanding of items may in fact be an integral part of the assessment process.

The test stimuli in the Rorschach and MMPI-2 could not be more different. Whereas the MMPI-2 items can be characterized as statements selected to elicit certain facts about persons, such as whether their sleep is regular or fitful or if they are worried about their health, the Rorschach stimuli are artistic-looking designs created by pressing ink onto paper. Some of the abstract designs are black and white whereas others are colored. These images are not clear, exact representations of specific things, although one can easily find areas in the inkblots that resemble recognizable objects, persons, or animals, sometimes quite closely and sometimes only in an impressionistic manner. Traditionally, the rationale for using these designs in personality assessment has been that subjects can produce an almost unlimited number and variety of responses when asked to react to ambiguous stimuli. The way in which subjects perceive, organize, and interpret these unstructured images is thought to reflect fundamental aspects of their conscious and unconscious psychological functioning, including their needs, defenses, conflicts, and thought processes (Frank, 1939).

Exner (1991) presented data from a series of studies that examined whether the inkblots are as ambiguous as has been assumed. These studies found that the Rorschach images are not completely ambiguous and that each card has a particular stimulus pull that is altered if the inkblot is altered. For instance, the most common responses to Card I are of a winged animal, such as a bat or butterfly. In one study, a group of 24 subjects was asked to write at least four responses for Card I after being shown the card for 24 seconds. A second group of subjects was shown a modified version of Card I in which the winged details had been deleted. They were also asked to write at least four responses after seeing the modified image for 24 seconds. Although all subjects who saw the standard inkblot produced one or more responses involving winged objects, only one subject who viewed the modified image reported a winged object. Exner found that responses to other cards also changed significantly if the image was changed. For instance, although the most common response to Card IV involves a human or human-like figure, the frequency of human responses increased substantially if one detail (D1) was removed from the card. On the basis of these and similar findings, Exner concluded that the inkblots are not completely ambiguous. Although they are not exact representations of particular objects, the inkblots have specific features that make certain percepts and ways of organizing the card more likely than others.

Thus, the MMPI-2 stimuli are not as completely objective as may be thought whereas the Rorschach stimuli are not as completely subjective as may be thought. There are degrees of subjectivity and objectivity involved in each test's stimuli. In both instances, it is the way in which subjects respond to the stimuli that is important in terms of obtaining data that provides information about their psychological functioning.

Scoring and Interpretation

Different approaches to administering, scoring, and interpreting the Rorschach exist. Exner (1969) pointed out that before the Comprehensive System was developed, there were at least five major Rorschach systems used in the United States, the Beck, Hertz, Klopfer, Piotrowsky, and Rapaport–Schafer systems. After comparing these systems, Exner (1986) concluded:

> The breadth of differences among the Systems was so great that the notion of the Rorschach was more myth than reality. In effect, five uniquely different Rorschach tests had been created. They were similar only in that each used the same Swiss stimulus figures, and that each had included most of Rorschach's original scores and basic interpretive postulates, but even some of those had been uniquely embellished by some of the systematizers. (p. 19)

These Rorschach systems, particularly those relying substantially on content interpretation, have been criticized harshly for lacking adequate psychometric properties, such as poor inter-rater reliability for scoring and test interpretation (Jensen, 1965; Peterson, 1978). Such criticism called attention to serious limitations in the psychometric properties of early Rorschach methods. Some critics, in fact, evaluated the early Rorschach systems so negatively that they recommended that the Rorschach be abandoned. Jensen (1965), for example, reviewed the empirical status of the Rorschach and emphatically concluded:

> The Rorschach as a clinical instrument has too inadequate reliability and meager validity even in the hands of the most expert to justify any claims for its practical usefulness. . . . The question of why the Rorschach still has so many devotees and continues to be so widely used is quite another problem and beyond the scope of this review. . . . the rate of progress in clinical psychology might well be measured by the speed and thoroughness with which it gets over the Rorschach. (p. 509)

Critics of the early Rorschach systems attacked not only the limited data establishing the Rorschach's reliability but also the limited data supporting its validity and therefore the basis for sound clinical interpretation. Anastasi (1988), for example, criticized projective assessment methods in general for the lack of objectivity in scoring and interpreting test data. She concluded that significant dangers exist when test interpretation relies on the subjective approach typical of projective assessment methods. In addition to the dangers associated with poor inter-rater reliability,

> the most disturbing implication is that the interpretation of scores is often as projective for the examiner as the test stimuli are for the examinee. In other words, the final interpretation of projective test responses may reveal more about the theoretical orientation, favorite hypotheses, and personality idiosyncracies of the examiner than it does about the examinee's personality dynamics. (p. 614)

During the past several decades Exner's work has been dedicated to developing a comprehensive system for administering, scoring, and interpreting the Rorschach based on a solid empirical foundation that corrects the limitations of past Rorschach systems. Among the strengths of the Comprehensive System is the use of clearly articulated rules and standardized procedures for test administration that reduce examiner effects and increase comparability across examiners. In addition, criteria for scoring responses are spelled out in considerable detail. When these criteria are followed, high levels of inter-rater reliability for scoring are found. For example, Exner (1993, p. 138) reported inter-rater agreement of 90% or above for 28 of 32 Rorschach variables in one study and for 31 of the same 32 variables in a second study. Inter-rater reliability for the remaining variables was greater than or equal to 88%. In fact, no scoring category was included in the Comprehensive System unless inter-rater agreement for that category could be reliably demonstrated at or above the .85 level (Exner, 1986, p. 23). Thus, acceptable levels of inter-rater reliability have been established when protocols are administered and scored according to the procedures of the Comprehensive System.

The Comprehensive System has also made advances in terms of establishing empirically verified interpretations of Rorschach data. A major thrust of the research conducted by Exner and colleagues has been to identify meaningful behavioral correlates of Rorschach variables. Their efforts to establish the external validity of Rorschach data have proceeded in two ways. The first approach has examined relationships between individual Rorschach variables and extratest variables. One example of this is research concerning differences between overincorporators ($Zd > +3.5$) and underincorporators ($Zd < -3.5$). On several experimental tasks, overincorporators and underincorporators differ significantly in how they approach new situations and problems. Overincorporators are more careful, cautious, and thorough than underincorporators and, as a result, tend to be slower, although they are not necessarily more effective (Exner, 1993).

Studies of subjects differing in the number of Texture responses they produce have supported the clinical observation that T is related to subjects' needs for interpersonal closeness. Normatively, it is expected that persons will produce only one Texture response. Increased needs for closeness are suggested when $T \geq 2$. This interpretation was supported when a group of recently separated or divorced subjects was compared to a matched control group with stable relationships. As predicted, the divorced group produced significantly more T than the control group. Conversely, a cautious, reserved, detached approach to relationships is expected when $T = 0$ because the absence of T suggests an individual lacks a sense of basic trust in others. This was confirmed in a study that compared children from stable families with children in foster care who had had placements lasting no more than 14 months. As expected, children in the foster care group produced fewer responses involving T than children living with their natural parents. Furthermore, whereas 3 of the 32 control subjects had records in which T was absent, 20 of the 32 children in foster care with multiple placements had no T in their records. In a laboratory setting, subjects without T sat farther from an experimental collaborator posing as a research subject than did subjects who had T in their records, whereas subjects who had elevations in T sat as close to the collaborator as possible (Exner, 1993). These studies illustrate how Rorschach interpretation is based on empirical findings rather than on intuition or unsubstantiated clinical lore.

A second approach to establishing extratest correlates of Rorschach data has proceeded by selecting groups of subjects with a particular psychological characteristic and then identifying a cluster of Rorschach variables that discriminate between that criterion group and other patient groups or normals. The Schizophrenia Index (SCZI), Depression Index (DEPI), and

Hypervigilance Index (HVI) are several of the indices developed using this approach. It should be noted that this method conceptually parallels the approach used to develop many MMPI scales. Thus, a positive score on one of these indices strongly suggests that a subject presents with some or many of the characteristics manifested by the criterion group. If interpretation is based on scores and indices that have empirical support, then Rorschach interpretations can no longer be dismissed as being subjective and reflecting the pet theories and personal idiosyncracies of the examiner rather than identifying salient aspects of the subject's psychological makeup. Agreement about the interpretation of Rorschach data between observers knowledgeable about the Comprehensive System should be enhanced because interpretation now involves clearly specified conclusions based on empirical research.

The advances in Rorschach methodology instituted by the Comprehensive System have resulted in the Rorschach achieving respectable levels of inter-rater reliability. Furthermore, interpretation of the Rorschach is now based on an empirical criterion approach similar to that used to develop many MMPI-2 scales. All told, current Rorschach methodology using the Comprehensive System can no longer be viewed as subjective and impressionistic but instead as having a firm psychometric foundation and a solid, empirically derived basis for interpretation. Anastasi (1988), a critic of the weak psychometric properties of previous Rorschach systems, concluded that the Comprehensive System's emphasis on standardized administration, scoring, and interpretive procedures and attention to issues of inter-rater reliability, temporal stability of scores, and construct validity have "injected new life into the Rorschach" (p. 599). Overall, the objective/subjective distinction is less of an issue for current assessment practice when the MMPI-2 and the Rorschach Comprehensive System are used than in the past when Rorschach systems lacking a proven empirical foundation were the standard of clinical practice.

IMPRESSION MANAGEMENT

Rorschach proponents have argued that the MMPI-2 is more susceptible to impression management than the Rorschach because of differences in the response format of these tests. The MMPI-2 stimuli are viewed as face valid and therefore easily manipulated, whereas it is unclear how to create a particular impression on the Rorschach. One might conclude that because the Rorschach is less obvious than the MMPI-2, there is less chance for "the impression management noted in MMPI profiles" (Acklin, 1993). For instance, if someone were trying to portray himself or herself as being paranoid, it would be easy to respond consistently to all MMPI-2 items related to paranoid beliefs, persecutory delusions, and so on. However, on the Rorschach it may be more difficult to elevate the Hypervigilance Index because many of the components of this cluster are not obvious. The person would need to know that to appear paranoid he or she cannot produce any Texture responses while simultaneously being knowledgeable about Rorschach signs indicating a careful, vigilant attention to detail and heightened concern about people.

The belief that the Rorschach is impervious to conscious attempts to shape what one reveals about oneself follows logically from traditional views about projective instruments. It has been assumed that the ambiguous stimuli used in projective testing taps unconscious processes that, by definition, are not consciously controlled and therefore cannot be intentionally manipulated. However, this assumption has not been supported empirically. Exner (1991), for instance, examined the extent to which subjects' responses to the Rorschach could be altered by a particular response set introduced by the examiner (pp. 113–115). In one study, subjects were recruited for a study about social sensitivity. Subjects were assigned to one of three groups. Subjects in the first group were told that people who are sensitive to other people find it easier to see responses involving cooperative movement. A second group was informed that people who are sensitive to others find it easier to see responses involving aggressive movement, whereas a third group was informed that people who are sensitive to others find it easier to see responses with morbid content. As predicted, these sets influenced the responses given by subjects in the three groups. Subjects in the first group produced more responses involving cooperative movement, subjects in the second group produced more responses involving aggressive movement, and subjects in the third group produced more responses involving morbid content. These results indicate that responses to the Rorschach can be affected by conscious response sets to a greater degree than has been thought possible in the past.

Perry and Kinder (1990) reviewed the research examining whether responses to the Rorschach can be deliberately skewed and concluded that no firm conclusions could be reached because of methodological limitations and inconsistent results across the existing studies. Studies since this review have suggested that subjects informed about a particular disorder may be able to alter their responses to the Rorschach in a manner consistent with the particular disorder being feigned, including schizophrenia (Netter & Viglione, 1994; Perry & Kinder, 1992) and post-traumatic stress disorder (PTSD), although the role-informed subjects asked to malinger PTSD did differ from diagnosed PTSD patients in important respects (Frueh & Kinder, 1994). Similar results have been found for the MMPI-2 when role-informed subjects were instructed to simulate a specific disorder (Wetter, Baer, Berry, Robison, & Sumpter, 1993). One limitation of the

Rorschach simulations studies is that all involved college students or community volunteers whose motivation to malinger may be different than in real-life, clinical situations. Ganellen, Wasyliw, Haywood, and Grossman (1996) compared the Rorschach protocols of two groups of criminal defendants, those who responded honestly to the MMPI and those who malingered on the MMPI. Even though the malingered group attempted to portray themselves as being extremely disturbed and suffering from psychosis on the MMPI, the two groups did not differ on Rorschach variables related to psychosis.

The studies discussed previously focused on whether the Rorschach is vulnerable to deliberate attempts to fabricate or exaggerate psychopathology. A different question concerns the extent to which the Rorschach may be affected by attempts to underreport or deny psychopathology. A small number of studies have examined the effects of denial or minimization of problems on the Rorschach. Some studies have reported that Rorschach protocols administered under standard as opposed to fake-good conditions do not differ (Carp & Shavzin, 1950; Fosberg, 1938, 1941). Seamons, Howell, Carlisle, and Roe (1981) administered the Rorschach to inmates at a state prison under two conditions, when subjects were instructed to appear well adjusted as opposed to mentally ill. Subjects in the fake-good condition gave more conventional, expected responses, fewer unusual, deviant responses, and fewer responses with dramatic content. Ganellen (1994) examined the Rorschach protocols of airlines pilots examined in the context of a fitness to return to work evaluation. Even though all subjects were quite defensive on the MMPI and during the clinical interview, their Rorschach protocols indicated significant emotional distress, self-critical ideation, and difficulties in interpersonal relationships. Ganellen (1994) suggested that some defensive subjects respond to the Rorschach in a constricted manner that does not reveal anything about their psychological state, whereas other defensive subjects reveal important information about their psychological functioning on the Rorschach, information that was denied during the clinical interview and on self-report measures.

Although some defensive subjects are able to conceal and deny negative information when completing the MMPI-2, other defensive subjects do reveal meaningful, and sometimes, unflattering information about themselves on the MMPI-2. This point was illustrated previously during the discussion of the MMPI-2 of a woman involved in a custody dispute (see profile at end of this chapter). Thus, it is not the case that attempts to consciously control the impression subjects make are always successful when they complete the MMPI-2 and always fail when they complete the Rorschach. Although it may be more difficult to consciously distort responses on the Rorschach than on the MMPI-2 because of differences in test formats, these studies suggest that the Rorschach is not impervious to conscious attempts to control responses. Efforts to create a particular impression are most likely to be successful on both the Rorschach and the MMPI-2 when a subject has been informed about how patients with a particular disorder present or when persons defensively limit what they reveal about themselves.

No research has addressed the extent to which subjects who either fake-good or fake-bad are successful at doing so on both the MMPI-2 and Rorschach. Several studies suggest that in many instances subjects may adopt a response set that skews the results from one test, without simultaneously spoiling the results of the other. This suggests that a multimethod approach to personality assessment using both the MMPI-2 and Rorschach is likely to yield the most complete, accurate description of an individual, particularly when response bias is suspected.

In summary, the previous discussion indicates that commonly held stereotypes about the MMPI-2 and Rorschach Comprehensive System are not accurate. Both the Rorschach and MMPI-2 provide valuable information about an individual's symptoms, behavior, emotions, interpersonal functioning, self-concept, defenses, and dynamics. Although much has been written about each test individually, little has been written about how to use the two tests together. The basic premise of this volume is that psychologists' armamentarium of assessment techniques can be strengthened by using the MMPI-2 and Rorschach together and that essential information may be lost if one test is used to the exclusion of the other. The remainder of this volume examines interrelationships between the MMPI-2 and Rorschach on several levels, including empirical and research findings, conceptual relationships, and integration of MMPI-2 and Rorschach results for clinical personality assessment.

Name _____ Mrs. N. _____

Address _____

Occupation _____ Date Tested __/__/__

Education __12__ Age __45__ Marital Status __Separated__

Referred By _____

MMPI-2 Code _____

Scorer's Initials _____

MMPI-2

Minnesota Multiphasic Personality Inventory-2™

Profile for Basic Scales

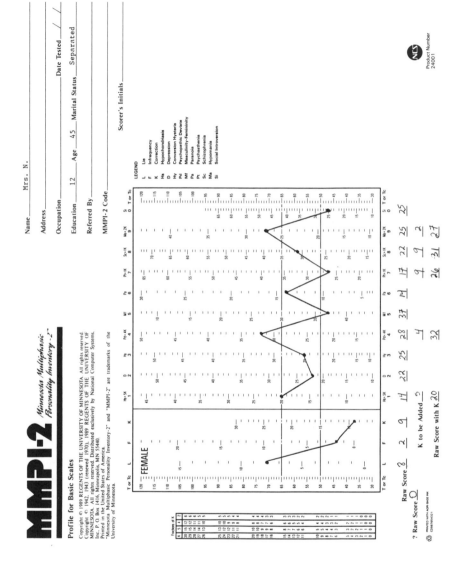

FEMALE

LEGEND

L	Lie
F	Infrequency
K	Correction
Hs	Hypochondriasis
D	Depression
Hy	Conversion Hysteria
Pd	Psychopathic Deviate
Mf	Masculinity-Femininity
Pa	Paranoia
Pt	Psychasthenia
Sc	Schizophrenia
Ma	Hypomania
Si	Social Introversion

	L	F	K	Hs+.5K	D	Hy	Pd+.4K	Mf	Pa	Pt+1K	Sc+1K	Ma+.2K	Si
Raw Score	8	2	9	14	22	25	28	37	14	17	22	25	25
? Raw Score 0			K to be Added	5			4			9	9	2	
			Raw Score with K	20			32			26	31	27	

22

2 Empirical Findings and Research Issues

(T)he best set of behavior data from which to predict a criterion is the set of data which are among themselves not correlated. This is well known and made use of in the combination of scales into (test) batteries.

—Meehl and Hathaway (1946)

As discussed in chapter 1, a relatively small number of studies have examined interrelationships among MMPI-2 and Rorschach data. These studies overall show generally weak relationships or no relationship between the two tests in adolescent and adult samples (Archer & Krishnamurthy, 1993a, 1993b). These results are unexpected, because the MMPI-2 and Rorschach were both developed to assess similar psychological constructs, such as emotional state, personality characteristics, and aspects of psychopathology. In their reviews, Archer and Krishnamurthy questioned whether the weak findings were obtained because of methodological limitations in the studies, such as the use of small sample sizes, variability in methods of administering and scoring the Rorschach, lack of control for multiple statistical tests, and failure to consider the power of the research design. In addition, the reliability of scores on the Rorschach in many of these studies is questionable because few studies reported interscorer agreement, a practice that is mandatory for publication of contemporary Rorschach research (Weiner, 1991).

The fact that the studies reviewed by Archer and Krishnamurthy involved a variety of methods for administering, scoring, and interpreting the

Rorschach is another significant methodological issue. For instance, Winter and Salcines (1958) examined the relationship between MMPI scales and scores on the Objective Rorschach, a forced-choice procedure in which the subject is asked to consider 12 alternative responses and choose the two responses that best represent the image on the card. This method differs markedly from how the Rorschach is administered according to the Comprehensive System in terms of a group versus individual and forced choice versus free association format.

It is difficult if not impossible to draw general conclusions about MMPI-2–Rorschach relationships from studies using disparate Rorschach methodology or to generalize from studies using multiple methods of administering, scoring, and interpreting the Rorschach to the system used most widely today, the Comprehensive System. Before any firm conclusions can be reached about MMPI-2–Rorschach interrelationships, a sufficient number of studies using contemporary assessment practices and adequate research methodology needs to be completed. In other words, there is insufficient data at this time on which to base a definitive judgment as to whether the Rorschach and MMPI-2 are correlated and, if they are, the magnitude of the correlation.

One might conclude that the generally low level of association between the MMPI-2 and Rorschach shows that the two tests are not related and do not overlap in measuring personality characteristics, emotional adaptation, and psychological problems. Before accepting this conclusion, however, a number of important methodological and conceptual issues must be considered. These issues are discussed here and recommendations for future research are suggested.

RELIABILITY, STABILITY, AND VALIDITY

The weak relationships between the MMPI and Rorschach could occur if they differed in their reliability and validity. This issue is particularly important to consider as the MMPI has traditionally been regarded as having better psychometric properties than the Rorschach. The MMPI is often described as the "standard of psychological assessment" (Kendall & Norton-Ford, 1982, p. 310) because of its solid empirical foundation, whereas the psychometric properties and scientific status of the Rorschach have been repeatedly challenged (Jensen, 1958; Zubin, Eron, & Schumer, 1965). Note, however, that such criticisms of the Rorschach were directed at methods used before the Comprehensive System was developed.

Several studies have examined the Rorschach's reliability and validity using meta-analysis, a procedure developed to statistically aggregate and objectively evaluate the results of a large number of studies (Smith & Glass, 1977). These meta-analyses concluded that weak support for the Rorschach was found among those studies that did not have a clear theoretical or empirical rationale, whereas studies guided by theory, prior research, or both supported the Rorschach's validity (Atkinson, 1986; Atkinson, Quarrington, Alp, & Cyr, 1986; Parker, 1983).

The relative validities and reliabilities of the MMPI and Rorschach have been compared using meta-analytic techniques (Parker, 1983; Parker, Hanson, & Hunsley, 1988). These reviews concluded that the MMPI and Rorschach are comparable in terms of their reliability, test–retest stability, and validity. These reviewers also concluded that the highest convergent validity values for both the Rorschach and MMPI were found in studies that examined specific hypotheses based on theory or prior empirical findings, whereas lower validity values were found for studies with no clear conceptual framework or rationale. Parker et al. (1988) concluded that "the MMPI and Rorschach are both valid, stable, and reliable under certain circumstances. When either test is used in the manner for which it was designed and validated, its psychometric properties are likely to be adequate for either clinical or research purposes" (p. 373). Thus, although personality assessment using the MMPI-2 and Rorschach involves different, nonoverlapping methods, extensive research has shown comparable reliability and validity for both methods.

The temporal stability of the Rorschach using the Comprehensive System and MMPI-2 can be compared by examining published test–retest data. Butcher, Dahlstrom, Graham, Tellegen, and Kaemmer (1989) reported 1-week test–retest reliability coefficients ranging between .67 for scale *6* (Paranoia) to .92 for scale *0* (Social Introversion) among males. Among the nine clinical scales (excluding *Mf*), six had test–retest reliability coefficients greater than .75. Exner (1993) presented test–retest reliability data over a 3-week period for seven Rorschach ratios and percentages central to the interpretive process. Of these, the test–retest value was greater than .75 for six of the seven variables, whereas one variable, a measure of situational distress, had a value of .59. Thus, the Rorschach and MMPI-2 have comparable test–retest reliability over a short period of time. MMPI-2 reliability data over a longer period of time was not reported by Butcher et al. (1989). Exner presented test–retest reliability data for the seven ratios and percentages described previously over a 1-year period. Again, six variables had a test–retest value above .75 whereas the measure of situational distress had a value of .64. This indicates considerable temporal stability for Rorschach data.

The data discussed previously indicate that the weak association between the MMPI and Rorschach cannot be attributed to differences in their respective reliability and validity values. Instead, other factors need to be considered to account for the low level of relationships found between them.

HYPOTHESIS TESTING VERSUS FISHING EXPEDITIONS

One limitation of many of the studies examining interrelationships between the MMPI and Rorschach is the lack of clear, theoretically based, experimental hypotheses that were tested by the researchers. Instead, a large number of studies examined data in a "shotgun" approach rather than testing specific hypotheses. For instance, researchers have looked at all possible correlations between standard MMPI scales and Rorschach variables (e.g., Dana & Bolton, 1982) or relationships between the 10 MMPI basic scales and Rorschach color responses without a clear rationale for doing so (Clark, 1948). Archer & Krishnamurthy (1993a) correlated 50 Rorschach variables with the raw scores of MMPI Scales L through Si. No a priori predictions concerning relationships among MMPI and Rorschach variables were made. Not surprisingly, of the 1,300 correlations computed (650 for each gender), few were significant.

The absence of a priori hypotheses to be tested in many studies is important not only because this violates an essential element of the scientific method on which contemporary psychological knowledge is based but also because of the effect this has on the predictive power of both the MMPI and the Rorschach. The dangers of this approach are described by Archer and Krishnamurthy (1993b) as follows: "Researchers who investigate a large number of potential relationships in an atheoretical manner may bias their research toward obtaining mostly nonsignificant findings because such investigations may be uninformed by previous research findings or sound theoretical predictions" (p. 285). A similar point was made by Kinder (1992) as he reflected on his experience reviewing manuscripts submitted for publication:

> I have encountered manuscripts in which 30, 40, or, in one case, over 60 Rorschach variables were subjected to analysis. It is unrealistic to expect that any experimental manipulation and/or comparison of two or more groups of subjects will result in meaningful differences on such large numbers of variables. Researchers should make specific predictions based on theory or previous research and analyze only those variables within any given study. (p. 257)

As described previously, several reviews have examined the Rorschach's reliability and validity using meta-analysis. These meta-analytic reviews concluded that the Rorschach's validity was supported by studies guided by theory, the results of prior research, or both, whereas little support for the Rorschach's validity was found in studies that lacked a solid theoretical or empirical foundation (Atkinson, 1986; Atkinson et al., 1986; Parker, 1983; Parker et al., 1988). Similarly, MMPI findings are weakest for undirected, exploratory studies and strongest for studies based on a clear rationale (Parker et al., 1988). Thus, the chances of obtaining significant relationships between the MMPI-2 and Rorschach are diminished greatly when research is conducted in a shotgun approach rather than being based on clearly articulated experimental hypotheses. Because many studies examining MMPI–Rorschach interrelationships were not based on a firm theoretical or empirical foundation (cf. Archer & Krishnamurthy, 1993a; Clark, 1948; Dana & Bolton, 1982), it is not surprising that many reports of weak or nonexistent relationships between the MMPI and Rorschach have been reported.

Future research should examine associations between MMPI-2 and Rorschach variables hypothesized to be related because findings from previous empirical studies show they are related to one another, because each are conceptually related to a specific construct, such as social discomfort or impulsivity, or because previous research has found each to be related to an external criterion variable, such as a diagnosis of depression or the use of intellectualization as a primary defense. Researchers should avoid tossing "everything but the kitchen sink" into statistical analyses and should instead include in their data analysis only variables identified on an a priori basis as relevant to the research questions they are addressing. Doing so will not only increase the chances of obtaining significant results, but will increase the chances that research findings are conceptually meaningful and increase our understanding of the construct validity of the MMPI-2 and Rorschach instead of simply showing the pattern of correlations between the two.

RESPONSE SETS AND VALIDITY

Another important limitation of previous studies examining relationships between the MMPI and Rorschach involves the limited application of criteria across studies to determine whether or not MMPI and Rorschach data were valid. In either research or clinical contexts one must have confidence that subjects completed the MMPI-2 and Rorschach in a reliable, genuine manner in order to consider the data useful, valid, and meaningful. For the MMPI-2 this means that subjects read and understood each item, conscientiously considered how the items applied to them, and responded honestly. For the Rorschach, this means that subjects attended to the inkblots and reported what the figures reminded them of without deliberate, excessive holding back or contrived embellishment of their percepts. When subjects respond in a genuine manner one can have confidence that test scores generated from their responses will provide accurate information about their personality functioning. In contrast, if subjects do not respond to the tests in a meaningful, honest manner significant concerns are raised as to whether test scores accurately reflect their psychological characteristics. Data derived from invalid protocols are likely to have limited value, if any, and may weaken or obscure significant findings if included in statistical analyses. Thus, it is extremely important to identify and exclude from statistical analyses data produced by subjects whose MMPI-2 and/or Rorschach protocols are invalid.

In the studies reviewed by Archer and Krishnamurthy (1993a, 1993b) criteria concerning MMPI and Rorschach profile validity were often not reported and may have been absent or applied in an inconsistent fashion. Many studies did not state whether profile validity was considered or how invalid profiles were handled if detected. Thus, it appears that many studies included all completed MMPI protocols in data analyses, whether or not they were valid. Furthermore, when researchers have explicitly addressed the validity of MMPI profiles, greater attention has been given to detection of fake-bad profiles than to fake-good profiles. For instance, Archer and Gordon (1988) reported that MMPI profiles with an F scale T-score greater than 100 were discarded, but no mention was made of criteria regarding inclusion or exclusion of defensive profiles.

Similarly, many studies do not state whether Rorschach protocols were assessed for validity and, if so, which criteria were used. The most important criterion for Rorschach profile validity, the number of responses produced by the subject, has changed over time. Initially, Exner (1986) recommended that any record with fewer than 10 responses be considered invalid and discarded. Records with 10 to 12 responses were to be reviewed as to their clinical usefulness. These criteria were modified in 1988 when it was recommended that protocols with fewer than 14 responses be discarded as they were most likely invalid (Exner, 1988). This modification was based on a reanalysis of data that led to the conclusion that a low number of responses ($R < 14$) indicated that the subject was resistant to the testing procedures, attempted to conceal information from the examiner, and most likely did not produce an interpretable record. In other words, one should not expect the information about subjects' personality functioning obtained from records with a low number of responses to be accurate, valid, and reliable. Because studies conducted prior to 1988 did not use the cutoff for profile validity now in effect ($R < 14$), they are likely to have included protocols that would be considered invalid in current practice. Results may be skewed if Rorschach records with a low number of responses are included in data analysis.

Considerations about profile validity refer not only to exaggeration of symptoms, or faking-bad, but also to minimization of symptoms, or faking-good. It is possible that a defensive response set has had a greater impact on past research examining MMPI-2–Rorschach interrelationships than exaggeration, because exaggerated MMPI-2 profiles are more likely to have been detected and discarded by researchers than defensive profiles. In clinical practice, a defensive response set does not automatically mean that the profile of clinical scales cannot be interpreted; traditionally the clinician attempts to correct for the extent to which this defensive approach lowered scores on the clinical scales by adding 5 to 10 T-score points to the scale scores (Friedman, Webb, & Lewak, 1989). For research purposes, however, including defensive protocols reduces the chances of finding a relationship between MMPI-2 and Rorschach variables since a fake-good response set lowers the value of scores and truncates the range of scores. Persons responding in a defensive manner may produce scores that do not accurately or fully describe relevant psychological characteristics. Nonsignificant findings obtained when analyses are conducted using samples containing a high percentage of defensive subjects are ambiguous: The nonsignificant results could be interpreted as accurately showing a lack of association between the variables being examined or as showing the result of a restricted range of scores.

The possibility that a defensive response set affects the pattern of correlations among psychological tests is illustrated by a study comparing levels of depression in a group of sexually abused girls and a matched sample of girls with medical illness (Shapiro, Leifer, Martone, & Kassem, 1990). Shapiro et al. predicted that the sexually abused group would score higher on measures of depression than the control group. Depression was assessed using a multimethod approach, including self-report measures, the Child Behavior Checklist, and the Children's Depression Inventory, and a projective measure, the Rorschach. Contrary to predictions, the sexually abused and control groups did not differ on self-report measures of depression. As expected, however, the sexually abused group produced significantly higher scores on Rorschach indices of depression than the control group. Correlations between the self-report measures and Rorschach variables were nonsignificant.

Shapiro et al. speculated that differences in results between the self-report measures and the Rorschach occurred because the sexually abused subjects attempted to conceal emotional distress on the self-report scales as a result of shame about their condition, threats made by the perpetrator to harm the children if they disclosed information about the abuse, or because they had learned to defend against experiencing dysphoria. In this instance the absence of correlations between self-report and Rorschach variables was thought to be meaningful: The self-report approach seemed to reflect primarily self-presentational concerns, whereas the Rorschach was thought to measure depression-relevant variables subjects were unable to censor or control. These findings strongly suggest that in many instances the most accurate picture of an individual's psychological functioning will be obtained when different assessment methods are used in combination rather than when one method is used alone.

Findings that conceptually parallel those of Shapiro et al. (1990) were reported by Ganellen (1994). Ganellen reported MMPI and Rorschach data for a sample of airlines pilots who were evaluated concerning their fitness to return to work after completing an inpatient alcohol treatment program. These subjects were all aware that the results of the psychological evaluation would be taken seriously when a decision was made by the Federal Aviation Administration whether or not to reinstate their pilots' license, a prerequisite for their return to work. Thus, all subjects had a considerable motivation to convince the examiner they were not troubled by emotional, psychological, or interpersonal problems. As would be expected in this situation (Butcher, 1979), all subjects denied any personal problems during the clinical interview, produced defensive MMPI profiles, and did not elevate any MMPI clinical scales. In spite of their attempt to create the impression of being psychologically healthy, well-adjusted, and normal, subjects' responses to the Rorschach showed emotional distress, a critical self-image, and difficulties in interpersonal functioning, consistent with the effects their histories of alcohol abuse had had on their lives and relationships and the serious threat to their livelihood caused by the alcohol abuse. Similar to the results of Shapiro et al., the absence of correlations among MMPI and Rorschach variables was considered meaningful.

The studies discussed thus far have focused on how response sets present when subjects complete the MMPI-2 affect MMPI/Rorschach relationships. Response sets present when subjects respond to the Rorschach can also influence whether or not relationships between these two tests are found. The Rorschach, unlike the MMPI-2, does not have validity indices designed specifically to detect such response sets, although several Rorschach variables are indirect measures of the extent to which an individual cooperated with test procedures. These include the number of responses produced and Lambda, an index comparing the number of responses containing only form to the number of responses containing other determinants.

As discussed earlier Exner (1991) cautioned that a low number of responses ($R < 14$) strongly indicates that subjects did not cooperate optimally during administration of the Rorschach. This position was supported by Finch, Imm, and Belter (1990), who found that among a sample of 439 adolescent inpatients, those who produced a low number of responses on the Rorschach also failed to complete other parts of the psychological evaluation significantly more often than did subjects who produced an acceptable number of responses. These results were not accounted for by group differences in intelligence or degree of emotional distress. Finch et al. concluded that subjects who gave few responses on the Rorschach were uncooperative and resistant to psychological assessment in general. The standard procedure for administering the Rorschach now attempts to avoid the effects of conscious resistance by explicitly instructing the examiner not to accept protocols with fewer than 14 responses. When a patient does produce a low number of responses, the standard procedure involves administering the Rorschach a second time after the examiner has attempted to increase the subject's compliance and motivation by addressing any questions or concerns and then encouraging the patient to increase the number of responses.

A second Rorschach indicator of cooperation with test procedures is *Lambda*, a variable related to the dimension of psychological openness as opposed to constriction. Subjects who are resistant to the Rorschach often earn high scores on Lambda (*Lambda* $\geq$ 1.00) as a result of efforts to avoid revealing much about themselves. Other subjects obtain high scores on Lambda as a result of a coping style that involves an attempt to simplify the stimulus field and to ignore or disregard the complexities of life (Exner, 1991). By definition, records from high Lambda subjects, who are psychologically closed and emotionally constricted, compared to records from low Lambda subjects, who are psychologically open, will contain proportionately more pure form responses and proportionately fewer responses that are not pure form, responses that generally reveal important information about subjects' psychological and emotional functioning.

The restrictive effects of Lambda on Rorschach variables may have had an important impact on the results of a study that examined relationships among MMPI and Rorschach variables associated with depression in a sample of adolescent psychiatric inpatients (Lipovsky, Finch, & Belter, 1989). The average age for this sample was 15. The mean value of Lambda was 1.75 in this sample as compared to a mean value of .65 in Exner's 15-year-old reference group. This indicates that these subjects were more psychologically constricted than the normative group and may have been quite resistant to testing procedures.

As would be expected given this high level of Lambda, the mean values for Rorschach signs of distress produced by Lipovsky et al.'s psychiatric sample were considerably lower than for the normative sample. For instance, the mean number of achromatic color responses was .77 for Lipovsky et al.'s sample of adolescent inpatients compared to 1.63 for the normative group, whereas the mean number of shading responses produced by their sample was .60 compared to 1.60 for the normative group. Taken at face value, these scores would suggest that the psychiatric patients were less distressed than the normative group. These low values are particularly unexpected because over 50% of Lipovsky et al.'s sample had a primary diagnosis of depression but may be understood in the context of the sample's high mean value for Lambda.

Nonsignificant relationships between the MMPI and Rorschach may be found if the sample being studied involves a disproportionate number of high *Lambda* subjects for the same reasons discussed previously concerning defensive MMPI-2 profiles: The constricted approach to the Rorschach associated with a high *Lambda* lowers the number of responses given containing a number of variables and restricts the range of scores overall. This may have been the case in a study that found no meaningful correlations between the Rorschach and MMPI in a sample of adolescent inpatients (Brinkman, Overholser, & Klier, 1994). In Brinkman et al.'s sample, the mean value for Lambda was significantly elevated, 1.55 for male subjects and 1.43 for female subjects, compared to a value of .65 for the normative sample. It is not surprising that nonsignificant correlations were found between self-report and Rorschach measures of distress as the high level of *Lambda* in this sample may have restricted the range of scores for Rorschach indices of emotional distress.

The unexpectedly low scores for Rorschach variables of distress in Lipovsky et al.'s and Brinkman et al.'s samples of adolescent psychiatric inpatients with high Lambda suggests that high scores on Lambda are conceptually similar to high scores on the MMPI-2 Lie scale: Both are indicators of a defensive, resistant attempt to avoid revealing information about oneself. This conceptual relationship was empirically supported in a study that divided a mixed group of adult psychiatric patients into those with high scores on *Lambda* (*Lambda* $\geq$ 1.00) and those with acceptable levels of *Lambda* (*Lambda* $\leq$ .99; Ganellen, 1995). As predicted, high *Lambda* subjects scored significantly higher than low Lambda subjects on the MMPI-2 Lie scale. Furthermore, the two groups did not differ on the *F* or *K* scales. Thus, Lambda appears to be associated with an unsophisticated defensive response set, rather than the more sophisticated defensiveness associated with elevations on *K*. These results suggest that when either Lambda or the Lie scale are elevated, scores on test indices of psychological problems and emotional distress are likely to be affected by a defensive response set. The effect of this defensive response set is to lower the absolute values of test scores as well as to restrict the range of scores. As a result, researchers who include a large proportion of subjects with high scores on either or both the Lie scale and Lambda are unlikely to find relationships between the MMPI-2 and Rorschach as a function of subjects' defensive response set, not necessarily because the two instruments are unrelated.

A related point was made by Meyer (1994), who showed how results examining associations among conceptually related MMPI-2 and Rorschach variables can be influenced by subjects' response styles. Meyer identified subjects as openly engaged or guarded and constricted when responding to these tests and predicted that significant associations would be found for subjects who responded to both tests in a similar manner but not for those subjects who responded in a dissimilar manner. Correlations between MMPI-2 and Rorschach indices of distress (e.g., MMPI-2 scales *2, 7, DEP, ANX,* and *OBS* and Rorschach *DEPI, S-CON,* and *OBS*) were nonsignificant for the entire sample ($N = 269$). For example, the correlation between scale *2* and *DEPI* was $- .08$.

Meyer then identified subsamples of subjects who responded to both tests in a similar or dissimilar manner. As predicted, significant positive relationships between MMPI-2 and Rorschach variables were found when subjects' response style was similar on both tests. Significant negative correlations were found among subjects with dissimilar response styles. For example, the correlation between scale *2* and *DEPI* was .32 ($p < .05$) in the former group and $- .42$ ($p < .01$) in the latter group. Meyer reported a similar pattern of findings for indices of psychosis (e.g., MMPI-2 scales *6, 8,* and *BIZ* and the *SCZI*). In each case, results were nonsignificant for the entire sample, whereas significant positive and negative correlations were found for the similar and dissimilar groups, respectively. Meyer (1994) concluded that these results "highlight the important role that response styles play in mediating relationships" between Rorschach and MMPI-2 variables (p. 12).

The implications of the previous discussion for future research is that relationships between MMPI-2 and Rorschach variables may be obscured if response style is not considered, particularly if a sample includes a proportionately high number of defensive or exaggerated protocols. Researchers should set clear criteria for inclusion and exclusion of both fake-good and fake-bad MMPI-2 and Rorschach profiles (cf. Butcher, Graham, & Ben-Porath, 1995; Weiner, 1995). Subjects identified as having fake-good or fake-bad response sets should be excluded from statistical analyses. In addition to analyzing MMPI-2–Rorschach relationships for the entire sample, researchers should consider conducting supplementary data analyses for groups of subjects identified as having similar response styles on the MMPI-2 and Rorschach and groups of subjects identified as having dissimilar response styles to determine whether significant relationships will be found for the former but not the latter group, as suggested by Meyer (1994).

SELECTION OF THEORETICALLY RELEVANT VARIABLES

A number of studies have examined correlations between MMPI-2 and Rorschach scales presumed to measure similar constructs, such as a diagnosis of depression or schizophrenia. If this were the question being investigated, it would be logical to examine relationships between scores on the MMPI-2 Depression scale and the Rorschach Depression index (*DEPI*) or between the MMPI-2 Schizophrenia scale and the Rorschach Schizophrenia Index (*SCZI*). It is not always the case, however, that scales that are purported to measure the same construct actually do. Particular caution must be taken when relationships are expected on the basis of scale names because the name of a scale does not always accurately reflect what the scale measures. For instance, the name of the Harris–Lingoes subscale Need for Affection (*Hy2*) suggests that it is a measure of interpersonal dependency. However, *Hy2* is more accurately viewed as a measure of denial of hostile, angry, resentful, or negative feelings towards others (Graham, 1993; Greene, 1991).

When two scales that are expected to correlate do not, one must determine whether one scale is more robustly correlated with the criterion variable than the other or whether the scales actually measure different constructs. Issues related to selection of theoretically relevant variables are illustrated next by a discussion of several studies that examined correlations between the Rorschach Egocentricity Index and various MMPI scales.

In one study, adolescent subjects scoring in the upper and lower thirds of the distribution of scores on the Egocentricity Index were compared on MMPI scales (Caputo-Sacco & Lewis, 1991). As predicted, subjects in the lower third of the Egocentricity Index, who would be expected to have low or negative self-esteem, scored significantly higher on the MMPI Depression scale than subjects in the upper third, who would be expected to have high or positive self-esteem. These results were expected because a central feature of depression is a negative, critical view of oneself. Furthermore, previous research has reported that adolescents who scored high on the MMPI Depression scale were rated by clinicians as guilty, ashamed, self-critical, and introspective (Archer, Gordon, Giannetti, & Singles, 1988). Thus, the significant relationship between the Depression scale and Egocentricity Index makes theoretical sense. This is an example of convergent validity that is established when predicted correlations are found between variables that theoretically should relate to one another (Campbell & Fiske, 1959).

Because adolescents who score high on scales *4* and *9* have been described as self-centered, egocentric, and grandiose (Archer, 1987), Caputo-Sacco and Lewis also predicted that subjects scoring in the lower and upper thirds of the Egocentricity Index would differ on scales *4* and *9*. These predictions were not supported. However, Archer et al. (1988) reported that adolescents with scale *4* elevations were rated by clinicians as having numerous prominent behavioral problems, including alcohol and substance abuse, lying, cheating, stealing, temper outbursts, aggression, family problems, and legal problems. An elevation on scale *4* does not indicate whether a person has some or all of the characteristics associated with scale *4*. In other words, scores on scale *4* can reflect a number of factors that are not directly related to egocentricity. Caputo-Sacco and Lewis (1991) interpreted the nonsignificant relationship between scale *4* and the Egocentricity Index as indicating that "the self-centered component of the Egocentricity Index as theoretically described is not reflected in the MMPI scales assumed to reflect this characteristic" (p. 33).

An alternative interpretation not discussed by Caputo-Sacco and Lewis is that the Egocentricity Index is not directly related to the behavioral problems associated with scale *4* elevations, including alcohol or substance abuse, lying, cheating, stealing, temper outbursts, aggression, family problems, and legal problems. Thus, correlating scale *4* and the Egocentricity Index is not an optimal test of whether the Egocentricity Index measures self-centeredness or grandiosity, because scale *4* is multidimensional and the variance is saturated with acting-out behavioral problems, many of which are theoretically unrelated to egocentricity.

Barley, Dorr, and Reid (1985) looked at the correlation between the Egocentricity Index and the MMPI Ego Strength scale (*Es*), a scale developed to predict response to psychotherapy (Barron, 1953). High compared to low scorers on *Es* tend to show more positive changes during psychotherapy and in general seem to be better adjusted psychologically (Graham, 1993). The rationale for exploring the relationship between *Es* and the Egocentricity Index was Barley et al.'s view that *Es* "is presumably related to self-esteem" (p. 137). However, Greene's (1991) review of Es concluded that in general Es is negatively correlated with MMPI indicators of emotional distress. Neither Graham nor Greene identified Es as specifically measuring self-esteem or self-focus, the dimensions tapped by the Egocentricity Index. Thus, the nonsignificant results of this study have little theoretical relevance concerning either the Egocentricity Index or the Es.

A later study examined the relationship between the Egocentricity Index and several MMPI special scales including the Narcissism–Hypersensitivity (*Mf1*) subscale (Brems & Johnson, 1990). Conceptually, one would expect the Egocentricity Index to be correlated with a measure of narcissism. Contrary to predictions, the correlation between Narcissism–Hypersensitivity and the Egocentricity Index was nonsignificant.

Before one can conclude that Brems and Johnson's results show that the Egocentricity Index is not associated with narcissistic self-involvement, however, two characteristics of the Narcissism–Hypersensitivity scale must be considered. First, an examination of interpretations associated with high scores on Narcissism–Hypersensitivity suggests that nonsignificant correlations between *Mf1* and the Egocentricity Index should be expected. While a high score on the Narcissism–Hypersensitivity subscale describes an individual who is self-centered, high scores are also related to being extremely sensitive and easily hurt, worrying constantly, concerns about one's physical appearance, preoccupation with sexual matters, resentment and hostility directed towards family members, and a view of others as insensitive and unreasonable (Graham, 1993; Greene, 1991). Thus, Narcissism–Hypersensitivity taps a number of dimensions that are not directly related to self-esteem or egocentricity. As with scale *4*, the nonsignificant relationship between Narcissism–Hypersensitivity and the Egocentricity Index may be due to the fact that Narcissism–Hypersensitivity is not a pure measure of the dimensions the Egocentricity Index measures.

Second, when discussing guidelines for interpreting the Serkownek (1975) subscales for scale *5*, one of which is Narcissism–Hypersensitivity, Graham (1987) cautioned that "because no validity data and only limited clinical experience are available for the subscales, the interpretive descriptions that follow are based on an examination of the content of items included in each subscale" (p. 137). Because the construct validity of the Narcissism–Hypersensitivity scale has not been firmly established, the meaning of significant or nonsignificant correlations between this scale and other variables is not clear. One cannot assume that Narcissism–Hypersensitivity does indeed measure egocentricity or inflated self-esteem, even though the item content suggests that it does, along with the other content areas described previously. The absence of validity data for Narcissism–Hypersensitivity and its mixed item content suggests that the nonsignificant correlation reported by Brems and Johnson does not directly show whether the Egocentricity Index is a measure of self-involvement or self-esteem.

Overall, the limitations of studies concerning the Egocentricity Index discussed previously illustrate the importance of using well-validated scales that are relatively pure measures of the constructs of interest. Researchers should avoid using scales that are multidimensional in nature, as interpretation of results using such scales is likely to be unclear. Researchers should be particularly careful to select scales not by their name but by the constructs involved.

INCREMENTAL VALIDITY AND CONVERGENT VALIDITY

Among the small number of studies that have examined empirical relationships among MMPI-2 and Rorschach data, even fewer studies have examined the issue of incremental validity, a determination that clinical decisions are more accurate when the MMPI-2 and Rorschach are used together than when one is used alone. Incremental validity is established when the accuracy and validity of clinical judgments improve after additional sources of information are added compared to decisions based on one source of information alone. A review of the literature concerning incremental validity concluded that the MMPI consistently performed better than the Rorschach or other projective tests and that adding the Rorschach did not increase judgment accuracy above levels obtained using only the MMPI (Garb, 1984). However, the extent to which this conclusion applies to current assessment practice is unclear because none of the studies included in Garb's review used the Exner Comprehensive System, which improved the psychometric properties of the Rorschach and bases interpretations on identified empirical correlates of test scores rather than on unspecified decision rules or subjective impressions.

Only one study has examined the issue of incremental validity using the MMPI and Comprehensive System for the Rorschach (Archer & Gordon, 1988). In this study, the original MMPI and Rorschach were administered to a sample of 134 adolescent inpatients. Subjects were grouped according to *DSM–III* discharge diagnoses. Archer and Gordon found no correlations between MMPI scale *2* and the *DEPI* or between scale *8* and the *SCZI*. Scale *8* was shown to have a slightly better hit rate than the *SCZI* (.76 vs. .69, respectively) in detecting schizophrenia, while showing a substantial advantage in sensitivity. The combination of scale *8* and the *SCZI* did not significantly increase hit rate accuracy compared to that achieved using scale *8* alone. Neither MMPI nor Rorschach data predicted depressive disorders accurately.

Several limitations of this study should be noted. First, the original MMPI was used as the form of the MMPI later developed specifically for use with adolescent populations; the MMPI-A (Butcher et al., 1992), did not yet exist. According to authorities in this area, significant problems exist when the original MMPI is used in adolescent populations (Archer, 1987). It is therefore quite likely that use of the original MMPI affected the results obtained in Archer and Gordon's study.

Second, subsequent to Archer and Gordon's (1988) study, the *SCZI* and *DEPI* were revised to correct deficiencies recognized in earlier versions of these indices, namely that they were not as sensitive or accurate as desired (Exner, 1991). Results using the MMPI-A and updated *SCZI* and *DEPI* may be quite different than those found using the original MMPI and original *SCZI* and *DEPI*. For instance, Ball, Archer, Gordon, and French (1991) reported findings using both forms of the *DEPI*. They showed little overlap in results using the original as compared to the revised *DEPI*. In an outpatient sample of 67 children and adolescents, for instance, none obtained scores on the original *DEPI* in the range significant for depression, whereas 11 subjects did on the revised *DEPI*. Similarly, among their sample of 99 inpatient adolescents, 1 scored in the positive range for depression on the original *DEPI*, whereas 23 scored in the positive range on the revised *DEPI*. Thus, Archer and Gordon's findings have only limited relevance for contemporary practice unless they are replicated using the MMPI-A and revised *SCZI* and *DEPI*.

Archer and Gordon's (1988) study raises several other important questions for future research and clinical practice. Their sample included 15 patients who met diagnostic criteria for schizophrenia. Of these 15 patients, 8 were correctly identified as being schizophrenic by scale *8*, whereas the original Rorschach *SCZI* correctly identified 7 as being schizophrenic. Archer and Gordon did not report the extent to which the Rorschach and MMPI overlapped in identifying these patients. It is conceivable that the 7 patients correctly identified by the Rorschach were among the 8 patients correctly identified by the MMPI. Alternatively, there may have been partial or no overlap among the patients correctly identified by the two tests.

The extent of agreement between the MMPI and Rorschach is a critical issue that has generally been neglected but that has the following implications. Assume, for instance, that there was a complete absence of overlap between patients correctly identified as being schizophrenic by the Rorschach and the MMPI in Archer and Gordon's study. If this were the case, it could suggest that these tests are differentially sensitive to subgroups within a particular disorder, in this case schizophrenia. Several implications for clinical practice would be suggested by this finding. First, if the Rorschach and MMPI were shown to be accurate for different purposes, then both tests should be administered routinely to insure adequate sensitivity to all subgroups within a disorder and to avoid inaccurate conclusions that could be reached if one test were administered alone. Second, a lack of agreement between the two tests would be expected to occur routinely. Rather than being a cause to question the validity or clinical utility of either the MMPI-2 or Rorschach, a lack of agreement would be viewed as a result of their relative strengths and weaknesses, attributes that would need to be carefully identified through empirical research.

Archer and Gordon (1988) reported a large number of false positive identifications of schizophrenia using both the MMPI (25 of 33 positive scores) and the Rorschach (31 of 38 positive scores). In their study, a substantial risk existed of inaccurately concluding that a patient was schizophrenic using either MMPI or Rorschach findings. Assume, however, that substantial overlap was found between the MMPI and Rorschach among those patients correctly identified as being schizophrenic. If the rate of true positives is higher when scores are positive on both the MMPI and Rorschach than when scores are positive on only one test, then a psychologist who observes positive signs of schizophrenia on both the MMPI and Rorschach would have considerable confidence in making a diagnosis of schizophrenia (Hegarty, Baldessarini, Tohen, Waternaux, & Oepen, 1994). Demonstrating that positive findings on these two assessment instruments strongly indicate a condition is more likely to be present than when only one test is positive would have an important implication for clinical practice, such as when a clinician is asked to make decisions having significant implications for treatment, likely course of illness, and prognosis. Although the issue of incremental validity is important, in some circumstances, convergent validity (agreement between two methods) may be more important, particularly before assigning a diagnosis that has as weighty and ominous implications as the diagnosis of schizophrenia.

As the previous discussion indicates, issues concerning the incremental validity and convergent validity for combined use of the MMPI-2 and Rorschach are far from being settled. These issues deserve careful and systematic attention. For instance, the issue of diagnostic agreement between the MMPI-2 and Rorschach could be examined empirically in future studies by computing the kappa coefficient.

CHANGES IN RORSCHACH SCORES

The Comprehensive System has continued to evolve over time as data accumulate and in response to demonstrated shortcomings of specific scores and indices. This has resulted in the development of new indices, such as the Hypervigilance index and the Obsessive index, as well as changes in scoring other indices. For instance, as mentioned previously, problems with the original *DEPI* prompted Exner to reexamine the variables comprising the *DEPI* and to alter it. Similar changes have been made in several other indices including the *SCZI*, the Isolation index, and the Intellectualization index (Exner, 1991). For instance, changes in how the Isolation index is computed were made after research showed that its accuracy increased when two of the variables in the index were weighted more heavily than the other variables.

Because of these changes, research using older, now discarded methods of calculating scores may not generalize to the revised Rorschach variables. For instance, one study reported nonsignificant correlations between the original Isolation Index and MMPI scores, including the Social Introversion scale (Simon, 1989). However, it remains to be seen whether similar results will be found for the revised Isolation index. This awaits further research.

CONTINUOUS OR CATEGORICAL VARIABLES?

Another factor that may have affected the outcomes of studies examining MMPI-2–Rorschach relationships is the choice of statistical tests. Most studies used parametric statistical procedures, such as Pearson product-moment correlations, analysis of variance, or t-tests. Although these statistics are generally quite robust, assumptions underlying parametric tests are violated when the distributions of variables are not normal and their ranges are quite restricted, as is the case for many Rorschach variables (Exner, 1991). For example, the tables for Exner's normative sample shows that 48 of 111 Rorschach variables are not normally distributed. Exner recommended that variables with skewed distributions and restricted ranges should not be analyzed using parametric statistics. Similarly, Kinder (1992) recommended that "when significant departures from normality occur, the appropriate nonparametric analyses should be employed" (p. 256).

Researchers also must consider whether Rorschach variables should be treated as continuous or categorical variables when conducting statistical analyses. When interpreted in clinical practice, many Rorschach variables are treated as categorical rather than continuous variables. For instance, Vista is described as a dichotomous variable: One or more Vista responses suggests that the patient is self-critical or guilty, whereas no Vista responses suggests an absence of self-punitive reactions. Although one assumes that the greater the number of Vista responses the more intense the patient's self-punitive feelings, there is no metric showing that two Vistas indicates twice as much self-criticism as one Vista or that four Vistas is twice as painful as two. In other words, these scores have not been shown to be continuous. Similarly, the presence of one or more Color Shading blends suggests a painful, confusing mixture of affective reactions. Again, Color Shading blends are treated as a dichotomous rather than a continuous variable. For clinical purposes, many Rorschach scores are treated as categorical rather than continuous variables, such as Lambda greater than or equal to 1.00, the presence of one or more Reflection answers, and an Intellectualization Index score greater than or equal to 4. In these instances plus many others, a score above or below a critical level or cutting score has interpretive significance. Investigators should analyze Rorschach variables in a manner consistent with how those variables are used clinically. If a Rorschach variable is interpreted in relation to a specified cutting score, such as *DEPI* less than or greater than 4 or Reflections less than or greater than 1, then these variables should be analyzed in a categorical rather than a continuous manner using the same cutting scores for research purposes as for clinical practice.

It is possible that weak MMPI–Rorschach relationships may have been found in previous studies because of inappropriate data analytic procedures. For instance, studies that computed large numbers of correlations between MMPI and Rorschach variables without considering whether to use parametric or nonparametric tests may have obtained nonsignificant results as a result of an inappropriate application of statistical procedures (Archer & Krishnamurthy, 1993a; Dana & Bolton, 1982). Researchers should determine whether Rorschach variables are normally distributed and use parametric statistics for variables that are normally distributed and nonparametric statistics for variables that are not. Researchers can easily refer to the normative tables for the Comprehensive System (Exner, 1993; Exner & Weiner, 1995) to determine whether or not variables are normally distributed and then analyze their data using the appropriate statistics.

Given the categorical nature of many Rorschach variables, one approach to studying MMPI-2–Rorschach relationships would be to group subjects on the basis of scores above or below a critical level on specific Rorschach variables. For instance, subjects could be assigned to high or low self-critical groups on the basis of the presence or absence of Vista responses. The two groups could then be compared on relevant MMPI-2 variables. For instance, one might predict that the high and the low self-critical groups would differ on MMPI-2 scales related to negative, critical self-evaluation, such as scales *2* and *7*, *DEP*, and *LSE*. This approach could be implemented with other Rorschach variables as well.

FUTURE DIRECTIONS

The weak associations between the Rorschach and MMPI-2 may lead some to conclude that one of the two tests is more strongly related than the other to specific criterion variables, such as clinical diagnosis, level of distress, or a particular personality characteristic. However, this conclusion does not necessarily follow, as each test may be independently correlated with a criterion variable even if they are only modestly correlated with one another. Rather than pitting the MMPI-2 and Rorschach against each other, these results could also suggest that the two tests measure different aspects of the same phenomena.

A parallel controversy exists in the neuropsychological literature concerning the relatively weak relationship consistently reported between two tests often described as measuring similar abilities, the Halstead Category test (HCT; Reitan & Wolfson, 1985) and the Wisconsin Card Sorting Test (WCST; Heaton, 1981). It is generally thought that successful performance on both tests requires abstract concept formation and reasoning; development of strategies to solve complex, unfamiliar problems; cognitive flexibility; and the ability to adapt to changing test demands. Despite the apparent similarities between the HCT and WCST, only modest correlations between them have been reported and, in a substantial number of studies, results from the HCT and WCST do not agree. As a result, some researchers have suggested that although the HCT and WCST share some characteristics, they assess nonoverlapping cognitive operations and therefore should not be considered interchangeable (e.g., Donders & Kirsch, 1991; Pendeleton & Heaton, 1982).

Perrine (1993) investigated the extent to which the HCT and WCST involved similar types of conceptual processing using a sophisticated research paradigm adapted from cognitive psychology. Perrine found that the modest relationship between the two tests was explained by the fact that different cognitive processing demands were differentially associated with each test. For instance, performance on the HCT was most strongly related to deducing rules and determining abstract principles used to classify unfamiliar stimuli, whereas performance on the WCST was most sensitive to attribute learning and perseverative tendencies.

The studies designed to explain the modest correlations between the HCT and WCST might serve as a model for future research concerning MMPI-2–Rorschach interrelationships in several respects. First, the spirit of the studies described previously reflect a fundamental respect for the clinical usefulness of both the HCT and WCST, rather than a partisan attempt to prove that one was right and the other wrong. Ideally, a similar spirit will infuse research examining MMPI-2–Rorschach relationships. Second, these studies attempted to identify specific dimensions along which the HCT and WCST converged and differed. This strategy may be quite useful for future MMPI-2–Rorschach research. For example, one might predict that relationships between MMPI-2 scale *8* and the *SCZI* would be weak even though both were developed to identify patients with a psychotic disorder, because items on Scale 8 are heterogeneous, involving not only psychotic experiences, but also social alienation and problems with impulse control, whereas the variables comprising the *SCZI* involve cognitive slippage, thought disorder, and distorted perceptions of stimuli. A weak correlation might be expected between a measure of thought disorder (*SCZI*) and a measure of psychotic experiences, social alienation, and poor impulse control (scale *8*) without calling into question the construct validity of each scale. Based on the differences between scale *8* and *SCZI*, one could hypothesize that scale *8* and *SCZI* will be differentially associated with different aspects of a psychotic disorder.

Similarly, although one might expect to find significant correlations between MMPI-2 scale *6* and the Hypervigilance Index (*HVI*), the two indices do not overlap completely. Items on scale *6* involve suspiciousness, sensitivity, delusions of persecution and/or grandeur, ideas of reference, resentment, feelings of being mistreated, and a sense of getting a raw deal out of life. In contrast, the HVI is related to a suspicious distrust of others, cautious watchfulness, apprehensive anticipation of trouble, and a cynical view of the world but do not directly involve psychotic, delusional symptoms. Thus, although the MMPI-2 and Rorschach should be expected to share some characteristics, they may assess nonoverlapping psychological variables and therefore should not be considered interchangeable. Future research should examine to which specific aspects of personality, emotional functioning, and psychopathology each is related.

CONCLUSIONS

The previous discussion indicates that no definitive conclusions about empirical relationships between the MMPI-2 and Rorschach can be reached at this point given the methodological limitations of existing studies, particularly the limited number of studies that used contemporary assessment procedures. In addition to these methodological issues, consideration must be given to whether the MMPI-2 and Rorschach should be expected to be correlated. If so, the clinician or researcher must specify the circumstances in which agreement is expected as well as the significance of disagreement between the two.

Because the Rorschach and MMPI-2 were developed to measure similar psychological constructs, it is reasonable to expect that the two should be correlated in many instances. The magnitude of the correlation between the MMPI-2 and Rorschach, however, should be expected to be in the low to moderate range given the differences in response format. In general, higher correlations are expected between two tests using similar formats to assess a psychological construct than between two tests using different formats. For example, two self-report measures of depression, such as the Beck Depression Inventory and Zung Depression Inventory, would be expected to be more strongly correlated with one another than with the Rorschach.

As earlier sections of this chapter indicate, however, there are circumstances in which the Rorschach and MMPI-2 would not be expected to correlate or to show a low magnitude of correlation. This may occur, for instance, if the two procedures are related to a construct, such as a psychotic disorder, but tap different aspects of that disorder, such as poor reality testing and thought disorder as opposed to hallucinations, delusions, and social alienation.

It is also possible that disagreement between the MMPI-2 and Rorschach may occur if each independently measures aspects of an individual's psychological makeup not measured by the other. For instance, patients meeting criteria for one of the *DSM-IV* Somatoform Disorders are typically focused on, aware of, and concerned about physical problems. In many cases, these physical symptoms are the result of emotional distress or a psychological conflict patients are not aware of and that is not overtly manifested. It is possible that in these cases the MMPI-2 will identify one aspect of patients' condition whereas the Rorschach identifies another. This can also occur when patients split off from awareness aspects of themselves that although not consciously recognized, have an important influence on their psychological functioning. For instance, an individual who is overtly polite, compliant, and emotionally constrained may have developed these characteristics as a means of inhibiting expressions of anger and resolving conflicts related to an impulse to be independent and autonomous while needing to remain submissive and dependent (Millon, 1969).

It is possible that the MMPI-2 and Rorschach may be differentially sensitive to different aspects of the individual's psychological condition, somatic symptoms as opposed to emotional distress in the first example or polite and formal behavior as opposed to submerged hostility and oppositionality in the second. Thus, apparently contradictory findings can in some cases yield meaningful information that enriches the interpretation of clinical personality assessment when MMPI-2 and Rorschach data are integrated. Furthermore, the previous discussion suggests that in many instances personality assessment will be incomplete if one test is administered without the other, as important information about a patient provided by one test may not be provided by the other. Approaches to identifying, weighing, and reconciling similar and dissimilar MMPI-2 and Rorschach findings are discussed in detail in chapters 3, 4, and 5, which focus on integrating MMPI-2 and Rorschach findings and on general issues of test interpretation.

3 Test Interpretation I: Conceptual Relationships

The primary areas addressed during a psychological evaluation include an assessment of profile validity, current symptomatology, interpersonal relationships, self-concept, defenses, and dynamics. Test results pertaining to these dimensions form the foundation for the complex clinical decisions demanded in psychological evaluations, including differential diagnosis, formulation of the dynamics of patients' behavior, identification of specific problems to be targeted during treatment, recommendations about specific intervention strategies, and identification of factors that could contribute to resistances to treatment.

As discussed in Chapter 1, relatively few empirical studies have examined MMPI–Rorschach interrelationships, and the conclusions that can be drawn from these studies are limited by the methodological shortcomings discussed in chapter 2. In this chapter, conceptual relationships between individual MMPI-2 scales and Rorschach variables and several dimensions of clinical interest are presented, including test-taking attitudes, mood and emotional functioning, contact with reality and indicators of psychosis, characteristic patterns of interpersonal functioning, self-concept, coping strategies and defenses, and alcohol/substance abuse. MMPI-2 and Rorschach variables related to each of these domains are identified on the basis of reported empirical findings, review of the conceptual meaning of specific variables, review of the content of items comprising individual scales, and clinical experience.

The tables presented later outline MMPI-2 and Rorschach variables related to a particular variable, such as depression or authority conflict. Although the test variables appear in parallel columns in these tables, this does not imply that there is a corresponding Rorschach variable for each MMPI-2 variable. The reader should assume that MMPI-2 scales indicate a particular feature is present only if scores on that scale are elevated, with the exception of low scores on scales when specifically noted. After conceptual relationships between the MMPI-2 and Rorschach are presented, a general framework for test interpretation is discussed in chapter 4. This includes discussion of potential sources of bias or error in clinical decision making and recommendations for avoiding these biases. Issues to consider when interpreting MMPI-2 and Rorschach data in an integrated manner are discussed in detail in chapter 5.

TEST-TAKING ATTITUDES

An important issue in any personality assessment is a judgment about the quality of the test data that is used during the interpretive process. Issues to consider include the degree of cooperation with the evaluation, subjects' ability to understand test procedures, and how honestly patients described themselves. For a variety of reasons, patients may be motivated to create a particular impression during the psychological evaluation by attempting to appear more disturbed than they actually are, trying to deny or conceal difficulties they actually have, or claiming to have more positive character-istics than is actually the case. Thus, an integral part of any clinical assessment is an examination of the patients' truthfulness and identification of any bias in their presentation during the evaluation (Rogers, 1988).

Recognition of response sets that may skew or invalidate the test results is critical when evaluating patients' psychological condition, assessing the presence or absence of a psychiatric disorder, and formulating treatment recommendations. Although psychologists are generally quite concerned about profile validity when assessments are conducted in a legal context, response bias can also affect how patients present in clinical contexts, even when they have no involvement with the legal system. This may occur, for instance, when patients feel they have to call attention to their problems to receive treatment and therefore present with a "plea for help", when patients deliberately try to maintain a particular image through impression management strategies, or when they attempt to protect their self-image and unconsciously deceive themselves by denying or ignoring problems (Paul-haus, 1986). Thus, the first step in the interpretive process should involve an assessment of subjects' approach to the evaluation, level of cooperation, and consideration of whether there were any indications of a fake-good or fake-bad test-taking attitude.

The MMPI-2 validity scales were developed specifically to objectively assess these test-taking attitudes, profile validity, and cooperation with evaluation procedures. Detailed discussions concerning the development, validity, and clinical use of MMPI-2 validity scales can be found in standard MMPI-2 texts (e.g., Butcher & Williams, 1992; Friedman et al., 1989; Graham, 1993; Greene 1991). In brief, the validity scales provide the clinician with objective information to use to make judgments about individuals' ability to read, concentrate on, and understand MMPI-2 items; whether they avoided responding to certain content areas; whether they answered in a consistent as opposed to an inconsistent manner; and whether signs exist of attempts to fake-bad or fake-good. A meta-analytic review showed that MMPI validity scales accurately differentiated between subjects attempting to fake-bad or exaggerate symptoms and subjects who reported symptoms honestly (Berry, Baer, & Harris, 1991). Similarly, a meta-analytic review showed that subjects attempting to fake-good differed from subjects responding honestly on standard MMPI validity scales and on special scales designed to detect underreporting of symptoms (Baer, Wetter, & Berry, 1992).

The Rorschach does not have validity indices parallel to the MMPI-2 with which to identify deviant response sets. The primary way in which validity is assessed on the Rorschach involves examining the number of responses produced and the percentage of responses given involving pure form compared to other determinants. Protocols are viewed as invalid if too few responses are produced ($R < 14$) and, in some instances, if responses predominantly involve pure form (*Lambda* ≥ 1.00; Exner, 1991). There are no scores that reliably identify a fake-bad or fake-good response set, although some studies have suggested that subjects who fake-bad produce a high number of responses with dramatic content (Ganellen et al., 1996; Netter & Viglione, 1994; Perry & Kinder, 1990; Seamons et al., 1981). In some cases an elevated number of personalized responses (*PER* > 2) indicates a defensive response set. However, neither dramatic responses nor personalized responses are uniquely associated with distortions in self-presentation. The extent to which fake-good or fake-bad response sets influence scores on the Rorschach is not clear, although recent reports suggest that valid Rorschach results can be obtained even when naive subjects consciously attempt to conceal or to exaggerate problems (Ganellen, 1994; Ganellen et al., 1996; Perry & Kinder, 1990).

In summary, the MMPI-2 validity scales provide important, objective information about subjects' cooperation with evaluation procedures and the presence of response sets that might bias their report of symptoms. In contrast, the Rorschach does not address these critical validity issues directly and provides limited information concerning response bias. In clinical practice, therefore, one should rely on the MMPI-2 validity scales to determine whether results from a psychological evaluation were skewed by a fake-good or fake-bad response set. When the MMPI-2 indicates that patients' presentation involved an attempt to exaggerate or minimize psychological difficulties, the clinician must judge whether their test-taking attitude influenced responses on the Rorschach or whether the Rorschach data can be interpreted meaningfully.

MOOD STATES

The MMPI-2 and Rorschach both provide information about individuals' current mood states, including depression, anxiety, guilt, and anger. Test variables related to each of these dimensions are presented in Table 3.1.

TABLE 3.1
Test Variables Related to Mood States

MMPI-2	*Rorschach*
Depression/Distress	
Scale *2*	$DEPI \geq 5$
Low scale *9*	$CDI \geq 4$
DEP	$C' > 2$
D1 (subjective depression)	Color shading blends > 0
D2 (psychomotor retardation)	$FV + VF + V > 0$
D4 (mental dullness)	$FD > 2$
D5 (brooding)	$MOR > 2$
Hy3 (lassitude-malaise)	$es > 10$
Sc2 (emotional alienation)	$SumC < 6$
Sc4 (lack of ego mastery—conative)	
Anxiety	
Scale *7*	D score < 0
ANX	$FY + YF + Y > 2$
FRS	$m > 2$
PK	$es > 10$
PS	$Sum\ Y > Fm + m$
Guilt	
Scale *2*	$FV + VF + V > 0$
Scale *7*	
D1 (subjective depression)	
D5 (brooding)	
Pd5 (self-alienation)	
Ma4 (ego inflation)—low	
Anger	
Scale *4*	$S > 2$
Scale *6*	
ANG	
Type A	
Hy5 (inhibition of aggression)—low	
Sc5 (defective inhibition)	

In addition to information concerning the presence or absence of specific mood states, the Rorschach provides information concerning individuals' control over emotions ($FC:CF+C$) and how open the individual is to processing emotional experience (Afr; $Lambda$; C':$WSumC$). For example, the Rorschach may show that two individuals differ in the extent to which emotions dominate their reactions and their ability to modulate their feelings and keep a reasonable perspective on events ($FC:CF+C$ = 6:3; $Lambda$ = .70; Afr = .64) as opposed to a tendency to being flooded by emotions ($FC:CF+C$ = 3:6; C = 2: $Lambda$ = .22; Afr = .98). The MMPI-2 clinical and supplementary scales do not address these issues directly, although information about regulation of emotions is contained in the behavioral correlates associated with many MMPI-2 codetypes.

PSYCHOTIC DISORDERS

The MMPI-2 and Rorschach identify psychotic disorders in different ways. The MMPI-2 relies on patients' report of the deviant, unusual experiences typical of psychotic disorders, such as hallucinations, delusions, ideas of reference, thought disorder, and strange and peculiar beliefs. In contrast, the Rorschach detects psychotic disorders by identifying inaccurate, distorted perceptions of stimuli (e.g., $X + \%$, $X - \%$) and by scoring instances of cognitive slippage and thought disorder (Special Scores). Specific test variables related to psychotic and paranoid disorders are presented in Table 3.2.

INTERPERSONAL FUNCTIONING

Several MMPI-2 scales were developed to measure specific aspects of interpersonal functioning, such as a rebellious, defiant attitude toward authority figures (scale 4; Antisocial Practices [ASP]) and a tendency to be introverted and uncomfortable with others (Scale 0; Social Discomfort [SOD]). There are no parallel Rorschach indices measuring these dimensions, although individual Rorschach variables are conceptually associated with oppositionality and social discomfort. Other aspects of interpersonal functioning, such as dependence and interpersonal exploitation, can be inferred from the characteristics associated with various MMPI-2 scales and Rorschach variables. Additional information about interpersonal functioning is also contained in descriptions of behavioral correlates associated with specific MMPI-2 codetypes. Test variables related to specific aspects of interpersonal functioning are presented in Table 3.3.

In addition to the dimensions described previously, Rorschach protocols

TABLE 3.2
Test Variables Related to Psychotic and Paranoid Disorders

MMPI-2	*Rorschach*
Psychotic Disorders	
Scale *F*	SCZI $\geq$ 4
Scale *8*	$X-\% > .29$ and $X-\% > Xu\%$
Scale *6*	*Sum6* special scores > 6
Scale *9*	*WSum6* special scores > 17
BIZ	$M- > 1$
Sc3 (LEM − cognitive)	$FQ- \geq FQu$ or $> FQo+FQ+$
Sc6 (bizarre sensory experiences)	
Paranoid Ideation	
Scale *6*	*HVI* positive
BIZ	$T = 0$
Pa1 (persecutory ideation)	$S > 2$
Pd4 (social alienation)	$AG > 2$
Sc1 (social alienation)	$H+(H)+Hd+(Hd) > 6$
	$Cg > 3$
	$X+\% < .70$
	$X-\% > .29$ and $X-\% > Xu\%$
	$M-\% > 1$
	$Sum C \leq 6$
	$Dd \geq 3$

describe qualitative aspects of interpersonal relationships not contained in all MMPI-2 profiles. For instance, Rorschach data might show that one views others as real, unique, and separate individuals who have their own needs (Pure $H >$ Non-pure H), as opposed to perceiving others as important principally because they gratify one's own psychological needs (Pure $H <$ Non-pure H). Rorschach data may also provide information clarifying the reasons for interpersonal difficulties identified on the MMPI-2. For instance, the MMPI-2 might show that two people are equally uncomfortable in social situations (scale $0 = 72$), whereas the Rorschach might identify different reasons for their interpersonal discomfort. One of these individuals may avoid social involvement because he or she anticipates others will be attacking and hostile ($AG = 3$; $COP = 0$), whereas the second person anticipates friendly cooperation ($COP = 2$; $AG = 0$) but avoids social encounters because of feelings of inferiority and inadequacy (*Egocentricity index* $= .22$). Additional information about interpersonal functioning may also be gleaned through analysis of the content of responses involving human movement and human content. Although some MMPI-2 scales and codetypes do address these issues, not all MMPI-2 profiles contain the information about qualitative features of personal interactions routinely provided by the Rorschach.

TABLE 3.3
Test Variables Related to Interpersonal Functioning

MMPI-2	Rorschach
Rebelliousness/Conflict with Authority	
Scale *4*	$S > 2$
49/94	$Fr + rF > 0$
ASP (antisocial practices)	$a{:}p > 2{:}1$
Pd2 (authority conflict)	Egocentricity ratio $> .45$
*Ma*1 (amorality)	$PER > 2$
MAC-R	
CYN (Cynicism)	
Social Discomfort/Avoidance	
Scale *0*	$FT + TF + T = 0$
Scale *7*	$COP \leq 1$
SOD (social discomfort)	Isolate cluster $> .25$
LSE (low self-esteem)	*HVI* positive
*Hy*1 (denial of social anxiety) − low	$CDI \geq 4$
*Pd*3 (social imperturbability) − low	$H < (H) + Hd + (Hd)$
*Si*1 (shyness/self-consciousness)	
*Si*2 (social avoidance)	
*Ma*3 (imperturbability) − low	
Dependence/Passivity	
Scale *3*	$p > a + 1$
Scale *4* − low	$Mp > Ma$
Scale *5* (males − high; females − low)	Food > 0
*Hy*2 (need for affection)	$FT + TF + T > 1$
*Ma*4 (ego inflation) − low	Populars > 8
*Si*3 (self/other alienation)	
LSE (low self-esteem)	
Do (dominance) − low	
Interpersonal Manipulation/Exploitation	
Scale *4*	$Fr + rF > 0$
Scale *9*	Egocentricity index $> .45$
ASP (antisocial practices)	$AG \geq 2$ and $COP \leq 1$
*Pa*3 (naivete) − low	$H < (H) + Hd + (Hd)$
*Ma*1 (amorality)	
*Ma*4 (ego inflation)	

SELF-CONCEPT

Psychological test data provides information about individuals' self-image, the characteristics individuals value as opposed to those that are viewed as unimportant, and their self-esteem, how individuals evaluate themselves and the extent to which they feel positively or negatively about their talents, strengths, weaknesses, accomplishments, and failures. MMPI-2 and Structural Summary data directly assess how positively or negatively individuals feel about themselves. Other information about self-concept, such as valued traits, characteristics one wishes for, and aspects of one's identity that are feared, are not measured directly but may be inferred from specific MMPI-2 scores or the content of Rorschach responses. For instance, a low score on Scale 5 may indicate that traditional masculine values are quite important to a man. Listed in Table 3.4 are test variables related to positive and negative self-evaluations.

COPING STRATEGIES AND DEFENSES

Identification of characteristic coping strategies and defense mechanisms is important for a comprehensive understanding of individuals' personality functioning, how psychological difficulties are likely to be expressed, and response to psychotherapy. Few MMPI-2 or Rorschach variables were developed to identify specific defense mechanisms, with the exception of the MMPI-2 Repression scale (Welsh, 1956) and the Rorschach Intellectualization index (Exner, 1991). However, elevations on various MMPI-2 scales are associated with specific defenses, such as elevations on L and scales 1 and 3 suggesting the use of repression and denial as primary defenses, whereas an elevation on scale 4 suggests the use of acting out, rationalization, and projection as primary defenses (Trimboli & Kilgore, 1983).

TABLE 3.4
Test Variables Related to Positive and Negative Self-Evaluations

MMPI-2	*Rorschach*
Negative Self-Esteem/Self-Criticism	
Scale *2*	Egocentricity index $< .33$
Scale *7*	$FV + VF + V > 0$
Scale *0*	$FD > 2$
LSE (low self-esteem)	$MOR > 2$
D1 (subjective depression)	
Pd5 (self-alienation)	
*Si*1 (shyness/self-consciousness)	
*Si*3 (self/other alienation)	
Positive Self-esteem/Narcissism	
Scale *4*	Egocentricity index $> .44$
Scale *9*	$Fr + rF > 0$
LSE (low self-esteem) — low	
*Ma*4 (ego inflation)	
*Pd*3 (social imperturbability)	

TABLE 3.5
Test Variables Related to Coping and Defense Mechanisms

MMPI-2	Rorschach
	Repression and Denial
L scale	*Lambda* > .99
K scale	Color projection > 0
Scale *3*	*Afr* < .45
Repression	*Sum* color > 7
Hy2 (need for affection)	*Sum Y* > 2
Hy5 (inhibition of aggression)	
Pa3 (naivete)	
Ma1 (amorality) — low	
	Intellectualization/Rationalization
Scale *6*	$2AB + Art + Ay \geq 4$
Scale *4*	Obsessive index positive
Scale *7*	*Dd* > 3
OBS (obsessiveness)	*Zd* > 3.5
	$X + \% \text{ and/or } F + \% > .89$
	Pervasively introversive
	$FC:CF + C > 2:1 \text{ and } C = 0$
	SumC′ > WSumC
	Somatization
Scale *1*	$An + Xy \geq 3$
Scale *3*	$FC′ + C′F + C > 2$
Conversion V	*CP* (color projection) > 0
HEA (health concerns)	
D3 (physical malfunctioning)	
Hy3 (lassitude malaise)	
Hy4 (somatic complaints)	
Sc6 (bizarre sensory experiences)	
	Acting Out
Scale *4*	*D* score and/or *Adj D* < 0
Scale *9*	*Lambda* > .99
ASP (antisocial practices)	*CF* + *C* > *FC*
MAC-R	*C* > 0
Pd2 (authority problems)	*CDI* ≥ 4
Pd4 (social alienation)	*S* > 2
Sc5 (defective inhibition)	*AG* > 2
Ma2 (psychomotor acceleration)	$X + \% < .70$
OH (overcontrolled hostility) — low	Populars < 5
	$S - \% > .40$
	Pervasive extratensive
	a:p > 3:1
	Retreat into Fantasy
Scale *8*	$Mp > Ma + 1$
BIZ	Pervasive introversive
	$M- > 0$
	Formless *M* > 0

Defensive operations on the Rorschach have traditionally been identified on the basis of analysis of the content and sequence of Rorschach responses, as well as specific determinants (Rappaport et al., 1945; Schafer, 1954). One can infer that MMPI-2 scales and variables from the Structural Summary are related to certain defenses based on examination of the extratest correlates and conceptual underpinnings of individual test variables.

Not all defense mechanisms are assessed adequately by the MMPI-2 and Rorschach. In particular, neither the MMPI-2 nor the Rorschach Structural Summary directly provides information about the defenses associated with more primitive character pathology, such as splitting, idealization, or devaluation. These defensive operations may be assessed more directly on the Rorschach by analysis of content or by scales not included in the Comprehensive System constructed to incorporate recent developments in psychodynamic theory. Lerner (1991) described the theoretical underpinnings and preliminary findings of many of these scales. Even though several of these scales appear to be quite promising, they cannot be recommended for routine use in clinical practice until their reliability and validity are adequately demonstrated.

ALCOHOL/SUBSTANCE ABUSE

Several MMPI-2 scales identify persons at risk for alcohol and substance abuse including scale *4*, the MacAndrew Alcoholism (MAC) scale (1965), and the Addiction Potential and Addiction Admissions scales(Weed, Butcher, McKenna, & Ben-Porath, 1992). A considerable amount of research has been generated by the original and revised MacAndrew scales. This research strongly indicates that clinicians should not automatically assume that individuals abuse alcohol simply on the basis of an elevated MAC or MAC-R given the substantial risk of false positive and false negative identifications of alcohol and substance abusers (Gottesman & Prescott, 1989). The substantial risk of misidentification is not surprising because alcohol and substance abuse are not associated with one specific personality type and because alcohol abuse can co-occur with many different types of psychopathology, including depression, antisocial personality disorder, anxiety disorders, and schizophrenia, among others. However, an elevation on scale *4* or the MAC/MAC-R can alert the clinician that patients share many of the characteristics exhibited by persons who abuse alcohol or other substances and the possibility of alcohol and substance abuse should therefore be explored thoroughly (Greene, 1991). Only limited data concerning the utility of the APS and AAS are available, although initial findings are promising. However, the accuracy with which alcohol and substance abuse are detected by the AAS and APS has not yet been established.

   The Rorschach contains no scores or indices specifically developed to identify persons at risk for alcohol or substance abuse. Although substance abusers often obtain positive scores on certain indices, such as the Coping Deficit Index (*CDI*), elevations on these indices are not specific to alcohol and substance abuse. Thus, clinicians should not expect the Rorschach to make reliable contributions to identification of alcohol and/or substance abuse above and beyond the information provided by the MMPI-2.

4 Test Interpretation II: Stages of Test Interpretation

Interpretation of data from a psychological evaluation proceeds by considering the various and sometimes conflicting interpretive possibilitites suggested by the test data, weighing and deciding among competing interpretations, and integrating the many separate conclusions suggested by the data into a meaningful, theoretically consistent description of patients' current symptoms, problems in psychological adaptation, and need for psychological treatment. In this chapter, a framework is presented for interpreting the complex array of data collected during a psychological evaluation to answer specific referral questions, assist in differential diagnosis, and formulate treatment plans. Detailed guidelines for integrating MMPI-2 and Rorschach findings are presented in chapter 5.

There is a remarkable consistency across writers who have described the stages involved in interpretation of data obtained during a psychological evaluation (Exner, 1993; Friedman et al., 1989; Graham, 1993; Greene; 1991; Lerner, 1991; Rappaport et al., 1945). Although differences exist in the number of stages described and in the labels given to each step in the interpretive process, all agree that after the test data is gathered and scored, the clinician first generates preliminary hypotheses from a careful review of all test data, decides which hypotheses to retain and which to discard, and then integrates the various findings into a comprehensive formulation to describe patients' personality organization, assist in differential diagnosis, identify characteristic patterns of interpersonal functioning, assess their self-concept, and highlight issues for treatment planning. The remainder of this chapter describes these three stages of test interpretation.

The approach to test interpretation presented below assumes, first, that test interpretation will be most accurate and meaningful if it is data driven rather than theory-driven. This statement reflects the view that what is learned from a psychological evaluation differs from what is learned from a clinical interview or a psychotherapy session in that the clinician gathers and interprets information during a psychological evaluation using standardized, empirically validated procedures. Thus, the clinician's understanding of an individual client based on the results of the MMPI-2 and Rorschach does not rely primarily on what that client says about himself or herself, observations of the patient's behavior, or intuitive reactions to the person. Instead, the psychologist uses psychological test data to develop a conceptualization of an individual's psychological functioning based on specific test findings that have been shown empirically to be associated with relevant extratest behaviors, including symptoms, interpersonal relationships, organization of thinking, emotional control, self-concept, and defenses, among others. These findings are then compared to and integrated with information from other sources, including clinical history and observations of the client during the evaluation, to generate a comprehensive, theoretically coherent formulation of the patient's psychological makeup.

Some theorists and clinicians have taken the position that test interpretations that rely on empirically validated findings are impersonal and ignore what is unique and distinctive about an individual's personality structure (Aronow et al., 1995; Sugarman, 1991). Other writers have countered that empirically validated conclusions are more accurate than conclusions based on clinical judgment, even if informed by theory and intuition, especially when guidelines for clinical decision making have been empirically validated (Meehl, 1954; Sarbin, 1986; Sawyer, 1966; Wiggins, 1973). In the context of this discussion on the stages of test interpretation, the emphasis placed on the objective nature of a psychological evaluation does not imply that there is no room for theory during interpretation of psychological test data; as discussed later, theoretical concepts related to personality development, psychological organization and functioning, and psychopathology play an important role in test interpretation, particularly during the second and third stages of the interpretive process.

Finn and Kamphuis (1995) recognized that many clinicians are reluctant to rely on empirically derived guidelines in their clinical practice because doing so feels as if they are treating a client as "a number" rather than as a unique individual:

> As clinicians, we may believe that we are caring more about clients when we avoid using statistics to make decisions that affect them. In fact, however, the costs of such decisions are likely to far outweigh their benefits. We show our greatest caring when we use all the information available to make the most accurate decisions possible about out clients. (p. 233)

Thus, there is little justification for ignoring what can be learned about an individual based on the impressive body of research that has accumulated for the MMPI-2 and the Rorschach Comprehensive System in favor of an approach relying primarily on clinical intuition and judgment.

The previous should not be taken to imply that clinical judgment has no place in the interpretive process. Although statistically derived interpretations are more likely to be accurate than clinical judgment in situations that have been adequately researched, clinical inferences are quite justified in the many situations for which empirically derived decision rules have not yet been articulated and validated, for highly unique circumstances, and for those decisions that are not readily translated into statistical formulae (Kleinmuntz, 1990; Meehl, 1967). Furthermore, currently there are no empirically validated guidelines to integrate multiple test findings in clinically meaningful ways. In other words, it would be a mistake to conclude that the controversy between clinical and statistical approaches to test interpretation must be resolved by adopting either one or the other approach; in the real world it is most effective to utilize both approaches in a thoughtful manner, recognizing the strengths and weaknesses of each.

The discussion of test interpretation presented below also takes into account research that has identified biases and distortions affecting how most people make decisions, whether they are professionals or laypersons (Hogarth, 1987; Kahneman & Tversky, 1973; Tversky & Kahneman, 1978). This research has found that biases in thinking that operate unintentionally, automatically, and outside of conscious awareness can lead to errors in judgment, such as the complex judgments involved in differential diagnosis or in describing a patient's personality characteristics. Because the effects of these biases are nearly universal, researchers suggest that the processes affecting judgment and choice are a byproduct of how human thinking evolved to increase efficiency and simplify decision making by using shortcuts, commonly referred to as heuristics. Anyone involved in decision making, such as a clinician interpreting psychological test data, can avoid being influenced by these heuristics only if they recognize that the heuristics exist and then consciously attempting to minimize their effects on the decision making process (Arkes, 1981; Hogarth, 1987).

PRELIMINARY HYPOTHESES

The first stage in the interpretive process involves generating initial hypotheses about an individual's psychological functioning based on a review of each discrete test score, such as individual MMPI-2 scales and codetypes or Rorschach clusters and the distribution of variables. The goal of the first stage of the interpretive process is to identify meaningful findings about an individual grounded in the results of the empirical literature, rather than in developing a theoretically based explanation about the person's presentation. At this point, all interpretive hypotheses should be entertained and none discarded lest the examiner prematurely dismiss a potentially meaningful finding. Greene (1991), for instance, recommended that "each [MMPI-2] scale should be analyzed sequentially with notes made on what each score means and any hypotheses recorded that occur to the clinician" (p. 288). Similarly, Exner (1993) advocated reviewing all the Rorschach data in the sequence directed by the search strategy to formulate initial interpretive proposition and hypotheses: "At this point, it is important that no reasonable hypothesis be rejected simply because it does not seem compatible with other propositions generated from the review. It is also quite important that all of the components are studied, not simply those that are unusual or dramatic" (p. 324). In other words, the initial stage of interpretation should be data driven rather than theory driven. For example, during the first phase of test interpretation there is a difference between concluding that the data are consistent with an episode of depression as opposed to conceptualizing a depressive reaction as the result of anger turned inward, object loss, learned helplessness, cognitive distortions, or a reaction to a narcissistic injury, conclusions that should be reserved for later stages in the interpretive process.

The importance of systematically reviewing all of the interpretations suggested by the psychological test data cannot be emphasized enough. One reason why it is important to systematically consider the interpretive implications of each test score is to avoid making biased interpretations of test data. One trap that can influence clinical judgment during the first stage of test interpretation is termed a *confirmatory bias*, the tendency for an individual to prematurely make a decision and then maintain that conclusion without considering evidence contradicting one's initial impressions. For instance, people are more likely to selectively attend to information that confirms their initial thoughts than to information that challenges or conflicts with their initial hypotheses. Information consistent with one's initial impressions are also treated preferentially and given the greatest weight in decision making, whereas inconsistent data is commonly dismissed or explained away. In other words, there is an automatic tendency for people to be selectively "open" to evidence confirming their initial hypotheses and selectively "closed" to evidence disconfirming them.

The danger of the confirmatory bias for clinical personality evaluations is clear because it is rare for clinicians to interpret test data "blindly." Usually, clinicians interview the persons they test and, in some cases, also have information from other sources, such as family members, clinical records, the referral source, or other members of a treatment team. It is natural and expectable that clinicians will develop hypotheses based on this nontest information. In fact, research has shown that mental health professionals form clinical impressions quite quickly. This point was made clearly in one rather extreme example: Psychiatrists shown a filmed interview formed diagnostic impressions about the person they observed within the first 30 to 60 seconds of the interview (Gauron & Dickinson, 1969). It is quite likely that other mental health professionals also quickly form impressions about their clients. A bias towards accepting information that confirms initial impressions can influence how clinicians approach and organize data from a psychological evaluation: according to the confirmatory bias, clinicians are more likely to focus on test data that reinforces their initial hypotheses and ignore, discredit, or reinterpret information that contradicts their initial conclusions, even though they do not intend to do so and are not aware of instances when they have (Arkes, 1981; Arkes & Harkness, 1980).

For instance, a woman raised in the Philippines who attended college in the USA before beginning to work as a computer programmer was referred for psychotherapy by her physician after a thorough medical work-up found no medical explanation for recurrent headaches. The patient and therapist identified a relationship between the onset of these debilitating headaches and stressful interpersonal interactions at work. She explained that these interactions occurred because she was Asian; was assigned a heavier work load than her coworkers, who were predominantly White; and was given the least desirable assignments. The therapist initially planned to reduce the patient's tension by teaching deep muscle relaxation and eventually to increase the patient's ability to handle these upsetting encounters more assertively.

When only minor improvement occurred after these interventions were implemented the therapist arranged a consultation with another colleague. The consultant suggested a psychological evaluation to objectively assess the patient's level of stress, coping style, and tendency to react to stress by developing psychosomatic symptoms. The patient's MMPI-2 profile was remarkable for an unexpected elevation on scale 6 (Paranoia; $T = 81$), with secondary elevations on scales 1 ($T = 76$) and 2 ($T = 72$). The therapist initially rejected the consultant's interpretation that the troubling interpersonal interactions might occur because the patient could be irritable, grouchy, stubborn, and overly sensitive to criticism. The therapist saw no inconsistency when he discounted the elevation on Scale 6 as due to the patient's upbringing outside of the USA, while accepting that the elevations on scales 1 and 2 were valid. In other words, the therapist engaged in a confirmatory bias.

The antidote for the confirmatory bias is to deliberately review the test data in a systematic, impartial manner to develop hypotheses using test data alone and to systematically check whether the data confirms or contradicts initial impressions based on nontest data, as well as the clinician's first reactions to the test protocol. The risk of confirmatory bias may also be minimized if the clinician deliberately thinks about alternative interpretations after initial hypotheses are formulated (Hogarth, 1987; Ross, Lepper, Strack, & Steinmetz, 1977). Ideally, this systematic review of the test data will permit the clinician to generate impartial, unbiased hypotheses about the test data that can then be evaluated further in the second and third stages of test interpretation.

EVALUATE AND REFINE HYPOTHESES

In the second stage of the interpretive process, the clinician identifies points of agreement and disagreement among the initial interpretive findings to determine whether the preliminary hypotheses should be accepted, modified, or discarded. During this stage of interpretation the clinician examines relationships among MMPI-2 and Rorschach findings and identifies points of agreement and disagreement. The framework described in chapter 3 is one approach to organizing these findings. In general, the clinician can have considerable confidence that a particular interpretation is correct if it is confirmed by several pieces of data, particularly if the same conclusion is suggested by independent sources. Holt (1968), for example, stated that "convergence of interpretations arising from different tests and different types of interpretive principles is the soundest basis of all for the tester's having enough confidence in his point to include it in his report" (p. 20).

Ideally, all findings related to a specific hypothesis will mesh and agree. In clinical practice, however, one should expect to find both agreement and disagreement among related test scores in nearly every case. While discussing MMPI-2 interpretation, for instance, Greene (1991) noted:

> Inferences or hypotheses that are suggested by several scales are important to note since they may represent central features of the client. It is a rare profile, however, that does not also contain inconsistent information; the contradictory inferences that result are important since they will somehow need to be resolved in interpreting the profile. (p. 289)

Greene's recognition that discrepancies within a test are commonplace occurrences that need to be reconciled has an important implication for the way in which clinicians view inconsistent findings between tests, such as the MMPI-2 and Rorschach. Whereas MMPI-2 within-test differences are regarded as routine occurrences that do not call into question the validity of the MMPI-2 and discrepancies among Rorschach variables do not call into question the validity of the Rorschach, discrepancies between the MMPI-2 and Rorschach are sometimes viewed as quite significant, to the point that some clinicians become concerned with determining which test is right and which is wrong. Because the validity and reliability of the Rorschach and MMPI-2 are comparable (Parker et al., 1988) and, as discussed in chapter 2, apparent disagreement between the MMPI-2 and Rorschach can occur for a variety of reasons without necessarily invalidating either test, there is little rational justification for reacting to between-test differences as a sign that one must decide between the Rorschach or the MMPI-2. Instead, between-test differences should be treated exactly as within-test differences are treated, namely as common occurrences to be resolved in a thoughtful, meaningful, clinically useful manner. Guidelines for making these determinations are discussed in detail in chapter 5.

INTEGRATION

During this stage of the interpretive process the clinician organizes, refines, and integrates hypotheses generated from the test data to describe the person's psychological functioning as fully and completely as possible. The clinician does not simply list the discrete, independent signs and symptoms suggested by individual test scores during the first two stages of test interpretation in a piecemeal fashion but instead develops an in-depth, theoretically coherent description of an individual patient's current psychological makeup based on an integration of test findings, information about the individual's past history and current clinical presentation, and the clinician's knowledge of psychopathology, human behavior, and clinical theory. These conclusions should address various aspects of psychological functioning including the person's symptoms, self-concept, organization of thought processes, contact with reality, self-control, defenses, potential for acting out, and interpersonal functioning. In addition, the clinician can use the integrated results from a psychological assessment to address questions concerning differential diagnosis, personality structure, dynamics of behavior, and probable response to treatment.

As discussed in chapter 1, both the MMPI-2 and the Rorschach Comprehensive System are atheoretical. Although neither assessment instrument is linked to a specific personality theory, the clinician can use empirically derived MMPI-2 and Rorschach findings as the basis on which higher order inferences about an individual's psychological characteristics can be developed. Use of a clinical theory can help the clinician organize and integrate diverse test findings and also allows the clinician to generate additional inferences not contained specifically in the test data (Lerner, 1991; Sugarman, 1991). For instance, if the clinical history and pattern of test findings are consistent with a Borderline Personality Disorder, the clinician might link test findings of clinically significant depression (scale $2 = 85$, $DEPI =$

6), interpersonal neediness ($T = 2$; Food $= 4$), and anger and resentment (scale $4 = 70$; scale $6 = 72$, $S = 4$) as indicating that the patient is likely to react to abandonment with intense depression and rage. Furthermore, the clinician could infer that this patient is likely to alternate between idealization and hostile devaluation of other people, including the therapist. The latter inference could reasonably be suggested based on current conceptualizations of the disorder even though this specific interpretation is not suggested directly by the test data.

Questions of differential diagnosis can also be addressed during the third stage of the interpretive process. It should be noted that neither MMPI-2 nor Rorschach results translate directly into many of the behavioral and symptom criteria needed to make *DSM–IV* diagnoses. However, MMPI-2 and Rorschach results can be used to describe patients' psychological organization, personality structure, and the symptoms, characteristics, and behaviors associated with particular configurations of test data (Exner, 1991; Graham, 1993). Thus, MMPI-2 and Rorschach data can confirm the presence or absence of symptoms reported by patients, such as depression or psychosis, and can show whether an individual patient responded similarly to patients with a particular disorder. In some instances this data can support or rule out a specific diagnosis. For instance, a psychotic disorder may be ruled out if no signs of psychotic experiences, thought disorder, and cognitive slippage are apparent on either the MMPI-2 or the Rorschach. Test results can also identify similarities and differences among patients who meet criteria for the same *DSM–IV* diagnosis, information that can be useful for tailoring treatment strategies to the individual patient.

Two heuristics, the *availability heuristic* and *hindsight bias*, potentially can affect the conclusions reached during the integrative stage of the interpretive process. The availability heuristic is based on research showing that an individual's choice among several, equally plausible alternative explanations for a particular situation can be influenced by how familiar they are with and how recently they have been exposed to the different explanations: the explanation the individual has been exposed to most recently is the one most likely to be chosen, presumably because it is cognitively more accessible than other, competing explanations (Hogarth, 1987). For instance, the availability heuristic predicts that a therapist is more likely to think about and address countertransference issues immediately after attending a workshop about countertransference than a month later because the knowledge acquired during the workshop is "fresher," more readily available, immediately after the workshop than at a later point in time. Thoughts about countertransference issues come to mind more readily than thoughts about other issues because the therapist is "primed" to attend to this topic and to organize the clinical data within that framework. This does not necessarily mean that other conceptual frameworks are less applicable, only that the therapist's thinking and interventions are guided by the framework uppermost in his or her mind. Note that the availability heuristic influences an individual's choice of explanations not as a function of knowledge about or understanding of the various theoretical concepts but simply as a result of which explanation has been thought about and processed most recently or which explanation is most familiar.

Awareness of the availability heuristic has an important implication for the integrative stage of psychological assessment, namely that a psychologist who routinely interprets test data using a particular theoretical perspective is likely to interpret other cases using the same theoretical perspective, not necessarily because the theory fits the clinical data best, but because that theoretical framework is most accessible. For instance, a psychologist who usually uses self-psychology as a framework to organize test results is more likely to explain a patient's symptoms as a function of a disorder of the self rather than of cognitive distortions, whereas a cognitive therapist, given the same data, is more likely to conclude that the patient's problems are due to errors in thinking than to a lack of self-cohesion. Rather than relying on the theoretical constructs with which they are most familiar, clinicians should challenge themselves to consider which theoretical position is most consistent with the test data delineated in the first two stages of the interpretive process, as well as which has the greatest explanatory power.

A second heuristic, the hindsight bias, can also influence how test data is interpreted, particularly when clinicians attempt to construct causal explanations for a client's current behavior. The hindsight bias involves the tendency for people who know a specific outcome has already occurred to have unrealistic confidence they could have accurately predicted that outcome before it occurred (Fischoff, 1975). In other words, the probability that an event will occur is judged to be more likely when one knows that the event has occurred; people are much more confident about their ability to predict an outcome in hindsight as opposed to their ability to predict the same event in foresight. Furthermore, knowing that an outcome has happened affects how the person organizes, integrates, and weighs information related to the outcome so as to create the impression that the outcome was inevitable (Hawkins & Hastie, 1990). For instance, a clinician performing a psychological evaluation of a female who presented with an eating disorder learned that the patient was sexually abused on one occasion as a child. The clinician might conclude that the patient's eating disorder was the inevitable results of these events, even though an association between sexual abuse and eating disorders has not been demonstrated (Finn, Hartman, Leon, & Lawson, 1986). Similarly, after hearing that a murderer was physically abused as a child, one might conclude with utter certainty that the murder was the inevitable outcome of the childhood abuse, even though most victims of childhood abuse do not murder as adults. This phenomenon is recognized in popular culture by the label "Monday morning quarterback," a term that captures how easy it is for a person to feel they "knew" a particular outcome was clear after the fact, as though the chain of events was simple, easily understandable, and predictable. These errors in judgment may also be attributed to failures to consider or take into account base rate information, the actual as opposed to perceived probabilities that events are associated (Finn & Kamphuis, 1995). In the latter case, the base rate fallacy concerns the failure to consider how often victims of childhood abuse murder.

The hindsight bias may play a role in how clinicians explain a person's current psychological functioning (the outcome) based on knowledge of the person's past history. This is particularly relevant to the accuracy and confidence with which genetic reconstructions are made. For example, a clinician might conclude that a male patient is emotionally constricted and interpersonally detached because the man's father died when he was 9. Although this explanation is compelling, the hindsight bias warns clinicians to be cautious about stating that a specific outcome (emotional constriction and interpersonal detachment) was caused entirely and inevitably by specific events, because it is possible the clinician does not know everything there is to know about the factors contributing to the development of these problems.

Schafer (1954) warned against using Rorschach data as the basis for genetic reconstructions for reasons quite similar to those discussed previously related to the hindsight bias. For instance, Schafer critiqued an interpretation of a response to Card IV on the Rorschach as indicating a negative attitude toward a domineering, critical, overwhelming type of father-figure as:

> *gratuitous* because it is nothing more than a statement of a psychoanalytic proposition concerning the genesis of overwhelming father-figures. It is in no way derived from the Rorschach test responses. . . . [A genetic reconstruction] infers sequences of early relationships and details of the personalities involved from what the patient emphasizes at present. It thereby neglects the inevitable selectivity, distortion and other retrospective falsification in current representations of remote experience. How a patient spontaneously represents his past tells us how he needs to see his past *now*. At best this account is only fairly well correlated with the actual past. It is by no means identical with it. The present "autobiography" cannot therefore be taken at face value. Often it is only late in treatment before certain vital corrections are introduced into the patient's account of his past. . . . For these reasons and those mentioned earlier, Rorschach images cannot be considered reliable indicators of the actual past. (p. 144)

Recognition that retrospective analyses are likely to be limited in a number of important respects suggests that clinicians should be cautious in presenting explanations as to why particular symptoms, character traits, or interpersonal difficulties developed. This may relieve pressure from those psychologists who believe that a diagnostic evaluation is not complete unless they have "discovered" the historical bases for a patient's problems, conflicts, and interpersonal relationships in the test data they gathered. The biasing effects of judgments made in hindsight can be minimized by presenting discussions of how problems developed as inferences that are probable or likely, rather than as inevitable outcomes given the unique circumstances of the person's life history (Brehmer, 1980; Einhorn, 1986; Garb, 1989).

5 Test Interpretation III: Integrating MMPI-2–Rorschach Findings

As discussed in chapter 4, during the interpretive process, the clinician must account for and understand the points of agreement and disagreement suggested by MMPI-2 and Rorschach results. Examination of these relationships may permit the clinician to modify or clarify the meaning of certain data, suggesting, for instance, that an interpretation be moderated in one case and emphasized in another. Thus, test results can be viewed as agreeing with, conflicting with, or complementing one another. The definitions and implications of these relationships are discussed here.

SIMILAR FINDINGS

Conjoint use of the MMPI-2 and Rorschach can be viewed as a multimethod strategy to assess an individual's psychological functioning using two tests with nonoverlapping assessment methods that have comparable psychometric properties. One's confidence in a particular conclusion should be quite strong when the results of both tests agree. For instance, if a referral question centers on the presence or absence of schizophrenia, the clinician should view agreement between the MMPI-2 (elevations on scales F, 6, 8, and BIZ) and Rorschach ($SCZI = 6$) as providing powerful support for a diagnosis of schizophrenia. Similarly, robust evidence for a diagnosis of depression might be seen on both the MMPI-2 (elevations on scale 2 and DEP) and Rorschach (positive DEPI, $C = 3$, $V = 2$, $MOR = 4$). In general, the clinician can be quite confident in stating a particular conclusion that has been confirmed by multiple sources, particularly when agreement is found among tests using different approaches (cf. Holt, 1968; Weiner, 1995b).

The examples provided previously illustrate agreement between the MMPI-2 and Rorschach at the level of individual test scores. This is the level most research examining MMPI–Rorschach interrelationships has focused on. The MMPI-2 and Rorschach may also be related at the level of psychological constructs associated with or inferred from a pattern of test scores. For instance, one important feature of interpersonal functioning associated with a *23/32* codetype is a tendency to be dependent and passive in relationships. The Rorschach may similarly show signs of a passive-dependent orientation towards interpersonal relationships ($a{:}p = 2{:}6$; $T = 2$; Food $= 3$; $COP = 4$; $AG = 0$). Another behavioral correlate associated with the 23/32 codetype is overcontrolled feelings and being "bottled up" emotionally. Several Rorschach scores are directly related to how freely and comfortably an individual expresses emotions. Scores on these variables can also show emotional constriction (e.g., $EA = 6{:}1.0$; $FC{:}CF+C = 2{:}0$; $SumC{:}WSumC = 3{:}1$; $Afr = .38$). It is possible that meaningful agreement between the MMPI-2 and Rorschach will be found at the level of specific constructs, such as those outlined in chapter 3, as well as at the level of individual test scores. To date, however, relationships between the MMPI-2 and Rorschach at the level of psychological constructs have not been examined empirically.

As discussed in chapter 2, issues concerning convergent validity may be of critical importance when clinical decisions are made. In a time when rapid clinical work and cost containment are emphasized and demanded, it is particularly important to stress the significance of accurate clinical decision making, the results of which can have significant effects on the treatment patients receive. For example, determining whether the first psychotic decompensation for a young adult reflects a schizophrenic process or an affective psychosis can have profound implications for the type of treatment the patient receives, decisions about realistic vocational goals, and the explanations and education given to family members about the patient's clinical condition and prognosis.

DIVERGENT FINDINGS

Resolving conflicting findings in data obtained during a psychological evaluation is a major challenge for clinicians. As discussed in chapter 4 and previously in this chapter, there are few cases in which all findings from all sources agree. Much more frequently the data suggests ambiguous and/or contradictory interpretations. The challenge for the clinician is to thoughtfully and carefully consider the various interpretive possibilities and decide which are the most accurate and most meaningful.

As noted previously, inconsistent and contradictory hypotheses occur not only between the MMPI-2 and Rorschach but within a test as well. For example, several MMPI-2 clinical scales have parallel content and supplementary scales that tap similar, if not identical, domains. These include scale *2* (Depression) and *DEP* (Depression), scale *8* (Schizophrenia) and *BIZ* (Bizarre Mentation), and scale *4* (Psychopathic Deviate) and *ASP* (Antisocial Practices), among others. An elevation on a clinical scale (e.g., scale *8*), however, is not always accompanied by an elevation on parallel content and supplementary scales (e.g., *BIZ*). The lack of correspondence between the two scales does not automatically invalidate the findings of one or the other of these scales. When an elevation occurs on one scale but not scales related to it, the clinician must wrestle with these findings and explain why this has occurred. Similarly, the clinician must also wrestle with and explain conflicting findings between tests. Guidelines for addressing and reconciling within-test and between-test discrepancies are discussed here.

What Does Each Measure?

Although the names of related MMPI-2 clinical, content, and supplementary scales suggest they are identical, some scales do not necessarily overlap completely and may actually tap different aspects of a particular domain. For instance, scale *8* can be elevated because a patient endorsed items related to psychotic experiences, confused thinking, social isolation and alienation or difficulties in impulse control and judgment. In contrast, *BIZ* is a "purer" measure of the disturbed thought processes and strange experiences associated with a psychotic disorder. Thus, finding that scale *8* is elevated while *BIZ* is not could suggest that scale *8* was elevated because the patient differentially endorsed the nonpsychotic items found on scale *8*. In this instance, the clinician should be quite cautious before concluding that the patient presented with a psychotic disorder. Alternatively, strong evidence that a patient is psychotic may occur when elevations are seen on both scale *8* and *BIZ*.

A lack of agreement between related MMPI-2 and Rorschach scales might also occur because the scales do not overlap completely. For instance, a patient may produce a positive Rorschach Hypervigilance Index (HVI) and an average MMPI-2 score on scale *6* (Paranoia). The positive *HVI* could indicate that the person is apprehensive and vigilant, interpersonally distant and reserved, and concerned about accounting for the meaning of discrete, unrelated bits of information without feeling suspicious, overly sensitive, and resentful about being mistreated, picked on, or persecuted, as would be suggested if scale *6* were elevated. In other words, the clinician must consider the extent to which related scales on the MMPI-2 and Rorschach are actually tapping overlapping constructs as opposed to measuring different aspects of a specific dimension of psychological functioning.

Scale 8 and the SCZI provide another example of how related MMPI-2 and Rorschach scales can overlap to a considerable degree while also measuring different aspects of a particular phenomenon. Although elevations on both are reliably associated with a psychotic disorder, they do not tap identical aspects of psychotic disorders. Whereas items on scale 8 involve psychotic experiences, mental confusion, peculiar perceptions, difficulty distinguishing between fantasy and reality, social alienation, unusual sensory experiences, and poor judgment, the components of the SCZI involve inaccurate, distorted perceptions, cognitive slippage, and thought disorder. Examination of the SCZI shows that four of its six components involve perceptual inaccuracy; thus, it is quite sensitive to unusual, distorted, or idiosyncratic perceptions. Although both scale 8 and SCZI are sensitive to disordered thinking and disturbances in reality testing, it is possible for one to be elevated but not the other. For instance, an individual can produce a positive SCZI and normal scale 8 because of poor perceptual accuracy without exhibiting signs of thought disorder. Just as the clinician must understand the implications of discrepant findings between scale 8 and BIZ, as discussed previously, the lack of agreement between the SCZI and scale 8 in this example should prompt the clinician to carefully consider why the SCZI was positive, how that relates to the low score on scale 8, and what this combination says about the presence or absence of a psychotic disorder.

Do the Psychometric Properties of the Scales Differ?

A second question to be asked when related scales yield conflicting results involves whether the scales' psychometric properties are equivalent. Of particular interest is the extent to which the scales' external validity, the strength of association with a nontest criterion variable, has been demonstrated. Graham (1993), for instance, suggested that inconsistent interpretations suggested by different MMPI-2 findings should be reconciled by relying on the codetype or scale that has the greatest empirical support. For instance, a patient may produce a score within the average range on scale 2 ($T = 50$), suggesting that the patient is not clinically depressed, while also obtaining an elevation on D5 (Brooding; $T = 79$), suggesting that the patient is unhappy, feels useless, and questions if life is worth living. Graham suggested that greater weight be given to findings from scale 2 because the meaning of scores on scale 2 have been empirically validated to a greater extent than the meaning of scores on D5.

In other words, if discrepant results are found on related scales, the clinician should place the greatest emphasis on findings from the scale that has been shown to be the more reliable, powerful predictor of the psychological variable of interest.

Associations between MMPI-2 scales and specific disorders and between Rorschach indices and specific disorders have been well established (Exner, 1993; Graham, 1993; Greene, 1991). There is a dearth of empirical research addressing the issue of the relative sensitivity and specificity of the MMPI-2 and Rorschach for specific disorders using both instruments in the same sample. Thus, at present it is difficult to weigh whether scores from the two tests show similar or different patterns of association with specific criterion variables, such as a diagnosis of an affective disorder or the presence of schizoid personality characteristics.

Clinical experience suggests that the MMPI-2 and Rorschach may be differentially sensitive in certain areas. For instance, the MMPI-2 seems to identify patients with somatic preoccupations and concerns more reliably than the Rorschach. Elevations on MMPI-2 scales *1* and *3* are generally considered to be robustly associated with excessive concerns about health and to identify patients whose physical complaints involve a significant psychosomatic component (Graham, 1993; Greene, 1991). In contrast, the Rorschach has relatively weak indicators of psychosomatic concerns. The primary Rorschach variable associated with health-related concerns is the sum of Anatomy and X-ray responses $(An+Xy)$. Exner (1993) suggested that some bodily concern may be present when $An+Xy$ is 1 or 2, whereas excessive preoccupation with health issues and bodily integrity can be identified when $An+Xy$ is greater than or equal to 3. Although an elevation on $An+Xy$ is infrequently seen without some health-related concerns, patients with psychosomatic disorders frequently do not elevate this Rorschach index. In other words, a low score on $An+Xy$ is likely to result in a large number of false negative clinical decisions (e.g., saying patients do not have excessive somatic concerns when they do).

In the event that a clinician has determined that certain scores on one test are more reliably associated with a specific criterion variable than a score on the other test, discrepancies between the two tests should be resolved in favor of the more robust measure. Following the example given previously, if a patient's protocol includes $An+Xy = 0$ and elevations on MMPI-2 Scales *1* $(T = 82)$ and *3* $(T = 85)$, the clinician should conclude that the MMPI-2 data are meaningful and should be accepted with little hesitation regardless of the Rorschach findings.

Do the Data Identify a Conflict?

Findings that initially appear to be inconsistent or contradictory may in some instances point to meaningful aspects of an individual's personality that surface at different times or in different situations. In other instances, inconsistent test findings may be due to different aspects or phases of a psychiatric disorder. For instance, one might not expect scales *3* (Hysteria) and *4* (Psychopathic Deviate) to be elevated simultaneously because scale *3* usually indicates denial, suppression, and inhibition of emotions, particularly anger, as well as a high level of concern about conformity and pleasing others. In contrast, scale *4* is often associated with acting out and impulsive discharges of feelings, including anger, without concern for the effects this has on others. Thus, concurrent elevations on both scales *3* and *4* may seem to be counter-intuitive. One important interpretation of simultaneous elevations on scales *3* and *4* is that the person experiences a conflict concerning impulse control and has difficulty expressing anger in an appropriate, modulated manner. As a result, *34/43* individuals are usually emotionally overcontrolled and express anger indirectly without showing any signs of distress or displeasure until they have an angry outburst and blow up, often to the surprise of others. Thus, what may at first appear to be a contradiction in the test findings may provide meaningful information about the persons' tendency to act one way at one point in time and a different way at a different point in time, ways that deviate to a significant degree from their customary behavior. This can occur because of a conflict, such as over expression as opposed to inhibition of angry, hostile feelings, or because of shifts in their clinical condition, such as between depressed and manic phases of a bipolar disorder.

Differences between the MMPI-2 and Rorschach can also highlight aspects of a person's personality that are expressed at different points in time or may identify a conflict. For instance, one man complained to his physician that he lacked energy and felt constantly tired. After finding no physical explanation for these symptoms, the physician referred the man for a psychological evaluation to determine whether he was depressed. During the clinical interview the patient denied all symptoms of depression. The MMPI-2 profile was notable for a moderately high score on scale *4* ($T = 67$) and a markedly low score on scale *5* ($T = 35$). The high 4 and low 5 indicates he was very invested in portraying himself as being masculine, independent, and in control (Friedman et al., 1989). Consistent with this, during the clinical interview he repeatedly expressed his philosophy that his auto supply company succeeded because of his hard work, initiative, and self-reliance: "When I started I had nothing, but I earned each customer's loyalty. Nobody hands you business on a silver platter. People don't just come knocking at your door. Each and every day I wake up knowing I have to prove to them that no one takes care of them better."

Although the MMPI-2 profile showed how much this man valued being strong and independent, his responses to the Rorschach revealed strong dependency needs (Texture = 2; Food = 2), needs that were not acknowledged during the clinical interview or on the MMPI-2. The discrepancy between MMPI-2 and Rorschach findings suggests that one important aspect of this man's functioning is a conflict between the side of him that is strong and independent as opposed to the side of him that wants to be close to and comforted by someone. In other words, these findings suggest that his emphasis on the traditional masculine values of strength and self-reliance reflect counter-dependent dynamics. After formulating this hypothesis, the clinician recalled that the patient had mentioned in passing that his wife traveled out of state for an indeterminate period of time to care for her ailing mother several days before he visited his physician but then quickly informed the examiner that he was perfectly capable of cooking for himself and had plenty to do to occupy his time.

Is the Client Consciously Skewing Responses?

Not all clients respond openly on both the MMPI-2 and the Rorschach. Some produce interpretable MMPI-2 but not Rorschach protocols, and others produce interpretable Rorschach but not MMPI-2 records. This can occur for many different reasons including a conscious attempt to deny or minimize problems or a conscious exaggeration of problems. For instance, patients may successfully avoid revealing emotional difficulties on a face-valid self-report inventory because they can selectively decide which items to endorse, while producing responses on a projective test indicating a psychological problem does exist because they are unaware of how responses to projective tests are related to the psychological variables they are trying to conceal (cf. Ganellen, 1994; Shapiro et al., 1990). Conversely, some clients may be more comfortable responding to self-report measures than to projective techniques and produce a valid MMPI-2 profile and a defensive Rorschach protocol that reveals little about their psychological state, either because the record is constricted (e.g., *Lambda* ≥ 1.00), or because they produce few responses (cf. Brinkman et al., 1994). In other instances individuals who deliberately attempt to fabricate or exaggerate the severity of psychological difficulties on the MMPI-2, such as having a psychotic disorder, may be unable to do so on the Rorschach (Ganellen et al., 1996).

Do the Data Reflect Different Levels of Awareness?

Admission of psychological difficulties on the MMPI-2 but not the Rorschach can occur either as a result of a conscious response set, as just discussed, or as a result of unconscious processes and defenses. For instance, individuals with a conversion disorder typically repress and deny anxiety, depression, worry, and emotional concerns and are therefore likely to produce scores within the normal range on MMPI-2 scales related to depression and anxiety. It is possible that some of these patients will produce a Rorschach protocol indicating they experience significant emotional distress (e.g., *DEPI* = 6; *D* score = -1; *Y* = 4; Color Shading Blends = 2) even though they did not endorse MMPI-2 items related to .emotional distress (e.g., scale *2* = 53; *DEP* = 55; scale *7* = 55; *ANX* = 52).

The apparent disagreement between the MMPI-2 and Rorschach in this example can be understood in terms of differences in the methods by which the two measures identify and assess emotional distress; the MMPI-2 relies on the patient's acknowledgment of distress using a verbal self-report format, whereas the Rorschach relies on the presence or absence of specific contents and determinants such as morbid content, shading, inanimate movement, and achromatic color, and scores on specific ratios such as the Egocentricity Ratio and Isolation Index. Thus, the two tests assess the same psychological construct using different methodologies. It is possible that the psychological operations involved in these related, but nonoverlapping approaches are differentially accessible to conscious awareness. In other words, in some instances MMPI-2 and Rorschach findings will be discrepant because what individuals consciously "know" and are able to say about their psychological makeup is at odds with aspects of themselves about which they have little or no conscious awareness. Clinically, identifying the thoughts, feelings, and impulses individuals cannot acknowledge or express consciously is critical to developing the most complete, accurate description of their psychological functioning possible.

It is well recognized that the results of personality assessments can be affected both by factors consciously acknowledged by individuals and by factors they do not consciously acknowledge. In a discussion of defensive response sets, for instance, Greene (1991) distinguished between two explanations for minimization of psychological troubles, impression management and self-deception. *Impression management* refers to instances in which individuals consciously attempt to create a particular impression as a strategy to achieve a desired goal. This often occurs when individuals know that a desired outcome is contingent on the results of a psychological evaluation, such as being judged suitable for a job or being awarded custody of one's children. Issues pertaining to test interpretation when impression management skews psychological test data are discussed in the immediately preceding section.

Self-deception, in contrast, occurs when individuals acknowledge one aspect of themselves while simultaneously being motivated to avoid acknowledging other, conflicting aspects of their psychological condition. That is, many individuals protect themselves from recognizing unflattering aspects of their personality and behavior or from experiencing painful or unacceptable emotions by denying, repressing, disavowing, projecting, or splitting off from conscious awareness some parts of their experience. This can occur in many different ways, such as when patients develop somatoform or psychosomatic disorders because they have difficulty expressing psychological distress directly; when patients externalize responsibility for their problems and instead blame others, as is characteristic of many antisocial and narcissistic patients as well as many patients with a history of alcohol or substance abuse; or when patients develop a dissociative disorder because they are unable to integrate various aspects of their identity, emotions, or memory (cf. Meyer, 1994).

A similar point was made in a provocative article by Shedler, Mayman, and Manis (1993) who argued that objective personality instruments do not distinguish between self-reported genuine mental health and the appearance of mental health created when individuals deny psychological distress because of a need to see themselves as well adjusted and healthy, a condition they labeled *illusory* mental health. Persons in the latter group were characterized as preserving a belief they are well adjusted by disavowing negative aspects of their emotional life and thereby lacking awareness of unacceptable needs, wishes, and feelings. Shedler et al. (1993) identified subjects as having an illusion of mental health if there was a discrepancy between self-report and a projective measure of mental health, the Early Memories test. Other subjects were classified as genuinely healthy if they reported no distress on a self-report measure and were judged to be healthy on the projective measure or as manifestly distressed if they reported being distressed on a self-report measure and were judged to be distressed on the projective measure. As predicted, defensive deniers, subjects with illusory mental health, differed from the genuinely healthy and manifestly distressed groups on physiological measures when exposed to laboratory induced psychological stressors: subjects classified as having illusory mental health showed the greatest physiological reactivity to the stressors. Shedler et al. vigorously asserted that inaccurate conclusions about individuals' psychological adjustment can be reached if clinicians rely on self-report measures of psychological adjustment alone, particularly for those subjects who defensively deny psychological distress on self-report measures.

Some writers have asserted that the Rorschach is particularly well suited to uncover those aspects of patients' psychology they generally keep concealed and hidden, not only from others but often from themselves. In a discussion of the process by which responses to the Rorschach are formed and expressed, for instance, Schafer (1954) described how patients' feelings, personal issues, conflicts, and defenses interact with the imagery, colors, and shadings of the inkblots to produce responses that are "dramatically revealing of the adaptive and defensive strengths and weaknesses of the patient, his pathological trends, his conscious and unconscious values, yearnings, fears, wrath, guilt and joy, and the overall color and tone of his personality" (p. 113).

The possibility that objective and projective assessment approaches access information at different levels of conscious awareness has also been proposed by researchers who have repeatedly found weak relationships among objective and projective measures of personality functioning and different patterns of association among the objective and projective personality measures and the variables with which they were predicted to be correlated. McClelland, Koestner, and Weinberger (1989), for instance, summarized the results of a series of studies conducted over a 40-year period showing, first, that projective and objective measures of specific psychological characteristics, such as achievement needs, affiliation needs, and power needs, typically are either not correlated or have a low magnitude of correlation with one another and, secondly, have different patterns of correlations with a variety of outcome measures. Similarly, Bornstein, Bowers, and Robinson (1995) found that dependency needs assessed by valid, reliable projective and objective measures were unrelated to one another and were differentially related to ratings of the frequency and impact of interpersonal life events: as predicted, dependence assessed using the Rorschach Oral Dependency scale (Masling, Rabie, & Blondheim, 1967) was significantly correlated with ratings of interpersonal life events but not life events in other domains, whereas dependence assessed using a self-report measure was unrelated to any of the dependent measures.

Based on these results, McClelland et al. (1989) and Bornstein et al. (1995) speculated that projective measures identify implicit or underlying motivational and emotional themes in a person's life that influence their behavior in an automatic manner outside of conscious awareness. In contrast, self-report measures were characterized as identifying psychological characteristics, traits, and values individuals consciously attribute to themselves and report as being descriptive of themselves, even though these attributes may not influence their behavior in a consistent, meaningful way. They also argued that the personality characteristics identified using projective techniques are more strongly related to behavior than are objective measures of the same construct.

The implication of this discussion for clinical personality assessment is that MMPI-2 and Rorschach data should be expected to disagree in those instances in which the two instruments measure aspects of personality functioning at different levels of awareness, particularly when a marked discrepancy exists between the patients' conscious and unconscious experience, values, needs, and perceptions of self or others. To return to the example given earlier of individuals with an MMPI-2 "conversion V" who produce no elevations on MMPI-2 scales associated with emotional distress while elevating the Rorschach Depression Index, careful attention should be given to the possibility that the individual is vigorously defending against conscious acknowledgment of negative emotions including sadness, pessimism, self-criticism, and negative views of the world. These results suggest that these individuals will have difficulty openly acknowledging their painful emotional state if asked directly, and instead are likely to present with a "smiling depression," to express emotional pain by developing somatic symptoms, or to manifest behavioral signs of depression while insisting they are not sad, upset, or distressed.

Based on the discussion just given, it may be tempting to conclude that projective tests, such as the Rorschach, in general more accurately capture those aspects of individuals' psychological makeup that are outside of conscious awareness than self-report, objective tests such as the MMPI-2. This is likely to be true either if MMPI-2 interpretation does not take into account the effects of self-presentational concerns or defensiveness or if MMPI-2 interpretation is based entirely on elevations of individual clinical, content, or supplementary scales. However, as discussed in chapter 1, this is not likely to be the case when MMPI-2 interpretation is based on the clinical correlates associated with specific two-point and three-point codetypes as research has identified the clinical presentation, emotional characteristics, defensive operations, interpersonal functioning, and areas of conflict typically associated with each codetype.

For instance, the *36/63* codetype identifies angry, hostile individuals who are difficult to get along with because of their deep-seated, chronic hostility and hypersensitivity to others. *36/63* individuals characteristically do not recognize the presence or extent of their anger, "even though these attributes are apparent to every one but themselves. . . . They perceive their relationships in positive terms and have difficulty understanding why others react to them the way they do" (Greene, 1991, p. 272). In this example, *36/63* individuals are not likely to describe themselves as being angry, nor are they likely to be aware of their hostility, even though anger has a significant impact on their interactions with others. Thus, both MMPI-2 and Rorschach data have the potential to reveal more about individuals' psychological functioning than they say about themselves or are consciously aware of.

The example just given suggests that when MMPI-2 and Rorschach data disagree, clinicians should consider whether this discrepancy reflects a conscious attempt to skew the data, differential comfort with the format of one test as opposed to the other, or differences in the level of subjective awareness tapped by the methods of each assessment instrument. Decisions as to which of these possibilities apply in an individual case can be made by examining MMPI-2 validity indices, the patient's involvement during administration of each test, the defensive operations the patient typically relies on, and whether the clinical disorder with which the patient presents is generally recognized as involving a split between what is consciously acknowledged and what is blocked from awareness.

COMPLEMENTARY FINDINGS

The previous sections discussed the interpretive implications of instances when test data presumed to measure related variables agree or disagree. Conjoint use of the MMPI-2 and Rorschach also provides an opportunity to interpret test data in a complementary manner, either by identifying information in one test that was not present in the other or by using findings from one test to enrich interpretations based on the other test (Weiner, 1995b).

One model for complementary test interpretation is suggested by Duckworth and Anderson (1995). They illustrated how interpretation of MMPI-2 high-point scales can be modified by consideration of how the behavior and emotions associated with a scale elevation will either be accentuated or suppressed by elevations on other clinical and supplementary scales. For example, the behavior of a person with a Spike 4 codetype may be different than the behavior of a person with a *49/94* or a *34/43* two-point codetype. Friedman et al. (1989) made a similar point when they stated that "the way in which individuals [with elevations on scale *4*] handle the resentment and asocial impulses may differ greatly, depending on elevations of other aspects of the profile" (p. 177). An individual with a Spike 4 codetype is likely to be impulsive and rebellious, have poor relationships with parents and other authority figures, and exhibit poor frustration tolerance. The combination of *4* and *9* accentuates these characteristics as the *49/94* individual would be expected to be even more impulsive, irresponsible, and restless than an individual with a Spike 4 profile. In contrast, the combination of *4* and *3* moderates the impulsive, aggressive aspects of Scale 4. The *34/43* individual would be expected to show the behavioral problems typically associated with elevations on scale *4* relatively infrequently, usually as a sudden, explosive outburst of anger rather than a pattern of chronic, repeated acting out.

Although Duckworth and Anderson focused only on the use of within-test (MMPI-2) data in a complementary manner, the approach they described can be applied to complementary relationships using between-test results as well. In other words, Rorschach data can modify interpretation of MMPI-2 findings and vice versa. For example, an elevation on scale *4* may have less pathological implications if persons show adequate self-control and frustration tolerance on the Rorschach (e.g., $FC:CF+C = 5:2$; D score $= 0$) than if they show poor ability to control emotional reactions, limited frustration tolerance, and a high potential to act in an impulsive, unrestrained fashion (e.g., $FC:CF+C = 2:5$; D score $= -2$). Furthermore, the interpersonal relationships of Spike 4 individuals who show an interest in and concern about others on the Rorschach ($COP = 3$; $H:(H)+Hd+(HD) = 6:3$) are likely to be very different than the relationships of Spike 4 persons whose Rorschach responses indicate they are extremely egocentric, have a strong sense of entitlement, and view others as pawns to be used to achieve their goals ($Fr = 2$; $COP = 0$; $H:(H)+Hd+(Hd) = 3:6$).

MMPI-2 data can also augment interpretations based on Rorschach findings. For instance, the Rorschach may show that a man evaluated prior to starting psychotherapy is depressed ($DEPI = 6$), obsessively preoccupied with details, perfectionistic, and extremely concerned about acting in a conventional manner (positive OBS; $Dd = 5$; $Zf = 14$; Populars $= 9$). These interpretations may be modified on the basis of his MMPI-2 profile. Suppose for instance that one man with this Rorschach protocol obtains a *27/72* codetype whereas another man with an identical Rorschach record produces a *274* codetype. The individual who produces a positive *DEPI*, positive *OBS*, and *27/72* codetype is likely to be quite tense, anxious, and depressed and worries constantly, usually about personal deficiencies and failures to live up to high standards. Interpersonally, *27/72* persons are usually rather passive, dependent, and uncomfortable with expressing anger. The second patient is also likely to present with symptoms of anxiety, depression, and deeply ingrained feelings of inadequacy and guilt. In contrast to 27 individuals, persons who produce a *274* codetype are likely to be dependent, demanding, immature, and angry and frequently use alcohol excessively, often in an attempt to alleviate their depression. Thus, MMPI-2 results may help differentiate between two patients with similar Rorschach protocols by identifying problems that are not shown in the Rorschach results, such as the potential that alcohol abuse plays a significant role in the clinical picture or by highlighting issues in interpersonal functioning.

When used in a complementary manner, results from the MMPI-2 and Rorschach can highlight and emphasize certain interpretations and tone down or minimize others. Complementary relationships among the two tests may add considerable depth and richness to clinical interpretation of personality test data and are invaluable in identifying unique features of an individual's psychological functioning, features that may not be otherwise captured in MMPI-2 two-point codetypes or clusters of Rorschach variables.

A series of psychological evaluations illustrating the approach to integrating the MMPI-2 and Rorschach described in chapters 3, 4, and 5 is presented in the next section of the volume. Each patient was administered both the MMPI-2 and Rorschach during the same testing session. The format for the case presentations includes the circumstances of the evaluation; the patient's history, test data, interpretations of each test individually; and an integrated interpretation of these findings. Relationships between MMPI-2 and Rorschach findings and *DSM–IV* diagnoses are also discussed. The purpose of these case presentations is to demonstrate how combined findings from the MMPI-2 and Rorschach are more powerful than either test used alone when psychologists are asked to conduct psychological evaluations to answer specific referral questions; describe the individual's psychological functioning, symptoms, and dynamics; and formulate appropriate treatment recommendations.

The discussion of test data in these cases refers to specific MMPI-2 scores and codetypes and specific Rorschach indices at each step of the interpretive process. Rorschach data are approached following the interpretive search strategy developed by Exner (1991). Although the step-by-step interpretation and reference to specific scores may make the text cumbersome, it is our hope that the awkwardness of this method is balanced by the reader's ability to clearly see what each interpretation is based on and to follow the logic of the clinical inferences made by the author.

6 Case 1: Compulsive Cosmetic Surgery

REASON FOR EVALUATION

Mr. B is a 25-year-old, single, White male who was recently discharged after a 2-week stay on an inpatient psychiatric unit for treatment of anxiety, depression, and work-related stress. One central feature of Mr. B's psychological condition involves his concern about and preoccupation with a perceived physical deformity of his lip and chin. This concern began when he was 14. Although he has had three cosmetic surgeries, Mr. B continues to be bothered by his appearance and believes additional cosmetic surgery is needed. It should be noted that the patient looked normal with no visible defect or abnormality to the psychologist who examined him. A psychological evaluation to assess Mr. B's psychological status and aid in clarifying his diagnosis was requested by the psychiatrist who began treating Mr. B a month before the most recent hospitalization. In particular, the presence of an affective disorder as opposed to a psychotic disorder was questioned.

BACKGROUND INFORMATION

Mr. B. is the youngest of three brothers. His father, a prominent businessman, and his mother were both described in primarily positive terms. Mr. B described himself as doing well academically, being involved in athletics, and being socially active until age 14 when he started to notice and be disturbed by the size and shape of his lower jaw and lip. He thought this was noticeable to others who he feared would be "turned off" by his appearance.

As a result of these concerns, he began to withdraw from involvement with others. When asked to explain his concerns, he told the examiner it was similar to how a person with a serious physical deformity would feel, but less intense.

During high school, Mr. B continued to obtain above average grades and be involved with sports but described himself as becoming socially withdrawn, apparently because of concerns about his appearance. He became preoccupied with his facial features and with the possibility that surgery would correct the defects in his appearance. He did not tell family or friends about these concerns until age 17 when he approached his parents about his condition. Mr. B became extremely upset when his parents did not agree that his appearance was abnormal and caused problems in social relationships or that cosmetic surgery was needed. After this discussion, Mr. B's parents arranged for him to begin psychodynamically oriented psychotherapy and paid for this treatment. He reported deriving little benefit from this treatment, which lasted a year.

Mr. B has been distressed that his parents have never understood his reasons for wanting surgery and do not share his concern about his appearance. He stated a number of times that he does not believe they have been honest with him about this. When the examiner asked Mr. B why his parents would not be honest, he indicated he tried to understand this but can't; he would not elaborate further when asked what he meant. Mr. B has had several intense arguments with his father over the years when Mr. B tried to convince father that cosmetic surgery was needed to correct the defect in his appearance. One of the psychiatrists who has treated Mr. B suggested that further fights might be prevented if he and his father avoided discussing whether surgery is needed; both Mr. B and his father have complied with this ground rule.

At age 18, Mr. B saw a plastic surgeon who agreed to reconstruct the lower jaw and lip. This involved three surgeries. He delayed attending college a year so that the surgeries could be completed. The plastic surgeon required Mr. B to participate in insight-oriented psychotherapy during the course of these surgeries. Mr. B agreed to this condition and began treatment with a different therapist. He reported this helped him deal with the anxiety of surgery but was not helpful in other respects. At father's insistence, Mr. B terminated insight-oriented psychotherapy and began treatment with a biologically oriented psychiatrist who prescribed antidepressant medications and used cognitive therapy.

Mr. B was pleased with the results of the cosmetic surgeries. He then attended college where he majored in accounting and international finance. He was not involved in psychotherapy during college. After graduation, he was accepted into a training program for financial analysts at a large financial services institution. Mr. B reported doing well in the training program, which he completed with about a dozen trainees from other branches of the company.

Several days after beginning to work as a financial analyst, however, he became anxious, depressed, and overwhelmed. He contacted the psychiatrist who had treated him prior to the surgeries. She advised Mr. B to take a leave of absence from work. When his condition did not improve, the psychiatrist arranged admission to a hospital for inpatient psychiatric treatment. Mr. B attempted to return to work after being discharged from the hospital but again became so depressed and anxious that he was readmitted for psychiatric treatment. During the second hospitalization, he and his psychiatrist had a conflict about the need for an additional cosmetic surgery; Mr. B insisted the surgery was necessary, whereas his psychiatrist challenged his beliefs. As a result, he terminated treatment with her and was referred to a new psychiatrist (who requested this evaluation). Over time he has questioned whether the previous psychiatrist truly understood his concerns about his appearance and supported him, or whether she had humored him during the course of treatment. He feels their relationship was ruined when she appeared sceptical about the need for further surgery.

During the clinical interview, Mr. B acknowledged feeling depressed about "what I've been through the past several years," referring to the distress concerned by the defect in his appearance and conflicts with his parents. Sleep is normal. Appetite has been poor, and he has had to force himself to eat. He is active and enjoys working out, aerobics, and playing on a soccer team. Concentration was poor at work but has improved. He continues to feel self-conscious about his appearance and reported wanting an additional surgery to change the shape of his lower lip. The surgeon who operated on him in the past has told Mr. B this was not possible and could even be dangerous. He has subsequently consulted with another surgeon about this operation but was advised against further surgery. He asked his brothers to speak to the second surgeon on his behalf, and when they refused to do so, he exchanged angry words with them. He reported having suicidal thoughts and seriously contemplated suicide 4–5 months ago after conflict with father and his previous psychiatrist, neither of whom supported his desire to have additional cosmetic surgeries. He denied current suicidal intent.

At the time of this evaluation, Mr. B was being treated with antidepressant and anxiolytic medications. His "new" psychiatrist did not change the medication regimen prescribed by the previous psychiatrist pending clinical observation and the results of this evaluation. Mr. B denied use of alcohol or recreational drugs. He reported no family history of psychopathology.

DIAGNOSTIC CONSIDERATIONS

Mr. B's history is consistent with a *Body Dysmorphic Disorder,* which is defined in the *DSM–IV* as an intense preoccupation with an imagined or minor defect in physical appearance that causes emotional distress, self-consciousness, withdrawal from social involvement, and impairment in social, marital, or occupational functioning. One complication of this disorder is that patients often seek unnecessary cosmetic surgery or other medical procedures to correct perceived defects in their appearance.

In a review of the literature concerning Body Dysmorphic Disorder, Phillips (1991) noted that this condition may exist in its own right or may be a nonspecific symptom that occurs in a variety of psychiatric disorders including schizophrenia, delusional disorder with somatic content, depression, obsessive–compulsive disorder, social phobia, monosymptomatic hypochondriasis, or anorexia nervosa. The phenomenology of Body Dysmorphic Disorder is quite similar to obsessive–compulsive disorder, as both involve persistent, intrusive, distressing thoughts that are difficult to suppress or ignore. Phillips also observed that body dysmorphic disorder and delusional disorder, somatic type share several important characteristics that may make it difficult if not impossible to distinguish between the two. Patients whose preoccupation with their appearance is due to a delusional disorder, somatic type may improve when treated with antipsychotic medications, whereas nonpsychotic patients with body dysmorphic disorder are more likely to respond poorly to antipsychotic medications.

As the previous discussion indicates, the diagnosis of body dysmorphic disorder may be associated with or be the result of a wide range of psychiatric disorders. Although no specific MMPI-2 or Rorschach profile is associated with body dysmorphic disorder, different patterns of test results would be expected if Mr. B's presentation was due to schizophrenia, depression, obsessive–compulsive disorder, a delusional disorder, or hypochondriasis. Thus, the test data may provide important diagnostic information concerning Mr. B's preoccupation with the defect he perceives in his appearance, information that may have critical significance for treatment planning.

MMPI-2 Data

Validity.   The raw score of 5 on *L* is higher than expected for a college graduate, particularly because Mr. B's family of origin is upper middle class (Graham, 1993). This suggests he was defensive when completing the MMPI-2 and attempted to deny and minimize psychological problems and personal faults or shortcomings. In addition, he may be overly concerned with self-control and moral virtues and attempts to conform to social norms

MMPI-2

NR Hathaway and J C McKinley

Minnesota Multiphasic
Personality Inventory -2

Profile for Basic Scales

Minnesota Multiphasic Personality Inventory-2
Copyright © by THE REGENTS OF THE UNIVERSITY OF MINNESOTA
1942, 1943 (renewed 1970), 1989. This Profile Form 1989.
All rights reserved. Distributed exclusively by NATIONAL COMPUTER SYSTEMS, INC
under license from The University of Minnesota.

"MMPI-2" and "Minnesota Multiphasic Personality Inventory-2" are trademarks owned by
The University of Minnesota. Printed in the United States of America.

Name ___ Mr. B. ___

Address ___

Occupation ___ Date Tested __/__/__

Education __16__ Age __25__ Marital Status __Single__

Referred By ___

MMPI-2 Code ___

Scorer's Initials ___

MALE

	?	L	F	K	Hs+.5K	D	Hy	Pd+.4K	Mf	Pa	Pt+1K	Sc+1K	Ma+.2K	Si
Raw Score	5	3	12	5	29	21	20	26	20	22	23	13	41	
K to be Added					6			5			12	35	2	
Raw Score with K				11				25			34	35	15	

? Raw Score __0__

NATIONAL
COMPUTER
SYSTEMS

24001

Case 1 MMPI-2 Content and Supplementary Scales

	Raw Score	T Score
FB	6	67
True Response Inconsistency (TRIN)	9	50
Variable Response Inconsistency (VRIN)	7	57
Anxiety	18	61
Repression	21	63
MAC-R	14	33
Ego Strength (Es)	33	40
Dominance (Do)	13	38
Social Responsibility (Re)	24	61
Overcontrolled Hostility (O-H)	17	65
PTSD - Keane (PK)	24	77
PTSD - Schlenger (PS)	26	69
Addiction Potential (APS)	24	52
Addiction Admission (AAS)	2	46

Content Scales (Butcher et al., 1990)		
Anxiety (ANX)	13	65
Fears (FRS)	4	51
Obsessiveness (OBS)	5	50
Depression (DEP)	13	66
Health Concerns (HEA)	5	51
Bizarre Mentation (BIZ)	2	51
Anger (ANG)	6	50
Cynicism (CYN)	7	46
Antisocial Practices (ASP)	1	35
Type A (TPA)	5	43
Low Self-Esteem (LSE)	2	45
Social Discomfort (SOD)	21	81

Depression Subscales (Harris-Lingoes)		
Subjective Depression (D1)	16	74
Psychomotor Retardation (D2)	6	54
Physical Malfunctioning (D3)	6	75
Mental Dullness (D4)	6	67
Brooding (D5)	4	62

Hysteria Subscales (Harris-Lingoes)		
Denial of Social Anxiety (Hy1)	1	34
Need for Affection (Hy2)	7	51
Lassitude-Malaise (Hy3)	7	70
Somatic Complaints (Hy4)	1	42
Inhibition of Aggression (Hy5)	4	55

```
                                                Raw Score   T Score

Psychopathic Deviate Subscales (Harris-Lingoes)
        Familial Discord (Pd1)                      2           51
        Authority Problems (Pd2)                    2           42
        Social Imperturbability (Pd3)               2           40
        Social Alienation (Pd4)                     6           62
        Self-Alienation (Pd5)                       7           67


Paranoia Subscales (Harris-Lingoes)
        Persecutory Ideas (Pa1)                     3           58
        Poignancy (Pa2)                             6           76
        Naivete (Pa3)                               9           70


Schizophrenia Subscales (Harris-Lingoes)
        Social Alienation (Sc1)                     9           76
        Emotional Alienation (Sc2)                  3           69
        Lack of Ego Mastery, Cognitive (Sc3)        4           66
        Lack of Ego Mastery, Conative (Sc4)         7           76
        Lack of Ego Mastery, Def. Inhib. (Sc5)      3           61
        Bizarre Sensory Experiences (Sc6)           3           55


Hypomania Subscales (Harris-Lingoes)
        Amorality (Ma1)                             1           42
        Psychomotor Acceleration (Ma2)              4           44
        Imperturbability (Ma3)                      1           35
        Ego Inflation (Ma4)                         4           56


Social Introversion Subscales (Ben-Porath et al., 1989)
        Shyness/Self-Consciousness (Si1)           13           74
        Social Avoidance (Si2)                      6           62
        Alienation -- Self and Others (Si3)         7           56
```

in a rigid, inflexible manner. These concerns about appropriate behavior and high moral standards may be related to a fear that others will judge him as being unacceptable. An elevation on *L,* particularly for a college graduate, suggests a lack of insight and psychological mindedness.

Clinical Scales.   The low scores seen on scales *1* and *3*, the two clinical scales most directly related to concerns about one's physical condition, are surprising given Mr. B's reported preoccupation with his appearance. Consistent with this, he produced an average score on the Health Concerns Content Scale (*HEA* = < 49). The scores on scales *1*, *3*, and *HEA* argue against his condition involving a somatoform disorder or conversion disorder.

The *26/62* codetype suggests Mr. B's current condition involves a combination of depression and strong, underlying anger directed both at others and at himself. Other indications of depression include the low score on Scale 9 and elevations on supplementary scales (*DEP* = 68, *D1* = 74, *D4* = 67, *Hy3* = 70, *Sc2* = 69, *Sc4* = 76). These scores suggest the depression may be manifested by withdrawal from the environment, a lack of energy, reduced motivation, fatigue, and a despairing sense that life is not worthwhile. The level of current emotional distress after two psychiatric hospitalizations and ongoing treatment with antidepressant and anxiolytic medications is noteworthy.

The *26/62* codetype also suggests that Mr. B has a long history of interpersonal distrust related to an excessive sensitivity to criticism. He may be described as being "touchy" and overly sensitive. He is prone to read hostile, malevolent intent into neutral situations, which contributes to considerable discomfort and anxiety in social situations (scale *0* = 68; *SOD* = 78; *Hy1* = 34; *Pd3* = 40; *Ma3* = 35; *Si1* = 74). His social discomfort is related to an anticipation that others will criticize, reject, or attack him. He may defensively reject others before they have the opportunity to reject him. It is possible that his angry, resentful, hostile behavior alienates others who then avoid and/or reject him. Unfortunately, he does not recognize the ways in which his own behavior elicits negative responses from others. When others react to him with anger or rejection, it reinforces his belief that others will inevitably treat him negatively.

Given the level of elevation on scale *6*, paranoid trends are likely to exist and a psychotic disorder is possible. At the least, he feels lonely, misunderstood, and unsupported by others (*Pa2* = 76; *Sc1* = 76).

A second two-point codetype is the *60/06* codetype that occurs relatively infrequently. The correlates of the *60/06* codetype are described differently in different contexts. Greene (1991), for instance, described *60/06* patients in a relatively benign manner as not experiencing any emotional distress and as seeing themselves as happy, well-adjusted, and in good health, although noting that *60/06* individuals are generally shy, self-conscious, and easily embarrassed. A slightly different description of *60/06* individuals is provided by Friedman et al. (1989), who suggested that Mr. B is particularly sensitive to criticism, anticipates that others will not like or accept him, and expects he will be rejected because of feelings of inferiority related to concerns about his physical attractiveness.

Rorschach Data

Several key variables are positive including the *SCZI*, elevated Lambda, and Hypervigilance index (*HVI*). The most important of these is the positive *SCZI*, as the probability of schizophrenia is high when the *SCZI* is $\geq$ 4. The search strategy when *SCZI* is positive begins by examining variables related to organization of thinking and perceptual accuracy.

In terms of his ideation, Mr. B has a markedly introversive style (*EB* = 7:1.5), indicating that he is oriented toward thinking and internal fantasy rather than emotions. In general, he prefers avoiding emotional reactions if possible (*EBPer* = 4.7; *L* = 1.31). What is of considerable concern for a man who is as oriented towards and relies on thinking as much as Mr. B is the high percentage of distorted, flawed, and unrealistic responses (*X* + % = .33; *X* − % = .43; *M*− = 3). The higher than expected number of *M* − responses suggests significant disturbance in his thinking and distorted perceptions of others. The minus responses are scattered throughout the record and occur with a wide range of content, which indicates that the distortions are not elicited by specific stimuli or themes. Instead, this suggests his perception of stimuli in general are quite unusual, inaccurate, and idiosyncratic. One finding inconsistent with schizophrenia is the absence of signs of serious cognitive slippage or bizarre thinking (*ALOG* = 0, *FABCOM2* = 0, *CONTAM* = 0). The majority of special scores were *DR*s which suggested an odd, tangential quality to his verbalizations, rather than thought disorder.

The positive *HVI* indicates that Mr. B is quite guarded and mistrustful of others. He makes a considerable effort to be alert to as many of the cues in his environment as possible. This is reflected in a heightened concern for details including minor, unusual details others would ignore or view as unimportant (*Dd* = 7). This contributes to his being more careful, conscientious, and cautious than most people, characteristics that could be positive for a career in financial analysis and accounting. However, these characteristics may also lead him to become bogged down in detail because of a diligent, persistent effort to account for, explain, and interpret the significance of all of the data he encounters (*Dd* = 7; *Zd* = +6.5). His interpretations of events are likely to be distorted because they are based on inaccurate perceptions, as described previously, and because of his focus on

Case 1 Rorschach Protocol

Card	Response	Inquiry
I	1. S: Its not just 1 thing? 　　E: Most p c more than 1 thing on each card. 　　S: It lks kind of like a dog's face. Got the ears, the outline.	E: (Rpts S's response) S: The ears, snout, eyes. E: Show me where y're lkg. S: Here. Shape of the snout & the ears. Floppy ears. E: Floppy? S: Yes.
	2. See, the same thing miniature? Same thing in profile.	E: (Rpts S's response) S: Yeah. At the bottom. The profile, snout, ears. Roth sides. E: Miniature? S: Yeah. It is.
	3. Cld be a p's heart. 4 chambers, 2 atrium, & 2 ventricles.	E: (Rpts S's response) S: 2 atrium & 2 ventricles. 4 chambers of the heart. If u got rid of this projection L.l a heart.
	4. I c a little A's head w ear up & the snout.	E: (Rpts S's response) S: Here & here. E: What abt the card gave it that impression? S: Again the profile. He's facing that way. E: Ear up? S: Yes.
	5. These 2 l.l eyes. It lks kind of angry.	E: (Rpts S's response) S: Yeah. Here & here. Little spots l.l eyes. It lks angry. E: Angry? S: Way the eyes are slanted.
II	6. Almost like a little face. 2 eyes & nose in center part.	E: (Rpts S's response) S: Up in here. Can c 2 eyes, nose & eyebrows. No mouth. Bridge of the forehead.
	7. Again, this lks alm like a heart, 1 an organ here.	E: (Rpts S's response) S: Here. E: Show me the heart. S: Just the general shape. The C.

8. See, 2 faces here. I
d't k if they're spitting
at e.o or just talking.

E: (Rpts S's response)
S: 2 faces up here.
E: Spitting?
S: Got little red spittle marks.
Got mouth open.
E: Open?
S: The red outline.

III 9. See, again, alm like
an A profile with ears on
top. Maybe some kind of
rabbit or s.t.

E: (Rpts S's response)
S: Yeah. See the ears here, face,
a little snout. Front legs & back
legs. Ears.

10. 2 p. Either they're
carrying s.t of ripping
s.t apart in the center.

E: (Rpts S's response)
S: 2 p here. They look female.
L.1 they're carrying s.t.
E: U said they were carrying or
ripping s.t.
S: It 1.1 its b split apart.
E: Split?
S: Part in the center, its left
over.
E: I'm not sure what u mean.
S: L.1 residue left over where it
was split apart, the lighter gray
area.

11. This 1.1...a baby,
attached to an umbilical
cord. I think both are
female. Has s.t to do
with birth.

E: (Rpts S's response)
S: Here.
E: What made it 1.1 that?
S: The 2 women, 1.1 what they may
be carrying, a crib or some kind
of baby. The whole female subject
made me think of a baby with an
umbilical cord.

IV 12. L.1 a dog. A big
one, with floppy ears.

E: (Rpts S's response)
S: Yes. Here, the ears, really
what made me see it. The snout.
D't r c the eyes.
E: Big?
S: It does.
E: What abt the card makes it look
big?
S: It just lks big.

13. Then, a small face
inside. 2 eyes & a nose.

E: (Rpts S's response)
S: Down here. See 2 eyes.
eyebrows. Maybe a bit of a nose
of some sort.
E: Eyebrows?
S: There, the part over the eyes.
Got little piece protruding over
the eye socket.

E: Protruding?
S: It just does.

V 14. L.l some kind of bat.
The top view of it, s.t
flying. Wings, ears,
legs stretched out behind
it.

E: (Rpts S's response)
S: Yes. Wings, feet projecting
out. Head. C't c the facial
features, so lkg down at back of
head.

15. Then it l.l the
profile of s.t. The
snout, mouth, & ears.

E: (Rpts S's response)
S: Out here. Maybe an alligator.
S.t w a very long snout & little
ears.

16. Maybe here the
profile of a person. The
nose, head.

E: (Rpts S's response)
S: Here's the nose & forehead.

17. This l.l s.b sitting
down maybe & reading a
book.

E: (Rpts S's response)
S: I remember saying it...I
c't...D't see it.
E: Take yr time.
S: Maybe the same thing...C't
really c it.

VI 17. Lks kind of like a
ship, floating. Maybe
there's a refl in the
water. L.l abt to run
into s.t there, some kind
of obstruction.

E: (Rpts S's response)
S: Yes. This l.l some kind of
smokestack, front of the boat. A
chimney & it l.l the bow sticking
out on a sailboat. Then this is
the refl.
E: Abt to run into s.t?
S: Yeah. Here, it l.l s.t is
there. Going to run into s.t.
S: Yeah. Here it l.l s.t there.

VII 18. I c a face here.
Side of the face. Can c
eye & nose. On left side
by position of the eye it
l.l the person is angry.

E: (Rpts S's response)
S: Yes. This one is angry. It
dsn't l.l 2 sides of the same
face.
E: Angry?
S: The slant of the eye.
E: Slant of the eye?
S: L.l the eyebrow is the way I
alw used to draw s.o angry.

19. I c an A again.
Eyes. On both sides.

E: (Rpts S's response)
S: There's an ear sticking up.
The ear & snout.

VIII 20. Just l.l a H
skeleton. Spine, rib
cage, shoulders.

E: (Rpts S's response)
S: The spine is here. The ribs
coming off & conneecting. A
pelvic area here. Shoulders.

21. This l.1 some kind of A, on both sides.

E: (Rpts S's response)
S: 4 legs. Crawling on 4 legs.
E: Crawling?
S: Or walking on 4 legs.

22. I guess this wld be part of the body, of the anatomy.

E: (Rpts S's response)
S: This part. Prob the pelvis of a female.
E: Female?
S: Way its spread out, way its opened. Hips or s.t
E: Open?
S: The refl. The same thing on both sides.
E: I'm not sure what u mean.
S: Seems wider. Female anatomy opens wider than the male part.

IX 23. L.1 a person here. And here. Again.

E: (Rpts S's response)
S: On top. Like a nose. Maybe wearing some k of hat. Mostly a face.

24. Down here, also, some kind of face on bottom.

E: (Rpts S's response)
S: Here. A profile w eyes. Nothing else is very descriptive.
E: Show me where y're lkg.
S: There. Can c forehead above it.

25. L.1 s.t is being ripped aprt.

E: (Rpts S's response)
S: Maybe stuff in the middle.
E: Ripped apart?
S: L.1 2 pieces of s.t that fit together are split apart now.

26. This k of l.1 the state of Maine. With some kind of lake in the middle.

E: (Rpts S's response)
S: Yeah, the green part. On a map. Just the shape. Just on the right side.
E: Lake?
S: This white part. I d't k if there's really a a lake in Maine. There may be.

27. Some kind of figure in the middle with a mouth & 2 eyes. L.1 a cat's eyes, way they're vertical.

E: (Rpts S's response)
S: Yeah. I c 2 eyes here. The eyes are vertical, so I thgt abt a cat.
E: Explain that again, the vertical part.
S: That's how I thght cat's eyes were.

28. I d't k. Maybe the 2
p are pointing at e.o,
maybe shooting at e.o.

E: (Rpts S's response)
S: Here. Whatever that is,
pointing s.t.
E: What made it l.l that?
S: At first I thgt it cld be an
arm, but lks more unnatural. Cld
be pointing a gun or s.t.
E: Shooting?
S: Yes. Pointing the gun &
shooting.

X   29. Again, I thnk abt the
H body. With the spine
& ribs.

E: (Rpts S's response)
S: Here is the upper part of the
spine. Ribs connecting to the
upper part, prob.
E: Spine?
S: Just this grey part here.

30. It lks female in
here. 2 legs coming
together. Maybe these
are female organs, s.t
having to do with
reproduction. That's abt
it.

E: (Rpts S's response)
S: Here.
E: Help me c it.
S: Just l.l in betw the 2 legs.
Maybe this is s.t on the inside.
E: On the inside?
S: Cld be the crotch area.
E: What abt the card reminded u of
that?
S: I think here, seeing inside of
legs, coming down. This going up
to the crotch area. It lks more
female than male.
E: Female?
S: Just the shape. Of this little
piece here.

```
CASE01.R3==================== SEQUENCE OF SCORES ===============================

CARD NO LOC   #  DETERMINANT(S)     (2)  CONTENT(S)    POP Z   SPECIAL SCORES
======= ======  ===============    ===  ==========    === =   ===============
  I  1 WSo   1  Fu                      Ad            3.5
     2 Do    7  Fu                 2    Ad
     3 DdSo     F-                      An            3.5
     4 Ddo  21  Fu                 2    Ad
     5 Ddo      Mp-                2    Hd                    AG

 II  6 Ddo      F-                      Hd                    DV
     7 Do    3  FC-                     An
     8 D+    2  Ma.CF-             2    Hd            5.5 AG
     9 Do    1  Fo                      A

III 10 D+    1  Ma.YFu             2    H,Id          P 3.0 AG,MOR
    11 D+       Mau                2    H               4.0 DR,COP

 IV 12 Do    7  Fo                      A
    13 Ddo      FD-                     Ad                    DR

  V 14 Wo    1  FMa.FDo                 A             P 1.0
    15 Do   10  Fo                      Ad
    16 Ddo  33  F-                      Hd

 VI 17 W+    1  mp.Fru                  Sc,Id           2.5 INC

VII 18 Do       Mpo                     Hd            P     AG,DR2,PER
    19 Do    3  Fo                 2    Ad

VIII 20 Do   8  F-                      An
     21 Do   1  FMao               2    A             P     DR
     22 Do   7  Mp-                     Hd,Sx

 IX 23 D+    3  Fo                 2    H,Cg          P 2.5
    24 Do    4  Fo                      Hd
    25 Dd/      ma-                     Id                    AG
    26 DSo   1  F-                      Ge              5.0 DR2
    27 DSo   8  F-                      Ad              5.0
    28 D+    3  Mao                2    H,Id          P 4.5 AG

  X 29 Do   11  Fu                      An
    30 D+   10  F-                      Hd,Sx           4.5


============================= SUMMARY OF APPROACH ==============================

    I  :  WS.D.DdS.Dd.Dd           VI  :  W
   II  :  Dd.D.D.D                VII  :  D.D
  III  :  D.D                    VIII  :  D.D.D
   IV  :  D.Dd                     IX  :  D.D.Dd.DS.DS.D
    V  :  W.D.Dd                    X  :  D.D
```

97

```
CASE01.R3==================== STRUCTURAL SUMMARY ==============================

LOCATION              DETERMINANTS              CONTENTS        S-CONSTELLATION
FEATURES         BLENDS          SINGLE                         NO..FV+VF+V+FD>2
                                           H   = 4, 0           NO..Col-Shd Bl>0
Zf    = 12       M.CF           M  = 5      (H) = 0, 0          NO..Ego<.31,>.44
ZSum  = 44.5     M.YF           FM = 1      Hd  = 8, 0          NO..MOR > 3
ZEst  = 38.0     FM.FD          m  = 1      (Hd)= 0, 0          YES..Zd > +- 3.5
                 m.Fr           FC = 1      Hx  = 0, 0          NO..es > EA
W   =  3                        CF = 0      A   = 4, 0          NO..CF+C > FC
  (Wv = 0)                      C  = 0      (A) = 0, 0          YES..X+% < .70
D   = 20                        Cn = 0      Ad  = 7, 0          YES..S > 3
Dd  =  7                        FC'= 0      (Ad)= 0, 0          NO..P < 3 or > 8
S   =  4                        C'F= 0      An  = 4, 0          NO..Pure H < 2
                                C' = 0      Art = 0, 0          NO..R < 17
   DQ                           FT = 0      Ay  = 0, 0           3.....TOTAL
........(FQ-)                   TF = 0      Bl  = 0, 0
  +  =  7  ( 2)                 T  = 0      Bt  = 0, 0          SPECIAL SCORINGS
  o  = 22  (10)                 FV = 0      Cg  = 0, 1                Lv1    Lv2
 v/+ =  1  ( 1)                 VF = 0      Cl  = 0, 0          DV  =  1x1    0x2
  v  =  0  ( 0)                 V  = 0      Ex  = 0, 0          INC =  1x2    0x4
                                FY = 0      Fd  = 0, 0          DR  =  3x3    2x6
                                YF = 0      Fi  = 0, 0          FAB =  0x4    0x7
                                Y  = 0      Ge  = 1, 0          ALOG = 0x5
      FORM QUALITY              Fr = 0      Hh  = 0, 0          CON  = 0x7
                                rF = 0      Ls  = 0, 0          Raw Sum6 =    7
        FQx  FQf  MQual  SQx    FD = 1      Na  = 0, 0          Wgtd Sum6 =  24
  +  =   0    0    0     0      F  =17      Sc  = 1, 0
  o  =  10    6    2     0                  Sx  = 0, 2          AB  = 0    CP  = 0
  u  =   7    4    2     1                  Xy  = 0, 0          AG  = 6    MOR = 1
  -  =  13    7    3     3                  Id  = 1, 3          CFB = 0    PER = 1
none=    0   --    0     0      (2) = 10                        COP = 1    PSV = 0

==================== RATIOS, PERCENTAGES, AND DERIVATIONS =====================

R = 30         L =  1.31                FC:CF+C = 1: 1     COP = 1    AG = 6
----------------------------------      Pure C  =    0     Food       = 0
EB = 7: 1.5  EA =   8.5   EBPer= 4.7    SumC':WSumC= 0:1.5  Isolate/R  =0.03
eb = 4: 1    es =   5       D =  +1     Afr     =0.58      H:(H)Hd(Hd)= 4: 8
         Adj es =   4   Adj D =  +1     S       = 4        (HHd):(AAd)= 0: 0
----------------------------------      Blends:R= 4:30     H+A:Hd+Ad  = 8:15
FM = 2  :  C'= 0   T = 0                CP      = 0
m  = 2  :  V = 0   Y = 1
                           P   = 6         Zf  =12         3r+(2)/R=0.43
a:p   =  7: 4   Sum6  = 7   X+% =0.33      Zd  = +6.5      Fr+rF   = 1
Ma:Mp =  4: 3   Lv2   = 2   F+% =0.35   W:D:Dd = 3:20: 7   FD      = 2
2AB+Art+Ay= 0   WSum6 = 24  X-% =0.43      W:M  = 3: 7     An+Xy   = 4
M-    =  3      Mnone = 0   S-% =0.23      DQ+  = 7        MOR     = 1
                           Xu% =0.23      DQv  = 0

==============================================================================
SCZI = 5*    DEPI = 2    CDI = 1    S-CON = 3    HVI =YES    OBS = No
==============================================================================
```

minor details others pay little attention to. The features described are typical of persons with obsessional character features, such as an extraordinary attention to detail, a tendency to be excessively careful, and greater comfort with thoughts and idea than emotions.

Mr. B's efforts to be alert to his environment are related to a concern that others will act in a hostile, attacking manner ($S = 4$; $AG = 6$; $COP = 1$). He expects that aggression will be a central feature present in most interpersonal interactions and fears that he will be the victim of aggression. The effort he expends in trying to account for all details, even minor, trivial details others ignore, by remaining alert and vigilant may be understood in terms of a defensive attempt to detect early signs of the impending attack he is convinced will occur. Thus, he approaches interpersonal interactions with guarded distrust. While with others, he is likely to be preoccupied with trying to figure out whether their actions or words contain or imply hostile intent and is likely to distort and mispeceive interpersonal interactions ($M- = 3$). After an interaction ends, he is likely to ruminate about happened to figure out what the other person "really" meant or intended.

Somewhat surprisingly given how recently he was discharged from a psychiatric hospital, Mr. B showed no signs of emotional distress, anxiety, or depression ($D = +1$; $Adj\ D = +1$; $DEPI = 2$). In fact, the positive Adjusted D score suggests he may have a sturdy tolerance for stress and a greater capacity than most people to maintain control when responding to difficult situations. However, as the Adjusted es is lower than average (4), the positive ADj D score may actually overestimate his stress tolerance. This indicates a potential for Mr. B to develop distress in response to difficult, negative circumstances. The data described previously indicates that the likelihood of developing distress is greatest in circumstances in which he perceives himself as attacked, criticized, or humiliated by others.

Mr. B's self-perception involves an inflated sense of self-importance ($Fr = 1$). He has a strong and exaggerated need for obtaining positive responses from others in order to maintain feelings of self-worth. The combination of this narcissistic orientation and the suspicious, distrustful attitude described previously (HVI) suggest he is extremely sensitive to how others respond to him, interprets events as having special personal significance, searches for cues regarding others' perceptions of him, and is likely to interpret benign, innocuous behavior as being hostile or critical. He is not critical of himself ($V = 0$; $FD = 2$), appears to have a positive view of himself, and may attempt to defend his self-esteem through the use of denial, externalization, or rationalization. However, his self-image is based on distorted, fantasized ideas rather than a realistic assessment of his strengths, abilities, and personal assets ($H:(H)+Hd+(Hd) = 4:8$). Thus, he may have rather unrealistic but grandiose ideas about his abilities, talents, and potential.

One important aspect of Mr. B's self-perception is an unusual preoccupation concerning body image ($An + Xy = 4$). This suggests he ruminates about and is overly concerned with his physical appearance. Of the 4 responses related to bodily concerns, 3 have minus form quality, whereas the form quality of the other was unusual, which suggests that his perceptions in this area are distorted and unrealistic. He may be unusually focused on himself and preoccupied with issues concerning his value and self-worth, which have crystalized around his appearance ($Fr = 1$; $An + Xy = 4$). This relates, of course, to the distress he reports concerning his appearance and suggests that his insistence on having a further surgery to correct defects in his looks reflects a distorted self-image.

Although the possibility of schizophrenia is suggested by the Rorschach *SCZI*, the protocol overall is not supportive of this diagnosis for several reasons. The majority of special scores are *DR*s and *DV*s with only one INCOM. This reflects peculiarities in thinking but not the bizarre percepts and cognitive slippage characteristic of schizophrenia.

Comment

The data from the MMPI-2 and Rorschach agree in several important respects. Both describe Mr. B as overly sensitive to perceived attacks and criticism in interpersonal situations and as anticipating that anger will be present when he interacts with others. Both also describe how this wariness contributes to his feeling extremely uncomfortable and anxious when interacting with people.

The MMPI-2 suggests that Mr. B's emotional state includes both depression and anger, whereas the Rorschach identifies his emotional state as involving primarily anger with no clear indication of emotional distress. The Rorschach suggests he may present as having adequate ability to cope with stress when he is outside of a difficult situation but is likely to experience considerable distress, particularly when forced to be involved with persons he does not know well and whom he fears will criticize, attack, or humiliate him.

The Rorschach data describe Mr. B's cognitive style in greater depth than the MMPI-2 in that the Rorschach shows he processes information in a careful, cautious, conscientious manner and diligently attempts to account for all data. He attempts to focus on thought processes and to screen out or ignore emotions as much as possible. These features are suggestive of obsessional characteristics. The Rorschach also characterizes thought processes as distorted, idiosyncratic, and illogical to a greater extent than does the MMPI-2, with little evidence of cognitive slippage or thought disorder on either test.

Data from the MMPI-2 and Rorschach suggest different conclusions about Mr. B's self-image that are relevant to an understanding of Mr. B's preoccupations with his appearance. The *60/06* codetype suggests that he anticipates being rejected because of feelings of inferiority and concerns about his physical attractiveness. The high number of $An + Xy$ responses on the Rorschach also point to unusual preoccupations with somatic concerns and, as most of these responses have minus form quality, indicate perceptions about his body are likely to be distorted. However, the Rorschach also suggests that his self-image involves an unrealistic, if not exaggerated, sense of self-importance and a need to vigorously defend himself when his self-esteem is challenged or threatened. These findings may be reconciled if one views Mr. B's feelings of inadequacy as having crystalized around distorted, negative ideas about his appearance.

MMPI-2-Rorschach Integration

Mr. B responded to the MMPI-2 in a defensive manner and attempted to minimize and disavow problems ($L = 5$). He may deny, rationalize, or externalize responsibility for difficulties and, as a result, does not recognize how his actions contribute to the problems he experiences ($L = 5$; $Fr = 1$). These defenses interfere with his insight into the nature of his condition and suggest he is not psychologically minded. He may reject efforts to explain his problems in psychological terms rather than as caused by or related to his appearance. In addition, Mr. B is overly concerned with self-control and moral virtues, and attempts to conform to social norms in a rigid, inflexible manner. His concerns about appropriate behavior and high moral standards may be related to a fear that others will judge him as being unacceptable and will shame or humiliate him.

Mr. B's current emotional state involves a combination of depression and strong, underlying anger directed both at others and at himself (*26/62*; *DEP* $= 68$; $S = 4$; $AG = 6$). The depression may be manifested by withdrawal from the environment, a lack of energy, reduced motivation, fatigue, and a despairing sense that life is not worthwhile ($D1 = 74$, $D4 = 67$, $Hy3 = 70$, $Sc2 = 69$, $Sc4 = 76$).

Mr. B has a long history of interpersonal difficulties related to excessive sensitivity to criticism and to his chronic anger and hostility (*26/62*; *60/06*; *HVI*). He anticipates that interpersonal relationships will involve an aggressive component and fears that he will be the target of a hostile attack (*26/62*; *HVI*; $S = 4$; $AG = 6$). As a result of this suspicious distrust of others, he is vigilant, alert, and on guard in an effort to detect cues that signal others harbor aggressive intentions towards him. He carefully scrutinizes what others say and do but is prone to misinterpret or distort their actions by attributing hostile intent to them, even when none is intended ($X - \% = .43$; $M - = 3$). In other words, he projects hostility onto others and then fears being the victim of their aggression and malice.

His views of events may also be biased by how self-focused and self-absorbed he is, which contributes to interpreting events in a self-referential manner ($Fr = 1$). After an interaction, he is likely to ruminate about what happened to figure out what the other person "really" meant and may interpret benign interactions as having hidden meanings involving attempts to demean or ridicule him.

Mr. B feels quite uncomfortable in interpersonal situations, particularly when meeting people for the first time (scale $0 = 68$; $SOD = 78$; $Hy3 = 70$; $Ma3 = 35$; $Si1 = 74$). He generally approaches others in a cautious, emotionally detached manner because he anticipates others will not like or understand him ($60/06$; $T = 0$; HVI). As described previously, he views others with considerable distrust and apprehension and fears being ridiculed, humiliated, or rejected. He may be overly sensitive to how others respond to him and reads criticism and threatened hostility into innocuous comments. He may also be reluctant to confide in others, so they will not be able to use what he says against him. He is particularly focused on being ridiculed and rejected by others because of his physical appearance. His excessive preoccupation with and concern about his attractiveness reflect a distorted, unrealistic self-image and feelings of inferiority about his physical attractiveness ($60/06$; $An+Xy = 4$; $Fr = 1$). His distorted self-image and worries about others' reactions to his appearance contribute significantly to the development of emotional distress and insistence that he have further cosmetic surgery to "correct" defects in his looks. The likelihood that further surgery will alleviate distress about his appearance is low, given his distorted body image.

Mr. B's recent psychological difficulties that required inpatient psychiatric treatment may reflect the discomfort with others described previously, as he became depressed, anxious, and stressed after entering a new work setting in which he was forced to interact with many new people. This appears to be the situation in which he is most likely to respond with considerable distress given his concerns about being attacked, criticized, and humiliated. The likelihood of his functioning successfully at work will depend in large part on his developing comfort with coworkers, so that he does not dwell excessively on how they act towards him. He may function best in a position that requires limited direct contact with others.

When he feels attacked, rejected, misunderstood, or humiliated, Mr. B reacts strongly with considerable anger and then ruminates and broods about this. Given his distrust of others, it may be difficult for him to regain confidence in a person whom he perceives as having attacked him. These reactions are relevant to the bitter fights he has had with his parents, particularly his father, as well as to his recent termination of treatment with the therapist with whom he had worked for an extended period of time. In both situations, Mr. B became enraged when his demands for another cosmetic surgery were challenged rather than supported.

Although Mr. B's self-image involves feelings of inferiority and inadequacy about his physical appearance, he also has an inflated sense of self-importance $(Fr = 1)$. The positive aspects of his self-image are based on distorted, fantasized ideas about his strengths and abilities rather than a realistic assessment of his personal assets $(H:(H)+Hd+(Hd) = 4{:}8)$. Thus, he may have rather unrealistic but grandiose ideas about his abilities, talents, and potential. He has a need to vigorously defend himself when his self-esteem is challenged or threatened and does so through the use of denial, externalization, or rationalization. Because of the unusual degree of self-preoccupation, concerns about his value, adequacy, and self-worth appear to have crystalized around distorted, negative ideas about his appearance $(Fr = 1; An+Xy = 4)$.

In spite of Mr. B's guarded, defensive attempt to deny and minimize problems, his responses indicated peculiar, unusual thinking and strained reasoning $(X+\% = .33; X-\% = .43; M- = 3)$. Although there were no indications of thought disorder, cognitive slippage, or active psychosis at present (scale $8 = 65$; Special Scores), his responses indicate his interpretations of events are based on significant distortions and illogical thinking. He is generally careful, conscientious, and cautious in his attempts to account for all the details in a situation $(Dd = 7; Zd = +6.5)$. These features are typical of persons with obsessional character features, such as an extraordinary attention to detail, a tendency to be excessively careful, and greater comfort with thoughts and ideas than emotions. Although these characteristics may be positive in a work context, his efforts to be thorough and complete are excessive and result in his giving unwarranted significance to minor, irrelevant details. This contributes to inaccurate, idiosyncratic perceptions of events. His efforts to be alert to the environment may be understood as reflecting a defensive effort to detect early signs of the attack he is convinced will inevitably occur.

Diagnostic Impression

DSM-IV   Axis I   300.70 Body dysmorphic disorder
                    297.10 Delusional (paranoid) disorder, somatic type
                    296.25 Major depression, single episode, in partial
                           remission

          Axis II   300.01 Paranoid personality disorder with obsessive-
                           compulsive features

TREATMENT RECOMMENDATIONS

Indications that Mr. B's condition is best characterized as a delusional disorder suggest that careful consideration be given to treatment with antipsychotic medication given reports that similar patients have responded to neuroleptics (Phillips, 1991). Findings from the psychological test data raise significant concerns about the prognosis for individual psychotherapy, particularly if an insight-oriented approach is used for several reasons. First, Mr. B was defensive and attempted to deny psychological problems, personal faults, or shortcomings. Although he has experienced significant personal problems including conflict with family members, psychiatric hospitalization, and a leave of absence from work, he does not seem to feel responsible for his situation. The rigid, inflexible reliance on projection, denial, externalization, and rationalization indicates he is reluctant to consider, let alone accept, personal responsibility for any aspect of his problems. Instead, he insists that all his difficulties are due to his physical appearance and a lack of sympathy from others.

Second, Mr. B is distrustful of others, fears being ridiculed or humiliated, and reads criticism and hostility into innocuous comments. When he feels attacked, rejected, or misunderstood, he reacts with considerable anger and broods about being hurt; he is not one to forgive and forget. His confidence in a person can be profoundly shaken if he believes that person has attacked him, no matter what the nature of their past relationship has been. This is as likely to be true of his relationship with a psychotherapist as with other people, particularly given his past psychotherapy experiences. It is particularly important to note that his involvement in psychotherapy has occurred at the insistence of his parents or his physician rather than because of his own interest in seeking help. This sets up a dynamic in which Mr. B can, with some justification, view the therapist as being an agent of people who do not support or understand him, rather than being on his side.

The above suggests that a central issue in psychotherapy will be Mr. B's trust and mistrust of the therapist, particularly in relation to his perception of whether or not the therapist supports Mr. B's desire to have additional cosmetic surgery. The therapist treating Mr. B should be alert to signs that Mr. B feels misunderstood or criticized by the therapist's comments and address this immediately in order to maintain the therapeutic alliance. The therapist should also be prepared for a conflict that will inevitably arise in the transference in the following manner: Mr. B will adamantly insist that all of his difficulties stem from his physical defect. Should the therapist attempt to "do therapy" by suggesting, no matter how gently, that other factors may also apply, that some of these factors are psychological in nature, and that some of his difficulties are unrelated to his appearance, Mr. B will feel hurt, angry, and misunderstood, and his confidence in the therapist will be sorely threatened. The therapist should expect that these reactions will occur and be prepared to talk about Mr. B's disappointment, suspicious withdrawal, and anger in a nondefensive fashion. The therapist's ability to weather these storms and to use them in a therapeutic manner is essential to increase Mr. B's sense of safety and trust.

These considerations suggest that the chances of success are extremely slim if the therapist assumes that the goal of therapy is to attempt to persuade Mr. B to renounce concerns about his appearance by challenging and confronting him. Instead, the odds of success may be increased if treatment is conceptualized as helping Mr. B accept that further surgery is not possible and to develop more effective ways of coping with his social discomfort than withdrawing from others. Should these goals be met and a solid therapeutic alliance established, therapy may begin to examine Mr. B's beliefs about others as well as the unrealistic aspects of his self-image.

Case 2: Unexplained
Reactions to an Insect Bite

REASON FOR EVALUATION

Mrs. S is a 48-year-old, married, White female who had no physical problems until she was bitten on the left hand by an insect 2 months prior to this evaluation. Her hand and arm became swollen over several days following the insect bite. The swelling receded, but shortly after this, she developed a wide range of physical symptoms including pain in her back, neck, left breast, and eyes; weakness; fatigue; and difficulties with memory. After a thorough work-up found no medical explanation for these problems, her physician requested a psychological evaluation to assess whether psychological factors play a role in her presentation.

BACKGROUND INFORMATION

After graduating high school, Mrs. S married a high school boyfriend knowing that he had been drafted into the military and was going be sent to Viet Nam. During his 3-year tour of duty, they saw each other only when he was on leave. After his discharge from the military, they lived together for a brief period and then agreed to a divorce. She remarried 2 years later and has had 6 children with her second husband. Her children now range in age from 12 to 23. She and her family live in a small town in a rural area.

Mrs. S worked part time for short periods while her children were younger. About a year ago, she decided to work full time and obtained a position as a child care worker at a residential treatment facility for patients with developmental delays. Her position involved feeding, dressing, bathing, and watching children who were severely retarded. Her description of her job was unusual in that she repeatedly referred to the residents with whom she worked as "my children" and stated "I love them like my own children." She became very attached to the residents with whom she worked. For instance, she obtained permission to take residents to her home on her days off, voluntarily baked treats for them, and brought candy to work for them.

Mrs. S sought this position at the residential treatment center after a member of her church group described the special needs of these children. Shortly after this, she was in church and saw a bright flash of light. She explained that this was a sign for her to care for these children.

Mrs. S described herself as having no problems until 2 months prior to this evaluation when she was bitten on the left hand by an insect while at work. Her hand, wrist, and arm gradually became swollen over several days. The swelling subsided within a day or two. Since then, however, she has developed a wide range of symptoms including weakness, fatigue, diffuse tingling, headaches, and difficulties with concentration and memory. She also reported experiencing pain in her eyes, back, and left breast. She nearly refused a mammogram as she claimed it was too painful to endure. She has been seen by an internist, gynecologist, opthamologist, rheumatologist, neurologist, and neuropsychologist, none of whom has found a medical explanation for her symptoms.

While describing the effects of the insect bite, Mrs. S mentioned that a representative from the facility's personnel department had suggested she might be avoiding work because of a conflict with coworkers. Mrs. S initially disclaimed this in a heated manner but later acknowledged having differences with coworkers and supervisors concerning care of the residents. She emphatically insisted, however, that she was correct and the others wrong in each instance. When asked about previous conflicts with coworkers, Mrs. S responded by describing how much she cares for the residents and the lengths to which she goes to provide service to them above and beyond what other staff members do. She eventually acknowledged having filed three complaints against coworkers in the year she has worked at the facility for actions she believes involved either neglect or abuse of the residents. She repeatedly insisted she was correct in doing so.

When asked about her current mood, Mrs. S responded that she misses the residents since being off work for the past 2 months and wishes she could visit with them at her home. She acknowledged that not doing so makes her feel sad but insisted she is not depressed. Sleep is interrupted when she has pain in her left arm. Appetite is decreased, and she believes she has lost weight since September without dieting. Energy is decreased, and she becomes tired easily. She remains interested in activities and enjoys them. Libido is markedly decreased. She feels critical of herself for not taking care of household responsibilities and for asking her children to help with household chores, something she never did in the past. She denied suicidal ideation or intent.

Past psychiatric history is significant for a suicide attempt at age 16 related to her father's alcoholism and conflict with a boyfriend. Her stomach was pumped after she swallowed some pills. There was no follow-up psychiatric treatment.

Mrs. S also reported becoming "terribly" depressed 5 years ago after a daughter was killed in an automobile accident. After her daughter's death, Mrs. S did not come out of her bedroom for months. She was helped by support from her fundamentalist Christian community but did not seek help from a mental health professional. She reported "going bananas" a year later after being told that the passenger riding with her daughter when the accident occurred now admits that the accident was his fault and not her daughter's. Because of her condition, she was admitted to an inpatient psychiatric unit where she stayed for a month. It was difficult to obtain information from her about the reasons for this hospitalization or the treatment she received. She was treated with medications but did not recall their names. After discharge, she discontinued the medications that had been prescribed for her and has not pursued any further outpatient treatment. No records from this hospitalization were available for review.

Mrs. S denied alcohol or substance abuse. She attributed this to having grown up in a family in which her father was an alcoholic who was verbally abusive and who acted inappropriately when he was intoxicated.

Behavior during the evaluation was notable for being dramatic with rapid speech. It was difficult to have her focus on a specific topic during the interview as she digressed and provided many irrelevant details. She also indicated several times that she was preoccupied with her own thoughts, such as not responding to a question and spontaneously saying, "My mind wandered. I'm just missing people." She also commented on being confused during the testing. Mrs. S appeared depressed although she denied feeling so.

DIAGNOSTIC CONSIDERATIONS

Mrs. S's history of multiple, unexplained medical problems following a minor physical trauma suggests she may present with one of the somato-form disorders, such as a conversion disorder, hypochondriasis, or a pain disorder associated with psychological factors. According to the *DSM-IV* (American Psychiatric Association, 1994), a *Somatoform Disorder* is diagnosed when a patient presents with physical symptoms suggestive of a medical disorder that is not fully explained by any medical findings or diagnosable condition. Several MMPI-2 codetypes are associated with somatoform disorders, including the "conversion V" and elevations on scales *1, 2,* and *3* in various combinations.

One may question whether patients with diagnosed medical disorders elevate MMPI-2 scales related to health concerns. This question was addressed by Swenson, Pearson, and Osborne (1973), who collected MMPI data for approximately 25,000 male and 25,000 female medical patients seen at the Mayo Clinic. All subjects were either being worked up for or treated for a medical illness. The mean MMPI profiles for these subjects were within normal limits, with only mild elevations on scales *1, 2,* and *3*. These results demonstrate quite clearly that a medical disorder does not necessarily drive up scores on MMPI indices of emotional distress or of health concerns and worries. Given the continuity between the MMPI and MMPI-2, one would expect to find similar results with the MMPI-2.

As discussed in chapter 5, Rorschach indicators of health-related concerns ($An + Xy \geq 3$, $FC + CF + C' > 2$, $CP > 0$, *Lambda* ≥ 1.00) are not as robust as parallel MMPI-2 indicators. Clinical experience indicates that patients whose complaints about their medical condition are colored by psychological factors frequently do not produce positive scores on these indices. Although the sensitivity of these indices may be low, they do seem to be quite specific; one rarely sees elevations on these indicators when somatic concerns or preoccupations are not present, although patients with psychosomatic disorders frequently do not elevate these Rorschach indices.

The history reported by Mrs. S also raises questions about the presence or absence of an affective disorder. Although she denied being depressed during the clinical interview, when asked about specific symptoms, the examiner noted behavioral signs of depression during the interview. In addition, she described a past episode of depression following the tragic death of one of her daughters.

Finally, the difficulties in relationships with coworkers described by Mrs. S are noteworthy. These difficulties could occur for any of a number of reasons. However, the description of friction with a number of people raises questions about personality characteristics that might irritate and alienate others.

MMPI-2 Data

Validity Scales.   The elevations on both the *L* and *K* scales are usually high. Interpretation of the high score on scale *L* must take into account her involvement in a fundamentalist church, socioeconomic status, and residence in a rural area. Even with these factors in mind, however, the high scores on scale *L* and scale *K* indicate that Mrs. S attempted to create an

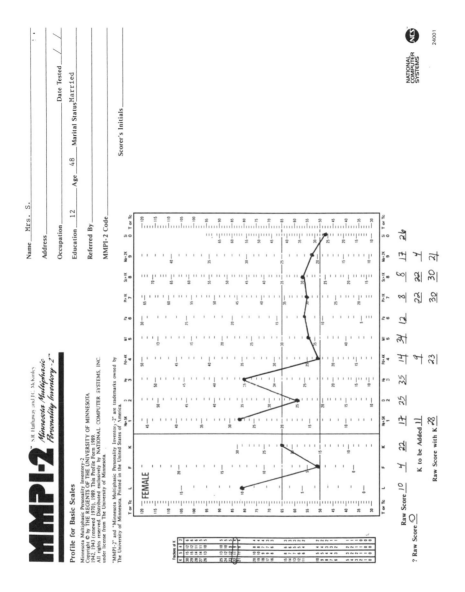

Case 2 MMPI-2 Content and Supplementary Scales

	Raw Score	T Score
FB	2	50
True Response Inconsistency (TRIN)	11	65T
Variable Response Inconsistency (VRIN)	9	66
Anxiety	5	43
Repression	26	75
MAC-R	18	45
Ego Strength (Es)	30	41
Dominance (Do)	17	54
Social Responsibility (Re)	23	56
Overcontrolled Hostility (O-H)	19	70
PTSD - Keane (PK)	5	45
PTSD - Schlenger (PS)	10	48
Addiction Potential (APS)	17	33
Addiction Admission (AAS)	0	19

Content Scales (Butcher et al., 1990)		
Anxiety (ANX)	3	43
Fears (FRS)	4	43
Obsessiveness (OBS)	2	41
Depression (DEP)	1	39
Health Concerns (HEA)	11	61
Bizarre Mentation (BIZ)	0	39
Anger (ANG)	5	47
Cynicism (CYN)	2	38
Antisocial Practices (ASP)	1	36
Type A (TPA)	3	38
Low Self-Esteem (LSE)	2	44
Social Discomfort (SOD)	5	46

Depression Subscales (Harris-Lingoes)		
Subjective Depression (D1)	10	56
Psychomotor Retardation (D2)	4	41
Physical Malfunctioning (D3)	7	78
Mental Dullness (D4)	4	57
Brooding (D5)	0	37

Hysteria Subscales (Harris-Lingoes)		
Denial of Social Anxiety (Hy1)	6	61
Need for Affection (Hy2)	9	60
Lassitude-Malaise (Hy3)	7	67
Somatic Complaints (Hy4)	6	62
Inhibition of Aggression (Hy5)	5	62

```
                                                   Raw Score   T Score


Psychopathic Deviate Subscales (Harris-Lingoes)
     Familial Discord (Pd1)                           2          50
     Authority Problems (Pd2)                         2          48
     Social Imperturbability (Pd3)                    5          60
     Social Alienation (Pd4)                          3          45
     Self-Alienation (Pd5)                            1          39


Paranoia Subscales (Harris-Lingoes)
     Persecutory Ideas (Pa1)                          1          45
     Poignancy (Pa2)                                  2          46
     Naivete (Pa3)                                    8          65


Schizophrenia Subscales (Harris-Lingoes)
     Social Alienation (Sc1)                          0          37
     Emotional Alienation (Sc2)                       1          49
     Lack of Ego Mastery, Cognitive (Sc3)             2          55
     Lack of Ego Mastery, Conative (Sc4)              1          43
     Lack of Ego Mastery, Def. Inhib. (Sc5)           0          72
     Bizarre Sensory Experiences (Sc6)                4          59


Hypomania Subscales (Harris-Lingoes)
     Amorality (Ma1)                                  2          54
     Psychomotor Acceleration (Ma2)                   4          45
     Imperturbability (Ma3)                           4          56
     Ego Inflation (Ma4)                              4          56


Social Introversion Subscales (Ben-Porath et al., 1989)
     Shyness/Self-Consciousness (Si1)                 1          38
     Social Avoidance (Si2)                           3          51
     Alienation -- Self and Others (Si3)              1          38
```

extremely favorable impression by denying unacceptable feelings, impulses, or behavior and minimizing any problems. The high score on scale L also suggests she views herself as an exceedingly conscientious, responsible, virtuous woman whose self-image and lifestyle is conventional and above reproach. She approaches issues involving morality in a rigid, inflexible, and self-righteous manner, particularly when her own integrity is at stake.

This validity scale configuration, as well as the high score on the Repression scale ($T = 75$) and the low score on the Anxiety scale ($A = 43$), indicates that she utilizes denial, repression, and externalization as primary defenses. Her reliance on these defenses allows her to deny, rationalize, or gloss over aspects of herself and her behavior that could be viewed as socially unacceptable. Furthermore, she views any psychological difficulties as ego-dystonic, if acknowledged at all. The use of these defenses interferes with her having insight into her feelings, motivations, or behavior. As a result, it is unlikely that she would benefit from traditional psychotherapy.

Clinical Scales.   The elevations on scales *1* and *3* with a low score on scale *2* is a classic "conversion V" that indicates that Mrs. S unconsciously uses somatic symptoms to avoid dealing with or thinking about psychological problems. A wide variety of symptoms may be produced including headaches, chest pain, back pain, numbness, fatigue, dizziness, and sleep disturbance (D3 = 78; Hy3 = 67). The onset and severity of these physical symptoms is associated with emotional stress. Her physical complaints are reinforced by secondary gain, such as eliciting sympathy and reassurance from others, avoiding responsibility, or escaping from a troubling situation. Despite her complaints, she is likely to continue functioning, although at a reduced level of efficiency.

Mrs. S has a strong need to convince both herself and others that she does not have any psychological or interpersonal problems and to portray herself as normal, responsible, and virtuous. To do so, she denies troubles in her life and minimizes personal inadequacies. The use of somatization serves to explain any difficulties she experiences as due to physical problems entirely rather than to anything psychological. Although she may report some tension, she is unlikely to admit to experiencing emotional distress, depression, or anxiety.

Mrs. S has very strong, immature dependency needs. She seeks attention, affection, and sympathy from others to reassure herself others care about her and feels insecure if others do not express their interest in and concern about her frequently enough. She may not be comfortable with her dependency needs and may experience conflict because of it. She is generally outgoing and comfortable in social settings and is able to engage others and attract their attention. Although superficially friendly towards others, her relationships may lack depth as she approaches social relationships in an attempt to gratify her own needs for affection. At times, she may act in an egocentric, selfish, demanding, and even manipulative manner. Physical complaints may serve the purpose of eliciting sympathy and support from others.

As noted previously, it is important to Mrs. S to act in a socially acceptable manner. Because of this, she is likely to deny and suppress negative emotions, particularly anger, which she fears would be met with disapproval if expressed. Thus, she generally does not voice negative feelings directly. She is likely to store up anger and resentment, most likely related to times when she felt others disappointed her or did not fulfill her demands for attention. For the most part, her anger is discharged in passive, indirect ways, although she may occasionally have uncharacteristic outbursts of anger, much like a temper tantrum.

Because of her strong need to deny psychological problems and to maintain an impression of being reasonable, moral, and normal, she is unlikely to respond to traditional psychotherapy. She much prefers to view her difficulties in terms of physical complaints and will likely vigorously resist any suggestion that psychological processes play any role whatsoever in her condition. If caregivers make direct interpretations along these lines, she is likely to terminate therapy prematurely. She may be most comfortable with a supportive, reassuring therapist who employs a problem-focused model of psychotherapy.

Rorschach Data

The first key variable to attend to is the positive Depression Index ($DEPI$ = 6) that strongly suggests that Mrs. S's current condition involves an affective disorder. The $DEPI$ is an empirically derived cluster of variables that identifies patients who experience the emotional and/or cognitive features of depression. It should be noted that the $DEPI$ was validated on a pool of patients described as having an "affective disturbance" rather than on patients selected because they met strict DSM-III-R diagnostic criteria for depression. Thus, patients who obtain positive scores on the DEPI are likely to have the emotional and/or cognitive features frequently seen in depression even though they may not meet DSM-III-R diagnostic criteria for a depressive disorder.

When a positive $DEPI$ is found, the path for reviewing the Rorschach data involves first examining the subject's affective experience and controls over emotions. These data suggest a number of important findings. Because Mrs. S has an extratensive style (EB = 3:5.5), her feelings generally play an important role in her thinking and behavior. She trusts her intuition and relies on emotional impressions more than on reason and logic when reacting to situations and making decisions. At present, Mrs. S experiences

Card	Response	Inquiry
I	1. God. It just ll this cld either be a bat,	E: (Rpts S's response) S: OK, this is the eyes, head, head area. L little things. I d't k what bat have. Never seen 1. Wings. Only thing I c in that mass of black. Its the only poss thing it cld be. Dsn't ll a.t. animal. Dsn't ll a.t human. If y're searching for s.t., that's my best choice.
	2. or a spider.	E: (Rpts S's response): S: I dk. Just the arms all coming off. Legs. The body.
	3. A fly. That's it. Its ugly. Its uniform. The sides are equal. Its symmetrical.	E: (Rpts S's response) S: Yeah. E: What reminded you of a spider? S: I dk. E: Where were u lkg? S: Same image. Like an insect. Its ugly. E: Ugly? S: Its black, dark. Its not pretty. The opp of pretty. I dk.
II	4. All I c is a blob. A complete blob. Its not pretty, not stimulating. It has no character. E: E.b. sees s.t. Take yr time. S: 2 rabbits. There. 2 black rabbits & they have bloody red feet. It ll they're spitting blood out of their mouths. 2 dead rabbits on the road, spitting blood, or were until deceased.	E: (Rpts S's response) S: Oh, yeah. This is the easiest. Ears. That's all the red blotches. Maybe internal bleeding. Flattened, like car ran over it. Red coming out, so I thght bood and internal bleeding.
III	5. This 1 is fun. 2 people, a man & lady. They're happy. In love.	E: (Rpts S's response) S: Yeah. It just ll they're k of bent over. Head, body, arms,

A BF or s.t. They have a
baby...Yeah.

& legs. Why a baby, I d.k. Cld
j be a baby. This is a BF. I
d.k. Like a symbol of love. Or
on the sides, cld be 2 hearts
meshed together.
E: Symbol of love?
S: Yeah. Unity.
E: Happy?
S: 2 people. The baby. A
couple. Bonding, not sep, like
the others. Maybe they j had
the baby, and this is the cradle
or s.t.

IV   6. The end of time
     prophecy! The man w 10
     horns, from the Book of
     Revelations.

E: (Rpts S's response)
S: It j ll it cld be some of the
10 horns.
E: Where were u lkg?
S: Here. Can see a blob, an eye
here. Can see on this side, not
there. These are horns to me.
E: Eye?
S: Here. The dot. There's
white. A speck of white.

7. Dreary. Dark.
Desolate...J very
cold...They cld be lions
or s.t. Very forsaken.
Just lost.

E: (Rpts S's response)
S: I d.k.
E: Where were u lkg?
S: I don't even know.
E: U said it was dreary, dark, &
desolate.
S: Yeah. It does.
E: Dreary & desolate?
S: Just bec its a mess. And its
just like...lost.
E: Help me see it.
S: It ll that to me. The
coloring is dark. It lks as if
it were dark & desolate. It lks
symbolic.
E: Symbolic?
S: Just all the end of time
prophecy, before Jesus is
coming. If j ll that. It dsn't
really ll lions.

V   8. This just ll a flying
     bat. Yeah, a flying bat.

E: (Rpts S's response)
S: Yeah. It still does.
E: Bat?
S: Its head, antenna, wings,
legs. It cld j be flying.

9. It also reminds me of
my kids. Saw at Hallo-

E: (Rpts S's response)
S: Oh yeah. We made bats. Cut

117

ween, for decoration.
Its a little different.
Bats, witches, Hallo-
ween. A happy time.
Thought this bat looks a
little on the sad side.
He's j lost and
foresaken, all by
himself. Lonely.

them out & painted them. Made
me think of that.
E: What abt the card reminded
you of that?
S: Bec its a bat. Several years
ago I had an idea I wanted to
hang bats outside in the yard.
I saw this at Great America.
They had a graveyard with bats
and skeletons.
E: U said the bat looked sad.
S: This 1 looks lost bec its all
by itself. Ours was happy, a
big family. We made abt 20 of
them, hung them in the yard.

VI 10. Well, this thing
still has eyes & a little
bitty antenna & a long
tail. Its skin looks
flattened out. Dark.
These pictures are all
gloomy, except the 2
people with the baby.
None of them are pretty.
None are beautiful. A
flattened bat, car ran
over it.

E: (Rpts S's response)
S: It just ll an eye, an
antenna. Some type of flattened
bat or s.t. An A skin rug.
E: Bat?
S: I d.k. Just ll a bat, except
for this, what may be a tail.
Maybe it got run over by a car.
That's why its so flat.
E: Dark?
S: Yeah. Dismal. All of them
are.
E: Flattened?
S: It just does. Prob bec both
sides are the same & its
uniform. This is the spine. It
j looks flattened out.

VII 11. My 2 dogs! Yeah!
Absolutely. Wagging
their tails. Ears r up.
Really happy. That's
Romeo, that's Julie.
What's that in the
middle? Cld be 2 dogs
and 2 bones, but knowing
them they d't share a.t.,
so 2 bones. 2 steak
bones. Thy're wagging
tails. Thy're happy.

E: (Rpts S's response)
S: Head, ear, body. Long little
tail. There's Romeo, there's
Julie. Short stubby feet. It
cld be 1 bone, but my dogs d't
share a.t., so 2 bones. This
cld be a little on the happy
side. Even though th color is
gloomy & dismal. My dogs r
happy.

VIII 12. Well, these pink A's.
They cld be like, not
bears, coyotes, crossing
over. Like thr a
mountain. This is water.
When they meet on the o
side of the mtn they'll

E: (Rpts S's response)
S: These are the 2 coyotes.
Here's a mtn. The coyotes are
jumping. Here's a big river.
They're both going to the o
side, so I thght they were
happy. I think of C's so think

be together. Crossing the mtn so they can be tog.

it looks happy.
E: Crossing over the water?
S: The blue. Saw 4 feet. This foot is way up in the air & these were on the edge. Just made it over. Happy they're g to be tog inst of being sep.

IX 13. 2 big dinosaurs. Involving, evolving s.t out of the earth. That's the earth in the center. And they're dying fr exposure to the sun or s.t. The orange stuff.

E: (Rpts S's response)
S: This wld be the earth. These are dinosaurs. This looked hot bec its a warm C. The sun is radiating down on them. For whatever reason, thght they were getting overexposure. The sun is radiating down on them and destroying them. Too intense. Cldn't take the heat.
E: Evolving?
S: They seem like they're coming out of here, the Earth.
E: Coming out?
S: Cld be like a little lake or the earth. Seems like they're pulling out from there.

X 14. (Seems very irritated) Just a lot of sep C's. No sense of family. They all seem sep. A lot of C's.

E: (Rpts S's response)
S: Yes. Just blotches of diff color.
E: Separate?
S: Yes. Bec e.t. is sep. When I think of closeness or bonding, I think of family. Because this is all sep I think of aliena-tion. No unity. For me, family is closeness. This wasn't that.

15. You k, there's a person, hanging from the top. A very small person...As if she's swinging from some tree or s.t. Got legs, arms are up. 1 small p suspended fr tree branches. The blue cld be water. I d.k., it does nothing for me.

E: (Rpts S's response)
S: It ll a girl. This ll tree branches. Skinny little green legs & green arms & head. These wld be tree branches. If you have to stretch yr imag to find s.t., this wld be it. The yellow wld be the sun, the warm color of the sun. The brightness & intensity. She's suspended over the blue, the water.
E: Water?
S: This ll the splashing waves. Ll water splashing. We go to the lake alot, have a boat. Our kids are alw swinging from the trees. That's prob why. I d.k.

```
CASE02.R3===================== SEQUENCE OF SCORES ==============================

CARD NO LOC  #  DETERMINANT(S)      (2) CONTENT(S)    POP Z  SPECIAL SCORES
======= ======  ===============     === ==========    === =  ==============
   I  1 Wo   1  FC'o                    A             P 1.0  DR
      2 Wo   1  F-                      A               1.0
      3 Wo   1  FC'u                    A               1.0

  II  4 W+   1  FC'.CF.mao          2   A,Bl            4.5  MOR,FAB2

 III  5 D+   1  Mpo                     H,A           P 4.0  AB

  IV  6 WSo  1  FC'-                    (H)             5.0
      7 Wv   1  C'                      Id                   AB

   V  8 Wo   1  FMao                    A             P 1.0
      9 Wo   1  Mpo                     A,Art           1.0  INC,DR2,PER

  VI 10 Do   1  FC'u                    A                    MOR,DR,DV

 VII 11 W+   1  FMa.FC'u            2   A,Fd            2.5  PER,DR

VIII 12 W+   1  FMa.CF.FD+          2   A,Na            4.5  ALOG

  IX 13 W+   1  FMa.ma.CF.FD-       2   (A),Na          5.5  MOR,AG,DV

   X 14 Wv   1  C                       Id                   DR2
     15 D+   5  Mp.CF.mpu               H,Na            4.5  DV,PER,INC


=========================== SUMMARY OF APPROACH ==============================

     I  :   W.W.W                        VI  :   D
    II  :   W                           VII  :   W
   III  :   D                          VIII  :   W
    IV  :   WS.W                         IX  :   W
     V  :   W.W                           X  :   W.D
```

120

```
CASE02.R3==================== STRUCTURAL SUMMARY ==============================

LOCATION              DETERMINANTS              CONTENTS        S-CONSTELLATION
FEATURES         BLENDS          SINGLE                         NO..FV+VF+V+FD>2
                                           H   = 2, 0          YES..Col-Shd Bl>0
Zf    = 12     FC'.CF.m         M  = 2     (H) = 1, 0          YES..Ego<.31,>.44
ZSum  = 35.5   FM.FC'           FM = 1     Hd  = 0, 0          NO..MOR > 3
ZEst  = 38.0   FM.CF.FD         m  = 0     (Hd)= 0, 0          NO..Zd > +- 3.5
               FM.m.CF.FD       FC = 0     Hx  = 0, 0          YES..es > EA
               M.CF.m           CF = 0     A   = 9, 1          YES..CF+C > FC
W  = 12                         C  = 1     (A) = 1, 0          YES..X+% < .70
  (Wv = 2)                      Cn = 0     Ad  = 0, 0          NO..S > 3
D  = 3                          FC'= 4     (Ad)= 0, 0          NO..P < 3 or > 8
Dd = 0                          C'F= 0     An  = 0, 0          NO..Pure H < 2
S  = 1                          C' = 1     Art = 0, 1          YES..R < 17
                                FT = 0     Ay  = 0, 0          6.....TOTAL
   DQ                           TF = 0     Bl  = 0, 1
.........(FQ-)                   T  = 0     Bt  = 0, 0          SPECIAL SCORINGS
 +  = 6  ( 1)                   FV = 0     Cg  = 0, 0                Lv1    Lv2
 o  = 7  ( 2)                   VF = 0     Cl  = 0, 0          DV  =  3x1    0x2
 v/+ = 0 ( 0)                   V  = 0     Ex  = 0, 0          INC =  2x2    0x4
 v  = 2  ( 0)                   FY = 0     Fd  = 0, 1          DR  =  3x3    2x6
                                YF = 0     Fi  = 0, 0          FAB =  0x4    1x7
                                Y  = 0     Ge  = 0, 0          ALOG =  1x5
    FORM QUALITY                Fr = 0     Hh  = 0, 0          CON =  0x7
                                rF = 0     Ls  = 0, 0          Raw Sum6 =   12
       FQx  FQf  MQual  SQx     FD = 0     Na  = 0, 3          Wgtd Sum6 =  40
 +  =   1    0     0     0      F' = 1     Sc  = 0, 0
 o  =   5    0     2     0                 Sx  = 0, 0          AB  = 2    CP  = 0
 u  =   4    0     1     0                 Xy  = 0, 0          AG  = 1    MOR = 3
 -  =   3    1     0     1                 Id  = 2, 0          CFB = 0    PER = 3
none=   2    --    0     0      (2) =  4                       COP = 0    PSV = 0

=================== RATIOS, PERCENTAGES, AND DERIVATIONS =====================

R = 15        L = 0.07          FC:CF+C = 0: 5    COP = 0    AG = 1
-----------------------------------     Pure C  =   1    Food        = 1
EB = 3: 5.5  EA  = 8.5   EBPer= 1.8  SumC':WSumC= 7:5.5  Isolate/R =0.40
eb = 7: 7    es  = 14       D  = -2    Afr     =0.36    H:(H)Hd(Hd)= 2: 1
           Adj es = 12   Adj D = -1    S       =   1    (HHd):(AAd)= 1: 1
-----------------------------------     Blends:R= 5:15   H+A:Hd+Ad =14: 0
FM = 4  :  C'= 7   T = 0                 CP      = 0
m  = 3  :  V = 0   Y = 0
                            P   = 3     Zf   =12          3r+(2)/R=0.27
a:p    =  6: 4   Sum6  = 12  X+% =0.40  Zd   = -2.5       Fr+rF    = 0
Ma:Mp  =  0: 3   Lv2   = 3   F+% =0.00  W:D:Dd=12: 3: 0   FD       = 2
2AB+Art+Ay= 5    WSum6 = 40  X-% =0.20  W:M  =12: 3       An+Xy    = 0
M-     =  0      Mnone = 0   S-% =0.33  DQ+  = 6          MOR      = 3
                            Xu% =0.27  DQv  = 2

=============================================================================
 SCZI = 3   DEPI = 6*   CDI = 4*   S-CON = 6   HVI = No   OBS = No
=============================================================================
```

121

significant emotional distress ($es = 14$) involving depressive affect ($C' = 7$) and a sense of helplessness ($m = 3$).

Several variables indicate that Mrs. S is a woman who experiences emotions very intensely while struggling to exert control over her feelings. On the one hand, she can display affective reactions in a very strong, at times exaggerated, manner that calls attention to herself ($FC:CF+C = 0:5$; $C = 1$). The absence of any FC responses suggests that when emotional reactions are triggered, she lacks control over herself and is unable to stop or hold back from expressing everything she feels. She can become easily overwhelmed and flooded by emotions as her capacity to use reason or logic to regulate her internal state is ineffective ($C = 1$; $FC = 0$; $Lambda = .07$). Although some people may respond to her emotional style as genuine, warm, and expressive, others may view her as immature, overly dramatic, and excessive and may even question if her reactions are genuine or reflect an exaggerated desire for attention.

Perhaps because of this, Mrs. S attempts to avoid emotional stimuli and to inhibit herself from becoming emotionally aroused or worked up ($Afr = .36$; $C = 7$; $SumC:SumC = 7:5.5$). That is, she tries to prevent uncontrolled affective outbursts or overreactions either by distancing herself from an emotional response or by suppressing and burying feelings. She may also try to detach herself from feelings through the use of intellectualizing defenses ($2AB+Art+Ay = 5$). Although able to maintain an emotional equilibrium in stable, structured situations, she is continually vulnerable to being overwhelmed and disorganized by emotions ($Adj\ D = -1$). Thus, she expends considerable effort to contain emotions but at times may display overly intense emotional reactions that are uncontrolled and out of proportion to the situation.

Mrs. S feels inferior and inadequate compared to others (Egocentricity index $= .27$; $MOR = 3$). Her negative self-image contributes to a vulnerability to becoming depressed in reaction to stressful events. These concerns about her self-worth have not developed in response to recent events ($FV = 0$; $FD = 2$) but are longstanding in nature. Although one might predict that a person with a negative self-image would react to conflicts with coworkers and supervisors in a self-critical manner, there is no indication that Mrs. S has done so. Her responses suggest that she did not react to this conflict by becoming self-critical or even by thinking about how her actions may have contributed to the problems, even though she has the capacity to do so ($FD = 2$). To the contrary, she apparently interprets this type of confrontation as a challenge to her self-worth and then responds with a defensive assertion that she was indeed correct and the other person wrong ($PER = 3$). In defense of herself, she may rationalize and explain her actions in a rigid, inflexible manner that does not take into account the points made by others ($PER = 3$; Intellectualization Index $= 5$).

The positive Coping Deficit Inventory ($CDI = 4$) indicates that Mrs. S is less socially mature than typical and frequently has difficulties in interpersonal relationships. This is related in part to a conflict concerning her unusually strong dependency needs ($Food = 1$). She seeks reassurance from others that they care for and are concerned about her. Because of her desire for approval from others, she may turn to them for direction and guidance even in situations that she could manage on her own ($Food = 1$; $Ma:Mp = 0:3$). At the same time, however, she is more cautious than most in terms of establishing close emotional bonds with others and keeps a distance from them ($T = 0$; $H+(H)+Hd+(Hd) = 3$), because she does not anticipate that interactions with most people will be positive ($COP = 0$; $AG = 1$). This suggests she experiences a conflict about dependency needs such that she wants others to show they love her while also needing to maintain a safe distance from others and from becoming overly attached to them. The compromise she has reached in terms of her involvement with others is not satisfying, as she feels lonely and isolated from others (Isolation Index = .40).

As noted previously, affect has an unusually strong influence on Mrs. S's perception and interpretation of events such that logic and reasoning are overshadowed by emotion ($Lambda = .07$; $FQnone = 2$). The degree to which emotions affect her processing of stimuli contributes to her interpreting stimuli in unusual and overly personalized ways ($X + \% = .40$; $Xu\% = .27$; Populars = 3). Her thinking is often immature, illogical, digressive, and strained that can contribute to poor judgment ($WSum6 = 40$). Thinking may also be strange at times because of her attempts to search for symbolic meanings in events others would accept at face value ($2AB+Art+AY = 5$). Although the number of Special Scores is much higher than expected, a review of the responses involving Special Scores shows that none of them is bizarre. There is no indication of thought disorder. Instead, these slips reflect the disruptive impact on her thought processes of emotions and of preoccupations concerning closeness with others (Responses 5, 9, 12, and 14). These processing characteristics may relate to her having interpreted the bright light at church as a sign directing her to work with the residents of the treatment facility.

Mrs. S has a marked tendency to respond to unpleasant situations with a "flight into fantasy" ($Ma:Mp = 0:3$). She uses fantasy to deny painful aspects of reality and avoids dealing directly with the situation that upsets her.

Comment

The MMPI-2 and Rorschach agree in important respects, and complement one another by offering unique information not provided by the other. Both describe Mrs. S as having unusually strong, immature dependency needs about which she experiences a conflict. Both also indicate that she is apt to defensively deny having problems and to explain or justify her actions as reasonable, understandable, and correct. The MMPI-2, however, shows more clearly the extremely strong need Mrs. S has to portray herself as being virtuous, responsible, and above reproach.

The MMPI-2 "conversion V" profile provides information not contained in the Rorschach, namely that emotional conflicts are expressed by focusing on physical complaints thath allow her to avoid admitting to or dealing with psychological issues. The high number of C' responses on the Rorschach might be interpreted as consistent with this defensive maneuver, as it is associated with an effort to internalize reactions, but does not directly suggest the presence of a conversion disorder. Note that she did not produce any Rorschach responses suggesting unusual concerns about her body.

The MMPI-2 profile suggests the absence of depression whereas the Rorschach strongly suggests Mrs. S's current condition involves significant depressive features. The discrepancy between the MMPI-2 and Rorschach concerning identification of signs of sadness and depression may be due to her extremely defensive approach to the MMPI-2 and the extensive reliance on denial, repression, somatization, and intellectualization. As discussed in chapter 5, a patient may avoid revealing emotional difficulties on a self-report inventory while producing responses on a projective test indicating a psychological problem exists or vice versa. This may occur because of deliberate attempts to deny problems or because the two tests measure emotional distress at different levels of conscious awareness. Given the pattern of findings overall, the conflicting findings between Mrs. S's MMPI-2 and Rorschach indicate that she is troubled by underlying feelings of sadness but tries not to acknowledge these upsetting feelings, perhaps because of how painful it would be if these feelings were experienced more directly.

The Rorschach also describes Mrs. S as having significant difficulty modulating emotional reactions and having the potential to become flooded with and overwhelmed by her feelings. As a result, she attempts to contain emotions by trying not to react in the first place but may still respond on occasion in an overly emotional, uncontrolled manner.

As noted previously, both the MMPI-2 and Rorschach indicate that Mrs. S has unusually strong dependency needs and experiences conflicts about her dependency needs. Both also describe her as having rather superficial relationships with others. The MMPI-2 appears to explain the lack of depth in relationships as due to her egocentric approach towards others. In contrast, the Rorschach suggests she keeps a distance from others in spite of her needs for attention and affection because she anticipates that interactions with most people will be negative. The Rorschach also suggests that the amount of contact she has with others does not fulfill her, as she feels lonely and unsupported.

The Rorschach data concerning how she processes and interprets data suggests that thought processes may be immature, overly personalized, and illogical because of the disruptive effects of emotions, preoccupations concerning closeness with others, and an effort to infer symbolic meaning in situations. This may result in unusual, irrational interpretations of events that others may find peculiar or strange. The MMPI-2 does not suggest this.

MMPI-2–Rorschach Integration

Mrs. S's responses indicate she attempted to minimize and deny having any problems (Lie = 80; K = 65). She has a very strong need to portray herself as an exceedingly virtuous, responsible, and conscientious woman whose self-image and lifestyle are above reproach. She does not admit to having any personal faults, flaws, or foibles. If difficulties arise, she externalizes responsibility for the problems and focuses on the behavior of other people without considering or acknowledging her own contribution to the situation (Lie = 80; PER = 3; Intellectualization Index = 5). Her reliance on denial, repression, intellectualization, and externalization allows her to explain, rationalize, or gloss over aspects of herself and her behavior that others could judge as socially unacceptable. Given her strong need to appear morally correct, she may justify and rationalize her behavior in a way others experience as self-righteous. The use of these defenses interferes with her having insight into her feelings, motivations, or behavior, as well as prevents her from listening openly to points made by others that might challenge her self-image.

Mrs. S expresses emotional difficulties in somatic complaints that allow her to avoid dealing with or thinking about her own psychological problems (*13/31* "conversion V"). Common complaints associated with this profile include headaches, chest and back pain, numbness, fatigue, weakness, and sleep disturbance that are not explained by medical work-up. The onset and severity of these symptoms are related to emotional stress. These symptoms are reinforced by how others respond to her as well as by explaining any problems she experiences as due to physical rather than psychosocial difficulties. It is likely that the unexplained physical symptoms she reports serve to allow her to escape from a work situation in which she experienced repeated difficulties with coworkers and supervisors.

Mrs. S has very strong, immature dependency needs (*13/31* codetype; Food = 1). She seeks attention, affection, and sympathy from others to make her feel worthwhile, needed, and valuable. She feels insecure if others do not provide frequent expressions of interest and concern. Although superficially friendly, her relationships may be characterized as involving difficulties (*CDI* = 4) and as lacking depth because of her constant attempts to elicit from others reactions that show they care about her (*13/31* codetype). Others may experience her efforts to win their approval as demanding or manipulative and may become irritated, impatient, and intolerant of her as a result.

At the same time that she desires contact with others, Mrs. S is cautious about establishing close bonds with others and keeps a distance from them because she anticipates that interactions with others will turn out badly and that she will be hurt ($T = 0$; *H content* $= 3$; $COP = 0$; $AG = 1$). Her need to maintain a distance from others may have been learned from childhood experiences with a verbally abusive, volatile, unpredictable, alcoholic father. The compromise she has reached in terms of the amount of involvement she allows herself to have with others is not satisfying as she feels lonely, isolated, and unsupported (Isolation Index $= .40$).

Mrs. S may acknowledge experiencing some tension but is unlikely to openly admit to any significant emotional distress (*13/31* codetype; *Afr* $= .36$; $C' = 7$). In spite of her tendency to deny emotional difficulties, her responses suggest she has experienced feelings of depression for an extended period of time (*DEPI* $= 6$; $C' = 7$; $m = 3$; *Adj D* $= -1$). One might speculate that the episode of depression precipitated by the death of her daughter has never fully resolved, in part because her defensive style interferes with recognizing, focusing on, and working through emotional issues, or in reaction to frustrated dependency needs.

In general, Mrs. S is a woman who experiences emotions in a very intense manner ($FC:CF+C = 0:5$; $C = 1$) and struggles to maintain control over how feelings are expressed to avoid becoming overwhelmed and disorganized by strong affect (*Afr* $= .36$; $C' = 7$; $SumC':SumC = 7:5.5$). When emotional reactions are triggered, she is vulnerable to losing control over herself and becoming flooded with emotions, as she lacks the capacity to use logic or reason to regulate her internal state or to modulate behavior (*Adj D* $= -1$; $FC = 0$; $C = 1$; *Lambda* $= .07$). Although some people may respond to her style of expressing emotions as warm and expressive, others may view her reactions as immature, overly dramatic, and exaggerated. She attempts to contain affective reactions by trying to suppress or bury feelings ($C' = 7$) or by detaching from feelings through the use of intellectualizing defenses (Intellectualization Index $= 5$). In spite of the considerable effort Mrs. S expends trying to contain her emotions, she is vulnerable to overreacting to situations and responding in a manner that is out of proportion to the situation.

Affect can adversely affect Mrs. S's interpretations of events and lead to illogical, strained thinking and poor judgment (*Lambda* $= .07$; *FQnone* $= 2$; $X + \% = .40$; $Xu\% = .27$; Populars $= 3$). Her thought processes may be immature, overly personalized, and illogical because of the disruptive effects of emotions, preoccupations concerning closeness with others, and an effort to infer symbolic meaning in situations. This may result in unusual, irrational interpretations of events that others may find peculiar, strange, and hard to understand ($WSum6 = 40$; Intellectualization Index = 5).

Mrs. S's self-esteem has been negative for a long period of time (Egocentricity Index = .27; $MOR = 3$). This did not develop in response to the recent conflicts at work ($FV = 0$; $FD = 2$). She often feels inadequate and inferior to others. The lack of a positive self-image contributes to a vulnerability to becoming depressed in response to stress. Rather than becoming self-critical in reaction to recent conflicts with coworkers and supervisors, she responded with a vigorous defensive effort to prove that she was correct and others wrong (Lie = .80; $PER = 3$; Intellectualization Index = 5). In her efforts to do so, she may rationalize and justify her actions in a manner that dismisses the point of view of the other people involved. Her rigid insistence that she was correct and her adamant refusal to consider other points of view may be perceived by others as self-righteous and inflexible.

One may speculate that Mrs. S found working with the developmentally disabled residents so rewarding because her relationships with this population gratified her strong dependency needs without threatening her. Taking care of these helpless, intellectually limited children who require a great deal of attention and patience made her feel important, needed, and wanted. One must wonder why her relationships with her husband and her own children did not fulfill these needs. It is possible that her need to maintain a distance from others and to inhibit expressions of emotions played a role in this. This suggests that further investigation of her relationships with her husband and children is needed to assess whether conflict or distance exists that could be addressed in psychotherapy.

The conflicts Mrs. S described with staff concerning treatment of the residents may be understood in terms of the psychological characteristics described previously. Her overprotective responses concerning treatment of the children reflect her strong dependency needs, her tendency to overreact when emotions are triggered, and her tendency to respond in emotional situations with poor judgment. In addition, she reacts to problems by attributing blame to the other persons involved and justifying her own actions as necessary, correct, and above reproach. This stance makes it difficult to resolve differences with others and may have offended co-workers further, leading to increasing conflict with them. This escalating tension is critical in terms of understanding the development of physical symptoms that has not been explained by thorough medical work-up.

Diagnostic Impression

DSM-IV   Axis I   300.11 conversion disorder
296.25 major depression, in partial remission

Axis II   301.50 histrionic personality disorder

TREATMENT RECOMMENDATIONS

Because of Mrs. S's strong need to deny psychological problems and to maintain an impression of being reasonable, normal, and moral, she prefers to view her difficulties in terms of physical symptoms and will likely vigorously resist any attempt to suggest her physical condition is related to her psychological reactions. She is not likely to accept a recommendation for traditional psychotherapy if the stated aim is to alleviate the multiple, vague physical symptoms she reports. She may, however, accept a recommendation for psychotherapy if it is presented as a means of helping her cope with her symptoms and the stress that has developed as a result of her situation. She is likely to be resistant to insight-oriented psychotherapy given the defensive style described previously and her insistence that she has no psychological problems.

Mrs. S is likely to need repeated reassurance from her physician that she does not suffer from a serious medical condition. Her physician should be educated about her condition to be prepared to deal with her with support and comfort rather than exasperation and disbelief.

An attempt should be made to resolve the conflict Mrs. S experiences with coworkers concerning treatment of the developmentally disabled residents she cares for in order to facilitate her return to work. This may be difficult, as she is not likely to acknowledge her own role in creating this conflict and may respond with a self-righteous conviction that she acted in a virtuous and correct manner. The odds of resolving this conflict are greatest if discussions about it are focused primarily on ways to enhance the residents' welfare rather than on an attempt to determine who was right and who was wrong.

Although the test data suggest that Mrs. S's condition involves significant depressive elements, she is unlikely to admit to being sad. Thus, traditional psychotherapy may not be helpful in terms of treating the depression. As she responded to support from members of her church in the past, one might recommend that she increase or simply continue involvement with church activities to obtain support.

Finally, the finding that Mrs. S feels lonely, isolated, and unsupported by others is unexplained. This may signify family and/or marital problems that were not reported during the clinical interview or might be due to her constricted emotional style. These possibilities should be investigated further to assess whether there are any reasons for family and/or marital therapy.

8 Case 3: Adolescent Alienation – or Psychosis?

REASON FOR EVALUATION

Mr. R is a 19-year-old, single, White, college freshman who began outpatient psychotherapy 2 months after entering college. His parents made arrangements for this treatment after he told them about troubles he was having adjusting to college life, including feelings of social isolation, distress, and marked problems with motivation. His parents were concerned about him and immediately arranged outpatient treatment with a psychiatrist who recommended individual psychotherapy. The psychiatrist also prescribed Loxitane, an antipsychotic medication, after the second session. Two months later, Mr. R's father asked for a consultation with a second psychiatrist because he was concerned about the slow rate of improvement in his son's condition. A psychological evaluation was requested by the second psychiatrist to assist in determining whether Mr. R's presentation was consistent with Schizophrenia or an affective disorder with psychotic features.

BACKGROUND INFORMATION

Mr. R is currently a freshman at a large, academically rigorous university. When asked about his adjustment to college, he reported having difficulties in functioning because of a lack of motivation, minimal interest in academics and social activities, and limited effort to become involved in campus life. It was difficult to get a more detailed understanding of his functioning as his descriptions of life at college were vague.

Mr. R attended private schools from kindergarten through high school. He maintained an A average until the second semester of 12th grade when his motivation declined and he started withdrawing from social activities. At that time he began to feel detached from others, even friends he had been close to in the past, and felt as though he were "going through the motions" when he was with them. He often listened to his friends talk but felt he was "not with them. Never felt on the same par. I had the feeling people hated me because I couldn't get up and get going." Mr. R became angry and frightened as he felt more and more left out and isolated. When asked why he was frightened, he replied that he felt he had to "hide under a rock. Like somebody was whipping me." He also frequently thought common, everyday situations seemed strange and unreal. He tried to manage these situations by talking to himself and telling himself to "look at a wall for 15 seconds and then things would make sense. People would talk and I had no idea what they were saying."

As events began to feel increasingly strange and unfamiliar, Mr. R tried to establish and follow set patterns of activity to maintain a constant routine in his life. In spite of this, he felt that "everything fell through. I never completed anything, never followed a train of thought. To tell you the truth, I wasn't thinking. Like I was comatose." He was surprised no one seemed to notice his problems at work but explained that his job was not very demanding, he could be alone as much as he wanted, and there was little supervision.

When asked whether he felt depressed during this period in high school, Mr. R acknowledged feeling sad, upset, and guilty. There was no precipitant he could identify that triggered feelings of sadness, guilt, or detachment from others. He could not recall experiencing any particularly stressful events during his senior year in high school. It was not clear whether these dysphoric feelings occurred prior to or concurrent with feelings of detachment and social withdrawal or whether they developed in reaction to these experiences. He did not acknowledge having hallucinations or delusions, although the examiner wondered whether Mr. R was being evasive when asked about this.

Mr. R initially denied being depressed when seen for this psychological evaluation but then later said he had been feeling sad and upset. He acknowledged feeling extremely anxious much of the time. This anxiety was not limited to any particular situation, subject, or concern. He often had difficulty waking up in the morning. He tried to work around this by registering for college classes offered in the late morning and afternoon but still frequently misses classes because he oversleeps. He denied any change in appetite. He has difficulty concentrating and tries to force himself to pay attention to lectures. He feels guilty about these problems and at having worried his parents. He stated he has lost respect for himself, no longer feels proud of his abilities, and fears his father will be critical if he cannot succeed in college. He denied suicidal ideation and intent. As stated previously, he is currently being treated with Loxitane 25 mg., which Mr. R feels has helped clear up his thinking.

Mr. R expressed ambivalent feelings about his parents. His father is a high ranking executive with a large corporation, a job which is quite demanding in terms of time and travel. Father's background is in accounting and finance. Mr. R respects his father and wants to please him but perceives his father as someone who is hard to talk to and hard to get close to.

Mr. R feels his mother is easier to talk to than his father. However, he expressed angry feelings at mother who experienced repeated episodes of severe depression while he was in Grades 2 through 6. He recalled coming home from school and being happy about the events of his day, but then her depressed mood would "spoil my fun." He also described becoming extremely angry at her on several occasions when she remained in bed after his father went to work and the patient would yell at her to "get up and do something! What are you doing? Get up!" Her condition was serious enough that inpatient psychiatric treatment was required on more than one occasion. She improved with psychotherapy and medication treatment. She has maintained a positive adjustment without medication for several years.

In addition to mother's recurrent depression, family history of psychiatric disorder is positive, as Mr. R's maternal grandfather committed suicide at the age of 24. No further information concerning the reasons for his suicide was available.

Mr. R denied a history of current or past alcohol or substance abuse. There is no family history of alcohol or substance abuse.

DIAGNOSTIC CONSIDERATIONS

Mr. R reported significant difficulties in academic and social functioning that has worsened over time. Symptoms included markedly diminished interest in activities; difficulties with motivation, concentration, and thinking; feelings of detachment from others; sleep disturbance; social withdrawal and isolation; sadness; anxiety; and guilt. These symptoms could be consistent either with an episode of major depression, possibly with psychotic features, or with negative symptoms of schizophrenia, which include apathy, emotional withdrawal, avolition, anhedonia, and attentional impairment (Andreasen & Olsen, 1982; Crow, 1985). The available history does not clearly differentiate one diagnosis from the other.

It is extremely important to make an accurate diagnosis between schizophrenia and major depression, as these conditions are treated very differently and have very different prognostic implications (*DSM–IV*, 1994). In terms of treatment, it is generally accepted that the primary treatment modality for schizophrenia involves the use of antipsychotic medications, whereas depression may be treated effectively with antidepressant medication, psychotherapy, or a combination of the two. In terms of prognosis, depression is typically more responsive to treatment and has a less ominous prognosis than schizophrenia. Although individuals with schizophrenia may show significant improvement in symptomatology with treatment, most suffer from a chronic disorder and never fully return to their premorbid level of functioning (Hegarty et al., 1994). In contrast, the majority of individuals who develop major depression show a complete remission of symptoms, and their functioning is not chronically impaired, although a sizable minority do experience persistent symptoms of depression for an extended period of time. Furthermore, negative symptoms of schizophrenia are often more enduring and respond less well to antipsychotic drug treatment than positive symptoms (Mayerhoff et al., 1994; Pogue-Beile & Harrow, 1985). Thus, the results of this psychological assessment can provide extremely valuable diagnostic information so that the most effective treatment interventions can be implemented and so Mr. R and his family can be educated about the long-term implications of his condition.

The history of familial affective disorder is quite important, because both mood disorders and schizophrenia have been shown to have a strong genetic component. For example, the *DSM–IV* reports that first-degree biological relatives of individuals with schizophrenia have a risk for developing schizophrenia that is about 10 times greater than that of the general population, whereas the risk for developing major depression among first-degree biological relatives of individuals with major depression is about 2 times greater than for the general population. Thus, the positive family history of depression and of completed suicide suggests Mr. R has a higher risk of developing an affective disorder than the general population.

One study specifically examined the MMPI-2's ability to differentiate between schizophrenia and depression (Ben-Porath, Butcher, & Graham, 1991). Ben-Porath et al. found that for men the only MMPI-2 standard clinical scale that discriminated between groups of depressed and schizophrenic patients was the Depression scale, with depressed subjects scoring significantly higher than schizophrenic subjects on scale *2*. No significant between-group difference was found on scale *8*.

When MMPI-2 content scales were examined, it was found that schizophrenic men scored significantly higher than depressed men on Bizarre Mentation (*BIZ*), whereas depressed subjects scored significantly higher on Depression (*DEP*) and Social Discomfort (*SOD*). The results of multiple regression analyses showed that the BIZ and DEP content scales discriminated between these diagnostic groups and contained more information than found in the standard MMPI-2 clinical scales alone. This suggests that MMPI-2 content scales may yield valuable information independent of the information provided by MMPI-2 clinical scales when a question is raised concerning differential diagnosis between schizophrenia and depression.

Two Rorschach indices are of particular relevance to distinguishing between schizophrenia and major depression, the Schizophrenia Index (*SCZI*) and the Depression Index (*DEPI*). Both indices were empirically developed by comparing a group of patients with a specific diagnosis (e.g., schizophrenia or depression) with groups of normal controls and groups of psychiatric patients with other diagnoses. Exner (1991) compared *SCZI* scores obtained by patients with schizophrenia and with an affective disorder. Of the schizophrenic subjects in these samples, 82% produced an elevated *SCZI*, whereas only 9% of the patients with an affective disorder produced a positive *SCZI*. In a sample of 315 psychiatric inpatients with a diagnosis of depression, 11% obtained a positive *SCZI*, although most of the positive *SCZI* scores were 4, a score that must be viewed with considerable caution given the possibility of false positive identification of schizophrenia. In the same sample, 75% of the depressed inpatients obtained positive scores on the *DEPI*. In a sample of 320 inpatient schizophrenics, 82% obtained a positive *SCZI* and 19% produced a positive *DEPI*. Thus, examination of the *SCZI* and *DEPI* may yield important information when the clinician attempts to differentiate between major depression and schizophrenia.

MMPI-2 Data

Validity. The MMPI-2 validity scale configuration is noteworthy given the elevations on the *F* and *F-Back* scales. His endorsement of an unusually large number of deviant items could be due to one of several factors including lack of reading ability, inconsistent responding, an acute psychotic decompensation, or exaggeration of symptoms. Mr. R's reading skills are not an issue given the fact that he obtained above average grades in high school and is currently enrolled at a competitive university. Consistent with this, his score on the Variable Response Inconsistency scale (*VRIN*) was acceptable ($T = 54$). This suggests he was able to read and understand test items, sustain attention, and respond to MMPI-2 items in a consistent manner. Thus, the elevations on *F* and *F-Back* cannot be attributed to carelessness, confusion, or poor reading ability. In the absence of any external incentive to exaggerate symptoms, this validity scale configuration suggests the presence of emotional turmoil, difficulties in functioning, and serious psychopathology, possibly involving a psychotic decompensation.

134

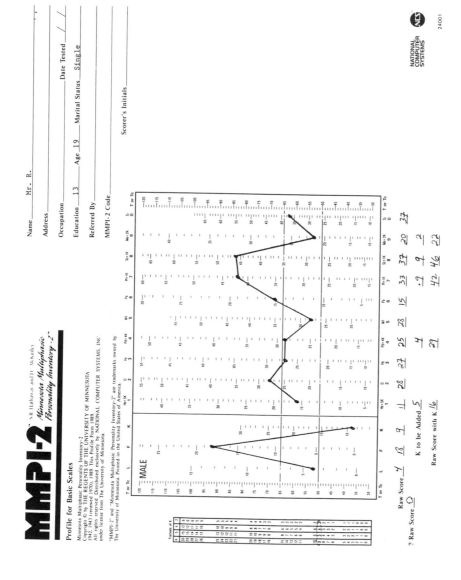

MMPI-2™
Minnesota Multiphasic Personality Inventory-2™

by S.R. Hathaway and J.C. McKinley

Profile for Basic Scales

Minnesota Multiphasic Personality Inventory-2
Copyright © by THE REGENTS OF THE UNIVERSITY OF MINNESOTA
1942, 1943 (renewed 1970), 1989. This Profile Form 1989.
All rights reserved. Distributed exclusively by NATIONAL COMPUTER SYSTEMS, INC
under license from The University of Minnesota.

"MMPI-2" and "Minnesota Multiphasic Personality Inventory-2" are trademarks owned by
The University of Minnesota. Printed in the United States of America.

Name _____Mr. R._____

Address _____

Occupation _____ Date Tested __/__/__

Education __13__ Age __19__ Marital Status __Single__

Referred By _____

MMPI-2 Code _____

Scorer's Initials _____

NATIONAL
COMPUTER
SYSTEMS

24001

MALE

Raw Score   4   18   9   11   28   27   25   28   15   33   37   20   37

K to be Added   5   4   .9   9   2

Raw Score with K   16   29   42   46   22

? Raw Score   O

Case 3 MMPI-2 Content and Supplementary Scales

	Raw Score	T Score
FB	14	100
True Response Inconsistency (TRIN)	12	72T
Variable Response Inconsistency (VRIN)	6	54
Anxiety	32	81
Repression	18	56
MAC-R	26	58
Ego Strength (Es)	29	31
Dominance (Do)	8	20
Social Responsibility (Re)	16	39
Overcontrolled Hostility (O-H)	14	55
PTSD - Keane (PK)	30	87
PTSD - Schlenger (PS)	41	88
Addiction Potential (APS)	29	65
Addiction Admission (AAS)	2	46

Content Scales (Butcher et al., 1990)		
Anxiety (ANX)	7	56
Fears (FRS)	5	54
Obsessiveness (OBS)	7	56
Depression (DEP)	20	78
Health Concerns (HEA)	8	58
Bizarre Mentation (BIZ)	13	88
Anger (ANG)	6	50
Cynicism (CYN)	15	59
Antisocial Practices (ASP)	8	49
Type A (TPA)	10	53
Low Self-Esteem (LSE)	14	75
Social Discomfort (SOD)	10	54

Depression Subscales (Harris-Lingoes)		
Subjective Depression (D1)	19	82
Psychomotor Retardation (D2)	10	76
Physical Malfunctioning (D3)	5	59
Mental Dullness (D4)	9	82
Brooding (D5)	6	74

Hysteria Subscales (Harris-Lingoes)		
Denial of Social Anxiety (Hy1)	3	45
Need for Affection (Hy2)	5	43
Lassitude-Malaise (Hy3)	8	75
Somatic Complaints (Hy4)	6	67
Inhibition of Aggression (Hy5)	5	63

135

	Raw Score	T Score
Psychopathic Deviate Subscales (Harris-Lingoes)		
Familial Discord (Pd1)	1	45
Authority Problems (Pd2)	3	47
Social Imperturbability (Pd3)	3	45
Social Alienation (Pd4)	11	87
Self-Alienation (Pd5)	9	77
Paranoia Subscales (Harris-Lingoes)		
Persecutory Ideas (Pa1)	12	112
Poignancy (Pa2)	6	75
Naivete (Pa3)	3	41
Schizophrenia Subscales (Harris-Lingoes)		
Social Alienation (Sc1)	11	84
Emotional Alienation (Sc2)	5	88
Lack of Ego Mastery, Cognitive (Sc3)	7	84
Lack of Ego Mastery, Conative (Sc4)	8	82
Lack of Ego Mastery, Def. Inhib. (Sc5)	6	82
Bizarre Sensory Experiences (Sc6)	9	85
Hypomania Subscales (Harris-Lingoes)		
Amorality (Ma1)	3	58
Psychomotor Acceleration (Ma2)	10	73
Imperturbability (Ma3)	1	35
Ego Inflation (Ma4)	4	56
Social Introversion Subscales (Ben-Porath et al., 1989)		
Shyness/Self-Consciousness (Si1)	6	53
Social Avoidance (Si2)	3	49
Alienation -- Self and Others (Si3)	13	74

Clinical Scales.   The *78/87* codetype occurs frequently among persons seen by mental health professionals (Greene, 1991). This codetype is produced about as often by patients with a psychotic disorder as by patients with a neurotic disorder. Some authors (Graham, 1993; Greene, 1991) recommend examining whether scale *7* or *8* is higher to determine whether this codetype indicates the presence of a psychotic as opposed to a neurotic disorder. They suggest that the likelihood of a psychotic disorder increases when scale *8* is greater than scale *7*, particularly if the scales comprising the neurotic triad (scales *1, 2,* and *3*) are relatively low. A psychotic disorder is less likely to be present if scale *7* is higher than scale *8*. In the latter case, persons are likely to be distressed and upset by the unusual thoughts and behaviors they experience and may be struggling to maintain control over themselves.

Mr. R's scores on scales *7* ($T = 83$) and *8* ($T = 84$) are nearly identical. The relative elevations on scales *7* and *8* do not clarify whether the *78/87* codetype indicates a vulnerability to a psychotic decompensation or a current psychotic disorder. However, the latter possibility is supported by scores on several content and supplementary scales, including elevations on the Bizarre Mentation scale ($BIZ = 88$), Lack of Ego Mastery, Cognitive ($Sc3 = 84$), and Lack of Ego Mastery, Defective Inhibition ($Sc5 = 82$). Thus, Mr. R endorsed a higher than average number of items on scales that tap the strange thoughts and unusual experiences often associated with psychosis, such as feelings of unreality, concerns others are trying to harm him, hallucinations, or delusions.

The *78/87* codetype suggests Mr. R currently experiences considerable turmoil that includes worry, anxiety, depression, and tension (scale *2* = 70; *DEP* = 78; *ANX* = 70; *D1* = 82; *Sc2* = 88). He is likely to be withdrawn, to lack the energy needed to try to cope with everyday activities, and to feel immobilized ($D2 = 76$; $D4 = 82$; Hy 3 = 75; $Pd5 = 77$). These reactions may be overwhelming at present. He is likely to ruminate and be preoccupied with worries, particularly related to feelings of personal inadequacy ($D5 = 74$; $Sc4 = 82$). This degree of rumination, worry, and tension may produce inefficient thinking and disrupt concentration.

In general, Mr. R lacks self-confidence and is troubled by feelings of inferiority. His self-concept is negative, he views himself as a failure, and he is likely to give up easily (Low Self-Esteem = 75; *Si3* = 74). His lack of self-confidence affects social interactions as he feels shy, nervous, and inadequate. As a result, he avoids social situations. He is particularly threatened by heterosexual interactions because of self-doubts and feelings of inadequacy as a male. He may also be uncomfortable with dating because of guilt concerning sexual impulses and sexual activity (*78/87*). However, he may have rich sexual fantasies and daydreams that function to compensate for doubts about his adequacy as a male.

Overall, the MMPI-2 clinical and supplementary scales provide strong support both for a current psychotic disorder and for significant emotional turmoil and affective disturbance. However, the clinical and content scales do not clearly distinguish between a psychotic decompensation associated with schizophrenia as opposed to a mood disorder with psychotic features.

Rorschach Data

The search strategy for the Rorschach is determined by the positive Schizophrenia Index ($SCZI = 5$). The $SCZI$ is an empirically derived cluster of 10 Rorschach variables that was developed to identify the presence of Schizophrenia. The variables comprising the $SCZI$ were identified on the basis of discriminant function analyses that differentiated among groups of schizophrenic patients, normals, and psychiatric patients with diagnoses other than schizophrenia. Scores on the $SCZI$ range from 0 to 6. Scores of 4 or more indicate a significant probability that a patient is schizophrenic or has a psychotic disorder. The results of these procedures found a low rate of false positives, that is, identifying an individual as being schizophrenic or psychotic when they are not. Most of the false positive cases occurred when the $SCZI$ was 4, whereas the probability of accurate identification of schizophrenia was greatest when the $SCZI$ was 5 or 6.

When $SCZI$ is ≥ 4, the search strategy begins by examining the character and quality of clients' thinking and the way in which they organize, interpret, and conceptualize stimuli. Mr. R does not have a consistent ideational style, as he is an ambitent ($EB = 4:5.5$). This lack of consistency in responding is associated with inefficient decision making, vacillation as he attempts to solve problems, and a vulnerability to errors in judgment. He is easily distracted, inattentive, and unfocused at present because disturbing thoughts and concerns interfere with attention and concentration ($m = 3$). His patterns of thinking, opinions, and values are quite fixed and rigid, which makes it difficult for him to shift or change ideas ($a:p = 8:1$). His thinking is likely to be quite gloomy and pessimistic ($MOR = 5$).

The number of special scores, scores designed to detect the presence of cognitive slippage and illogical, idiosyncratic thinking, is considerably higher than would be expected ($Sum6 = 12$; $WSum6 = 42$). This suggests Mr. R's thinking is markedly disorganized and notable for peculiar logic. Responses involving special scores sometimes reflect limited educational background or membership in a particular subculture. This was not the case for Mr. R who was raised in an upper middle-class home and attended a well-known university. His responses contained several instances of cognitive slippage, such as when he incorrectly used words he would be expected to know (e.g., on Card IV, he described a monster's arms as being "all dangled up," whereas on Card IX, he commented that a fountain was

Card	Response	Inquiry

I   I. I noticed 2...This up here l.l the earth. 2 mountains coming out. And a canyon inthe middle. 2 little hills in the middle of the canyon

E: (Rpts S's response)
S: That includes the upper 1/3 area. I c these as cliffs, land, 2 hills, rock formation.
E: What made it ll that?
S: Bec the shapes are so random & misshapen. Things happ in nature without organization or structure. Nature came to my mind when I lkd at the cards bec it seems so jumbled up. Figures seem so inanimate.
E: Inanimate?
S: Bec it dsn't have wings on the side. It l.l, no resemblance to a living being.

     2. That's it.
E: Most p c more than 1 thing on e card.
S: I noticed the holes in it. It seems l it was a complete object before, but now its just deteriorating. It resembles a BF. The black spots wld be the wings falling off. L.l a black BF y'd find in a field, dead, withering away. That's it.

E: (Rpts S's response)
S: Pretty much the whole thing. Just l.l its been torn apart.
E: BF?
S: 2 areas repr wings. These l.l eyes, maybe. BF's are symmetrical.

II   3. I noticed the red blotches. Reminds me of blood. L.l s.o took a hammer to a moth & it just went splatter on the ground.

E: (Rpts S's response)
S: Yeah. Blood smears. The red dsn't seem l it makes the picture more alive. Just bec its colored red makes it morbid.
E: Moth?
S: It l.l a moth bec I tried to identify it w s.t. I saw symmetry & some shape of wings.

     4. Grey & black l.l a continent. L.l Antarctica. Most ll countries,

E: (Rpts S's response)
S: Yeah, it resembles that.
E: Show me.

& the grey & black...is sort of smeared. Not 1 complete C. Diff shades of black. these seem 1 ridges on a country.

S: It just l.1 a big, massive body of earth. Antarctica is huge.
E: Help me c it.
S: The way its shaped, l.1 a country. Countries have no form. Not a happy place, a desolate place where e.t is dark & grey. Only attached to s place 1 Antarctica.

III 5. This reminds me of 2 A's playing ball or s.t Top l.1 cat's heads. Dsn't serve much of a purpose. Just sit w a glum look & pass this red ball betw them.

E: (Rpts S's response)
S: That's the ball.
E: Cats?
S: Their pointed noses & their small heads.
E: Glum?
S: Yeah. Just a look of despair.
E: U mentioned it didn't serve much purpose.
S: Yeah, lks sort of like a statue. Dsn't seem active.

6. Only thing I c, down the middle, l.1 a shrine, little thing that comes out.

E: (Rpts S's response)
S: Down here, in the middle. Sort of l.1 a shrine.
E: Shrine?
S: Bec of the way its structured. Like a tower or bldg.

IV 7. This l.1 an overwhelming terror creature. L.1 a big mammoth. Overwhelming size. His arms are all dangled up. Bottom here seems 1 the feet.

E: (Rpts S's response)
S: All of this, excluding this. makes it appear he's out to get s.t.
E: Out to get s.t.?
S: The way he's in sort of an active pose. Got 2 arms, prob his weapons. Just l.1 an evil guy.
E: Evil?
S: His head, the way his head, its 1 a creature's head. Not a normal head. The way the eyes, head has no eyes. Size l.1 it has no purpose but to destroy.

8. This part, I d't underst why this is here bec the monster wld be complete without this. It l.1 a shrimp sort of. He (monster) has no thought

E: (Rpts S's response)
S: Down here, in the middle. Sort of l.1 shrimp.
E: Shrimp?
S: Here, the way its shaped somewhat.

except for killing &
pillaging & that sort of
thing. He is a single-
minded being.

V   9. This sort of resembles   E: (Rpts S's response)
     a BF, too.   S: This way its happy lkg.
                                   (Turns card upside down, then
                                   right side up) Get the feeling
                                   of BF bec it lks so fragile.
                                   Like black substance is v
                                   frail.
                                   E: Fragile?
                                   S: No structure, just ridges &
                                   bumps. Yr shoe has structure &
                                   a BF has structure, but this
                                   has no structure. Just lks
                                   torn apart.
                                   E: Downcast?
                                   S: Bec of the wings. Dsn't
                                   seem to be a happy creature.
                                   In my head, like s.o who gave
                                   up, put arms down, & gave up.

     10. But when I turn it   E: (Rpts S's response)
     (turns card upside down),   S: Wings, still. These cld be
     it l.1 a happier, more   antennae.
     upbeat, like holding yr   E: Upbeat?
     arms up in joy BF or   S: The fact the wings are up.
     thing. More structured &
     happy. Turned the o way
     lks downcast, like the BF
     gave up & fell to the
     ground.

VI   11. L.1 a big shell for a   E: (Rpts S's response)
     turtle. The top part is   S: Yeah, its sort of just
     working its way out.   budging out.
                                   E: Where were u lkg?
                                   S: This is the shell. This is
                                   where he came out.
                                   E: What abt the card reminded u
                                   of a turtle shell?
                                   S: Bec it reminded me of a
                                   being that has a...has a...has
                                   an outer coating or
                                   outer...This lks more inanimate
                                   & this lks more animate bec s.t
                                   is coming out.

     12. (Turns card upside   E: (Rpts S's response)
     down) This way it l.1 a   S: Yeah. Top of earth & this
     coal mine shaft. Top of   is the shaft that goes down.
     canyon. 2 little hills &   E: Coal mine?

goes straight down. Seems like its pointing at s.t.

S: It dsn't...It gets blacker, or has black on the side. This cld be coal on bottom, what they're digging for.
E: Hills & canyons?
S: Yeah, here in middle. 1/2 circles.
E: U said they were pointing at s.t.
S: Yeah. Like pointing in 1 direction.

VII   13. 2 guys arguing at e.o. Neither 1 will let the o get a word in edgewise. 2 heads at top, shouting out insults. Ripping on e.o. left & right.

E: (Rpts S's response)
S: These. Their mouths s wide open. Heads are pointed away, not pointed directly at the o person.

14. These 2 heads lk more like possessed demons. Can c eyes that l.l a firey monster w emaciated heads and no goodness within these 2. Basically j evil.

E: (Rpts S's response)
S: Yeah. Just bad creatures. Got mangled faces & eyes.
E: What gave u that impression?
S: Well, not demons, but s.t similar.
E: Evil?
S: 1st, all lkg in diff directions. None l.l thy're cooperating w e.o. They seemed unfriendly just bec of that.
E: Emaciated?
S: The head is not...seems... like this face here wld be covered w...I d.k.

15. Whole thing reminds me of a horeshoe crab.

E: (Rpts S's response)
S: The last time I did it, it remined me of that.
E: Show me where u were lkg.
S: The entire form. When I go to Bethany I've seen those. Just popped into my head.

VIII 16. This is more of a picture w the C's. Seems like 2 A's climbing up a tree on the side. Its more alive & colorful.

E: (Rpts S's response)
S: Yeah. The entire picture, mainly the pink seems more...
E: Seems more?
S: More pleasing than dark green or blue.
E: A's?
S: Here.
E: Tree?
S: Its bec -- it l.l these guys are climbing up the side of it.

142

IX 17. The C's again are
    vivid. And it lks to me,
    1st impr, this is a
    fountain w a base & this
    little area is where the
    fountain is. This area is
    sprouting out water. The
    dome in the backgr, l.l
    one. All the shapes are v
    misshapen. All l.l paint
    blots. The green & yellow
    is the fountain, sort of
    repr autumn, trees &
    bushes. Or it repr that,
    at least.

E: (Rpts S's response)
S: Here. The pink area is the
base of the fountain.
E: U saw a dome?
S: Yes. here. These little
pothole slits.
E: In the background?
S: Bec o C's are overlapping
it. I got the sense of green &
yellow, didn't find any
complete picture. If to be a
complete picture, s.b. put in
right area. This wld be a
complete picture that just
scattered. This is 1st decent
picture, like a fountain,
shooting up. L.l shrubs.
E: U said it repr autumn.
S: Yellow repr in the fall,
changing fr green to yellow.

X   18. A lot of things...The
    blue reminds me of the
    ocean. Many diff ideas &
    C's here. The blue
    reminds me of an ocean.

E: (Rpts S's response)
S: The blue, it l.l some
splashes, sort of. The
extensions, splashing.
E: Water?
S: The blue makes me identify w
water.

    19. (Upside down) U can
    alm make a head out of it.
    2 eyes, nose, side, &
    chin.

E: (Rpts S's response)
S: Here's the eyes, nose,
mouth, sides of head.

    20. The green demon lks
    weird with, shooting out
    fire. A Devil figure to
    tht guy. Its just very
    random. No structure,
    except for symmetry.

E: (Rpts S's response)
S: Yeah. Here.
E: Demon?
S: It l.l, bec of the way the
body is shaped. It seems l its
winged or s.t
E: U mentioned it was shooting
s.t.
S: These 2 green, sort of.
E: I'm not sure what u mean.
S: It reminds me of shooting
out fire or s.t. He's an
enraged beast or s.t.
E: Fire?
S: Bec of the direction its
going. Its going, l shooting
up. I assoc fire w a demon.
The 2 wings above the head.

```
CASE03.R3===================== SEQUENCE OF SCORES =============================

CARD NO LOC  #  DETERMINANT(S)   (2) CONTENT(S)   POP Z  SPECIAL SCORES
======= ======  ================ === ==========  === =  ==============
  I   1 Ddo     F-                   Ls                  DR
      2 WSo   1 FC'o                 A            P 3.5  MOR

 II   3 W+    1 CFu                  A,Bl           5.5  MOR,DR
      4 Dv      FY-                  Ls                  MOR

III   5 D+    1 Ma.FC-           2   A,Id           4.0  FAB2,MOR
      6 Ddo     Fu                   Id

 IV   7 Do    7 Mao                  (H)          P      AG,ALOG,DV2
      8 Do    1 F-                   A

  V   9 Wo    1 Fo                   A            P 1.0  MOR,ALOG,INC
     10 Wo    1 Mpu                  A              1.0  DR,INC2

 VI  11 Wo    1 FMa-                 A              2.5  DV
     12 D+    5 FC'o                 Ls             2.5

VII  13 D+    1 Mao              2   Hd           P 3.0  AG
     14 Do    3 Fu               2   (Hd)
     15 Wo    1 F-                   A              2.5  PER

VIII 16 W+    1 FMa.CFu          2   A,Bt         P 4.5

 IX  17 WS+   1 ma.FD.CFo            Id,Bt          5.5  AB,DV2

  X  18 Dv      CF.mau               Na
     19 Dd+     F-                   Hd             4.5
     20 D+   10 CF.ma-               (H),Fi         4.0  ALOG,AG


============================= SUMMARY OF APPROACH =============================

      I :  Dd.WS                   VI :  W.D
     II :  W.D                    VII :  D.D.W
    III :  D.Dd                  VIII :  W
     IV :  D.D                     IX :  WS
      V :  W.W                      X :  D.Dd.D
```

144

```
CASE03.R3==================== STRUCTURAL SUMMARY ==============================

LOCATION              DETERMINANTS              CONTENTS      S-CONSTELLATION
FEATURES          BLENDS          SINGLE                      NO..FV+VF+V+FD>2
                                          H    = 0, 0         NO..Col-Shd Bl>0
Zf    = 13    M.FC          M   = 3     (H)  = 2, 0         YES..Ego<.31,>.44
ZSum  = 44.0  FM.CF         FM  = 1     Hd   = 2, 0         YES..MOR > 3
ZEst  = 41.5  m.FD.CF       m   = 0     (Hd) = 1, 0         NO..Zd > +- 3.5
              CF.m          FC  = 0     Hx   = 0, 0         NO..es > EA
W  = 8        CF.m          CF  = 1     A    = 9, 0         YES..CF+C > FC
  (Wv = 0)                  C   = 0     (A)  = 0, 0         YES..X+% < .70
D  = 9                      Cn  = 0     Ad   = 0, 0         NO..S > 3
Dd = 3                      FC'= 2      (Ad) = 0, 0         NO..P < 3 or > 8
S  = 2                      C'F= 0      An   = 0, 0         YES..Pure H < 2
                            C'  = 0     Art  = 0, 0         NO..R < 17
  DQ                        FT  = 0     Ay   = 0, 0          5.....TOTAL
.........(FQ-)              TF  = 0     Bl   = 0, 1
  +  = 8  ( 3)             T   = 0     Bt   = 0, 2         SPECIAL SCORINGS
  o  = 10 ( 4)             FV  = 0     Cg   = 0, 0                Lv1    Lv2
 v/+ = 0  ( 0)             VF  = 0     Cl   = 0, 0         DV   = 1x1    2x2
  v  = 2  ( 1)             V   = 0     Ex   = 0, 0         INC  = 1x2    1x4
                            FY  = 1     Fd   = 0, 0         DR   = 3x3    0x6
                            YF  = 0     Fi   = 0, 1         FAB  = 0x4    1x7
    FORM QUALITY            Y   = 0     Ge   = 0, 0         ALOG = 3x5
                            Fr  = 0     Hh   = 0, 0         CON  = 0x7
       FQx  FQf MQual SQx   rF  = 0     Ls   = 3, 0         Raw Sum6 =  12
  +  =  0    0    0    0    FD  = 0     Na   = 1, 0         Wgtd Sum6 =  42
  o  =  6    1    2    2    F   = 7     Sc   = 0, 0
  u  =  6    2    1    0                Sx   = 0, 0         AB  = 1    CP  = 0
  -  =  8    4    1    0                Xy   = 0, 0         AG  = 3    MOR = 5
 none=  0   --    0    0    (2) = 4     Id   = 2, 1         CFB = 0    PER = 1
                                                            COP = 0    PSV = 0

=================== RATIOS, PERCENTAGES, AND DERIVATIONS ===================

 R = 20         L =  0.54           FC:CF+C = 1: 5      COP = 0     AG = 3
-------------------------------------   Pure C  =  0      Food        = 0
 EB = 4: 5.5  EA =  9.5  EBPer= N/A  SumC':WSumC= 2:5.5  Isolate/R  =0.35
 eb = 5: 3    es =  8      D =   0    Afr    =0.33       H:(H)Hd(Hd)= 0: 5
        Adj es =  6    Adj D =  +1    S      = 2         (HHd):(AAd)= 3: 0
-------------------------------------   Blends:R= 5:20    H+A:Hd+Ad =11: 3
 FM = 2  :  C'= 2  T = 0             CP      = 0
 m  = 3  :  V = 0  Y = 1
                           P   = 5       Zf   =13        3r+(2)/R=0.20
 a:p   =  8: 1   Sum6  = 12  X+% =0.30    Zd   = +2.5     Fr+rF   = 0
 Ma:Mp =  3: 1   Lv2   =  4  F+% =0.14    W:D:Dd = 8: 9: 3  FD    = 1
 2AB+Art+Ay= 2   WSum6 = 42  X-% =0.40    W:M  = 8: 4     An+Xy   = 0
 M-    =  1      Mnone =  0  S-% =0.00    DQ+  = 8        MOR     = 5
                             Xu% =0.30    DQv  = 2

=======================================================================
 SCZI = 5*    DEPI = 4    CDI = 3    S-CON = 5    HVI = No   OBS = No
=======================================================================
```

145

"sprouting out water"). His responses also involved unrealistic perceptions of stimuli and contained bizarre, strange reasoning. For instance, on Card III, he perceived two "glum" cats playing ball, whereas on Card IV he attributed aggressive, malicious intent to a creature because of its size. He explained that this creature "has no thought but killing and pillaging" because its "size looks like it has no purpose but to destroy." On Card X, he justified seeing a demon shooting fire by explaining that he perceived fire "because of the direction its going. Its going up – like shooting up." These responses overall indicate that his thinking is quite disturbed and is more likely to reflect internal preoccupations than an accurate appraisal of reality.

Mr. R perceives stimuli in an inaccurate, unconventional, distorted manner (Populars = 5; $X + \% = .30$; $Xu\% = .30$ and $X - \% = .40$). He sees events quite differently than most others do. His perceptions may be described as unrealistic, strange, and unusual given the lower than expected number of Popular responses produced and significant difficulties in perceptual accuracy ($X + \% = .30$; $X - \% = .40$). Although a lower than expected number of Popular responses and a lower than expected $X + \%$ could be produced by someone who is nonconforming, highly individualistic, or creative, the high $X - \%$ indicates marked difficulties in perceiving events in an accurate, realistic manner, particularly when $X - \%$ is elevated and is greater than $Xu\%$. Because minus answers were scattered throughout the protocol rather than clustered in specific segments of the record, these difficulties in perceptual accuracy cannot be explained by a lack of cooperation with testing procedures, negativism, or affective disruption. The combination of perceptual distortions and thought disorder described previously most often occurs when a psychotic disorder is present.

Surprisingly, given the history of difficulties in daily functioning and adaptation to college, Mr. R's capacity to handle stressful, difficult situations is greater than that of most people ($Adj D = +1$). This does not imply he is better adjusted than most others or does not have problems so much as that he generally has the psychological resources and self-control to prevent stress from disrupting behavior.

Also surprisingly, no signs of current emotional distress or frustration over unmet needs exist that would account for the difficulties with which he presented (D Score = 0; $FM = 2$; $C = 0$; $V = 0$; $T = 0$; $Y = 1$; $DEPI = 4$). Thus, these data provide no support for a diagnosis of an affective disorder.

Mr. R's control over his emotions tends to be much less than that of most people ($FC:CF+C = 1:5$). Because he often reacts with considerable intensity, others may view him as quite emotional, perhaps overly emotional or even high strung. Because of this tendency to react so intensely, he tries to contain expressions of affect as well as to avoid being in situations that arouse emotions. These efforts at self-control may result in his acting in a constricted, detached manner (Afr = .33). He is especially likely to have difficulty handling emotionally complex situations (Blends:R = 5:20). For instance, he may be particularly uncomfortable meeting new people or even interacting with people with whom he is familiar, as people express feelings directly and internal emotional reactions are frequently triggered in social situations. Thus, the tenuous self-control he struggles to maintain may be threatened by social situations that are often affectively charged.

Mr. R's sense of self-worth is quite negative (Egocentricity Index = .20; MOR = 5). This negative self-image appears to be chronic and long standing in nature rather than having developed in reaction to any recent difficulties or failures (FD = 1; V = 0). He lacks self-confidence and feels inadequate, inept, and inferior to others. His self-image is likely to be based on distorted ideas and fantasies rather than on actual experiences ($H:(H)Hd(Hd)$ = 0:5). A review of the content involved in the MOR responses suggests he now views himself as deteriorating, despairing, and hopeless. For instance, on Card I, he saw a butterfly lying in a field that is dead and withering away; on Card II, a moth smashed by a hammer; on Card III, two glum, despairing cats; and on Card V, a fragile butterfly who has been torn apart and appears downcast, "like someone who gave up." Thus, he now feels more discouraged, hopeless, and despairing than usual.

Mr. R approaches interpersonal relationships in a guarded, cautious, reserved manner (T = 0). His view of others is colored by distrustful, negative attitudes. He does not believe that people are dependable or trustworthy and anticipates that most people will act in an aggressive, hostile manner (COP = 0; AG = 3). As a result, he may choose to avoid social contacts to reduce the risk of having to defend himself against hostile attacks. His withdrawal from others results in feeling isolated, lonely, and distant from others (Isolation Index = .35). A review of the content of his responses also suggests Mr. R fears being the target of interpersonal aggression, such as his response to Card VII where he perceived two guys arguing, "shouting out insults, ripping on each other, left and right." In addition, his percept on Card IV is of a terrifying creature that "has no thought except for killing and pillaging . . . it has no purpose but to destroy." Although one may question whether Mr. R identifies with the destructive, aggressive aspects of this creature, it seems more likely that he fears being the victim of another hostile attack he would be powerless to defend against (Egocentricity Index = .20; MOR = 5).

Comment

The primary referral question to be addressed in this case involves differential diagnosis between Schizophrenia and Major Depression. Both the MMPI-2 and Rorschach provide data directly addressing this issue. As described previously, the *78/87* MMPI-2 codetype is seen as often in psychotic as in neurotic disorders. In some cases, the relative elevations on scales *7* and *8* can be examined to distinguish between a neurotic and psychotic condition. In this case, scales *7* and *8* were nearly identical. Thus, the MMPI-2 profile was ambiguous in terms of the primary referral question. MMPI-2 content scales were similarly ambiguous as scales related to psychotic experiences and scales related to emotional distress were both elevated.

In contrast, data from the Rorschach clearly showed signs of a psychotic disorder with no indication of an affective disorder. It should be noted that a negative *DEPI* does not rule out a mood disorder, although a negative *DEPI* provides no support for a mood disorder.

In this case, data from the Rorschach and MMPI-2 complement one another to address the primary referral question by emphasizing the psychotic features detected on both tests. Both tests agree that Mr. R presents with a psychotic disorder (*78/87; BIZ; Sc3; Sc5; SCZI; WSum6*). Given the strong evidence for a psychotic disorder and the limited evidence for an affective disorder (scale *2* = 70; *DEP* = 78; *ANX* = 70; *DEPI* = 4), it seems most reasonable to conclude that the thought disorder and cognitive disorganization are primary features of Mr. R's presentation and that the mood disturbance is secondary. It is not unusual for patients with Schizophrenia to experience a disturbance in mood during the course of their illness.

The MMPI-2 and Rorschach agree in describing Mr. R as lacking in self-confidence and having a negative self-image. The Rorschach data suggests that his low self-esteem has been a chronic problem rather than developing in response to recent life events (*FD* = 1; *FV* = 0).

Both tests describe Mr. R as having significant difficulties in interpersonal relationships. The MMPI-2 seems to explain his avoidance of social interactions as due to feelings of shyness and inadequacy, whereas the Rorschach data suggests his views of others are negative and distrustful because of fears that he will be the victim of a hostile attack he will be powerless to defend against. The MMPI-2 data specifically addresses Mr. R's difficulties in heterosexual relationships including both feelings of inadequacy as a male as well as guilt about sex, whereas the Rorschach does not address these issues directly. Furthermore the MMPI-2 suggests he may engage in rich sexual fantasies. No specific indications of sexual concerns were apparent on the Rorschach (*Sx* = 0).

MMPI-2–Rorschach Integration

Mr. R cooperated during administration of both the MMPI-2 and Rorschach. The MMPI-2 validity scales showed he was able to read and understand test items, responded in a consistent manner throughout the test, and was attentive as he answered MMPI-2 items (*F*; *F-Back*; *VRIN*). He responded openly and produced many indications of significant emotional turmoil, difficulties in functioning, and serious psychopathology.

Mr. R's responses overall are consistent with a current psychotic disorder (*78/87*; *BIZ* = 88; *Sc3* = 84; *Sc5* = 82; *SCZI* = 5). His responses indicate he has experienced many of the strange thoughts and unusual experiences often associated with psychosis, such as feelings of unreality, concerns others are trying to harm him, hallucinations, or delusions. Thought processes were notable for signs of cognitive slippage; peculiar, idiosyncratic logic; and marked cognitive disorganization (*SCZI*; *Sum6* = 12; *WSum6* = 42).

Mr. R perceives stimuli in an inaccurate, unconventional, distorted manner (Populars = 5; $X + \%$ = .30; $Xu\%$ = .30; $X -$ = .40). He sees events quite differently than most others do. His perceptions may be described as unrealistic, strange, and unusual (Populars; $X + \%$ = .30; $X - \%$ = .40). He is likely to be distressed and upset by the unusual thoughts and behaviors he experiences and struggles to maintain control over himself (*78/87*). The combination of significant perceptual distortions and thought disorder most often occurs when a psychotic disorder is present. It is important to note that these signs of a thought disorder were produced while he was being treated with an antipsychotic medication, Loxitane, which would be expected to reduce cognitive slippage and thought disorder. Thus, one would expect that more pronounced cognitive disorganization and perceptual inaccuracies would have been observed had he been tested during a period when he was not being treated with antipsychotic medication.

The *78/87* codetype suggests Mr. R currently experiences considerable turmoil that includes worry, anxiety, depression, and tension (scale *2* = 70; *DEP* = 78; *ANX* = 70; *D1* = 82; *Sc2* = 88). He is likely to be withdrawn, to lack the energy needed to try to cope with everyday activities, and to feel immobilized (*D2* = 76; *D4* = 82; *Hy3* = 75; *Pd5* = 77). He is quite indecisive, vacillates when a decision must be made, and is vulnerable to making errors in judgment (*EB* = 4:5.5). He is likely to ruminate and be preoccupied with worries, particularly related to feelings of personal inadequacy (*D5* = 74; *Sc4* = 82; *m* = 3). The extent of his preoccupation with these disturbing thoughts results in his being easily distracted, inattentive, and unfocused. This vacillation, inefficient thinking, poor concentration, and distractibility may be significant factors in his difficulties in academic functioning and in adjusting to college life.

Mr. R's control over his emotions tends to be much less than that of most people (FC:CF + C). Because he often reacts with considerable emotional intensity, others may view him as quite emotional and even high strung. He tries to maintain control over his reactions by avoiding affectively charged situations (*Afr*). These efforts at self-control may result in his acting in a constricted, detached manner. He may have particular difficulty dealing with emotionally complex situations (Blends:R). It is possible that his withdrawal from social involvement reflects in part an attempt to avoid becoming overwhelmed and disorganized by situations in which feelings are expressed directly and in which internal emotional reactions are frequently triggered.

In general, Mr. R's sense of self-worth is negative, he lacks self-confidence, and is troubled by feelings of inferiority (*78/87*; Low Self-Esteem = 75; *Si3* = 74; Egocentricity Index = .20; *MOR* = 5). He views himself as a failure and is likely to give up easily. His self-image has been chronically negative (*FD* = 1; *V* = 0), although he now feels more discouraged, hopeless, and despairing than usual (Rorschach content). His lack of self-confidence affects social interactions as he feels shy, nervous, inadequate, and inferior to others. As a result, he may avoid social situations. He is particularly threatened by heterosexual interactions because of doubts about his adequacy as a male. He may also be uncomfortable with dating because of guilt concerning sexual impulses and sexual activity. However, he may have rich sexual fantasies and daydreams that function to compensate for doubts about his masculinity (*78/87*).

Mr. R's view of interpersonal relationships is colored by negative, distrustful attitudes. He approaches interpersonal relationships in a guarded, cautious, reserved manner (*T* = 0). He does not believe that people are trustworthy or dependable and anticipates that most people will act in an aggressive, hostile manner (*COP* = 0; *AG* = 3). As a result, Mr. R may choose to avoid social contacts as he fears being the victim of a hostile attack he is powerless to defend against (Egocentricity Index = .20; *MOR* = 5). His withdrawal from others results in feeling isolated, lonely, and distant from others (Isolation Index = .35).

Diagnostic Impression

DSM-IV   Axis I   295.90 Schizophrenia, undifferentiated type

Axis II   Deferred

TREATMENT RECOMMENDATIONS

Several treatment implications are suggested by these results. First, treatment with antipsychotic medication is strongly recommended to control thought disorder and cognitive disorganization. One initial goal of treatment will be to educate Mr. R and his family about the nature of his condition and the need for ongoing maintenance medication. His family should be involved in monitoring compliance with medication management.

Second, these data suggest that Mr. R should seriously consider withdrawing from college. He is unlikely to succeed academically at the present time because of difficulty focusing and sustaining attention. Furthermore, trying to adjust to the unfamiliar social environment of a large college campus may be particularly stressful for Mr. R, as he is likely to react with fear and apprehension to being in an unfamiliar environment in which he is expected to interact with strangers. As noted previously, social situations may contribute to his becoming disorganized and to a loss of control over emotional reactions. If he has a strong desire to remain in college, Mr. R will have a better chance of succeeding at a smaller, local college that is not as demanding academically and that has less of a potential to overwhelm him socially.

One goal of psychotherapy should be to help Mr. R and his family understand the nature of his difficulties and establish realistic educational and vocational goals. In addition, psychotherapy can provide an opportunity for Mr. R to examine perceptions of interpersonal interactions to determine whether his interpretations of events are accurate or distorted.

Several factors are of considerable importance to inform Mr. R's therapist about to aid in planning the most effective treatment approach for him. First, Mr. R reacts with considerable emotional intensity and can be overwhelmed and disorganized by feelings. Second, when it is necessary to make decisions, Mr. R tends to be ineffective, vacillates, and may show poor judgment. Furthermore, he feels immobilized and has difficulty motivating himself to take action, even to perform basic, necessary tasks. Third, he is likely to be guarded and distrustful, especially during the early phases of treatment. These factors suggest that Mr. R is most likely to respond to a treatment approach that focuses on solving specific problems and developing strategies to achieve these his goals.

9

Case 4: Marital Separation, Depression, and Alcohol Abuse

REASON FOR EVALUATION

Mr. H is a 30-year-old, married, White male. He arranged to meet with a therapist 4 weeks after separating from his wife because of distress about the separation. A psychological evaluation was requested to assist with diagnosis and treatment planning. In particular, the therapist was concerned about reports of intense swings in Mr. H's mood as he described abrupt shifts from feeling calm to "plunging into depression" and questioned whether his mood swings are symptoms of a bipolar disorder given a positive family history of bipolar disorder.

BACKGROUND INFORMATION

Mr. H and his wife have been involved for $3\frac{1}{2}$ years and married for 2 years. He met her through acquaintances with whom he "partied" regularly and was initially interested in getting to know her after learning that she sold drugs and provided free cocaine to her friends. At first, they got together primarily to use drugs and alcohol but then became involved sexually. He spontaneously commented that he pursued a relationship with her because of a desire to "rescue" her. When asked what he meant by this, he explained he wanted to help her with the problems she disclosed to him, including concerns about her escalating use of drugs and a history of feeling hurt and rejected by men. He described her past relationships as short-lived and promiscuous.

Mr. H and his wife have had a volatile relationship including a number of physical fights during which they have pushed, punched, and scratched one another. He denied ever injuring her. These fights often occurred after he felt ignored by her or when she was friendly and flirtatious with other men. Mr. H reported being bothered by intrusive, upsetting thoughts about her past sexual relationships in these situations. He described several incidents while they were dating and shortly after they married when they went to a bar together, had a fight, and she left with another man and stayed out all night. A physical fight inevitably occurred when she returned home.

Mr. H and his wife decided to separate 6 weeks prior to this evaluation after agreeing that their fights were becoming too intense and destructive. They talked about beginning marital therapy, but neither has taken any action to look into this.

When asked about his current mood, Mr. H described himself as alternating between having a calm, steady mood and "plunging" into depression when "little things get me down." The triggers for these shifts in mood included his wife acting cold rather than warm, feeling overwhelmed by bills, and making a mistake at work. He stated these periods last several days during which he feels life is futile and he contemplates suicide. He has never acted on these thoughts, because he has not found a painless way to kill himself, but believes everyone would be happier if he were not around. He reported that his sleep cycle has always been erratic, although he now sleeps more than usual as a way to escape his problems. Appetite is normal. When depressed, he has less energy than usual, doesn't want to work, and doesn't feel like doing anything. He stated that the only activity he enjoys is drinking because he can forget about his troubles. Concentration is poorer than usual. He reported feeling self-critical but noted he has felt this way most of his life. At the same time, he also feels a pressure to "do something great. I can't be content to just be an average guy. I want to be the greatest carpenter or the wisest guy at the AA meeting. I feel pressure to perform and I feel terrible if I don't get a raise at work or if I'm not good in bed with my wife." He has felt down in the past but never for more than a day or 2 and never as sad as he is now.

As he described his mood, Mr. H commented that he thinks "I'm a very angry person down deep. It's an academic reason why." When he is drunk, he often feels angry "at people and at the world." When asked how he expresses this anger, he replied that he becomes verbally abusive toward whomever gets in his way, including his wife. He quickly added that he does not have a history of violent behavior.

When asked if he has experienced periods of elevated, expansive, or irritable mood, Mr. H reported that when things are going well, he feels a strong positive mood to the point of feeling "invincible." This mood can last for several hours or as long as several days but is often terminated by an upsetting event, such as a negative encounter with his wife. There is no change in his need for sleep during these periods. He believes his thoughts race, and his speech is faster during these episodes. When he feels this way, he wishes he had "telepathic powers to shoot my ideas into other people's heads." He does not recall anyone ever telling him that his speech is too fast or hard to follow. When he feels good, his concentration is sharper than usual. He denied an increase in goal-directed behavior or excessive involvement in pleasurable activities.

Mr. H reported periods of heavy consumption of alcohol alternating with periods when he does not drink for several days or weeks. When he does drink, he typically consumes at least 12 beers during an evening and drinks more if he binges over a weekend. Alcohol has caused repeated problems at work, as his attendance is often erratic, and he is "absolutely useless after a drunk." Although he has never been fired from a job, he has quit several jobs because he anticipated being fired for poor job performance. He has been arrested twice for Driving Under the Influence and has spent the night in jail on several occasions to "sleep off a drunk." Mr. H has attended Alcholics Anonymous meetings but never maintained sobriety for more than a month. During the past 3 years, he has used cocaine regularly but prefers alcohol to cocaine or other drugs.

Mr. H attended college where he majored in fine arts, concentrating on painting. He dropped out of college after 3 years, as he "couldn't keep it together because of my drinking." He also questioned whether he would be a success as an artist.

Mr. H currently works as a carpenter. His work performance is good when he does not drink but suffers when he does. Because he has a good reputation among tradespeople, he finds work easily, although he has not kept any job for more than several months. He reported being angry at himself for not pursuing his dream of becoming an architect; "I kick myself for not following through on anything, taking risks, like pursuing an education."

Mr. H grew up in a household in which both parents were alcoholics. His father was successful and accumulated a considerable amount of money but has not yet attained the level of wealth he sought. He described his father as an entrepreneur who was always on the verge of clinching a deal that would make him wealthy. His father was characterized as emotionally distant and uncommunicative except when he talked with great enthusiasm about plans for his next business venture.

Mr. H described his mother as very kind and very intelligent but plagued by guilt, anxiety, and insecurity. She became worried and anxious about family and household responsibilities and so avoided them. When Mr. H was 12, she attempted suicide by an overdose of pills. Mr. H saved her life when he returned home from school, found her unconscious, and called an ambulance. He attributed her suicide attempt and chronic depression to his parents' unhappy marriage that included violent fights. For instance, he recalled an incident when mother poured hot coffee over father's head and other fights when mother and father punched and kicked each other.

Family history is significant for alcohol abuse on both sides of the family. His maternal grandmother was diagnosed as having a bipolar disorder and treated with Lithium. He has been told that his father's sister has a bipolar disorder but does not know whether this is true.

DIAGNOSTIC CONSIDERATIONS

The major diagnostic issue raised by the referring therapist is whether Mr. H presents with a bipolar disorder. This diagnosis must be considered seriously because of a positive family history of bipolar disorder and because there is strong evidence that bipolar disorder is highly heritable (Goodwin & Jamison, 1990).

Evaluation of the presence of a bipolar disorder rests heavily on obtaining a detailed history both of the patient's presenting symptoms and of any past episodes of depression and/or mania. In other words, reliable diagnosis requires both a careful cross-sectional and longitudinal assessment (Goodwin & Jamison, 1990). The reason for this is that a bipolar disorder typically involves marked fluctuations in mood between euphoria and depression. Thus, a patient will present quite differently if seen in a depressed, manic, mixed, or euthymic state. For example, a patient may not manifest the elevated mood, hyperactivity, grandiosity, pressured speech, and flight of ideas associated with mania when depressed and may not appear sad, anergic, anhedonic, or guilt-ridden during the manic phase of the illness.

This description has important implications for interpreting personality test data when considering whether an individual meets diagnostic criteria for a bipolar disorder. Specifically, test data provides information both about an individual's current state, such as mood, as well as longstanding, stable characteristics, such as personality style or self-image. One must take into account that some psychological characteristics are state variables that change over time, whereas others are trait variables that remain constant over time. Thus, very different profiles would be expected if a patient with a bipolar disorder were tested while in a depressed as opposed to a manic or euthymic state (Nichols, 1988). One cannot conclude from a protocol indicating the presence of depression that a patient has a unipolar as opposed to a bipolar disorder. This distinction can only be made on the basis of a careful exploration of the onset, symptoms, duration, and clinical course of past and present episodes of affective disturbance.

In terms of MMPI-2 and Rorschach assessment of a patient's affective state, both tests reliably identify the presence of a depressed state (e.g., scale 2 and *DEPI*). However, no scale or set of scores exists on either instrument that reliably identifies whether a patient who is depressed has a unipolar or bipolar depression. An elevation on MMPI-2 scale *9* is often associated with features of a hypomanic or manic episode, although not necessarily so (Greene, 1991). For instance, Walters and Greene (1988) found that schizophrenic and manic patients did not differ on MMPI scale *9* and did not differ in percentage of patients with high point codetypes involving scale *9* (e.g., Spike 9 or *89/98*).

Few studies exist that have examined Rorschach responses of patients with a bipolar disorder. No empirically derived index of mania comparable to the *DEPI* or *SCZI* has been developed for the Rorschach. Singer and Brabender (1993) compared Rorschach protocols of bipolar manic, bipolar depressed, and unipolar depressed subjects and found differences between the three groups. The bipolar manic and bipolar depressed groups produced significantly more responses indicative of thought pathology than the unipolar depressed group, with the manic group producing responses involving cognitive slippage, difficulties with reality testing, and poor logic most frequently. The unipolar depressed group, in contrast, obtained positive scores on the Rorschach Depression Index (*DEPI*) more frequently than the bipolar depressed group and gave more responses indicating intense dependency needs (Food responses) than the manic group. These results suggest that patients with a bipolar disorder are likely to manifest signs of cognitive slippage (e.g., Special Scores) and deficits in reality testing ($X - \%$), particularly during a manic episode.

A second issue that complicates the clinical picture is Mr. H's history of alcohol and substance abuse. This issue is particularly important as both alcohol and cocaine can produce organic mood disorders and cause changes in behavior, mood, and cognition that resemble symptoms of a mood disorder. For instance, Mr.H reported experiencing episodes that involved racing thoughts and rapid speech. It was not clear whether the racing thoughts and rapid speech were associated with drug use or occurred independently of drug use. Both of these could be symptoms either of a bipolar disorder or of the effects of cocaine use.

MMPI-2 Data

Validity.   The standard validity scales indicate that Mr. H responded to the MMPI-2 in an honest manner and openly admitted to psychological problems. His score on the K scale is low for the general population and is particularly low for a person with a college education. This suggests he is quite self-critical and readily admits to problems. The low *K* score in

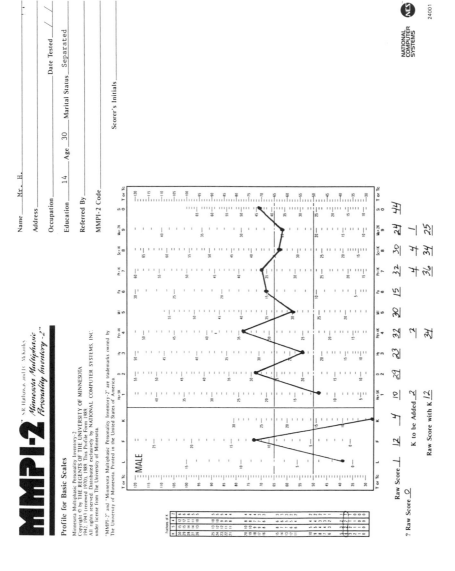

MMPI-2™
Minnesota Multiphasic
Personality Inventory -2™
SR Hathaway and JC McKinley

Profile for Basic Scales

Name __Mr. H.__

Address _____

Occupation _____ Date Tested __/__/__

Education __14__ Age __30__ Marital Status __Separated__

Referred By _____

MMPI-2 Code _____

Scorer's Initials _____

MALE

	L	F	K	Hs+5K 1	D 2	Hy 3	Pd+4K 4	Mf 5	Pa 6	Pt+1K 7	Sc+1K 8	Ma+2K 9	Si 0
Raw Score	1	12	4	10	29	23	32	30	15	32	30	24	44
K to be Added				2			2			4	4	1	
Raw Score with K				12			34			36	34	25	

? Raw Score __0__

Case 4 MMPI-2 Content and Supplementary Scales

	Raw Score	T Score
FB	11	87
True Response Inconsistency (TRIN)	11	64T
Variable Response Inconsistency (VRIN)	5	50
Anxiety	31	80
Repression	10	39
MAC-R	21	48
Ego Strength (Es)	38	40
Dominance (Do)	17	51
Social Responsibility (Re)	19	47
Overcontrolled Hostility (O-H)	8	35
PTSD - Keane (PK)	20	72
PTSD - Schlenger (PS)	29	74
Addiction Potential (APS)	24	52
Addiction Admission (AAS)	2	46

Content Scales (Butcher et al., 1990)		
Anxiety (ANX)	16	75
Fears (FRS)	8	64
Obsessiveness (OBS)	9	63
Depression (DEP)	23	83
Health Concerns (HEA)	14	70
Bizarre Mentation (BIZ)	4	58
Anger (ANG)	9	59
Cynicism (CYN)	16	63
Antisocial Practices (ASP)	14	65
Type A (TPA)	7	46
Low Self-Esteem (LSE)	15	77
Social Discomfort (SOD)	17	71

Depression Subscales (Harris-Lingoes)		
Subjective Depression (D1)	15	71
Psychomotor Retardation (D2)	5	48
Physical Malfunctioning (D3)	3	51
Mental Dullness (D4)	7	72
Brooding (D5)	7	84

Hysteria Subscales (Harris-Lingoes)		
Denial of Social Anxiety (Hy1)	1	34
Need for Affection (Hy2)	2	33
Lassitude-Malaise (Hy3)	9	79
Somatic Complaints (Hy4)	3	52
Inhibition of Aggression (Hy5)	3	48

```
                                          Raw Score  T Score

Psychopathic Deviate Subscales (Harris-Lingoes)
      Familial Discord (Pd1)                  9         97
      Authority Problems (Pd2)                5         71
      Social Imperturbability (Pd3)           4         52
      Social Alienation (Pd4)                13         97
      Self-Alienation (Pd5)                  11         87


Paranoia Subscales (Harris-Lingoes)
      Persecutory Ideas (Pa1)                 6         76
      Poignancy (Pa2)                         4         62
      Naivete (Pa3)                           5         51


Schizophrenia Subscales (Harris-Lingoes)
      Social Alienation (Sc1)                 9         76
      Emotional Alienation (Sc2)              3         60
      Lack of Ego Mastery, Cognitive (Sc3)    4         60
      Lack of Ego Mastery, Conative (Sc4)     8         82
      Lack of Ego Mastery, Def. Inhib. (Sc5)  4         68
      Bizarre Sensory Experiences (Sc6)       3         55


Hypomania Subscales (Harris-Lingoes)
      Amorality (Ma1)                         3         58
      Psychomotor Acceleration (Ma2)          8         63
      Imperturbability (Ma3)                  2         41
      Ego Inflation (Ma4)                     5         63


Social Introversion Subscales (Ben-Porath et al., 1989)
      Shyness/Self-Consciousness (Si1)       12         72
      Social Avoidance (Si2)                  7         71
      Alienation -- Self and Others (Si3)    13         74
```

combination with the low Ego Strength score ($T = 40$) suggests a deterioration in defenses and marked difficulty in coping.

Clinical Scales.   Mr. H produced elevations on scales *2, 4, 6, 7,* and *0.* With scale *4* as the highest elevation and *2* and *7* next at the same levels, this configuration can be viewed as a *247/427/472* three-point codetype. The *427* three-point codetype is commonly produced by passive–aggressive individuals who abuse alcohol and/or drugs. This codetype is associated with depression, guilt, irritability, worry, tension, and anxiety. Often, suicidal ideation is present. Conflict with family members, particularly his wife, exists related to substance abuse and to conflicts about expression of anger. Although Mr. H is likely to be resentful and verbally hostile, he has difficulty expressing anger directly and appropriately and instead expresses anger indirectly. After any direct expression of anger, he feels guilty, remorseful, and worried. He tends to be "highstrung" and reacts to minor difficulties as though they were catastrophic emergencies.

The *427* codetype suggests Mr. H has strong, unfulfilled needs for attention and support from others and quickly becomes overly dependent on them. The histories of men with this pattern often involved an extremely close relationship with a mother who emotionally "rescued" them (Friedman et al., 1989; Gilberstadt & Duker, 1965). These men frequently attempt to recreate a similar, dependent relationship with the women with whom they become involved as adults. One might speculate that Mr. H seeks involvement with a strong, dominating woman who he hopes will make him feel secure and whose strength will compensate for his underlying feelings of inferiority. Given this dependence on his wife, Mr. H is likely to feel extremely threatened if he anticipates being rejected by her and is likely to be distressed if he thinks he will lose her.

Mr. H's dependence on his wife must be understood in the context of his general discomfort with people (scale $0 = 71$; $Hy1 = 34$; $Pd3 = 97$; $Ma3 = 41$; $Si1 = 72$; $Si2 = 71$). In general, he feels shy, socially anxious, and awkward around others. As he easily becomes self-conscious and feels ill at ease around other people, Mr. H prefers to be alone or with persons with whom he has a close relationship. He is especially uncomfortable around members of the opposite sex. Difficulties in interpersonal relationships are likely to develop because he is overly sensitive and easily feels hurt, misunderstood, and resentful (scale $6 = 67$).

The *427* codetype is often associated with a history of underachievement in school and work. He is likely to have avoided competition or situations in which he would be evaluated because of a strong fear of failure. His reluctance to expose himself to failure reflects deepseated feelings of inferiority ($LSE = 77$; $Si3 = 74$). His lack of achievement may also be due to acting in self-defeating ways.

In terms of the question as to whether Mr. H presents with a bipolar disorder, his MMPI-2 profile is consistent with current depression as well as a passive–aggressive personality disorder. No signs of a current manic episode are present (scale $9 = 62$). As noted previously, the MMPI-2 cannot discriminate between an episode of unipolar as opposed to bipolar depression.

Rorschach Data

Interpretation of Mr. H's Rorschach protocol starts with the significant elevation on the Depression index that signals the presence of sadness and pessimistic, negative thinking associated with depression ($DEPI = 6$). Although the positive Coping Deficit index ($CDI = 4$) is not interpreted at this point, it is noteworthy and suggests that his present condition involves both current depression and longstanding difficulties in coping and interpersonal relationships. This indicates that the possibility Mr. H presents with a personality disorder in addition to a depression needs to be considered carefully.

The recommended search strategy when the $DEPI$ is positive begins by examining the role affect plays in coping, his ability to manage affect, and the nature of his current emotional state. In general, Mr. H does not have a consistent style of coping with stressful situations ($EB = 3:4.0$). That is, he does notrely either on thinking or intuition when responding to problems. He may be strongly influenced by thinking in one instance and by emotions in the next, even if the two situations are quite similar. Because he has not developed an effective way of reacting to stressful situations, he is quite vulnerable to being overwhelmed by feelings ($FC:CF+C = 2:4$; $Lambda = .29$) and disorganized by stress ($Adj D = -1$). His behavior is often driven by strong emotional reactions that cloud his judgment. A considerable potential for impulsive, rash, unpredictable behavior exists given his chronic lack of control over emotions and limited ability to respond effectively to stress ($Adj D = -1$; $CDI = 4$). In spite of his efforts to prevent losing control by avoiding or withdrawing from emotional stimuli ($Afr = .35$), a significant potential for acting out exists.

At present, Mr. H is overwhelmed by painful, negative emotions (D score $= -3$) and ruminates constantly about his problems. He is also preoccupied with feelings of guilt, self-blame, and self-recrimination ($FV = 1$; $FD = 8$). Distressing thoughts creep into his awareness, and it is difficult if not impossible for him to put these upsetting ideas out of his mind ($m = 5$). These negative ruminations disrupt concentration and impair his ability to function efficiently.

Mr. H's emotional state involves considerable anger and hostility ($S = 10$) in addition to depression; he is as angry as he is depressed. This anger

Card	Response	Inquiry
I	1. It 1.1 2 p, holding hands. Frolicking in the snow. That's it.	E: (Rpts S's response) S: Trailing arm, joined in the middle. Little hat. L twirling around, 1 when y're a kid, spin. Snow kicking up around them. E: Snow? S: Just the jagged edges, nor r precise. Not defined. Prob snowing now, a lot of snow on the ground. E: U said it 1.1 a lot of snow. S: Jagged edges & the feet are alm totally obscured. No appendages here. L.1 swirling, snow b blown away.
	2. E: Most p see more than 1 thing. S: A BF.	E: (Rpts S's response) S: Yeah, not as much. Antenna, wings. These white spots 1.1 coloring, markings.
	3. Well, 2 p & an A of some kind in the middle.	E: (Rpts S's response) S: The 2 p, like before. Hats, & arms. Here, these cld be antlers or horns on a cow. Y're looking down on it. E: Cow? S: The width of the body and bumps on head where horns grow. E: Looking down. S: Yes.
	4. I see a little, kind of a star. The neg space inside the inkblot.	E: (Rpts S's response) S: These are points of star, white spots. Within the dark framework 1.1 it cld be a rising sun or s.t. E: What makes it 1.1 that? S: Just 1 at 4 white points on black backgr, 1.1 a rising sun. From a childlike perspective. E: Rising sun? S: Yeah, only seeing part of it. Othr part is below. Light emenating from it. A kid's drawing.

5. Maybe a crown.

E: (Rpts S's response)
S: Same thing. Cld be on s.b's head.
E: Show me the crown.
S: It isn't exactly like a sun. Points cld be jewels on a crown that are shining. Shape is elongated & l.l a head.
E: Shining?
S: Bec thy're bright - white, not black.

II 6. A woman's genitalia. (lghs)

E: (Rpts S's response)
S: Here. Vulva & labia, major & minor. Kind of l.l the birth canal in the middle.
E: What reminded u of that?
S: Prob the red C in the lower portion. Not the upper portion.

7. A top. Spinning.

E: (Rpts S's response)
S: This in the center, l.l a top. Spinning on the axis in here. String, wrap it around to spin.

8. A cathedral steeple in the center.

E: (Rpts S's response)
S: This here lks knd of l a Greek Orthodox church steeple.
E: What gave u that impr?
S: The point, the center section creates a balance. K of a pire where inkblot was folded.

III 9. 2 p over a pot of food. A cauldron of some sort.

E: (Rpts S's response)
S: Bending over. Waists, feet, heads. Breasts - that's why they're women. Got hands on the pot here.
E: Over a pot of food.
S: Just the whole collective quality. Just the whole shape.

10. A glass, a wine glass w some wine in it. The red. C't really integrate parts of it. L.l it. L.l parts, but c't integrate into the imagery, 2 women over a cauldron.

E: (Rpts S's response)
S: If you remove the outside & look at this line & shadow, l.l the stem of glass & beverage inside it.
E: Wine?
S: The red cld be wine.

IV 11. Saskatch. Big Foot. U know. From below lkg up.

E: (Rpts S's response)
S: Big Foot is so big. Feet, big tial, arms & hands. Fore-

shortening, foreshortened view.
Head, a big hairy critter.
E: Lkg up?
S: Bec of the way it tapers to
top. L.1 its foreshortened.
E: Hairy?
S: All the waves & diff values
of dark, black. Like a layered,
hairy effect.

12. A bear or s.t, a large
bear.

E: (Rpts S's response)
S: Same thing. All the
hairiness of it. Bear on his
rear w legs rearing up. Didn't
see a.t too specific. Not 1 of
yr better inkblots.
E: Hairy?
S: Like I said, diff values of
black in actual inkblot. Its
fuzzy.
E: Rearing up?
S: Standing l a bear will do.
Getting ready to attack.

13. A p sitting on a chair
or pedestal.

E: (Rpts S's response)
S: This is the pedestal, legs, p
sitting there.
E: Show me.
S: Just reaching, nothing r
specific. Once again, the feet.
Whole thing is foreshortened,
obviously.
E: Foreshortened?
S: Way p is balancing themselves
in that position w their feet
stretched out.

V   14. A BF. Some k of
insect, a mature one...Its
so definitely an insect I
d't r see a.t else in it.

E: (Rpts S's response)
S: Tail here. A mature BF.
Wings & antenna. So much l a BF
I c't thk of a.t else.

VI   15. A skinned A.

E: (Rpts S's response)
S: Legs, central body portion,
head & snout.
E: Skinned?
S: Just that its spread out. L
bearskin rug or s.t Flattened
out or s.t. Edges are ragged.

16. A highway thr the
desert. From above.

E: (Rpts S's response)
S: This is highway in center
portion. Darker portion. Bleak
terrain on the sides. Mottling

of inkblots. I used to fly.
Like lkg down on desert in Ariz.
Get that effect, night or dusk.
E: Desert?
S: J the mottling of the
terrain, diff values of color.
Can imagine the sand near the
highway, c.b. boulders, make
that darker spot.

17. A phallus. A symbol
of some sort.

E: (Rpts S's response)
S: Just the long center section
with the head. L.l a phallic
symbol.
E: Symbol?
S: I interp any long, thin
objects as b phallic symbols.
Conveivably cld make a case for
it b symbolic that way. As
opposed to, say, more of a male
symbol than a female symbol, l
water, cultivated farmland.

VII 18. 2 rabbits.

E: (Rpts S's response)
S: Yeah, r reaching. Ears,
nose, tail, & feet. Kind of
perched on s.t.
E: Perched?
S: Just there.

19. Maybe 2 little
statuettes. Or 1
statuette, a decoration
that may sit on a table.

E: (Rpts S's response)
S: This cld be s form of
casting. Bec its darker on 1
side, its like there's shadows.
Like a light source. 3-
dimensional quality. Pedestal,
its connected.
E: Shadows?
S: Inside of it is darker, more
shadow. Prob 2 sources of
light.

20. Cross-section of a
bowl. We're r stretching
here.

E: (Rpts S's response)
S: Just, here's lip of bowl.
Here's little ornamental place,
l u wld keep s.t. there. This
is the inside.
E: Describe it.
S: The opening, cavity, & walls
of the outside.

VIII 21. Hmmm...Colors.
Colors. Pink, blue,
orange...

R: (Rpts S's response)
S: Yeah. Nice colors.

22. Or 2 bears or A's of
some sort. Rodents.
Walking around a pond of
water to get a drink.

E: (Rpts S's response)
S: These, front & rear legs,
tails, head. Looking down on
them. Water. Maybe a
reflection.
E: Did u see the refl
originally?
S: No. More 1 a circling thing.
Around the water.
E: Water?
S: Blue. That blue-green C.
E: Looking down?
S: Yeah. Just to make it
logical, conceivable for the 2,
have to be looking down to see
the 2.

IX   23. God, what do I see in
this... A vase. An urn of
some sort.

E: (Rpts S's response)
S: The whole thing 1.1 a vase.
E: What reminded u of a vase?
S: The shape. Bottom, sides,
lip. I've drawn many of these
before.

24. A rotating turbine
section. A turbine
section of an airplane.

E: (Rpts S's response)
S: This here 1.1 a flow. Axle -
spinning around the axle.
Manifold, intake manifold, &
exhaust manifold.
E: Rotating turbine?
S: It may not be rotating now,
but on an axle. From what I
know of turbines, they have
rotating blades & stationary
blades.
E: Flow?
S: Intake, passing air in that
direction.

25. An upside-down bell.

E: (Rpts S's response)
S: Mouth of bell, top, the rope
the bell is hanging from. C't
see the sriker, but its in
there.

X   26. Top of a skyscraper at
sunset.

E: (Rpts S's response)
S: The red outline & the
negative space inside. This is
like a tower on top. Building.
And red background 1.1 dusk.
Just that part.

27. Rocks & shells &
things in a tidal pool at
the edge of the ocean...
That's it.

E: (Rpts S's response)
S: That's more diff. The C's &
values of C 1.1 things I've seen
in ocean when diving. A
conglomerate of stuff. Things
disconnected, lying there in the
tidal pools.
E: Tidal pools?
S: Totally the C's. Seen C's in
shells before. Play of light &
C on shells, underneath the
water. And so disconnected.

```
CASE04.R3==================== SEQUENCE OF SCORES ===============================

CARD NO LOC  #  DETERMINANT(S)      (2) CONTENT(S)   POP Z  SPECIAL SCORES
======= ====== ===============     === ==========   === =  ==============
   I  1 W+   1  Ma.ma.FDu           2  H,Na,Cg       4.0 COP
      2 WSo  1  FC'o                   A           P 3.5
      3 Wo   1  FDu                 2  H,A,Cg        1.0
      4 WSo  1  FC'.mau                Na            3.5
      5 WSo  1  FC'u                   Cg,Hd         3.5

  II  6 WSo  1  FC-                    Hd,Sx         4.5
      7 DSo     mao                    Id            4.5
      8 DdSo    Fu                     Id            4.5

 III  9 D+      Ma+                 2  H,Sx,Fd       4.0
     10 DdSo    FCu                    Hh,Fd         4.5

  IV 11 Wo   1  FD.FTo                 (H)         P 2.0 DV
     12 Wo   1  FT.FMao                A             2.0 AG
     13 W+   1  Mp.FD+                 H,Hh        P 4.0

   V 14 Wo   1  Fo                     A           P 1.0

  VI 15 Wo   1  Fo                     Ad          P 2.5 MOR
     16 Wv   1  FD.YFu                 Ls                PER
     17 Do      Fo                     Hd,Sx             AB

 VII 18 Do      FMpo                2  A
     19 W+   1  FVo                    Art           2.5
     20 DSo     Fo                     Hh            4.0

VIII 21 Wv   1  Cn                     Id
     22 W+   1  FMa.FD.CF+          2  A,Na        P 4.5

  IX 23 Wo   1  Fo                     Hh            5.5 PER
     24 DSo     ma-                    Sc            5.0 PER
     25 Do      mp.FDu                 Id

   X 26 DdS+    CF.FDu                 Na,Sc         6.0
     27 W+   1  CFo                    Na            5.5 PER


=========================== SUMMARY OF APPROACH ===============================

   I  :  W.WS.W.WS.WS           VI  :  W.W.D
  II  :  WS.DS.DdS             VII  :  D.W.DS
 III  :  D.DdS                VIII  :  W.W
  IV  :  W.W.W                  IX  :  W.DS.D
   V  :  W                       X  :  DdS.W
```

169

```
CASE04.R3===================== STRUCTURAL SUMMARY =================================

LOCATION                DETERMINANTS              CONTENTS        S-CONSTELLATION
FEATURES          BLENDS            SINGLE                        YES..FV+VF+V+FD>2
                                                  H   = 4, 0      NO..Col-Shd Bl>0
Zf    = 22        M.m.FD            M   = 1        (H) = 1, 0      YES..Ego<.31,>.44
ZSum  = 82.0      FC'.m             FM  = 1        Hd  = 2, 1      NO..MOR > 3
ZEst  = 73.5      FD.FT             m   = 2        (Hd)= 0, 0      YES..Zd > +- 3.5
                  FT.FM             FC  = 2        Hx  = 0, 0      YES..es > EA
W   = 17          M.FD              CF  = 1        A   = 5, 0      YES..CF+C > FC
 (Wv = 2)         FD.YF             C   = 0        (A) = 0, 0      YES..X+% < .70
D   = 7           FM.FD.CF          Cn  = 1        Ad  = 1, 0      YES..S > 3
Dd  = 3           m.FD              FC'= 2         (Ad)= 0, 0      NO..P < 3 or > 8
S   = 10          CF.FD             C'F= 0         An  = 0, 0      NO..Pure H < 2
                                    C'  = 0        Art = 1, 0      NO..R < 17
   DQ                               FT  = 0        Ay  = 0, 0        7.....TOTAL
.........(FQ-)                      TF  = 0        Bl  = 0, 0
 +  =   7  ( 0)                     T   = 0        Bt  = 0, 0      SPECIAL SCORINGS
 o  =  18  ( 2)                     FV  = 1        Cg  = 1, 2               Lv1    Lv2
v/+ =   0  ( 0)                     VF  = 0        Cl  = 0, 0      DV   = 1x1     0x2
 v  =   2  ( 0)                     V   = 0        Ex  = 0, 0      INC  = 0x2     0x4
                                    FY  = 0        Fd  = 0, 2      DR   = 0x3     0x6
                                    YF  = 0        Fi  = 0, 0      FAB  = 0x4     0x7
                                    Y   = 0        Ge  = 0, 0      ALOG = 0x5
        FORM QUALITY                Fr  = 0        Hh  = 3, 1      CON  = 0x7
                                    rF  = 0        Ls  = 1, 0      Raw Sum6 =    1
       FQx  FQf  MQual  SQx         FD  = 1        Na  = 3, 2      Wgtd Sum6 =   1
 +  =   3    0     2     0          F   = 6        Sc  = 1, 1
 o  =  12    5     0     3                         Sx  = 0, 3      AB = 1      CP = 0
 u  =   9    1     1     5                         Xy  = 0, 0      AG = 1      MOR = 1
 -  =   2    0     0     2                         Id  = 4, 0      CFB = 0     PER = 4
none=   1   --     0     0          (2) =  5                       COP = 1     PSV = 0

==================== RATIOS, PERCENTAGES, AND DERIVATIONS =====================

R = 27          L =  0.29          FC:CF+C = 2: 4     COP = 1     AG = 1
-----------------------------------     Pure C =    0     Food       = 2
EB = 3: 4.0  EA =   7.0  EBPer= N/A  SumC':WSumC= 3:4.0  Isolate/R  =0.41
eb = 8: 7    es = 15       D = -3    Afr     =0.35      H:(H)Hd(Hd)= 4: 4
             Adj es = 11  Adj D = -1  S       =10        (HHd):(AAd)= 1: 0
-----------------------------------     Blends:R= 9:27     H+A:Hd+Ad  =11: 4
FM = 3  :  C'= 3   T = 2              CP      = 0
m  = 5  :  V = 1   Y = 1
                            P   = 6        Zf  =22        3r+(2)/R=0.19
a:p   =  8: 3   Sum6  = 1   X+% =0.56      Zd  = +8.5     Fr+rF   = 0
Ma:Mp =  2: 1   Lv2   = 0   F+% =0.83  W:D:Dd =17: 7: 3   FD      = 8
2AB+Art+Ay= 3   WSum6 = 1   X-% =0.07      W:M =17: 3     An+Xy   = 0
M-    =  0      Mnone = 0   S-% =1.00      DQ+ = 7        MOR     = 1
                           Xu% =0.33      DQv = 2

==============================================================================
  SCZI = 0    DEPI = 6*    CDI = 4*    S-CON = 7    HVI = No   OBS = No
==============================================================================
```

appears to be a chronic, enduring feature of his personality rather than a reaction to recent events. He harbors a resentful, hostile, negative attitude toward others and is quick to react to them with irritation, anger, and a conviction that he has been treated unfairly. When he becomes angry, there is a considerable potential for hostile outbursts given the combination of chronic, intense anger and limited control over the expression of emotions ($FC:CF+C$; $Adj\ D = -1$; EB). This is particularly likely to occur when his self-control is reduced further by abuse of alcohol or cocaine.

The depression, anger, and negative ruminations described previously, interfere significantly with Mr. H's current ability to manage daily responsibilities ($Adj\ D = -3$). He is likely to have considerable difficulty organizing himself to fulfill obligations at work or at home. His emotional turmoil (D score $= -3$; $es = 15$) was precipitated by the recent separation from his wife ($T = 2$). Most individuals produce only one Texture response. More than one Texture response indicates that the persons' need for interpersonal closeness is ungratified and they feel frustrated as a result. The clinician must determine whether this sense of deprivation reflects a reaction to a recent loss or chronic feelings of loneliness. In most cases, this can be determined by asking whether the individual has experienced a loss recently. Mr. H clearly has. Although this suggests that the greater than expected number of Texture responses represents a reaction to the separation from his wife and the possibility of a divorce, other test data suggest he also suffers from chronic feelings of frustration and deprivation. Specifically, his responses indicate he experiences persistent, very strong needs for attention, support, and affection from others (Food $= 2$).

Mr. H has a difficult time establishing and maintaining meaningful relationships with others and generally feels lonely, unconnected to others, and deprived of emotional support ($CDI = 4$; Isolation Cluster $= .41$) His relationships are quite troubled, frustrating, turbulent, and unsatisfying for several reasons. First, the combination of his strong dependency needs and chronic resentment suggests he can be quite demanding of others and reacts with outbursts of anger if his demands are not satisfied ($S = 10$). At the same time, he has a need to stubbornly oppose requests made by others, as he perceives their requests as demands. Second, he is defensive and touchy when interacting with others and is vulnerable to feeling hurt, misunderstood, criticized, or slighted. When this occurs, his first response is to angrily retaliate by acting in a provocative, insulting, aggressive manner ($PER = 4$). Given the difficulties he has with people in general, it is understandable that he would become deeply dependent on a person, such as his wife, who gratifies his needs for affection, nurturance, and warmth. It is also expected that he would react with profound hurt and rage if this relationship were threatened.

Mr. H has chronically felt inferior and inadequate compared to others

(Egocentricity Index = .19). At present, Mr. H feels extremely self-critical and guilty, most likely about his marital problems ($FV = 1$; $FD = 8$). The unusually high number of FD responses he produced is noteworthy. In Exner's (1991) normative sample, the mean number of FD responses was 1.16 (± 0.87) compared to the 8 responses he gave. This suggests one of Mr. H's personality characteristics is a tendency to frequently evaluate himself and look to find fault with his actions. The combination of feelings of inadequacy and a propensity to judge himself critically suggests he is vulnerable to react to events by becoming absorbed in self-critical, devaluing thoughts and ruminate about perceived failures, such as how he performed in a particular situation or how others perceived him. In this context, the greater than expected number of responses with sexual content ($Sx = 3$) suggests he is preoccupied with concerns about his sexuality and doubts about his adequacy as a man.

Mr. H made a considerable effort in processing ($Zf = 22$; $W > D + Dd$; $W:M = 17:3$). The high Zd score ($+8.5$) should be interpreted cautiously, however, as the unusually high number of space responses may have artificially inflated this value. With this in mind, his responses suggest he has a perfectionistic or obsessive style, consistent with the previous description of a tendency to ruminate about events ($Zd = +8.5$; $FQ+ = 3$). He does not use these characteristics in an effective manner, however, given his poor coping skills and resources. Although able to perceive stimuli in a conventional manner (Populars = 6), he has a tendency to interpret situations in an unconventional way ($X-\% = .56$). Rather than revealing serious difficulties in reality testing, this appears to reflect his sense of social isolation and rebelliousness ($Xu\% = .33$; $S-\% = 1.00$; $S = 10$). Thus, unconventional behavior may reflect a need to disregard social expectations and defy convention. No indications of cognitive slippage or a thought disorder exist.

The data from the Rorschach does not directly address whether Mr. H meets diagnostic criteria for a Bipolar Disorder. His profile differs from that of the manic subjects in Singer and Brabender's (1993) study in several respects. First, Singer and Brabender reported that the most common finding in patients with a Bipolar Disorder were indicators of thought disorder. Mr. H did not produce a higher than expected number of responses suggestive of thought disorder ($SUM6 = 1$). Second, they also reported that unipolar depressed subjects produced significantly more food responses than manic subjects, most of whom gave no food responses. This is noteworthy, as Mr. H produced a higher than expected number of Food responses. However, an elevated number of Food responses can occur in many conditions and is not sufficient to bipolar disorder. Overall, the results are consistent with both an episode of major depression and a personality disorder involving marked difficulties in interpersonal relationships, impulsivity, poor regulation of affect, and a negative self-image.

Comment

The MMPI-2 and Rorschach agreed in several important respects, including a description of Mr. H's current dysphoric mood, indicators of a personality disorder in addition to an Axis I diagnosis, difficulties in interpersonal functioning, pronounced dependency needs, and a negative self-image. Findings from the two tests also complement one another in several important respects.

Although both tests described Mr. H as angry, the Rorschach emphasized the intensity of his anger more than the MMPI-2. The MMPI-2 and Rorschach also differed in characterizing how the anger is likely to be expressed. The 427 codetype suggests Mr. H expresses anger in a passive-aggressive manner, whereas the Rorschach suggests a marked potential for impulsive, uncontrolled acting out. In this instance, Rorschach findings modify the interpretation suggested by the MMPI-2 codetype. The history reported by Mr. H of repeated verbal and physical fights with his wife is more consistent with impulsive outbursts of anger, as suggested by the Rorschach, than the indirect expression of anger typical of passive-aggressive individuals, as suggested by the MMPI-2. Although alcohol and cocaine abuse are likely to have played an important role in these outbursts, the available information suggests Mr. H has poor self-control, lapses in judgment, and little ability to check affective reactions. These characteristics may be worsened by the disinhibiting effects of alcohol and cocaine but are not caused by substance abuse.

Both tests identified Mr. H's dependency needs as extremely important. The MMPI-2 directly addressed his need to be involved with a strong, dominant woman to compensate for underlying feelings of inadequacy. As mentioned in chapter 1, some critics of the MMPI have characterized the test as providing superficial information related only to symptoms. In contrast to this stereotype, one should note that in this case the MMPI-2 addresses dynamic issues concerning his dependency needs and the historical basis for these dynamics. This dynamic is not clearly identified from the Rorschach Structural Summary. Other features that contribute to his difficulties in interpersonal functioning were identified by the Rorschach, including resentful reactions to requests made by others, defensiveness, and a tendency to react to others with an aggressive counterattack.

Mr. H's poor self-esteem and feelings of inferiority are addressed by both the MMPI-2 and Rorschach. The MMPI-2 links these issues to a history of underachievement. The Rorschach data complement this interpretation by describing his tendency to evaluate his actions, search for fault, and ruminate about perceived failures. In addition, Mr. H's concerns about his adequacy as a man are defined more clearly in the Rorschach than the MMPI-2.

MMPI-2-Rorschach Integration

Mr. H responded openly and honestly on both the MMPI-2 and Rorschach. His responses are consistent with longstanding difficulties in coping and interpersonal relationships (MMPI-2 427; $CDI = 4$; $Adj D = -1$), as well as clinically significant depressed mood, pessimistic thinking, worry, and guilt (427; $DEPI = 6$; $C = 3$; $m = 5$; $FD = 8$; $FV = 1$). He is overwhelmed by painful, negative emotions, ruminates constantly about his problems (scale 7; D score $= -3$; $Lambda = .29$), and is preoccupied with feelings of guilt, self-recrimination, and self-blame (427; $FV = 1$; $FD = 8$). He cannot stop dwelling on troubling thoughts that creep into his awareness, disrupt attention and concentration, and impair his ability to function effectively ($m = 5$). He is likely to have considerable difficulty organizing himself to manage daily responsibilities at work or at home (K; Ego Strength $= 51$; D score $= -3$). Feelings of sadness, hopelessness, anger, and guilt may be so severe that he has considered suicide as a solution to his problems (427).

Mr. H does not have a consistent approach to coping with stressful situations ($EB = 3:4.0$) and is quite vulnerable to being overwhelmed by feelings and disorganized by stress (K; Ego Strength $= 40$; $FC:CF+C = 2:4$; $Lambda = .29$; $Adj D = -1$). He tends to be highstrung and reacts to minor difficulties as though they were catastrophes (427). In general, his behavior is driven by strong emotional reactions that cloud his judgment. A considerable potential for impulsive, rash, unpredictable behavior exists given his chronic lack of control over emotions and limited ability to respond effectively to stress (427; $Adj D = -1$; $CDI = 4$). These characteristics result in a significant potential for acting out.

Mr. H's current emotional state involves pronounced anger and hostility in addition to depression ($S = 10$); he is as angry as he is depressed. This anger appears to be a chronic, enduring characteristic of his personality rather than a reaction to recent events. He harbors a resentful, hostile, negative attitude towards others and is quick to react to them with irritation, anger, and a conviction that he has been treated unfairly. When he becomes angry, there is a considerable potential for hostile outbursts given the combination of chronic, intense anger and limited control over the expression of emotions (427; $FC:CF+C = 2:4$; $Adj D = -1$; EB). This is especially likely to occur when his self-control is further compromised by abuse of alcohol or cocaine.

Mr. H's current emotional turmoil was precipitated by the recent separation from his wife and the threat of divorce. Mr. H has strong, unfulfilled needs for attention and support from others and quickly becomes overly dependent on them (427; $T = 2$; Food $= 2$). The pattern of his responses suggest that he wishes to be involved with a strong, protective woman who will make him feel secure and whose strength will compensate for underlying feelings of inferiority. His dependence on his wife may be so strong that he "clutches" onto and clings to her, even if their relationship is stormy and destructive. Given his dependence on his wife, Mr. H feels extremely threatened if he anticipates being rejected by her and is likely to develop symptoms of emotional distress if he thinks he will lose her.

Mr. H's dependence on his wife must be understood in the context of longstanding difficulties in interpersonal relationships. His relationships can be characterized as frustrating, turbulent, and unsatisfying. Mr. H has a difficult time establishing and maintaining meaningful relationships with others and feels lonely, unconnected to people, and deprived of emotional support ($CDI = 4$; Isolation Cluster $= .41$). In general, he feels shy, socially anxious, and awkward around others (scale $0 = 71$; $Hy1 = 34$; $Pd3 = 97$; $Ma3 = 41$; $Si1 = 72$; $Si2 = 71$). As he easily becomes self-conscious and feels ill at ease around people he does not know well, Mr. H prefers to be alone or with persons with whom he has established a close relationship. He is especially uncomfortable around members of the opposite sex. He is likely to be quite demanding of persons with whom he has established a relationship and reacts with outbursts of anger if his needs for attention and affection are not satisfied (427; $S = 10$; $T = 2$; Food $= 2$). After such an outburst, he may feel guilty and worried about whether his outburst damaged his bond with that person.

Although Mr. H expects others to respond to him, he has a strong need to stubbornly oppose requests made of him by others as he perceives their requests as demands ($S = 10$). He is defensive, touchy, and overly sensitive when interacting with others and is vulnerable to feeling hurt, misunderstood, criticized, or slighted (scale $6 = 67$; $PER = 4$). When this occurs, his first response is to angrily retaliate by acting in a provocative, insulting, aggressive manner. Given the difficulties Mr. H has with people in general, it is understandable that he became deeply dependent on his wife, who gratified his needs for affection, nurturance, and warmth and that he would feel extremely threatened by the possibility of losing her. He is likely to react with profound hurt and rage to any threat to their relationship. Mr. H apparently pursued a relationship with his wife because of his need to rescue her from her problems, especially her history of unhappy relationships with abusive men. This may reflect a need to reenact the relationship he had with his mother, who was chronically unhappy in a destructive, volatile marriage, and his feeling of responsibility to "save" her.

Mr. H has chronically felt inferior and inadequate compared to others (*427*; Egocentricity Index = .19). He tends to frequently evaluate himself and look to find fault with his actions (*FD* = 8). He is vulnerable to react to events by becoming absorbed in self-critical, devaluing thoughts and to ruminate about perceived failures, such as how he performed in a particular situation or what others thought of him. He avoids competition or situations in which he would be evaluated because of a fear of failing and then feeling ashamed, embarrassed, or humiliated (*427*; *LSE* = 77; *Si3* = 74; Egocentricity Index = .19). His fear of failure has contributed to a history of underachievement in school and work. He is preoccupied with concerns about his sexuality and doubts about his adequacy as a man (*Sx* = 3). Given these concerns, his preoccupation with his wife's sexual behavior is understandable. He readily becomes consumed with thoughts and fantasies about her involvements with other men that produce intense feelings of failure, inadequacy, and rage.

In terms of the specific question of whether Mr. H presents with a bipolar disorder, both the MMPI-2 and the Rorschach were consistent with a current episode of depression and a concurrent personality disorder. No signs of mania were present in the test data (scale *9* = 63; *SUM6* = 1). As noted previously, this in and of itself does not rule out a bipolar disorder. Assessing whether an individual meets diagnostic criteria for a bipolar disorder depends on careful review of longitudinal data concerning past episodes of depression and mania as well as their current symptom pattern. The history provided by Mr. H did not include discrete episodes that meet *DSM-IV* criteria for mania. Thus, no support for a diagnosis of a bipolar disorder was obtained.

Diagnostic Impression

DSM-IV   Axis I   296.22 Major depression, single episode, moderate
303.90 Alcohol dependence
305.60 Cocaine abuse

Axis II   310.9 Personality disorder NOS, with borderline and passive–aggressive features

TREATMENT RECOMMENDATIONS

Several issues for treatment are suggested by these results. First, Mr. H's alcohol and substance abuse should be confronted directly and, concurrent with individual psychotherapy, he should be referred for treatment of substance abuse, such as Alcoholics Anonymous.

The data provide an interesting contradiction concerning the prognosis for treatment. On the one hand, the MMPI-2 codetype suggests that his motivation for treatment will diminish when external stressors are reduced and as his life situation improves. Furthermore, the *427* codetype suggests an action-oriented style with little tolerance for reflection. These factors suggest that brief psychotherapy is a more appropriate treatment approach than insight-oriented psychotherapy.

In contrast, the Rorschach suggests Mr. H does have a capacity for self-reflection (*FD* = 8). This could be an asset in assisting him examine difficulties in interpersonal relationships, self-concept, control over emotions, and achievement, issues that may not be addressed effectively in a short-term approach given how entrenched these characterological features are. The longstanding nature of these difficulties suggests that long-term treatment could be of considerable benefit for Mr. H, should he decide to continue in psychotherapy once distress about his marital problems is resolved and if the therapist is able to establish a solid therapeutic alliance with him. However, the therapist should not be surprised if Mr. H decides to terminate treatment once the immediate distress is over.

The treatment relationship with Mr. H is likely to be colored by his social discomfort, strong dependency needs, resentment, and negative self-concept. Because Mr. H feels awkward, self-conscious, and uncomfortable with others, he is likely to have difficulty establishing trust and opening up to a therapist. The therapist should be alert to the possibility that Mr. H's discomfort may result in a decision to reject treatment soon after starting and should actively try to prevent this by being involved and concerned rather maintaining a traditional, detached stance. Given Mr. H's needs for attention and acceptance, during the early phase of therapy, he may be compliant and outwardly obliging. For instance, he may steer clear of revealing material he is afraid the therapist would disapprove of, such as open acknowledgment of anger. He is quite likely to be sensitive to comments made by the therapist that he perceives as critical or that cause him to feel ashamed, embarrassed, or inadequate.

Over time, Mr. H is likely to feel resentful of demands he perceives the therapist making of him but is more likely to act out these reactions than to talk about them directly. In order to assist Mr. H develop more effective ways of managing his reactions than impulsive acting out, the therapist should be prepared to confront these instances in a direct, firm manner while attempting to avoid becoming caught up in an angry battle. The therapist should be particularly alert to monitoring his or her own reactions to Mr. H's behavior in order to maintain a therapeutic perspective, rather than retaliating to his provocations.

10

Case 5: Communication With a Computer: Paranoia

REASON FOR EVALUATION

Mrs. J is a 32-year-old, married, Black female referred for a psychological evaluation by the personnel manager of the government agency where she has worked for 7 years after supervisors and coworkers observed her acting strangely. For instance, a coworker noticed Mrs. J staring at her computer screen with unusual intensity and a strange facial expression. When the coworker asked if anything was bothering her, Mrs. J said she was talking to her computer and it was talking back, but laughed this incident off. A psychological evaluation was requested to assess her current condition, the need for treatment by a mental health professional, and her ability to work.

BACKGROUND INFORMATION

Mrs. J was interviewed with her husband present. She is a high school graduate who earned average grades in school. She is the third of five children with two older sisters, a younger brother and a younger sister. Her parents divorced when she was 14. After the divorce, Mrs. J and her siblings lived with her mother, a school teacher, and had regular contact with their father who lived in the neighborhood several blocks away. She reported having a close relationship with her mother whom she described as a loving, strict, church-going woman who valued education, self-reliance, and a strong work ethic. Her parents did not discuss their marital problems with the children, so Mrs. J did not know the reasons for their divorce, although she had been aware of tension between her parents before they decided to separate. Her mother did not remarry.

Mrs. J's father, who worked in a steel mill, remarried a year or so after the divorce and had three children with his second wife. Mrs. J reported that she is not as close to her father as her mother. She described him as a quiet man who spent his free time watching sports events, working on his car, and performing maintenance projects around the two-flat building he owns. Mrs. J saw her step-brothers and step-sister regularly, but, as she was considerably older than them, has never felt close to them. She denied a history of physical or sexual abuse.

Mrs. J has worked in a secretarial position in a government agency for 7 years and has had a good work history. Her performance reviews to date have all been satisfactory or better. When asked about her current work situation and the reason for this evaluation, Mrs. J responded that she has been concerned about money being taken out of her paycheck that she did not authorize. She was angry as she reported this because she has not been able to save enough money to take a vacation. She believes her husband arranged for this money to be taken from her paycheck even though he stated this was not true. He reported that her wages have been garnished because of large credit card bills she has run up when she has made impulsive purchases. Mrs. J angrily denied making these purchases and claimed either that someone had stolen her card or that these purchases were made by another woman with the same name. It was difficult to follow her train of thought as she talked about these issues.

When the examiner asked Mrs. J about times when she told coworkers that she was talking to her computer and saw odd things, Mrs. J stated that she has never seen anything but acknowledged hearing the voices of family members talking to her. In fact, she heard their voices so clearly that on more than one occasion she called her siblings to ask them why they were in the building in which she works. When asked about the content of the voices, she seemed evasive and gave a vague response about being told to cut her hair. She did not seem to be frightened or bothered by these experiences nor to find them odd.

Mrs. J also reported developing problems with her arms that involve brief, recurrent periods of time when her arms feel numb, heavy, and weak. This started about 6 weeks prior to this evaluation. When asked for more details about these problems, Mrs. J recounted an incident several months ago when a supervisor touched her on the arm during a conversation in a friendly fashion. Mrs. J now believes that her supervisor's touch caused the unusual sensations in her arm and wonders if the supervisor was doing some "psychic stuff."

According to Mr. J, a clerk in a state government agency, his wife started voicing suspicions about him 3 months prior to this evaluation. For instance, Mrs. J told one of her sisters she was afraid he was trying to poison her and began refusing to eat any food he prepared. She has taken food he cooked to a hospital and to the police station to be tested for poison. These requests were denied. Mrs. J recently visited relatives in another state with her 13-year-old daughter and mother. Upon returning from this trip, Mrs. J threw out all the food staples in the house, such as flour and sugar, because of a fear that her husband had poisoned the food during her absence. According to her husband, Mrs. J has also accused him of having an affair with her younger sister. Mrs. J could not explain the basis for these accusations when asked by the examiner either in the presence of her husband or when interviewed alone. Mr. J expressed concern and puzzlement about his wife's current behavior and the accusations she voices. He characterized her as showing a gradual, but dramatic change in personality and attitudes toward others during the past several months, as she was not as suspicious, distrustful, or angry in the past. Neither Mr. J nor Mrs. J could identify any precipitant for these changes.

Mrs. J denied feeling depressed at the present time or in the past several months. She did not report being anxious, worried, or frightened. She acknowledged having difficulty concentrating at work. No changes in sleep, appetite, energy, or ability to enjoy herself were reported. However, her husband described her as irritable, restless, having difficulty sleeping, and pacing during the middle of the night. She denied a history of alcohol or substance abuse. No family history of psychopathology was reported.

The current evaluation was arranged by the personnel manager of the agency where Mrs. J works. The personnel manager, who told the examiner she has had no experience with psychological problems, seemed genuinely concerned about Mrs. J, bewildered by the recent changes in her behavior, and eager to obtain a better description of Mrs. J's condition so that appropriate treatment could be arranged.

DIAGNOSTIC CONSIDERATIONS

The paranoid ideation, auditory hallucinations, irritability, restlessness, and difficulty with concentration reported by Mrs. J and her husband could be symptoms either of schizophrenia or of the manic phase of a bipolar disorder with psychotic features. Although the paranoid symptoms may prompt one to first think of paranoid schizophrenia, paranoid features are also frequently seen during a bipolar disorder with psychotic features (Goodwin & Jamison, 1990). The history of running up large debts on her credit cards raises a question as to whether she has had spending sprees, which frequently occur during manic episodes, although her claim that she does not remember spending the money and that another person with the same name made the purchases is quite odd.

Distinguishing between schizophrenia and a bipolar disorder with psychotic features on the basis of symptomatology is quite difficult because the symptoms and behavioral problems associated with these disorders overlap considerably. For instance, both schizophrenia and a bipolar disorder can involve agitation; restlessness; irritability and hostility; grandiose and persecutory delusions; disorganized, illogical thought processes and speech; inappropriate sexual behavior; and excessive motor activity. Nichols (1988) suggested that it may be particularly difficult to discriminate between manic and schizophrenic disorders with prominent paranoid symptoms because "the former are less euphoric and hyperactive than manics in general, while the latter are less thought-disordered than schizophrenics in general" (p. 80).

In the past, it was thought that schizophrenia and mania could be distinguished by the presence or absence of thought disorder as disordered thinking was regarded as pathognomonic of schizophrenia (Arieti, 1974; Bleuler, 1950). However, research has clearly demonstrated that thought disorder is not specific to schizophrenia but is a central feature of both schizophrenia and bipolar disorder with psychotic features (Goodwin & Jamison, 1990; Harrow & Quinlan, 1977). Furthermore, the two disorders do not differ in severity of thought disorder. In fact, some studies have found a trend toward greater levels of thought disorder in manic compared to schizophrenic patients (Harrow, Grossman, Silverstein, & Meltzer, 1982). However, whereas psychotic symptoms occur exclusively during periods of mood disturbance in bipolar disorder, in schizophrenia psychotic symptoms occur independently of the presence or absence of a mood disturbance (*DSM–IV,* 1994). It is important to note, however, that patients with schizophrenia may meet diagnostic criteria for an affective disorder at some point during their illness. Goodwin and Jamison (1990) suggested that because presenting symptoms are often quite similar in schizophrenia and mania, an attempt to differentiate between these disorders should include attention to factors other than manifest symptomatology, including the patient's level of premorbid functioning, family history, course of the disorder, and characteristics of any previous episodes of psychopathology.

Nichols (1988) reviewed MMPI studies of mood disorders and concluded that for manic patients scale *9* is usually the first or second highest clinical scale, whereas elevations on scales *4, 6,* and *8* also occur frequently. It is quite uncommon for elevations to occur on scales *1, 2, 3,* and *7* in manic patients. The two-point codetypes seen most frequently in manic samples are the *49/94, 69/96,* and *89/98* codetypes (Nichols, 1988; Wetzler & Marlowe, 1993). Winters, Newmark, Lumry, Leach, and Weintraub (1985) compared groups of patients with schizophrenia, depression, or bipolar disorder and reported that only two codetypes were associated specifically with a single disorder: The *68/86* codetype was associated with schizophrenia, whereas the *984* codetype was associated with mania.

There are relatively few studies examining Rorschach responses of samples of manic patients, and none was found that specifically compared manic and schizophrenic patients. The existing Rorschach literature suggests that manic patients typically show significant thought disorder, cognitive slippage, and poor reality testing (e.g., Singer & Brabender, 1993). As a result, manic patients frequently produce a positive *SCZI*. Thus, one should not rely on the *SCZI* when attempting to distinguish between schizophrenia and a bipolar disorder with psychotic features. Clinical experience suggests that manic and schizophrenic patients differ in the types of Rorschach responses and special scores they earn; the responses of manics are often rambling (*DR2*), overly complex (Blends), and contain more features of affective turmoil than schizophrenic patients. The paucity of research comparing the Rorschach protocols of schizophrenic and manic patients suggests that this is a fruitful area for future empirical study.

MMPI-2 Data

Validity. The MMPI-2 validity scales are noteworthy for elevations on the F ($T = 106$) and *Fb* ($T = 89$) scales. *F* and *Fb* can be elevated at this level for a number of reasons including random responding, confusion, poor comprehension of test items, a plea for help, the presence of psychosis, or exaggeration of symptoms. Before interpreting the clinical scales, one must sort out which of these possibilities accounts for the validity scale configuration.

When *F* is high, the possibility of inconsistent or random responding can be examined by looking at the score on the *VRIN* scale. *VRIN* was designed specifically to assess whether a subject responded inconsistently to the MMPI-2 because of poor reading comprehension, confusion, or a random response set (Butcher et al., 1989). *VRIN* is interpreted based on the raw score rather than the *T* score. A raw score of 13 or more on *VRIN* indicates that the profile is invalid because the subject responded inconsistently. *VRIN* should be interpreted in conjunction with the *F* scale (Butcher et al., 1989; Graham, 1993; Greene, 1991). High scores on both *F* and *VRIN* suggest that the subject completed the MMPI-2 in an inconsistent manner. In contrast, a high *F* and low to moderate *VRIN* suggests that the subject completed the test consistently rather than randomly and that the elevation on *F* therefore reflects an open admission of psychopathology.

Because few empirical studies have examined *VRIN*, the MMPI-2 manual recommends (a) that *VRIN* be considered experimental until further research establishes its validity and (b) that interpretations based on *VRIN*

MMPI-2

S R Hathaway and J C McKinley

Minnesota Multiphasic Personality Inventory-2

Profile for Basic Scales

Minnesota Multiphasic Personality Inventory-2
Copyright © by THE REGENTS OF THE UNIVERSITY OF MINNESOTA
1942, 1943 (renewed 1970), 1989 This Profile Form 1989
All rights reserved. Distributed exclusively by NATIONAL COMPUTER SYSTEMS, INC.
under license from The University of Minnesota.

"MMPI-2" and "Minnesota Multiphasic Personality Inventory-2" are trademarks owned by
The University of Minnesota. Printed in the United States of America

FEMALE

Name ___Mrs. J.___

Address _____

Occupation _____ Date Tested __/__/__

Education __12__ Age __32__ Marital Status __Married__

Referred By _____

MMPI-2 Code _____

Scorer's Initials _____

	T or Tc	L	F	K	Hs+.5K 1	D 2	Hy 3	Pd+.4K 4	Mf 5	Pa 6	Pt+1K 7	Sc+1K 8	Ma+.2K 9	Si 0	T or Tc
Raw Score	5	20	14	8	19	17	20	24	19	17	27	23	28		
K to be Added				7			6			14	14	3			
Raw Score with K				15			24			21	41	26			

? Raw Score __7__

184

	Raw Score	T Score
FB	12	89
True Response Inconsistency (TRIN)	11	65T
Variable Response Inconsistency (VRIN)	12	78
Anxiety	14	53
Repression	18	54
MAC-R	23	58
Ego Strength (Es)	36	53
Dominance (Do)	16	49
Social Responsibility (Re)	18	41
Overcontrolled Hostility (O-H)	19	70
PTSD - Keane (PK)	20	68
PTSD - Schlenger (PS)	14	52
Addiction Potential (APS)	26	58
Addiction Admission (AAS)	3	56

Content Scales (Butcher et al., 1990)

	Raw Score	T Score
Anxiety (ANX)	8	53
Fears (FRS)	13	73
Obsessiveness (OBS)	6	50
Depression (DEP)	8	55
Health Concerns (HEA)	12	63
Bizarre Mentation (BIZ)	10	76
Anger (ANG)	6	50
Cynicism (CYN)	13	57
Antisocial Practices (ASP)	14	72
Type A (TPA)	10	56
Low Self-Esteem (LSE)	7	54
Social Discomfort (SOD)	9	52

Depression Subscales (Harris-Lingoes)

	Raw Score	T Score
Subjective Depression (D1)	10	56
Psychomotor Retardation (D2)	6	51
Physical Malfunctioning (D3)	2	41
Mental Dullness (D4)	5	61
Brooding (D5)	1	42

Hysteria Subscales (Harris-Lingoes)

	Raw Score	T Score
Denial of Social Anxiety (Hy1)	3	45
Need for Affection (Hy2)	1	26
Lassitude-Malaise (Hy3)	2	47
Somatic Complaints (Hy4)	5	57
Inhibition of Aggression (Hy5)	5	62

	Raw Score	T Score

Psychopathic Deviate Subscales (Harris-Lingoes)

	Raw Score	T Score
Familial Discord (Pd1)	4	62
Authority Problems (Pd2)	3	53
Social Imperturbability (Pd3)	3	47
Social Alienation (Pd4)	8	70
Self-Alienation (Pd5)	2	43

Paranoia Subscales (Harris-Lingoes)

	Raw Score	T Score
Persecutory Ideas (Pa1)	11	105
Poignancy (Pa2)	2	46
Naivete (Pa3)	3	41

Schizophrenia Subscales (Harris-Lingoes)

	Raw Score	T Score
Social Alienation (Sc1)	10	77
Emotional Alienation (Sc2)	0	40
Lack of Ego Mastery, Cognitive (Sc3)	2	55
Lack of Ego Mastery, Conative (Sc4)	2	49
Lack of Ego Mastery, Def. Inhib. (Sc5)	3	59
Bizarre Sensory Experiences (Sc6)	6	68

Hypomania Subscales (Harris-Lingoes)

	Raw Score	T Score
Amorality (Ma1)	4	70
Psychomotor Acceleration (Ma2)	6	55
Imperturbability (Ma3)	3	50
Ego Inflation (Ma4)	7	74

Social Introversion Subscales (Ben-Porath et al., 1989)

	Raw Score	T Score
Shyness/Self-Consciousness (Si1)	5	49
Social Avoidance (Si2)	1	42
Alienation -- Self and Others (Si3)	6	52

186

be made cautiously (Butcher et al., 1989). However, the guidelines concerning the relationships between *F* and *VRIN* discussed previously have been supported in several studies. Wetter, Baer, Berry, Smith, and Larsen (1992) assigned subjects to honest, random, or fake-bad groups. Significant between-group differences were found on MMPI-2 clinical and validity scales. Whereas the random group produced elevations on both *F* and *VRIN*, the fake-bad groups elevated *F* but not *VRIN*, which was within normal limits. Wetter, Baer, Berry, Robison, and Sumpter (1993) found that subjects instructed to malinger differed from psychiatric patients on the *F, F − K,* and *Ds* scales as expected but did not differ on *VRIN*. *VRIN* was below the cutoff of 13 for both the malingering and patient groups. Wetter et al. (1993) concluded that random responding elevates *VRIN* but that faking does not. As Mrs. J's score on *VRIN* is 12, the elevation on *F* cannot be attributed to random, inconsistent responding, confusion, or poor reading comprehension.

Several factors argue against the possibility that the high score on *F* is due to exaggeration of symptoms or faking-bad. First, no incentive was identified that would motivate Mrs. J to fake-bad. To the contrary, during the clinical interview, she did not focus on or seem bothered by the recent changes in her behavior that have alarmed and worried others. Second, whereas Graham (1993) characterized the fake-bad profile as having very high elevations on all clinical scales, the current protocol has elevations only on scales *6, 8,* and *9* with very low scores on scales *3* and *7*. Third, the score on another MMPI-2 index sensitive to faking-bad, the *F − K* Index (Gough, 1950), was within expected limits ($F - K = 6$). Wetter et al. (1992) reported that the *F − K* index accurately discriminated among subjects completing the MMPI-2 honestly and those instructed to answer randomly or fake-bad and among groups of fake-bad and psychiatric patients (Wetter et al., 1993). Thus, overall, there was little reason to think that the high *F* reflects faking-bad. Instead, the elevation on *F* suggests that Mrs. J's condition involves significant psychopathology.

Clinical Scales.   Elevations are seen on scales *6, 8,* and *9*. The *68/86* two-point codetype suggests the presence of serious psychopathology, thought disorder, and paranoid features. The *68/86* codetype is usually associated with a diagnosis of schizophrenia, although in some instances Cluster A personality disorders (e.g., paranoid personality disorder and schizoid personality disorder) are associated with this codetype (Graham, 1993). As noted previously, the *68/86* codetype is associated with schizophrenia to a greater extent than with a bipolar disorder (Winters et al., 1985). The likelihood of a psychotic disorder, most likely schizophrenia, is increased in Mrs. J's case given the "paranoid valley" configuration. The paranoid valley configuration, identified when there are elevations above a *T* score of 65 on both scales *6* and *8* and both *6* and *8* are more than 10 points higher than scale *7* (Friedman et al., 1989), is associated with psychotic symptomatology including hallucinations, delusions, and paranoid ideation. A psychotic disorder is also strongly suggested by the content scales (Bizarre Mentation = 76).

Persons with a *68/86* codetype present with difficulties in thought processes characterized by autistic logic; misinterpretations of situations; and a fragmented, illogical, rambling flow of ideas. As a result, she may have difficulty attending to tasks, poor concentration, and problems with memory. She is likely to express unusual ideas and hold peculiar if not bizarre, unrealistic beliefs involving paranoid ideation and persecutory delusions (*Pa1* Persecutory Ideas = 105). Systematized delusions may be present. She is apt to feel misunderstood and mistreated by others and to be preoccupied with concerns that others are trying to harm or take advantage of her (*Pd4* = 70; *Pa1* = 105; *Sc1* = 77). She views others with suspicious distrust and keeps a wary, cautious distance from them.

Adults with the *68/86* codetype often have a history of handling responsibilities at work and at home reasonably well. At the present time, however, Mrs. J's ability to manage adult responsibilities may be compromised because of fatigue, inefficiency, and difficulty concentrating as a result of her psychological decompensation. Work performance may suffer as a result of an apathetic withdrawal from everyday activities. In some cases, this decompensation occurs as a reaction to a stressful event, whereas in others, it occurs in the absence of any identifiable precipitant (Gilberstadt & Duker, 1965). She tends to respond to stress by withdrawing into fantasy and self-absorbed daydreams.

Mrs. J's current mood is dominated by an irritable resentment, although she may also report feeling tense, worried, and depressed. She reacts negatively to requests made of her by others, as she is primed to feel they are making unreasonable demands and trying to take advantage of her (*68/86*; *Hy2* = 26; *Pa3* = 41; *Sc1* = 77). Interpersonal interactions are likely to be colored by resentment, suspiciousness, and hostility. As a result, others may see her as angry, unfriendly, and difficult to get along with. Threatening, aggressive behavior may occur, especially following heavy alcohol use (Gilberstadt & Duker, 1965).

A secondary codetype to consider is the *69/96* codetype. Many of the characteristics associated with the *68/86* codetype also apply to the *69/96* codetype including psychotic symptoms, hallucinations, thought disorder, delusions, paranoid ideation, and anger and hostility. Persons with the *69/96* codetype also manifest difficulties with concentration, attention, and memory functioning. Whereas Graham (1993) reported that the *69/96* codetype is most frequently associated with schizophrenia, Greene (1991) suggested that the clinician consider whether the *69/96* codetype reflects "a mood disorder rather than a thought disorder."

Rorschach Data

The search strategy for Mrs. J's Rorschach protocol is determined by the positive Schizophrenia Index (*SCZI* = 4). Although a positive *SCZI* raises a strong possibility that a patient presents with schizophrenia or another psychotic disorder, there are several reasons that Mrs. J's record must be viewed cautiously before one can conclude with confidence that the Rorschach protocol supports this diagnosis. First, the risk of false-positives (e.g., concluding that she is schizophrenic when she is not) is greatest when the value of the *SCZI* is 4. Second, the low number of responses produced by Mrs. J (*R* = 14), her reliance on the form demands of the inkblots with relatively few other determinants (*Lambda* = 1.00), the low number of blends (1:14), and indicators of defensiveness (*PER* = 3) raise questions about how open Mrs. J was as she responded to this test. These factors may limit what can be learned about Mrs. J's current psychological state.

When the *SCZI* is positive, the search strategy begins by examining Mrs. J's thought processes to assess whether she shows the distortions in cognitive operations typical of schizophrenia. She has an introversive problem-solving style (*EB* = 3:0) that indicates that she typically considers all possibilities internally before making decisions, attempts to be logical when considering different ways to solve problems, and in general is not swayed by affect (*EBPer* = 3.0). The unexpectedly large number of special scores, particularly given the low number of responses, suggests her thinking and judgment are seriously disturbed, disorganized, and flawed and may include cognitive slippage (*Sum6* = 12). A review of the responses containing special scores suggests a peculiar use of language (Response 3 a "twin duet"; Response 4 the "breasts meet out together"), as well as immaturity (Response 6 material cut "zig-zag like"). The INCOM (Response 7 a bird with antennae), although unrealistic, is not bizarre. Thus, these responses suggest difficulties with thought processes but are not as bizarre, chaotic, or strange as is often the case in schizophrenia.

The higher than expected value for *Lambda* indicates a marked tendency to constrict or simplify complex and ambiguous stimuli (*L* = 1.00). She does not perceive things as most others do, even when the stimuli are clear and obvious, and misinterprets, distorts, and misunderstands events as a result of careless, incomplete processing of stimuli (Populars = 3; $X+\%$ = .43; *Lambda* = 1.00). These inaccurate perceptions and distorted interpretations most likely occur as a result of a tendency to maintain a distance from an environment she perceives as threatening and overly demanding.

Case 5   Rorschach Protocol

Card	Response	Inquiry
I	1. I wld say a BF. (puts card down)	E: (Rpts S's response) S: O.K. There are wings, body part, head. This is like the back, bottom part of it. It 1.1 BF's I've seen.
	2. E: Most p c more than 1 thing on e card. S: It cld be 3 p, like a dance. Little dance.	E: (Rpts S's response) S: Right. This is 1 a p here, hanging to the p's thighs. They swinging out, 1 its a ballet. These 2 p. Another p holding them up. They got they head down. This is 1 the hand holding onto. E: Head down? S: C't c a head, 1 a collar. Cld be a head under a collar.
II	3. Yeah, this is 1...a little, 1 a twin duet. With the hand clap & kneé being...That's it.	E: (Rpts S's response) S: Yeah. O.K. These are 2 bodies. head part, eyes. Got hand clap, hands tog. Knees coming tog here. Yet I d't see no feet. Maybe in the inside. E: Twin duet? S: Bec e body is the same to me. Mouth is the same, eyes. Little hats sticking up tog. Their uniform is made alike. Their knees tog. And I c no feet. E: No feet. S: No. D't show the feet.
III	4. Hmmm...This is 1 a little...twin figure. Of a...	E: (Rpts S's response) S: Well, the buttocks is pushed out the same. 1 leg the same. Got boots or heels. Their breasts meet out tog, 1 coming out to the bow. Their mouth, their nose is pointing tog. Their heads is shaped alike. E: Breasts meet? S: Yeah. Out to the bow.

	5. Little ducks. Little chicks or s.t	E: (Rpts S's response) S: Right. Down here. They form a duck or chicken, 1 I saw growing up. E: What abt the card reminded u of that? S: Ways its drawed. It cld be a profile of a duck. Or a p. But, yet, its still in a uniform, 1 a chicken or duck. E: Show me where y're lkg. S: The whole profile is a duck. Or it cld be a p wearing a uniform shaped 1 a duck.
IV	6. This is 1 a little...Cld be a statute holding a garment. Like a fur coat, yet its not a fur coat, its just material, cut zig-zag like. Yet here it has a rooster head at top. Got arms out.	E: (Rpts S's response) S: Here are arms. See this here? Its not a fur coat, but some type of material draped on the garment rack or s.t. Yet it cld be a chicken head. E: I'm not sure if y're seeing 1 thing or 2 things. S: Its s.t holding this garment. Yet its not a complete garment, 1 y started making s.t. On the rack. At the top its shaped 1 a turkey or chicken. E: Garment? S: L started making s.t. Not completely made. E: Statue? S: Right. Or rack or s.t.
V	7. This is 1 a wide bird or s.t. With its legs down. His wings out. Yet its got horns, so cldn't be a bird, right?...I c't...	E: (Rpts S's response) S: Yeah. This 1.1 the wings, the legs, how u see a hawk? But this looks more 1 a deer, so I c't say. I d.k. what y'd call it, but it 1.1 a bird down here. E: Did u see 1 thing or 2? S: Its tog. E: Wings out? S: Yeah, its getting ready to fly or its already in the air. Flying.
VI	8. I d.k...I wld say its a plant. With little stickers.	E: (Rpts S's response) S: Yeah. This part here, but its not a leaf type plant. Its a khaki type plant. Up here, its 1 the prongs of the

stickers. That's it.
E: Stickers?
S: This here & here.
E: Cactus?
S: Bec its not a leaf type
plant. A cactus, y always l.l
y c't set it out but y do set
it out. Its not a root for a
cactus plant.

VII   9. Just a...I c a
painting. Yet it has at
the end, I mean in the
middle it has l a
chicken, resembles it.

E: (Rpts S's response)
S: Yeah. Its more l a
painting.
E: Show me.
S: It has nothing to deal with
except this part here. It cld
be a stone or a stick or s.t
here. Cld be a piece of meat
or cut up chicken it l.l, but I
didn't see it at the beginning.
E: Painting?
S: Because sometime when u
start painting y're not aware
of the design & u start
painting with no shape to it.
Yet this little splinter shows
me some type of meaning. I
just c't see it.
E: Meaning?
S: I d.k. Just little
splinter.
E: Chicken?
S: Bec this painting, on e
side, generally it has a
similarity to wings.

VIII 10. This is more like fr
a science book I had in
school. S.t like the
body. Yet it has...I wld
say A's on e side. Cld
be l a...what u call it,
a rat, climbing on e
side, on the body. And
the body is similar to a
skeleton. Not showing
the head part, up to the
shoulder. More like a
man's skeleton than a
woman.

E: (Rpts S's response)
S: Yeah, it does. Like a
skeleton. This is more like a
man's skeleton to me. Its
showing his stomach part, here,
like L & R side of the body.
Here, this l.l 2 rats, O.K.?
They got their tail hanging to
his side. The feet here, l
they climbing up on him. Face
of the rat. Clinging to the
shoulder of it, of the body.
And up here, see it stops at
the shoulder. Dsn't show the
head of the body, but got the
whole, complete spine straight
up! There's not a bone
straight up the front, is it?

IX   11. This is more like a   E: (Rpts S's response)
      flower. It has roots.   S: Right. O.K., here 1.1
      And yet, no leaves or   roots. L shld have a turnip
      nothing. Not a khaki   root. Like went to green house
      plant either.   & already set out & get the
                                     bags. This part is not shaped
                                     1 leaves of a flower so...I d.k
                                     what it cld be.

      12. Just a design. Like   E: (Rpts S's response)
      a plant at bottom, got   S: Some type of design. I c't
      roots. The design part   make out what.
      at top dsn't favor a   E: What abt the card reminded u
      flower.   of a design?
                                     S: Cld be like a...what do u
                                     call it? Shrimp? L y're getting
                                     ready to fry?
                                     E: U didn't mention that
                                     before. Did u see that
                                     originally?
                                     S: No. Just saw it now.
                                     E: Design?
                                     S: Bec most times, u can, like
                                     snow melting, u c't picture
                                     what it 1.1 but u know snow is
                                     melting, that was snow. U know
                                     it was drawed, but u c't make
                                     out what it is.

X   13. Wld this be different   E: (Rpts S's response)
      position of ostrich?   S: Yeah. This 1.1 ostrich in
                                     here, like u have the tail.
                                     This 1.1 1, too, lying in a
                                     diff position. This 1.1 the
                                     mouth part of one & this 1.1
                                     mouth of one. Just 1.1 ostrich
                                     legs here & here.

      14. Snails or whatever?   E: (Rpts S's response)
      Sea A's? Sea fishes?   S: Yeah. This cld be, these
      L.1 a little ostrich   little yellow things.
      there, the tips.   E: Snails?
                                     S: C't recall.
                                     E: Sea A's?
                                     S: Here.

```
CASE05.R3=================== SEQUENCE OF SCORES ============================

CARD NO LOC  #  DETERMINANT(S)    (2) CONTENT(S)     POP Z  SPECIAL SCORES
======= ====== ===============   === ==========     === =  ==============
  I  1 Wo   1  Fo                    A              P 1.0  PER
     2 W+   1  Ma.FDo            2   H,Cg             4.0  COP

 II  3 W+   1  Mao              2   H,Cg             5.5  DV2

III  4 Do   1  Mpo              2   H,Cg,Sx        P       DR2
     5 Do   1  Fo               2   A,Cg                   PER

 IV  6 W+   1  mpu                  Ad,Art,Hh        4.0  DR

  V  7 Wo   1  FMao                 A                1.0  DV,INC

 VI  8 Wv   1  F-                   Bt                     DV,DR2

VII  9 Wv   1  Fu                   Art,A                  DR2

VIII 10 W+  1  FMa-             2   A,An           P 4.5  DR2,PER

 IX 11 Dd/     F-                   Bt               2.5  DR
    12 Dv   2  F-                   Id                    ·DR2

  X 13 Do      FMp-             2   A
    14 Do   2  Fu               2   A                     DV


============================= SUMMARY OF APPROACH =============================

     I :  W.W                        VI :  W
    II :  W                         VII :  W
   III :  D.D                      VIII :  W
    IV :  W                          IX :  Dd.D
     V :  W                           X :  D.D
```

194

```
CASE05.R3===================== STRUCTURAL SUMMARY ==============================

LOCATION            DETERMINANTS              CONTENTS        S-CONSTELLATION
FEATURES        BLENDS          SINGLE                        NO..FV+VF+V+FD>2
                                            H   = 3, 0        NO..Col-Shd Bl>0
Zf    =   7     M.FD            M   = 2     (H) = 0, 0        YES..Ego<.31,>.44
ZSum  = 22.5                    FM  = 3     Hd  = 0, 0        NO..MOR > 3
ZEst  = 20.5                    m   = 1     (Hd)= 0, 0        NO..Zd > +- 3.5
                               FC  = 0     Hx  = 0, 0        YES..es > EA
W  =  8                         CF  = 0     A   = 6, 1        NO..CF+C > FC
 (Wv =  2)                      C   = 0     (A) = 0, 0        YES..X+% < .70
D  =  5                         Cn  = 0     Ad  = 1, 0        NO..S > 3
Dd =  1                        FC'= 0     (Ad)= 0, 0        NO..P < 3 or > 8
S  =  0                         C'F= 0     An  = 0, 1        NO..Pure H < 2
                               C'  = 0     Art = 1, 1        YES..R < 17
   DQ                          FT  = 0     Ay  = 0, 0         4.....TOTAL
.........(FQ-)                  TF  = 0     Bl  = 0, 0
  +  =  4  ( 1)                 T   = 0     Bt  = 2, 0        SPECIAL SCORINGS
  o  =  6  ( 1)                 FV  = 0     Cg  = 0, 4               Lv1   Lv2
 v/+ =  1  ( 1)                 VF  = 0     Cl  = 0, 0        DV   =  3x1   1x2
  v  =  3  ( 2)                 V   = 0     Ex  = 0, 0        INC  =  1x2   0x4
                               FY  = 0     Fd  = 0, 0        DR   =  2x3   5x6
                               YF  = 0     Fi  = 0, 0        FAB  =  0x4   0x7
                               Y   = 0     Ge  = 0, 0        ALOG =  0x5
   FORM QUALITY                 Fr  = 0     Hh  = 0, 0        CON  =  0x7
                               rF  = 0     Ls  = 0, 0         Raw Sum6  =  12
     FQx  FQf  MQual  SQx       FD  = 0     Na  = 0, 0        Wgtd Sum6 =  43
  +  =  0    0    0    0        F   = 7     Sc  = 0, 0
  o  =  6    2    3    0                    Sx  = 0, 1        AB  = 0     CP  = 0
  u  =  3    2    0    0                    Xy  = 0, 0        AG  = 0     MOR = 0
  -  =  5    3    0    0                    Id  = 1, 0        CFB = 0     PER = 3
none=  0    --   0    0         (2) =  7                      COP = 1     PSV = 0

===================== RATIOS, PERCENTAGES, AND DERIVATIONS =====================

R = 14        L  =  1.00          FC:CF+C = 0: 0     COP = 1     AG = 0
---------------------------------      Pure C  =    0     Food       = 0
EB = 3: 0.0  EA  =   3.0  EBPer= 3.0   SumC':WSumC= 0:0.0  Isolate/R =0.14
eb = 4: 0    es  =   4        D =    0  Afr     =0.56      H:(H)Hd(Hd)= 3: 0
           Adj es =  4   Adj D =   0   S       = 0        (HHd):(AAd)= 0: 0
---------------------------------      Blends:R= 1:14     H+A:Hd+Ad =10: 1
FM  - 3   :  C'= 0   T = 0             CP      = 0
m   = 1   :  V = 0   Y = 0
                             P   = 3        Zf  = 7        3r+(2)/R=0.50
a:p    =  4: 3    Sum6  = 12  X+% =0.43     Zd  = +2.0     Fr+rF   = 0
Ma:Mp  =  2: 1    Lv2   =  6  F+% =0.29     W:D:Dd = 8: 5: 1   FD    = 1
2AB+Art+Ay= 2     WSum6 = 43  X-% =0.36     W:M  = 8: 3     An+Xy   = 1
M-    =  0        Mnone =  0  S-% =0.00     DQ+  = 4        MOR     = 0
                             Xu% =0.21     DQv  = 3

===============================================================================
SCZI = 4*    DEPI = 3    CDI = 3    S-CON = 4    HVI = No    OBS = No
===============================================================================
```

She is likely to act inappropriately as a result of this inefficient, careless view of situations.

A review of the Sequence of Scores shows that no minus responses occurred in the first five cards, whereas all minus responses occurred in the last five cards. Although this could reflect an acute decompensation of her psychological organization, a review of the protocol suggests instead that Mrs. J's effort waned during the second half of the test. The latter interpretation seems more likely than the former given the fact that the first minus response given by Mrs. J was also her first vague response, that three of her four minus responses also involved DQv or $v/+$, and the responses to the last five cards were less complex, less detailed, and not as fully elaborated as her responses to the first five cards. The quality of her processing tends to be simplistic, unsophisticated, and immature ($DQv = 3$; $DQv/+ = 1$). None of the minus responses was bizarre, and none violated the form demands of the cards. Instead, the minuses seemed to be associated with the limited effort suggested by the vague responses, rather than indicating severe distortions in perceptual accuracy. This pattern is not typical of schizophrenia as distorted, inaccurate percepts are usually scattered throughout the record of schizophrenic patients.

Although Mrs. J appears to have average capacity for control ($Adj D = 0$; $CDI = 3$), this finding may not be reliable given the complete absence of any color responses ($EB = 3:0$). It is extremely unusual for either side of the EB to be zero. The lack of color may suggest a considerable effort by Mrs. J to contain affect that threatens to overwhelm and disorganize her. Thus, the $Adj D$ score may overestimate her capacity to cope both because of the lower than expected EA ($EA = 3.0$) and because of the lower than expected $Adj es$ score ($Adj es = 4$).

Because the absence of any color responses on the EB suggests Mrs. J may try to defend against troubling, disturbing emotions, it is particularly important to examine carefully whether signs of an affective disturbance are present. There were no indications of current emotional upset or turmoil ($DEPI = 3$; $CDI = 3$; $es = 4$; D score $= 0$; $C' = 0$; $Y = 0$). The absence of color responses does not appear to be the result of an avoidance of feelings in general, as she appears to be comfortable responding to affective stimuli ($Afr = .56$). The lower than expected number of blends suggests impoverished psychological functioning, particularly given the high Lambda (Blends $= 1:14$).

Mrs. J tends to be quite self-focused and self-absorbed (Egocentricity Ratio $= .50$). This suggests she may be more involved with and attentive to her own thoughts and personal concerns to the relative neglect of external reality. She may have a higher than average sense of self-worth. The possibility that she is preoccupied with health-related issues or concerns about bodily integrity is suggested by an Anatomy response that has a minus form quality. No specific issues were suggested by the content of minus responses or responses involving movement.

In terms of interpersonal relationships, Mrs. J is quite cautious about becoming involved with other people and does not trust them easily ($T = 0$). Although she anticipates that most interactions will be positive ($COP = 1$; $AG = 0$), she lacks interest in social interaction and appears socially isolated and withdrawn $(H + (H) + Hd + (Hd) = 3)$. She tends to be defensive when she interacts with others ($PER = 3$).

As noted when beginning this discussion of Mrs. J's Rorschach protocol, a positive $SCZI$ should be interpreted cautiously, particularly when $SCZI = 4$, and does not automatically indicate an individual presents with schizophrenia or another psychotic disorder. Although her responses suggest thought processes are inaccurate, disorganized, and illogical and perceptions of stimuli are distorted, the findings were not robustly associated with schizophrenia. Overall, the review of Mrs. J's protocol does not clearly rule in or rule out schizophrenia, nor does the Rorschach data strongly suggest another diagnosis. For instance, no signs of an affective disturbance are present as would be expected in an affective psychosis. Instead, as a result of the constricted, defensive, and impoverished nature of her responses ($L = 1.00$; $DQv = 3$; Blends = 1:14; $PER = 3$), these results are ambiguous and provide only limited information with which to answer the referral questions.

Comment

Results from the MMPI-2 clearly describe Mrs. J as presenting with a psychotic disorder with paranoid features, most likely schizophrenia, paranoid type, whereas the Rorschach was ambiguous as to the presence of a psychotic disorder. Although the Rorschach suggested disturbed thought processes, cognitive slippage, and inaccurate reality testing, the paranoid features identified so clearly on the MMPI-2 were not detected on the Rorschach. In this case the MMPI-2 and Rorschach do not agree. However, the clinician can have confidence in results suggested by the MMPI-2 given the robust association between the *68/86* and *69/96* codetypes and a psychotic disorder. It is likely that clear conclusions could not be reached based on the Rorschach data either as a result of a constricted psychological style or inconsistent effort. Unlike the MMPI-2, the Rorschach did not indicate the extent to which Mrs. J's work performance, concentration, and efficiency are compromised by psychopathology. Although one might argue that the absence of color responses reflects the apathy and decreased motivation associated with the *68/86* codetype, this interpretation is post hoc and not supported by any empirical data concerning this variable.

In this case, relying on the Rorschach without the MMPI-2 would not have permitted the clinician to answer the referral question accurately. In other cases, the clinician may not be able to answer the referral question by relying exclusively on data from the MMPI-2 without the benefit of data from the Rorschach. This illustrates the basic premise of this volume, namely that one can obtain the most complete assessment of a patient's psychological status by routinely using the MMPI-2 and Rorschach together rather than individually. Relying on data from one test alone may limit the extent to which referral questions can be answered accurately and reliably, particularly because there is no way to predict in advance which patient will respond openly to the MMPI-2 as opposed to the Rorschach and vice versa.

MMPI-2–Rorschach Integration

Mrs. J endorsed an unusually large number of items on the MMPI-2 suggestive of serious psychological disturbance ($F = 106$; $Fb = 89$). The validity scale configuration was not due to random, inconsistent responding (*VRIN*), a failure to comprehend test items, or an attempt to exaggerate her problems.

The profile of MMPI-2 clinical scales suggests Mrs. J presents with serious psychopathology, such as hallucinations, delusions, thought disorder, and paranoid ideation. She is likely to exhibit difficulties in thought processes characterized by autistic logic, misinterpretations of situations, and a fragmented, illogical, rambling flow of ideas (*68/86*). As a result, she may have difficulty attending to tasks, poor concentration, and problems with memory. She is likely to express unusual, unrealistic ideas and hold peculiar if not bizarre beliefs involving paranoid ideation and persecutory delusions (*Pa1* = 105). Her belief that her husband has been trying to poison her and jealous suspicions that he is having a romantic relationship with her sister may reflect systematized delusions with persecutory and erotic content. Her conclusion that strange sensory experiences in her arm were caused by a supervisor's touch is another instance of delusional thinking.

Although in the past Mrs. J was able to handle responsibilities at work and at home reasonably well, at the present time, her ability to manage adult responsibilities is compromised because of fatigue, inefficiency, and difficulty concentrating as a result of a psychological decompensation. Work performance may suffer as a result of an apathetic withdrawal from everyday activities. In some cases, this decompensation occurs as a reaction to a stressful event, whereas in others, it occurs in the absence of any identifiable precipitant. She tends to respond to stress by withdrawing into fantasy and self-absorbed daydreams (*68/86*; EA).

In general, Mrs. J is likely to feel misunderstood and mistreated by others and to be preoccupied with concerns that others are trying to harm or take advantage of her (*68/86*; *Pd4* = 70; *Pa1* = 105; *Sc1* = 77). These characteristics may be related to her suspicions that money is being subtracted from her paycheck without her permission and that others benefit from this. She views others with suspicious distrust and keeps a wary, cautious distance from them (*68/86*; *T* = 0). She reacts negatively to requests made of her by others, as she is primed to feel they are making unreasonable demands and trying to take advantage of her (*68/86*; *Hy2* = 26; *Pa3* = 41; *Sc1* = 77). Interpersonal interactions are likely to be colored by distrust, resentment, suspiciousness, and hostility. As a result, others may see her as angry, distant, unfriendly, and difficult to get along with. Although she anticipates that interactions will be positive, (*COP* = 1; *AG* = 0), she is not interested in taking part in social interactions and appears socially isolated and withdrawn (*H+(H)+Hd+(Hd)* = 3).

Mrs. J's current mood is dominated by an irritable resentment, although she may also report feeling tense, worried, and depressed (*68/86*). Threatening, aggressive behavior may occur, especially following heavy alcohol use.

Diagnostic Impression

DSM–IV   Axis I   295.40 Schizophreniform Disorder

Axis II   None

TREATMENT RECOMMENDATIONS

These results are consistent with a current psychotic disorder. Although the MMPI-2 suggests a diagnosis of Schizophrenia, Paranoid Type, Mrs. J's history does not meet *DSM–IV* criteria for schizophrenia because her symptoms have been present less than 6 months (*DSM–IV*, 1994). The clinical history was not consistent with a Bipolar Disorder given the absence of clear episodes of mania or depression, and the test data was not typical of patients with Bipolar Disorder. A diagnosis of Schizophreniform Disorder is most appropriate, given the duration of her condition, although the diagnosis can be changed to schizophrenia should the disorder persist for 6 months or longer.

Referral to a psychiatrist for treatment with antipsychotic medication is strongly recommended given the findings of auditory hallucinations, delusional thinking, and paranoid ideation. Mrs. J's distrustful attitude towards others and constricted, defensive psychological state suggests that she is unlikely to benefit from traditional psychotherapy at the present time for several reasons, including difficulties establishing an effective working alliance with a therapist as well as the possibility that she may use therapy sessions to voice resentments rather than examining how her thoughts, feelings, actions, and motivations contribute to problems. Furthermore, Mrs. J is likely to distort and misinterpret the therapist's comments rather than using the therapist's input to modify inaccurate views of situations. Although one could argue that marital therapy should be considered on the basis of the presenting complaints, the results of this evaluation suggest otherwise, as she is not likely to respond to marital therapy in a reasonable, rational manner. For instance, Mrs. J may simply incorporate statements made by her husband into her delusional beliefs, such as interpreting his denial of any intent to harm her as evidence that he is concealing his malicious intent. It is unlikely that marital therapy would improve communication, increase trust, or resolve tensions in their relationship.

Initially, Mrs. J's treatment should have a psychoeducational focus to help her and her husband understand the nature of her diagnosis, the importance of ongoing medication management as a prophylaxis against future psychotic decompensations, and the implications of her condition for the future. An attempt should be made to actively involve family members in these therapeutic efforts as family members often find the changes in behavior exhibited by patients with schizophrenia difficult to understand (*DSM-IV*, 1994). These sessions can also address any questions or concerns family members have about causing her decompensation.

Every effort should be made to assist Mrs. J in continuing to work once an effective therapeutic regimen has been established. The chances for her being able to do so will depend in large part on how effectively medications control psychotic symptoms as well as whether she experiences medication side effects, particularly slowing in speed of psychomotor processing. In addition, work performance may be affected by the difficulties with attention, concentration, and motivation described previously. Finally, because the human resource and supervisory personnel at Mrs. J's place of work seem naive about psychological disorders, an effort to educate management and supervisors about her condition may help them figure out how to respond to Mrs. J and correct any outdated, biased, or unrealistic ideas they may have about schizophrenia. They may also learn what to do should Mrs. J exhibit any signs of a decompensation in the future. Of course, this intervention can be implemented only with Mrs. J's consent.

11 Case 6: Assessment of Suicide Potential

REASON FOR EVALUATION

Mrs. C is a 44-year-old, married, White advertising executive who began individual psychotherapy because of marital problems. She and her female therapist began meeting three times a week for intensive, psychodynamically oriented psychotherapy. After several months in treatment, Mrs. C reported experiencing several episodes of intense distress lasting from several hours to several days during which she was sad and tearful, reported feeling "out of control," and was troubled by intrusive thoughts about suicide. At this point, her therapist, Dr. K, requested a psychological evaluation to assess the severity of Mrs. C's depression, the risk of suicide, personality organization, and her potential for a psychotic decompensation.

BACKGROUND INFORMATION

Mrs. C arrived early for this evaluation. She was stylishly dressed and appeared poised and self-confident. She spoke openly about her past history and about the recent events that caused considerable concern both for herself and for Dr. K. No behavioral signs of depression were observed during this evaluation.

Mrs. C reported being excited about starting individual psychotherapy with Dr. K, who has an excellent reputation in the local community, and hopes to gain a better understanding of the tensions between her and her husband. Mrs. C expressed considerable puzzlement and concern about changes in her emotional state that occurred several months into treatment when she began having intense reactions to the issues discussed with Dr. K. At that point, she reported having days when she felt fine that alternated with hours or days when she felt there was no point in getting out of bed to go to work, had little interest in activities she had enjoyed in past, and was bothered by repetitive, intrusive thoughts about suicide. For instance, while driving on the highway, thoughts of driving into an embankment "came into my mind." Mrs. C became particularly concerned when she realized she had placed herself in harm's way on several occasions, such as walking into traffic on a busy street without first looking. She did not dwell on thoughts of suicide at other times, nor did she make specific plans to kill herself. She could not identify any clear precipitant for these shifts in mood, other than talking about painful issues in therapy sessions. Her mood became "blacker and blacker" during a week when Dr. K was on vacation, but this mood lifted after her therapist's return.

When asked by the examiner whether she was currently depressed, Mrs. C replied that she is moody and volatile. She did not report having a predominantly depressed mood most days for a 2-week period of time. She commented that she has been depressed off and on for many years and has frequently felt lonely and isolated. No changes in sleep have occurred, although she does view sleep as an escape when she feels more depressed. Her eating patterns have not changed. Mrs. C commented that since becoming an adult, she has made a conscious effort to control her eating habits and explained that as a child she often binged on sweets when she was upset. She attempted unsuccessfully to induce vomiting on one occasion when she was a teenager but found this so unpleasant she never tried it again. She denied use of laxatives. She has no difficulty concentrating at work. She described herself as feeling self-critical most of her life. She denied current suicidal ideation or intent.

Mrs. C works as an account executive in an advertising agency. Her responsibilities involve developing contacts with new clients, making sales presentations, acting as a liaison between the client and the creative team developing the ad campaigns, and insuring customer satisfaction with existing accounts. Her work is highly regarded both by her supervisors and clients. She described several instances when clients became so upset they threatened to cancel an account, and she was able to respond to their concerns, smooth over angry feelings, and, as a result, save the account. She does not believe her work performance has suffered during the past several months.

Mrs. C grew up in the South. She described her mother's side of the family as "blue-blooded Southern aristocrats." Her maternal grandfather became quite wealthy providing supplies for a local military base during World War I and subsequently developed a large trucking business. She described her mother as a homely woman who was "the most controlled, rigid woman I have ever met." In contrast, she described her father as a charming, sociable, handsome man who came from a poor family. He worked for his father-in-law and eventually took over the family business. She recalled with obvious affection that her father loved the "finer things in life," such as beautiful clothes, gourmet food, expensive wine, attending cultural events, and gambling on the thoroughbred horses he owned. He regularly flew to New York to attend openings at art galleries or gala benefits for the symphony and opera. On the majority of these trips, he was not accompanied by his wife. She recalls little affection being expressed between her parents.

Mrs. C's father died after a stroke during her senior year in college. When asked how his death affected her, she replied that "I just buried it," because there was too much to take care of between assignments for college classes during the week and helping her mother put her father's affairs in order on weekends.

While she was growing up, Mrs. C deeply wanted to please her mother and was "terrified" she would do something to cause mother to be angry with and reject her. In particular, Mrs. C was worried mother would be threatened by her appearance. She modeled her style of dress after her mother to avoid being more attractive than mother who had no interest in fashion, rarely bought new outfits, and generally wore clothes that were shapeless. Mrs. C concluded that mother did not want her to dress in a feminine or appealing manner as mother always chose clothes for her daughter that were too big or that were masculine in cut. She now wonders if she remained heavy as a teenager so she did not look attractive. During her senior year in high school, she gradually became aware that she could look more attractive if she lost weight and dressed more stylishly. However, she did not dare change her appearance until she went away to college when she began to diet, watch her weight, and select clothes that were more flattering.

Mrs. C did not date until she was in college. She believes that she was not asked out in high school because of her appearance. During her freshman year in college, she became involved with a senior and lived with him with during her sophomore year. She described him as a good person who was generous at some times and aloof and controlling at others. She initially indicated that their relationship ended by mutual decision but later stated he did not want her to accompany him when he moved out of state to attend graduate school. She was devastated by this rejection. She dated casually for several years until meeting the man she eventually married.

Mrs. C reported being happy with her marriage for the first several years, particularly when her two children were young. Over time, however, she became more and more dissatisfied with her marital relationship, as she felt her husband did not communicate with her. She perceives him as a man who "runs from his feelings." She contrasted feeling lonely at home with the friendly relationships she has with coworkers at the office. Although she suggested marital therapy, her husband refused to go with her. She eventually became so unhappy that she decided to leave home and move into her own apartment, hoping that this would force him to take her complaints seriously. After this he did agree to begin marital therapy. She feels marital therapy assisted in improving their communication.

Mrs. C denied a history of current or past alcohol abuse. There is no history of substance abuse.

DIAGNOSTIC CONSIDERATIONS

The referring therapist requested this evaluation to assess the severity of Mrs. C's current depression, the risk for suicide, personality organization, and the risk for a psychotic decompensation.

Depression.   Both the MMPI-2 and Rorschach are sensitive to identifying a current affective disorder. The MMPI-2 scale *2* is sensitive to symptomatic depression, poor morale, and general dissatisfaction with one's life circumstances. Because scale *2* was developed to be a measure of reactive depression, it is expected that scores on scale *2* will change over time depending on the individual's current mood state. Similarly, *DEP* appears to be sensitive to detecting the presence of depression.

The Rorschach Depression Index (*DEPI*) was empirically developed by examining the Rorschach data of a sample of patients with an affective disorder. Scores on the *DEPI* range from 0–7. *DEPI* scores of 5–7 indicate the presence of the cognitive and affective features commonly seen among patients diagnosed as having an affective disorder (Exner, 1991). Only 3% of a sample of nonpatient adults obtained positive scores on the *DEPI*, whereas 85% of a target sample of depressed patients obtained positive scores on the *DEPI*. However, the *DEPI* has not been cross-validated on an independent sample of depressed patients. In spite of this, these preliminary results suggest that the *DEPI* is sensitive to the presence of depression.

Suicide.   One should approach the question concerning Mrs. C's risk for suicide with considerable caution for several reasons. Most importantly, it is extremely difficult to accurately predict any phenomenon that occurs infrequently, such as suicide. Meehl (1973), for instance, demonstrated that the practical value of psychological test data depends not only on the discriminating power of the test results used to make a prediction but also on the frequency with which a particular clinical phenomenon occurs.

Meehl argued that when dealing with low base rate phenomenon, such as suicide, the clinician will be accurate more often than not simply by concluding that that particular phenomenon will not occur (e.g., that an individual patient will not commit suicide) because the frequency of occurrence is so rare. Furthermore, Meehl showed that even when the clinician's prediction about the occurrence of a rare event is based on a highly sensitive and valid measure, there is likely to be a high risk for false positives (i.e., concluding that an individual will commit suicide when they will not). Although one may argue that it is necessary or acceptable to make false positive predictions concerning suicide risk in order to identify persons who present a true risk for suicide, the clinician must be aware of the practical and ethical implications of identifying individuals as a risk for suicide when they are not (Rosen, 1954).

One must also be aware that the error rate for specific predictions will increase as the accuracy of the psychological measures used to make the predictions decreases. Research concerning prediction of suicide using the MMPI shows that MMPI data are not highly accurate in predicting suicide. Greene (1991), for instance, concluded that no single MMPI clinical scale, codetype, supplementary scale, or individual item is reliably associated with suicide. In spite of this, Greene recommended that the clinician examine the individual's responses to four MMPI-2 items that ask directly about suicidal ideation and attempts (Items 150, 506, 520, and 524). Note that although these items have face validity, their predictive validity has not been established.

What then is the clinician to do when asked to assess risk of suicide? According to Meehl, one would be accurate more often than not simply by saying that the patient will *not* commit suicide whenever this question arises. However, in clinical contexts, this begs a question that has important implications for treatment planning, such as taking the necessary steps to insure a patient's well-being or deciding whether there is a need for hospitalization. A different approach is suggested by Graham (1993). Like Greene, Graham (1993) concluded that no specific MMPI-2 scales or actuarial formula exist to accurately predict suicide. However, he suggested that the clinician can respond to referral questions about suicide risk by examining psychological test data, clinical findings, and history to make inferences about clinical factors related to an increased risk for suicide, such as severity of depression, energy level, impulsivity, a sense of hopelessness, and social isolation. The clinician should, of course, recognize that these inferences remain limited because of the infrequent rate of occurrence of suicide (Finn & Kamphuis, 1995).

The Rorschach Suicide Constellation (*S-CON*) is an empirically derived cluster of Rorschach variables developed to identify subjects at risk for self-destructive behavior. The *S-CON* was developed by examining

Rorschach protocols of a sample of 59 subjects who committed suicide within 60 days after a Rorschach had been administered. A cluster of variables was identified that correctly identified 75% of the suicide cases with a low rate of false positives for normals (0%) and schizophrenics (12%). However, 20% of a depressed sample obtained positive scores on the S-CON.

The original S-CON was refined and cross-validated on a second, independent sample of 101 suicide completers. The revised S-CON correctly identified 83% of the sample of suicide completers while misidentifying 0% of normals, 6% of schizophrenics, and 12% of depressives. Thus, the S-CON may incorrectly suggest a risk of suicide among depressed subjects who are not suicidal. Exner (1993) discussed these issues but encouraged the clinician to deliberately explore the possibility of self-destructive features when the S-CON is positive. It should be noted, however, that the revised S-CON has not been cross-validated on an independent sample. Furthermore, clinicians should be aware that the difficulties of predicting low base rate phenomena discussed previously apply as much to Rorschach data, including the S-CON, as to MMPI-2 data (Finn & Kamphuis, 1995). In spite of this, the S-CON appears to be a promising index of the risk for suicide that, when positive, should be taken seriously.

The previous discussion has several implications for assessment of suicidality in a clinical context. First, clinicians should be aware of their limitations in predicting suicidality accurately, because suicide occurs so infrequently. Second, no MMPI-2 scale score or profile associated specifically with suicide exists. Third, the risk for suicide should be explored if the Rorschach S-CON is positive, although the risks of false positives among depressed patients should be recognized. Fourth, clinicians may infer a risk of suicide if data from psychological tests and/or the clinical history show an individual exhibits psychosocial characteristics associated with an increased risk for suicide, such as severity of depression, energy level, impulsivity, a sense of hopelessness, or social isolation. The clinician can then make reasoned, cautious estimates about an individual's current risk for suicide but must recognize that firm predictions cannot be made reliably. Fifth, rather than using test data alone to make a decision concerning the risk for suicide, the clinician should inquire directly about suicidal ideation and intent during a clinical interview when suicidality is an issue.

Psychosis.   Similar to the previous discussion concerning depression, both the MMPI-2 and Rorschach are sensitive to psychotic ideation and experiences. Among MMPI-2 scales, scales 6 and 8 contain items related to directly to psychotic symptoms including paranoia; delusions of reference and persecution; peculiar, strange thought processes; and bizarre sensory experiences. The Bizarre Mentation scale also contains items that involve strange thoughts and experiences, paranoid ideation, and hallucinations.

Several Rorschach variables are related to psychosis. The Schizophrenia Index (*SCZI*) was developed specifically to detect schizophrenia, although other psychotic disorders can also result in a positive *SCZI*. A number of specific Rorschach scores are related to difficulties with accurate perceptions of stimuli ($F + \%$, $X + \%$, $X - \%$, Populars) as well as to cognitive slippage and disorganized thought processes (Special scores). For instance, normals rarely produce responses with Special scores (the mean number of the sum of Special scores for the normative sample is 1.62).

MMPI-2 Data

Validity. The validity scales are within expected limits. Mrs. C responded to the MMPI-2 in an open, honest, forthright manner. There were no indications of an attempt either to defensively minimize or to exaggerate symptoms of psychological difficulties.

Clinical Scales. Given the history of dysphoric mood, difficulties with motivation, and intrusive thoughts of suicide, the MMPI-2 profile is unexpected as all clinical scales are below a *T*-score of 65. Surprisingly, no indication of depression exists (scale *2* = 53; *DEP* = 56). As no clinical scales are greater than 65, this profile may be viewed as a within-normal-limits (WNL) profile. Although these scores suggest an absence of psychopathology, this conclusion is not consistent with the clinical history of recent emotional distress and suicidal ideation.

Duckworth and Barley (1988) reviewed the literature concerning MMPI WNL profiles and suggested that a WNL profile produced in a clinical setting may signify either a defensive response set, a lack of insight, or a relatively positive psychological adjustment. In this case, no signs of defensiveness were noted on the validity scales. Although Mrs. C does have a history of relatively high functioning in terms of academic and career achievements, her clinical history suggests it would be a mistake to conclude that she is well adjusted and that no personal issues exist that deserve clinical attention.

Duckworth and Barley (1988) presented several guidelines for interpretation of WNL profiles when MMPI clinical scales are below a *T*-score of 70. These guidelines should apply to interpretation of the MMPI-2 when clinical scale *T*-scores are below 65. Some authors (e.g., Lachar, 1974) suggested that WNL profiles can be approached by interpreting MMPI clinical scale *T*-scores in the range of 60 to 70, that is by approaching these scales as though they were elevated above 70. (On the MMPI-2, clinical scales with *T*-scores in the range of 55–65 would be similarly interpreted.)

208

Name _____ Mrs. C. _____

Address _____

Occupation _____ Date Tested ___/___

Education __16__ Age __44__ Marital Status __Married__

Referred By _____

MMPI-2 Code _____

Scorer's Initials _____

Profile for Basic Scales

Minnesota Multiphasic Personality Inventory-2
Copyright © by THE REGENTS OF THE UNIVERSITY OF MINNESOTA
1942, 1943 (renewed 1970), 1989. This Profile Form 1989.
All rights reserved. Distributed exclusively by NATIONAL COMPUTER SYSTEMS, INC.
under license from The University of Minnesota.

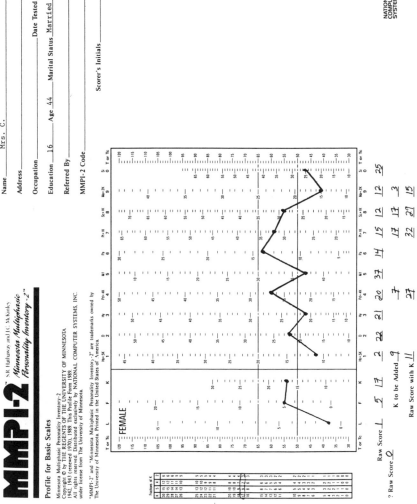

NATIONAL
COMPUTER
SYSTEMS

24001

Case 6 MMPI-2 Content and Supplementary Scales

                                                               Raw Score   T Score

FB   0   42
True Response Inconsistency (TRIN)   10   58T
Variable Response Inconsistency (VRIN)   4   46
Anxiety (A)   16   57
Repression (R)   19   57
MAC-R   15   37
Ego Strength (Es)   37   55
Overcontrolled Hostility (O-H)   16   59
Dominance (Do)   20   63
Social Responsibility (Re)   23   56
Post Traumatic Stress Disorder - Keane (PK)   9   51
Post Traumatic Stress Disorder - Schlenger (PS)   11   49
Addiction Potential (APS)   23   50
Addiction Admission (AAS)   2   50

Content Scales (Butcher et al., 1990)
        Anxiety (ANX)   9   55
        Fears (FRS)   4   43
        Obsessiveness (OBS)   3   44
        Depression (DEP)   8   56
        Health Concerns (HEA)   5   49
        Bizarre Mentation (BIZ)   0   40
        Anger (ANG)   4   45
        Cynicism (CYN)   9   50
        Antisocial Practices (ASP)   6   49
        Type A (TPA)   7   48
        Low Self-Esteem (LSE)   5   51
        Social Discomfort (SOD)   4   44

Depression Subscales (Harris-Lingoes)
        Subjective Depression (D1)   9   53
        Psychomotor Retardation (D2)   6   51
        Physical Malfunctioning (D3)   1   34
        Mental Dullness (D4)   1   42
        Brooding (D5)   5   63

Hysteria Subscales (Harris-Lingoes)
        Denial of Social Anxiety (Hy1)   5   56
        Need for Affection (Hy2)   6   46
        Lassitude-Malaise (Hy3)   2   47
        Somatic Complaints (Hy4)   1   41
        Inhibition of Aggression (Hy5)   5   62

```
                                              Raw Score   T Score

    Psychopathic Deviate Subscales (Harris-Lingoes)
         Familial Discord (Pd1)                   3         56
         Authority Problems (Pd2)                 2         46
         Social Imperturbability (Pd3)            4         54
         Social Alienation (Pd4)                  4         50
         Self-Alienation (Pd5)                    4         53


    Paranoia Subscales (Harris-Lingoes)
         Persecutory Ideas (Pa1)        .         2         51
         Poignancy (Pa2)                          4         59
         Naivete (Pa3)                            6         55


    Schizophrenia Subscales (Harris-Lingoes)
         Social Alienation (Sc1)                  3         50
         Emotional Alienation (Sc2)               3         67
         Lack of Ego Mastery, Cognitive (Sc3)     0         43
         Lack of Ego Mastery, Conative (Sc4)      4         59
         Lack of Ego Mastery, Def. Inhib. (Sc5)   1         46
         Bizarre Sensory Experiences (Sc6)        0         41


    Hypomania Subscales (Harris-Lingoes)
         Amorality (Ma1)                          1         45
         Psychomotor Acceleration (Ma2)           2         35
         Imperturbability (Ma3)                   3         50
         Ego Inflation (Ma4)                      4         56


    Social Introversion Subscales (Ben-Porath et al., 1989)
         Shyness/Self-Consciousness (Si1)         3         44
         Social Avoidance (Si2)                   3         51
         Alienation -- Self and Others (Si3)      5         49
```

However, other authors (e.g., Butcher, 1985; Graham, 1984) suggested that established correlates of MMPI codetypes can be used when clinical scales are mildly elevated but still within the normal range, although personality descriptors would be more applicable than psychopathologic correlates. Butcher (1985) advised that content scales may be better sources of personality description than clinical scales when interpreting WNL MMPI profiles, especially when T-scores on all clinical scales are between 60–64. However, a review of Mrs. C's content scales shows none is elevated above a T-score of 65.

Following these guidelines, the MMPI-2 profile can be viewed as a *46/64* two-point codetype. Although in some instances the *46/64* codetype is associated with serious psychopathology (e.g., Paranoid Schizophrenia), the present interpretation focuses on the personality descriptors associated with this codetype.

The *46/64* codetype suggests Mrs. C may experience depressed moods and guilt. As noted previously, the score on scale *2* ($T = 53$), indicates that her overall level of depression is well within the normal range. This finding is unexpected given the history of depressed mood, suicidal ideation, decreased energy, and poor motivation. Similarly, *DEP* is also within normal limits ($T = 56$). Although neither scale *2* nor *DEP* are elevated, scale *9* is lower than expected ($T = 41$). This low score may suggest decreased level of energy, lack of drive, and difficulties with motivation. Low scores on scale *9*, particularly when lower than a T-score of 40, are often associated with depression, even when scale *2* is not elevated (Friedman et al., 1989; Greene, 1991).

The *46/64* codetype suggests that Mrs. C frequently feels angry, resentful, and irritable. She typically tries to suppress, ignore, and conceal anger as she views being angry as shameful and does not want others to think she is a hostile, resentful person. As a result of her tendency to deny anger, she may not be aware of the intensity of her hurt and angry feelings. She typically expresses anger in indirect, passive ways that others may find difficult to deal with. Her passive–aggressive maneuvers may provoke angry attacks and retaliations by others after which she feels hurt and treated unfairly. She may not be aware of how her actions contributed to these upsetting situations. She instead focuses on how she has been hurt, neglected, mistreated, or ignored by others, particularly family members. She is quite sensitive to feeling criticized, rejected, and slighted. Her perceptions of personal relationships may emphasize the positive things she does while ignoring the role she played in creating difficult situations and problems. She rationalizes her behavior and blames others. She may also project angry feelings onto others.

Mrs. C experiences a conflict concerning dependency needs. She seeks approval from others and is likely to make many demands on others, particularly men, for attention and sympathy. At the same time, however, when others make requests or demands of her, she frequently feels unfairly burdened and then reacts with quick resentment if she feels rebuffed, ignored, or unappreciated.

No signs exist of a current psychotic disorder, nor were there any indications of an imminent psychotic decompensation (scale $8 = 55$; $BIZ = 39$). She did not endorse any of the four items Greene identified as specifically related to suicidal ideation or behavior.

Rorschach Data

The Rorschach protocol appears to be valid for interpretation, as Mrs. C produced 27 responses. The first positive key variable is the finding that the D score is less than the *Adjusted D* score. This suggests that Mrs. C currently experiences significant situational stress that may impact on her psychological adjustment. When $D < Adj\ D$, the search strategy proceeds by first examining the patient's ability to manage stressful situations in a deliberate, purposeful manner and then examining the sources and nature of the stress she experiences.

Mrs. C's *Adj D* score $(+2)$ is higher than expected, which suggests she generally has the psychological resources needed to tolerate stress and to manage difficult, unexpected, negative situations. The fact that $D = 0$ suggests Mrs. C's responses to stress are generally characterized by self-restraint, deliberation, and self-control rather than impulsivity. In other words, she generally has sufficient ego strength to weather life's ups and downs.

However, several pieces of data indicate that Mrs. C is currently troubled by significant emotional distress. First, whereas normatively the D and Adj D scores are expected to differ by one point, in this case D and $Adj\ D$ differ by two points. This suggests that in spite of her usual ability to handle unpleasant, difficult, or unwanted situations, Mrs. C's coping resources are currently ineffective to handle the stress she now experiences. Second, the left side of the eb ratio is always expected to be greater than the right side. When the right side of the eb ratio is greater than the left side, as it is in this case ($eb = 6:12$), the presence of significant situational distress is indicated. This involves a mixture of sadness, worry, and helplessness ($C = 2$; $Y = 7$; $m = 3$) and negative, critical feelings about herself ($V = 2$). It is quite noteworthy that Y is so much greater than m, which suggests that current stress has a greater impact on her emotions than on her thinking. The unusually high number of Y responses indicates Mrs. C feels quite anxious, helpless, and powerless. Third, the presence of three Color-Shading Blend responses is also quite unusual ($CF.FC$; $M.FC'.CF$; $FY.FC$), which indi-

Card	Response	Inquiry
I	1. It l.l a headless woman w 2 hands going up.	E: (Rpts S's response) S: That's the center. L.l her skirt comes down. L.l her breast. Arms g up & hand l this. But no head. E: Skirt? S: It lks fabricky. Got light & dark. Can see legs beh it.
	2. And...uhm...I d't k. (lghs) E: Take yr time. Most p c more than 1 thing on each card. S: This part is the woman. And a flying A or s.t. That's what it l.l. Like elephants or s.t. If I c more than 1 thing I shld tell u, right? E: That's right. There are no right or wrong answers. Just tell me what it l.l to u.	E: (Rpts S's response) S: These 2. And it l.l their ears are flying back as if moving in the air & ears pushed behind their tails and bodies. E: Ears pushed back? S: Bec the direction, pushing away as if wind is blowing & ears are pushed back. That's why it l.l they're moving.
II	3. God. I guess I'm into elephants! Well, it does l.l 2 elephants...And it l.l blood. Maybe they're wounded. Uh, I d't k.	E: (Rpts S's response) S: Right. E: Where were u lkg? S: Here. The trunks are touching. Have long trunks. Have same shape face, big heads, proportionate to their bodies. E: Blood? S: Here. Its red & its...It ll a blood stain. L blood kind of splatters, red spots on the elephant's grey skin.
	4. The things on top are kind of like spinning hats.	E: (Rpts S's response) S: These l.l spinning hats. E: What made it l.l that? S: I'm not r sure. Well, tall & conical, goes on head. E: Spinning?

S: Yeah. S.t abt the light &
dark or way its...to me, it
creates a sense of motion. And
the little pieces coming off, 1
an artist trying to convey a
sense of motion.

5. Or this kind of l.1
splashed paint.

E: (Rpts S's response)
S: Same as blood.
E: Paint?
S: I thk just the C & fact when
paint splashes it creates that
shape & that, u k, edges
splatter out in diff
directions.

III   6. Oh god. I d'k if I r c
this, but it 1.1 2 dancing
women so...but they 1.1
skeletal women. Have a r
macabre 1. Look
emaciated, 1 their bodies,
well, just 1 emaciated.
And they're holding s.t.
L.1 they're facing off, in
a struggle, pulling s.t.,
trying to keep s.t away
from the other.

E: (Rpts S's response)
S: Well, they're r skinny. Alm
1.1 part of their body has been
cut away.
E: What makes it l.1 that?
S: Upper part is full-bodied &
1.1 s.t. on bottom is missing.
Too skinny. And bec of the
white space. L.1 s.o took away
part of the body. What makes
it l.1 women? Bec of the
breasts. And faces. Oh, and
this l.1 high heeled shoes w
pointed toes.
E: Struggle?
S: Well, it l.1 they're pulling
apart this, whatever it is.
E: U said the red made u think
of anger.
S: I d't thnk the red 1.1
anger. Angry part comes from
this & this, s.t. pulled apart
& these are shreds. Also,
butts in the air in a v aggr
posturing.

7. The thing the center it
l.1 a red bow.

E: (Rpts S's response)
S: This just l.1 a red bow.
The shape & C.

IV   8. I thnk that's a
squished bear rug.

E: (Rpts S's response)
S: I'm not sure if I r c it.
Oh. There's the head, eyes.
L.1 the outline of body & legs.
Outside lks furry. And light &
dark lks furry. Like skin of
bear.
E: Furry?

214

S: Its got that furry texture.
Fuzzy.
E: Squished?
S: Yeah. Lks flattened.

9. That l.l a hippopotamus
head.

E: (Rpts S's response)
S: Oh, def l.l a hippo head.
There's 2 eyes & hippo mouth.
And 2 horns. D't k if they
have horns.

10. It l.l a giant, taking
out this part. It
l.l...not a menacing
giant. Just a mythical
giant. Looks more like
that to me than a bear
skin rug.

E: (Rpts S's response)
S: Right. Bec of -- here's the
head, arm & huge feet. Alm l
he's...u k. (motions with
hands)
E: Like he's?
S: Well, stalking comes to
mind, but like lumbering down w
huge feet.
E: Huge?
S: Just this size. Perspective
is so big compared to rest of
him. L.l he's walking bec his
toes are turned up, l he's abt
to step down.

V   11. (laughs) A bat.

E: (Rpts S's response)
S: The shape.

12. Well, I...it reminds
me of, these l.l dancing
legs. So, I suppose to me
it l.l a, a H face where
this is. Almost a
costume. Yeah. Like
maybe this is part of
costume, a headpiece & a
big feathery cape kind of
thing. And dancing legs.

E: (Rpts S's response)
S: Right. Here's dancing legs,
the shape. Headpiece, it l.l a
head. This l.l a costume.
Partly the light & dark makes
it l fabricky, l its billowing
out.
E: Billowing?
S: Well, the shape, the
direction of it. And maybe the
sense it just...the shape.
Kind of lks fabricky to me.
E: What do u mean?
S: As if its a costume & darker
& lighter material. Seems more
opaque.

VI   13. A cat, a smooshed cat.
Alm l.l a rug. An A skin
rug. And top part l.l a
cat's head. A flattened
A. That lks less benign
to me than a rug, like s.o
took an A & flattened it.

E: (Rpts S's response)
S: This l.l whiskers, the
snout, ears. Shape of it.
E: Smooshed?
S: It lks flattened bec of the
shape. Both sides flattened
out. And body, the symmetrical

nature of it.
E: Rug?
S: The same thing. Got outline
of A skin that's flat.

VII 14. Well, 1st thing I
thght of is 2 girls w
ponytails. I d't k if
that's...2 girls staring
at e.o. Sometime I thk
they look angry & s.t they
j lk intense. This part
feels 1 anger, 1 its
pulling away. But their
faces d't s angry.

E: (Rpts S's response)
S: Their faces, ponytails.
Shape of it. Staring at e.o.
E: U said they were angry or
intense.
S: I thk the darkness around
the mouth made them s angry.
And the fact this part of the
body is facing away lks angry.
Their body, breasts, the neck
comes down to the breast. Top
1/2 of body.

VIII 15. Oh...(lghs) 2 bears.
(lghs)

E: (Rpts S's response)
S: The shape.

16. These parts look
sexual to me, in some way.

E: (Rpts S's response)
S: The orangy, pinky part, k of
1.1 buttocks & legs spread out.
And k of pubic hair, vagina, &
anus.
E: What made it 1.1 that to u?
S: Well, the shape, I thk.
Shape of buttocks & legs, alm
in perspective. The darker
orange shading & light part in
center as if recessed back fr
the sexual organs.

17. This part k of 1.1 a
pink BF.

E: (Rpts S's response)
S: Right here.
E: BF?
S: The shape. U k, BF's have a
piece in center, the body. And
the C, pink.

18. This 1.1 an arm. L
the bear's holding the p's
hands.

E: (Rpts S's response)
S: Right. The shape. L.1
figure as if bear is clutching
one of the fingers, on both
sides.

IX 19. This alm lks to me l a
mythical dragon. That's
what comes to mind.

E: (Rpts S's response)
S: The shape.
E: Mythical?
S: I d'k. (lghs) I d't k. The
pointed top & the...I thk s.t
to do w the C, too. Wldn't

216

20. (Lghs) This l.l 2 girl's heads. Kind of l their faces are smooshed a little bit. Hmmm...

21. This l.l 2 old men, k of bowed over...(lghs) This k of l.l insect heads. It does l.l 2 old men w insect head even though I k... but that's what it l.l.

21. And this also lks sexual to me. Hmm...

22. Well, it l.l 2 crabs. Blue ones.

X   23. That l.l a wishbone, the orange thing.

24. These l.l...an A. L a squiggly, long k of A w its tail curling as it moves.

have said if j black. Maybe the orange l.l a mythical creature inst of a real creature

E: (Rpts S's response)
S: Oh, yeah! L.l the hair is back, l in a ponytail or bun. L.l a side view, a profile. Alm l.l the bottom part is flattened.
E: Flattened?
S: The shape & maybe bec of shading, its darker.

E: (Rpts S's response)
S: Oh, yes. The insect men, we c't forget them. Who knows. I d't k. L.l as if kneeling over. Backs & head are bowed, lkg down at the ground. I thk that the shading, this is darker, l in the shadows. Facing down. This is their butt & heads.
E: Insect head?
S: Yeah, these things. (lghs) The shape.

E: (Rpts S's response)
S: Oh, this part. Right...I thk the shape. This l.l a vagina, partly bec its lighter & the shape l.l labia & lips. Roundness k of l.l a butt. And maybe the pinky tone, k of l.l flesh.

E: (Rpts S's response)
S: There. The shape. Blue crabs.

E: (Rpts S's response)
S: The shape. An orange wishbone.

E: (Rpts S's response)
S: Here. The shape. Maybe the C, too. Kind of l.l, u k, some A's are green, l a little green worm.
E: Curling?
S: The shape & direction of it, l curling up.

E: I'm not sure what u mean, curling up.
S: Well, it l.l its moving. K of wiggling.

25. Hmmm...these l.l, they l real angry. L in a video game, a video game character, a video scene where glaring at e.o. (lghs)

E: (Rpts S's response)
S: L.l Nintendo men, l facing off. Their eyes, the lighter space. They l r angry. L Nintendo characters. Have little antenna. The kind u wt to get. I never can.

26. These l.l faces. But, boy, is that intense -- all I c are angry faces. They look angry. Alm l.l a seahorse to me, but more H than that. L they are floating. They cld be in the water. S k of creature with a H face, an angry H face, lkg at e.o.

E: (Rpts S's response)
S: The shape. L.l the forehead, nose, chin. I thk the C's def makes them l angry, deep purple to pink.
E: What abt the C's?
S: The intensity of it. The purple, j an angry C. L when y're r angry & face turns a diff shade. L their faces have darkened, r mad.
E: Floating?
S: Its not so much in water. I d't k. When -- I d't k what they l.l. They l.l women, floating.
E: Explain that.
S: L.l cld be floating in air or water, I g. Its the amorphous shape, I g, undulating.

```
CASE06.R3==================== SEQUENCE OF SCORES ===============================

CARD NO LOC  #  DETERMINANT(S)      (2) CONTENT(S)     POP Z  SPECIAL SCORES
======= ====== ================     === ==========     === =  ==============
   I  1 D+   4  Ma.FV+                  Hd,Cg,Sx        4.0  DV,MOR
      2 Do   2  FMa.mao                 A                    INC

  II  3 D+   1  CF.FC'o              2  A,Bl            P 3.0  MOR
      4 Do   2  ma.YFo                  Cg                   INC
      5 Dv      CFo                     Id

 III  6 DdS+    Ma.FC'.CFu           2  H,An,Sx,Cg      P 4.5  DV,AG,MOR
      7 Do   3  FCo                     Cg

  IV  8 Wo   1  FTo                     Ad              2.0  DR
      9 Do   1  Fo                      Ad
     10 Do   7  Ma.FDo                  (H)             P

   V 11 Wo   1  Fo                      A               P 1.0
     12 W+   1  Ma.ma.FY+               Hd,Cg           2.5  DR

  VI 13 Wo   1  Fo                      Ad              P 2.5  MOR,DR,PER

 VII 14 D+   2  Mp.FYo               2  Hd,Sx           P 3.0  AG,PER

VIII 15 Do      Fo                   2  A               P
     16 Do   2  Mp.FV-                  Hd,Sx
     17 Do   2  FCo                     A
     18 Dd+ 22  FMao                 2  A,Hd            P 3.0  FAB

  IX 19 Do   3  FCu                  2  (A)
     20 Do   1  FYu                  2  Hd
     21 Do   3  Mp.FYu               2  H,Ad,Sx              INC
     22 Do   6  FY.FC-                  Hd,Sx                DV

   X 23 Do   1  FCo                  2  A               P    INC
     24 Do   3  FCo                     Id                   INC
     25 Do   4  FMa.FCo                 A
     26 D+   8  Mp.FYo               2  (H)             4.5  AG,PER
     27 D+   9  Mp.CF-               2  Hd,A            4.5  AG,INC


============================= SUMMARY OF APPROACH ==============================

    I : D.D                      VI : W
   II : D.D.D                   VII : D
  III : DdS.D                  VIII : D.D.D.Dd
   IV : W.D.D                    IX : D.D.D.D
    V : W.W                       X : D.D.D.D.D
```

219

```
CASE06.R3===================== STRUCTURAL SUMMARY ===============================

LOCATION                   DETERMINANTS              CONTENTS        S-CONSTELLATION
FEATURES        BLENDS              SINGLE                           YES..FV+VF+V+FD>2
                                                H   = 2, 0           YES..Col-Shd Bl>0
Zf   = 11       M.FV              M   = 0        (H) = 2, 0           NO..Ego<.31,>.44
ZSum = 34.5     FM.m              FM  = 1        Hd  = 7, 1           YES..MOR > 3
ZEst = 34.5     CF.FC'            m   = 0        (Hd)= 0, 0           NO..Zd > +- 3.5
                m.YF              FC  = 5        Hx  = 0, 0           YES..es > EA
W  =  4         M.FC'.CF          CF  = 1        A   = 8, 1           NO..CF+C > FC
 (Wv = 0)       M.FD              C   = 0        (A) = 1, 0           NO..X+% < .70
D  = 21         M.m.FY            Cn  = 0        Ad  = 3, 1           NO..S > 3
Dd =  2         M.FY             FC' = 0        (Ad)= 0, 0           YES..P < 3 or > 8
S  =  1         M.FV             C'F = 0        An  = 0, 1           NO..Pure H < 2
                M.FY             C'  = 0        Art = 0, 0           NO..R < 17
  DQ            FY.FC            FT  = 1        Ay  = 0, 0            5.....TOTAL
........(FQ-)   FM.FC            TF  = 0        Bl  = 0, 1
 +  =  8  ( 1)  M.FY             T   = 0        Bt  = 0, 0           SPECIAL SCORINGS
 o  = 18  ( 2)  M.CF            FV  = 0        Cg  = 2, 3                   Lv1    Lv2
v/+ =  0  ( 0)                   VF  = 0        Cl  = 0, 0           DV  =   3x1    0x2
 v  =  1  ( 0)                   V   = 0        Ex  = 0, 0           INC =   6x2    0x4
                                 FY  = 1        Fd  = 0, 0           DR  =   3x3    0x6
                                 YF  = 0        Fi  = 0, 0           FAB =   1x4    0x7
                                 Y   = 0        Ge  = 0, 0           ALOG =  0x5
   FORM QUALITY                  Fr  = 0        Hh  = 0, 0           CON =   0x7
                                 rF  = 0        Ls  = 0, 0           Raw Sum6 =   13
       FQx  FQf  MQual  SQx      FD  = 0        Na  = 0, 0           Wgtd Sum6 =  28
 +  =   2    0     2     0       F   = 4        Sc  = 0, 0
 o  =  18    4     3     0                      Sx  = 0, 6           AB  = 0     CP = 0
 u  =   4    0     2     1                      Xy  = 0, 0           AG  = 4     MOR = 4
 -  =   3    0     2     0                      Id  = 2, 0           CFB = 0     PER = 3
none=   0    --    0     0          (2) = 11                         COP = 0     PSV = 0

===================== RATIOS, PERCENTAGES, AND DERIVATIONS =====================

R = 27        L =  0.17             FC:CF+C = 7: 4      COP = 0      AG = 4
-------------------------------     Pure C  =    0      Food   =     0
EB = 9: 7.5  EA = 16.5   EBPer= N/A SumC':WSumC= 2:7.5  Isolate/R =0.00
eb = 6:12    es = 18      D =   0   Afr      =0.93      H:(H)Hd(Hd)= 2:10
         Adj es = 10   Adj D = +2   S        =    1     (HHd):(AAd)= 2: 1
-------------------------------     Blends:R=14:27      H+A:Hd+Ad =14:12
FM = 3  :  C'= 2   T = 1             CP       =    0
m  = 3  :  V = 2   Y = 7
                                  P   = 9      Zf  =11          3r+(2)/R=0.41
a:p    = 10: 5   Sum6  = 13       X+% =0.74    Zd  = +0.0       Fr+rF  =    0
Ma:Mp  =  4: 5   Lv2   =  0       F+% =1.00    W:D:Dd = 4:21: 2 FD     =    1
2AB+Art+Ay= 0    WSum6 = 28       X-% =0.11    W:M = 4: 9       An+Xy  =    1
M-     =  2      Mnone =  0       S-% =0.00    DQ+ = 8          MOR    =    4
                                  Xu% =0.15    DQv = 1

===============================================================================
SCZI = 2     DEPI = 5*   CDI = 0    S-CON = 5    HVI = No    OBS = No
===============================================================================
```

220

cates that situational stress has created or contributes to intense, confusing emotional reactions.

After reviewing Mrs. C's abilities to cope with stress and the effects of recent stress, the search strategy proceeds by identifying the next positive key variable. In this case, however, none of the other key variable is positive. The search strategy therefore continues by examining Tertiary variables. The first positive Tertiary variable is *DEPI* = 5. Although the positive *DEPI* raises a possibility that Mrs. C's current condition involves an affective disturbance, *DEPI* = 5 does not necessarily indicate she will meet diagnostic criteria for a current affective disorder. Instead, *DEPI* = 5 indicates Mrs. C is prone to experience intense, disruptive episodes of distressing affect that may last for relatively brief periods of time. The combination of *DEPI* = 5 and the high *es* (18) emphasizes the importance of current emotional distress in understanding Mrs. C's presentation.

The search strategy continues by focusing on Mrs. C's characteristic ways of handling affect. Mrs. C does not handle emotions in a consistent manner. Sometimes her reactions are dominated by logic and reason, whereas at other times, her reactions and behavior are driven by feelings (*EB* = 9:7.5). This lack of consistency in handling emotions is noteworthy and suggests that, at times, emotions may have a greater than expected effect on her psychological functioning.

In some situations, Mrs. C shows considerable capacity to delay before responding and to carefully plan and deliberately respond to events in a logical, controlled, emotionally balanced manner (*M* = 9; *FC:CF+C* = 7:4). At other times, however, Mrs. C tends to be an extremely emotional woman who is more responsive to emotions than are most people (*Afr* = .93; *Sum C* = 11). She can become excessively involved with and overwhelmed by affect; in other words, feelings, rather than reason or logic, often dominate her awareness (*Lambda* = .17). As a result, she may overreact to situations. The high number of blends (14:27) suggests her psychological functioning is overly complex because of the powerful effect emotions have on her. In particular, intense emotional distress may overwhelm her ability to manage feelings (Blends created by *m* and *Y* = 7). The fact that she produced three Color-Shading Blend responses, two of which involve *C'*, suggests her emotional distress is not solely situational but is more longstanding in nature and involves a confusing mixture of both positive and negative reactions.

Mrs. C's self-image is colored by guilt, shame, and self-criticism (*V* = 2; *MOR* = 4). One important component of her current emotional distress involves these negative, punitive reactions to herself. Her negative self-image is not based on a realistic appraisal of her strengths and weaknesses but instead reflects a distorted view of herself (*H:(H)Hd(Hd)* = 2:10), particularly in terms of her body image and conflicts concerning sexuality.

Concerns about body image and her physical integrity were suggested by the unusual elaborations to the popular response on Card III (Response 6 two emaciated women with "part of their bodies cut away") as well as by the content of other Morbid responses (Response 1 "a headless woman" and Response 3 two wounded elephants).

Conflicts about sexuality are suggested by several findings. First, the higher than expected number of sexual responses suggests Mrs. C is preoccupied with issues related to sexuality ($Sx = 6$). Second, the possibility that she reacts to sexual issues with guilt and/or shame is suggested by the combination of Sx content with both of the *FV* responses she produced. Third, a review of the minus responses shows that two of three minus responses involved percepts of female genitalia (Response 16 and Response 22). Overall, these findings suggest a negative image of herself as a woman and perhaps a revulsion and abhorrence of female sexuality.

In general, Mrs. C appears much more interested in others than is typical (Human content = 12 vs. the expected range of 5–7 responses involving Human content). Although the higher than expected number of responses involving human content may reflect a healthy interest in others, it may also reflect a heightened sensitivity and concern about social interactions. The latter interpretation seems more likely than the former in this case for several reasons, including the higher than expected number of *(H)+Hd+(Hd)* contents and the higher than expected number of aggressive responses ($AG = 4$).

Mrs. C's involvement with others is shaped by two major factors, her anger ($COP = 0$; $AG = 4$) and a passive-dependent orientation ($Ma{:}Mp = 3{:}6$). The absence of any cooperative movement responses and the presence of 4 *AG* responses indicates Mrs. C expects hostility will be a core aspect of interpersonal interactions and that relationships with others will not be mutual. The unexpectedly high number of *(H)+Hd+(Hd)* responses suggests she views others not as whole, real, separate people but as part-objects who exist to fulfill the needs of one another ($H{:}(H)Hd(Hd) = 2{:}10$). She anticipates that in any relationship only one person's needs will be gratified, while the other person's needs are ignored or frustrated. As a result, Mrs. C tends to be quite sensitive and defensive in interpersonal interactions and reacts in a forceful, hostile manner when she feels threatened or insecure ($AG = 4$; $PER = 3$). The extent to which anger and aggression are significant factors in her psychological functioning is expressed vividly in Response 6 (two women engaged in a struggle to keep something away from the other), Response 14 (two girls staring at each other angrily), Response 26 (two Nintendo characters glaring at each other), and Response 27 (two figures who are so enraged their faces have turned a different shade of purple).

A passive-dependent orientation is suggested by the relationship between the number of M active to M passive responses ($Ma:Mp = 3:6$). Normatively, it is expected that Ma will be greater than Mp. It is quite unusual for a person to produce more passive than active M responses, as Mrs. C did. This unusual finding suggests that Mrs. C retreats from responsibility, avoids handling difficult situations independently, and responds to unpleasant situations by withdrawing into fantasy rather than taking direct action. This may contribute to her assuming a submissive, dependent role in relationships with others. Although she has the psychological resources to handle most stressful situations on her own ($EA = 16.5$; $Adj\ D = +2$), when difficulties arise, she wishes a strong, decisive individual would take charge so she can follow their directions in a compliant, submissive manner, rather than having to cope with the unpleasant situation on her own.

Mrs. C produced more Popular responses than expected (Populars $= 9$), which suggests she is quite concerned about conventionality and social expectations. The sensitivity to social interactions described previously ($H:(H)Hd(Hd)$) and her awareness of social expectations suggests Mrs. C is likely to be quite aware of how others view her, whether they approve of her actions and think her behavior is appropriate, and then tries to behave in line with their expectations. Her efforts to conform with others' expectations suggest she makes a considerable effort to please them and win their approval. In this context, the greater than expected number of clothing responses ($Cg = 5$ vs. an expected value of 1) might suggest that she attempts to cover over and conceal aspects of herself she is afraid others will disapprove of.

Mrs. C appears to be quite cautious, careful, and defensive in her approach to stimuli ($W < 1/2\ D + Dd$; $W:M = 4:9$). Given her intellectual strengths, this conservative approach is most likely a manifestation of a defensive withdrawal from social competition because of her negative self-image. This may also reflect obsessive tendencies. She tends to be precise if not perfectionistic ($FQ+ = 2$; $P = 9$). As expected, her perceptions of stimuli were accurate and conventional ($X+\% = .74$; $F+\% = 1.00$).

Mrs. C's record contains an unexpectedly high number of Special Scores ($Sum6 = 13$), particularly for an individual who has accomplished as much as she has. A review of the responses containing special scores suggests that most reflect immaturity rather than thought disorder or cognitive slippage. For example, many deviant verbalizations (DVs) seem somewhat adolescent in nature, such as calling material "fabricky" in both Response 1 and Response 12, describing a cat as "smooshed" on Response 13, or calling the color tone of buttocks "pinky" in Response 22. Similarly, the INCOM on Response 2 also has an immature quality (a flying elephant). Other responses involving Special Scores suggest that strong affective reactions may contribute to distortions in cognitive processing, especially when anger is involved (Response 6 and Response 27). The presence of two $M-$ responses suggests that Mrs. C is likely to have faulty judgment or errors in decision making. Overall, there were no indications of a current psychotic disorder, nor were there any indicators of a risk for a psychotic decompensation.

Comment

Neither the MMPI-2 codetype nor the Rorschach data are suggestive of an Axis I affective disorder, although the *46/64* codetype and the Rorschach both describe Mrs. C as experiencing depression, worry, and anger. The Rorschach more than the MMPI-2 describes a vulnerability to becoming preoccupied with and overwhelmed by intense, transient emotional reactions.

Both the MMPI-2 and the Rorschach agree in describing Mrs. C as presenting with significant dependent and passive–aggressive personality features. The degree of angry resentment that colors her affective reactions and interpersonal relationships is clear in both tests. However, the MMPI-2 more clearly than the Rorschach identifies passive–aggressive characteristics and the ways in which indirect expression of resentment contribute to a pattern of interpersonal difficulties. These MMPI-2 findings suggest that the aggression seen on the Rorschach is more likely to be expressed in an indirect fashion, than directly. Furthermore, both tests agree in describing Mrs. C as sensitive to feeling hurt, ignored, neglected, and unfairly mistreated by others. Her Rorschach responses help one understand the reasons for this given her perceptions that relationships are inevitably one-sided rather than mutual.

Although both tests identify Mrs. C as seeking attention and approval from others, the Rorschach brings into focus her need to please others and win their approval; the extent to which she acts in a compliant, submissive fashion; and her efforts to conceal reactions she fears others will disapprove of. Furthermore, the Rorschach reveals her desire to be able to depend on someone who is active, decisive, and in charge.

Both the MMPI-2 and Rorschach found that feelings of shame and self-criticism were important features of Mrs. C's current emotional state. However, the two tests focused on different aspects of her self-image. The MMPI-2 suggests that she feels ashamed of her anger and therefore tries to suppress, ignore, and conceal angry reactions, as she does not want other to conclude she is a hostile, resentful person. Her responses to the Rorschach add a different dimension by suggesting that she also experiences conflicts about her body image, physical appearance, and sexuality.

MMPI-2–Rorschach Integration

Mrs. C responded to the MMPI-2 and Rorschach in an open, honest way. There was no indication that a self-favorable or a self-critical response set biased her responses. However, the pattern of her responses suggests she may lack insight into herself (WNL MMPI-2 profile).

In general, Mrs. C has the psychological resources needed to tolerate stress and to manage difficult, unexpected, negative situations with self-restraint, deliberation, and self-control rather than impulsivity ($AdjD = +2$). In other words, she generally has sufficient ego strength to weather life's ups and downs. The test data provide no evidence for a current diagnosis of an affective disorder. At present, however, Mrs. C's ability to handle the stress she experiences is compromised. She appears to be chronically vulnerable to brief, transient, but disruptive episodes of intense emotional distress during which she is flooded by a mixture of sadness, anger, worry, and self-criticism (*46/64*; *C', Y, m, V*; *DEPI* = 5; Color Shading Blends). During these episodes, she can be overwhelmed by a sense of anxious helplessness and feels defenseless and powerless ($Y = 7$). She may also be bothered by decreased energy, lack of drive, and difficulties with motivation (scale *9*).

Mrs. C does not handle emotions in a consistent manner. Sometimes her reactions are dominated by logic and reason, whereas at other times, her reactions and behavior are driven by feelings (*EB* = 9:7.5). She has the capacity to delay before responding and to carefully plan and deliberately carry out coping strategies in a logical, reasonable, controlled manner (*M* = 9; *FC:CF+C* = 7:4). She can also be careful, precise, and obsessive, if not perfectionistic, in her approach to tasks (*FQ+* = 2; *P* = 9). These characteristics are important assets in her success at work, as she may be very effective in planning and carrying out assignments in a rational, deliberate manner. In these situations, she does not allow her feelings to sway her assessments of a situation or to influence her behavior.

At other times, however, Mrs. C is extremely emotional and has a tendency to overreact to situations (*Afr* = .93; *Sum C* = 11). She can be excessively involved with and overwhelmed by affect; in other words, feelings, rather than reason or logic, often flood her awareness and dominate her reactions (*Lambda* = .17). This suggests that Mrs. C may have strong reactions to psychotherapy sessions when she becomes aware of and focuses on upsetting emotions she typically avoids and then becomes preoccupied with and overwhelmed by intense feelings of sadness, anger, helplessness, and powerlessness.

Mrs. C's involvement with others is shaped by two major factors, her anger (*COP* = 0; *AG* = 4) and a passive-dependent orientation (*Ma:Mp* = 3:6). She expects hostility will be a core aspect of all interpersonal interactions and that relationships with others will not be mutual. She does not view others as whole, real, separate people but as part-objects who exist to fulfill the needs of one another (*H:(H)Hd(Hd)*). She seems to anticipate that in any relationship, one person's needs will be gratified whereas their partner's needs are ignored or frustrated, and therefore expects that tensions, conflicts, and struggles will occur concerning whose needs will be met and who will be disappointed and deprived. This model for relationships may have been learned by observing her parents' marital relationship. As a result, she is likely to focus on how she has been hurt, neglected, mistreated, or ignored by others, particularly family members, and is quite sensitive to feeling criticized, rejected, and slighted (*46/64*). She can be quite insistent that others respond to her and is "primed" to react in an angry, demanding manner when she feels they have not (*46/64*; *AG* = 4; *PER* = 3). At the same time, she is likely to feel unfairly burdened if others makes requests or demands of her.

Although Mrs. C frequently feels angry, resentful, and irritable, she tries to suppress, ignore, and conceal anger as she views anger as shameful and does not want others to think she is a resentful, hostile person. As a result, she may not be aware of the intensity of her hurt and angry feelings (*46/64*). She typically expresses anger in indirect, passive ways that others may find difficult to deal with. Her passive–aggressive maneuvers may provoke angry attacks and retaliations by others. As she is not aware of how her indirect expressions of anger affect others, Mrs. C is likely to feel they continually treat her unfairly, which adds to her resentment.

Mrs. C's involvements with others are also colored by her passive-dependent style (*Ma:Mp* = 3:6). She retreats from responsibility, avoids handling difficult situations independently, and responds to unpleasant situations by withdrawing into fantasy rather than taking direct action. This may contribute to her assuming a submissive, dependent role with others. Although she has the psychological resources to handle most stressful situations on her own, when difficulties arise, she wishes a strong, decisive, capable individual would take charge, so she can follow their directions in a compliant, submissive manner, rather than having to cope with the unpleasant situation on her own. She doubts herself, finds it difficult to make decisions without approval and reassurance from others, and has problems initiating independent action. One may speculate that Mrs. C is likely to become frustrated and resentful if she feels that others, such as her husband or therapist, do not take charge and provide the kind of direction, reassurance, and guidance she desires.

Mrs. C seems to be quite aware of how others view her, whether they approve or disapprove of her actions, and tries to behave in line with their expectations (Populars = 9). In other words, she may try to win others' approval by being compliant. Mrs. C's sensitivity to others and her ability to find ways to please them may be important assets in her professional role, which involves developing relationships with clients who can be difficult and demanding and maintaining those relationships when her clients are upset or unhappy. Her need to please others may also result in an attempt to cover over and conceal aspects of herself she is afraid others will disapprove of, such as feelings of resentment when her dependency needs are frustrated (Cg = 5). Mrs. C's submissive, compliant approach to interpersonal interactions may be viewed as a repetition of her childhood efforts to elicit approval from her mother by acting in ways that pleased mother and avoiding actions that displeased her, efforts that may have interfered with development of age-appropriate autonomy.

Mrs. C's self-image is colored by guilt, shame, and self-criticism (V = 2; MOR = 4). One important component of her current emotional distress involves these negative, punitive reactions to herself. Her negative self-image is not based on a realistic appraisal of her strengths and weaknesses but instead reflects a distorted view of herself ($H:(H)Hd(Hd)$ = 2:10), particularly in terms of her body image and conflicts concerning sexuality. As noted previously, feelings of guilt and shame may also be related to fears about how others will react if she expresses anger.

Mrs. C's concerns about body image are not unexpected given the history of conflicts concerning her appearance so as not to displease her mother, conflicts about her weight, and binging on sweets as a reaction to being upset. Her responses also suggest conflicts about sexuality, a negative image of herself as a woman, and, perhaps, a revulsion and abhorrence of female sexuality (Sx = 6; FV; content). It is likely that Mrs. C's negative feelings about herself as a woman developed as a result of an identification with her mother, a woman who seemed to disapprove of being feminine and discouraged looking attractive. One might also speculate that Mrs. C avoided heterosexual involvements by dressing in an unflattering manner and remaining overweight because of fears that her mother would angrily reject and disapprove of her if Mrs. C attracted more attention from males, including her father, than mother received. That is, Mrs. C may have been afraid that mother would be furious if Mrs. C were more attractive than she.

Mrs. C's perceptions of stimuli were accurate and conventional ($X+\%$ = .74; $F+\%$ = 1.00). There were no indications of cognitive slippage or thought disorder, although an immature quality did make some responses sound strained. Overall, there were no indications of a risk for a psychotic decompensation.

The test data contained no warnings suggestive of a current risk for suicide (S-CON; MMPI-2 items). However, the degree to which Ms. C becomes preoccupied with and overwhelmed by negative emotions suggests suicidal ideation may intrude into her thoughts when intense feelings of sadness, angry resentment, helplessness, powerlessness, and shame are triggered. Although she generally possesses sufficient ego strength to control her emotions and behavior, her self-control may be decreased during these brief episodes of intense distress.

Diagnostic Impression

DSM–III–R   Axis IV   61.1 Partner relational problem

    Axis II   301.9 Personality disorder NOS, with dependent
        and passive–aggressive features

TREATMENT RECOMMENDATIONS

Mrs. C is likely to present a challenge in psychotherapy in several respects. First, given Mrs. C's social sensitivity and need to please others, it is very likely that she will be quite sensitive to how her therapist reacts to her and will automatically try to conform to perceived expectations. She may be quite uncomfortable exposing information about her behavior, history, and feelings for fear that the therapist will judge her negatively. The therapist should be alert to the possibility that Mrs. C is saying and doing the "right" things in therapy rather than honestly expressing herself. For instance, Mrs. C may attempt to conceal negative, angry reactions for fear the therapist would disapprove of her and is likely to feel ashamed of herself if she does express anger.

The therapist should expect that during the course of treatment, Mrs. C will feel disappointed and frustrated with the therapist's neutrality and demand that the therapist take charge, make decisions for her, and be directive. For instance, in her efforts to elicit a relationship in which she can be compliant with the therapist's authority, Mrs. C may act in a helpless manner or repeatedly, insistently, and resentfully demand that the therapist make decisions and assume responsibility for the success of the treatment. Rather than complying with these demands or reacting to Mrs. C's resentment, the therapist should be prepared to explore and interpret these transference reactions to aid Mrs. C in increasing her ability to use her resources more effectively and to act more independently.

Mrs. C's manner of managing and defending against affect will be a major consideration in psychotherapy. As described previously, she tends to deal with conflict by suppressing negative feelings and avoiding thinking about disturbing problems. This may contribute to a lack of insight concerning the reasons for and the effects of her behavior. However, when Mrs. C becomes aware of her reactions she may become preoccupied with and overwhelmed by intense, disturbing emotions. This suggests the following. On a practical level, the therapist should refrain from bringing up new, emotionally charged issues towards the end of sessions and should make a deliberate effort to assist Mrs. C in achieving closure on emotionally charged issues within a session. The therapist should also attempt to activate Mrs. C's observing ego and the rational, reasonable side of herself when dealing with disturbing, emotionally charged issues.

As described previously, several issues are likely to be central in terms of understanding Mrs. C's marital difficulties. These include her passive-dependent, submissive, compliant role in relationships and passive-aggressive reactions when her needs are frustrated. She is unlikely to be aware of the extent of her anger, how she typically expresses anger indirectly, and how her actions affect others. She could benefit from learning to express anger more appropriately. Mrs. C's expectations about relationships should also be examined. For instance, she might assess whether her expectation that she must be prepared to fight to insure her needs will be responded to is realistic or should be modified. It is possible that these issues could be addressed most directly in marital therapy, which can take place concurrently with the ongoing individual therapy.

12 Case 7: Perpetrator of a Sexual Homicide

Mr. T is a 24-year-old, White male charged with the first degree murder of a 68-year-old widow. The murder occurred during an attempted robbery. Mr. T stabbed his victim 58 times with a butcher knife and had sexual relations with her. He confessed to this crime and is currently incarcerated while awaiting trial. There is no history of previous criminal activity, arrests, or violence. A psychological evaluation was requested by his attorney to assess his competence to stand trial, the presence of psychopathology that could be used to aid in his defense, and, given his bizarre behavior during the crime, to attempt to understand the psychological reasons for this brutal murder.

BACKGROUND INFORMATION

Information concerning Mr. T's developmental history was obtained by reviewing school records, medical records, transcripts of interviews with teachers and family members, as well as a clinical interview.

Developmental History.   Mr. T was born and raised on a small farm. He is the youngest in a sibship of five, with two older brothers and two older sisters. His father worked as a truck mechanic at a local truck stop until he lost his job and subsequently never worked off the family farm. Father drank alcohol on a regular basis before losing his job, and his alcohol consumption increased after he lost his job. He eventually developed cirrhosis of the liver as the result of long-term alcohol abuse. He supported the family by selling vegetables and livestock. According to Mr. T, his father was frequently verbally abusive towards family members but was never physically abusive towards the children, although he did slap his wife on several occasions. Father died of cancer when Mr. T was 18.

According to educational records, Mr. T was identified as having learning problems and low academic functioning in grade school. An evaluation by a school psychologist found his intellectual abilities to be in the low average range with significant delays in all areas of academic functioning. As a result, he was placed in a learning disabilities (LD) program. He made slow but steady gains in acquisition of academic performance during his involvement in a highly structured program. There was no history of behavior problems in school. His teachers described Mr. T as withdrawn, passive, and immature in comparison to children his age and as having few friends. He was frequently teased by classmates who made him the butt of their jokes. Although Mr. T's teacher advised his parents that he could benefit from psychotherapy, they did not make any arrangements for this. He continued in LD classes through high school and earned a high school degree.

After graduating high school, Mr. T worked at unskilled jobs. He was employed at the time of his arrest. He described himself as a loner who rarely saw others outside of his family. He made little effort to socialize or develop friendships.

During his childhood, Mr. T had a positive relationship with his maternal grandfather who was described as the only adult who consistently provided support and affection. Unfortunately, this grandfather died when Mr. T was 15. At his grandfather's funeral, Mr. T fell to the ground, appeared to lose consciousness, and exhibited jerky, uncontrolled movements. He was admitted to a local hospital where he reported sporadic tingling and numbness in his extremities and poor motor coordination. For example, he dropped silverware when eating and walked unsteadily. Two episodes of apparent loss of consciousness occurred in the emergency room. He had no memory for these episodes. A complete neurological evaluation was conducted to assess whether his condition was caused by a seizure disorder. The results of a CT scan, EEG, and neurologic evaluation were normal, and his symptoms were eventually attributed to anxiety, grief, and hyperventilation. Although follow-up with a mental health professional was recommended, Mr. T's mother insisted that her son's problems were caused by a physical illness and refused to believe that emotional variables had any bearing on his condition. As a result, there was no follow-up with a mental health professional. No further episodes of seizure-like activity were reported.

Mr. T reported being quite unhappy about the way he was treated by his oldest brother, who had assumed responsibility for running the family farm after their father's death. Mr. T felt that his brother, Timothy, constantly put him down and insulted him. When Mr. T protested about the amount of work expected of him in addition to paying room and board out of his salary, Timothy yelled at him, pushed him to the ground, and threatened to kick him. After this, Mr. T began saving money to move into his own apartment.

When he turned 19, Mr. T told his mother about his plan to get an apartment. Mother threatened to disown him if he left the family farm and did not obey Timothy. Several days later mother found Mr. T sitting in his bedroom holding a knife to his forehead. He was taken to a hospital emergency room and then admitted to an inpatient psychiatric unit because of suicidal ideation, anxiety, and depression. Hospital staff reported that he developed tremors and hyperventilated following a visit with mother and Timothy. The unit staff concluded that his distress was related to a conflict between his desire to leave home and fear that his family would reject him if he left home. His thinking was also described as having a "paranoid flavor."

During a family session, mother threatened never to speak to Mr. T again if he moved away from the farm and into his own apartment. She also expressed anger at him for "airing our dirty laundry in public." During this hospitalization, there were several instances in which he complained of feeling dizzy and "passing out." A neurological consultation was obtained, and no evidence of a neurological disorder was found. He was treated with medications including antidepressant (Desyrel), antianxiety (Xanax), and antipsychotic (Prolixin) medications. He was discharged after 10 days following improvement in mood and after suicidal ideation diminished. He returned to live at home and did not follow through on a recommendation for outpatient psychotherapy and treatment with psychotropic medications.

History of the Murder. Mr. T continued living at home until age 21 when he married. He and his wife argued frequently, and she often threatened to leave him. They eventually agreed to seek a divorce but decided to continue sharing the house they were renting until the end of the lease. Mr. T and his wife also agreed to start dating other people while they lived together. He commented that he knew his wife had become attracted to another man when her cat stopped sitting in his lap. During the time they lived together, Mr. T presented to a hospital emergency room with complaints of chest pain, numbness on the left side of his body, and transient episodes of slurred speech. A CT scan of the head obtained to rule out a CVA was normal, and other medical causes for this condition were ruled out. A psychiatric consultation was requested. The psychiatrist described Mr. T as worried, anxious, and depressed about his marital problems and recommended treatment with Xanax and Desyrel and outpatient psychotherapy. Mr. T did not follow up with treatment. Shortly after this the lease expired, and he and his wife separated.

Within a month after moving into a boarding house, Mr. T began dating a woman he knew from high school. They saw each other daily and started to talk about living together until her minister cautioned her about being involved with a married man. She was alarmed by her minister's admonitions and decided to curtail any involvement with Mr. T until his divorce was finalized. She agreed to continue seeing him when he explained that he had not been able to hire a lawyer because of financial problems but sincerely intended to do so when he saved enough money. However, she refused to resume their sexual relationship because he was still married and she did not want to commit a sin. This led to several heated arguments, including arguments on the day before and the evening of the murder.

On the day of the murder, Mr. T spent the afternoon and early evening drinking alcohol with a cousin who shared his half gram of cocaine, a drug Mr. T had used infrequently before. He estimated he consumed about 12–14 beers that day. His girlfriend joined Mr. T and his cousin after she got off work. During the evening, Mr. T and his girlfriend had a fight after he repeatedly asked her to sleep with him. During the fight, she threatened to end their relationship if he did not obtain a divorce. He convinced her not to leave him, and they wound up hugging one another and pledging their love for each other.

After his girlfriend went home, Mr. T continued to drink while he tried to figure out how to get the money he needed for his divorce. He remembered that a widow, who was known to be financially well off, lived a block from his cousin's house. He thought of a plan to rob her and immediately decided to carry this plan out. Mr. T walked to the woman's house, rang the bell, and asked if he could use her phone to call a tow truck. She recognized Mr. T and allowed him in. Mr. T then claimed to smell gas in the house and volunteered to check whether there was a gas leak in the basement. While they were in the basement, Mr. T demanded that the widow give him money. She told Mr. T she had no cash in the house but assured him she would withdraw money from the bank for him the next morning. Mr. T became frightened that she was going to call the police and began hitting her. He stated he does not recall any of the subsequent events.

Records of the murder concluded that Mr. T forced the victim upstairs and into her bathroom as he beat her. At one point, he left her in the bathtub, went into the kitchen, got a knife, and then began stabbing her. The police records showed he stabbed her 58 times. After this, he apparently undressed and sexually assaulted her. The police believe he was undressed during the sexual assault as there was no blood on his clothes. He then dressed and left the house without looking for money in her purse or in furniture drawers. No property was taken.

Mr. T was arrested after police matched a footprint at the murder scene with his footprint. He confessed to attempting to rob the victim, although he claimed that he did not recall the actual murder.

Mr. T denied having auditory or visual hallucinations prior to being arrested. There is no history of previous criminal activity nor of previous violent behavior.

Mr. T was evaluated by a prison psychiatrist shortly after he was incarcerated. His affect was described as tense, worried, and depressed with some agitation. Several days later, Mr. T complained of headaches, dizziness, and tingling in his chest and arms, as well as sadness and worry. Medical evaluation revealed no physical cause for these complaints. At that point, the psychiatrist began treatment with Xanax. A week after being taken into custody, Mr. T reported difficulties with sleeping because of hearing voices. When asked about these voices, he reported hearing the voice of the murdered woman crying out for him to stop and commented that he began hearing the voices the day after the murder. As a result, treatment with a low dose of Haldol was initiated on a PRN basis. The auditory hallucinations were reported to continue, and so a week later, daily treatment with Haldol was started, and the dose was increased. However, a guard reported overhearing Mr. T boast that he was going to beat the charges against him by acting "crazy." This medication regimen was in effect when this psychological evaluation was conducted 4 months after the murder.

DIAGNOSTIC CONSIDERATIONS

Malingering.   The first issue to be addressed involves Mr. T's truthfulness in reporting symptoms of psychological disturbance, particularly because a guard claims to have heard Mr. T boast about feigning mental illness. Although the issue of truthfulness as opposed to dissimulation should be considered in any clinical encounter, assessment of response bias is particularly important when individuals are involved in the legal system as powerful incentives may motivate persons to deliberately attempt to deceive the psychologist who evaluates them (Rogers, 1988). For instance, one person may attempt to create an extremely favorable impression by denying problems if his or her mental health is at issue in a child custody dispute, whereas another person may be motivated to exaggerate or fabricate psychological problems to obtain some payoff, such as an award for emotional damages or a reduced sentence for a criminal offense. In this case, a psychological disorder could potentially be used as the basis for a plea of not guilty by reason of insanity or, if Mr. T is convicted of murder, to attempt to avoid the death penalty.

The MMPI validity scales were developed specifically to identify efforts by individuals either to fake-bad or fake-good. Schretlen (1988) reviewed the use of psychological tests to identify deliberate attempts to malinger symptoms of mental disorders and endorsed the MMPI validity scales for this purpose. Ziskin and Faust (1988), who are quite critical of the assessment methods used by mental health professionals in general, also concluded that MMPI validity scales effectively and objectively detect malingering. Berry et al. (1991) reviewed the effectiveness of standard MMPI validity scales to detect malingering and concluded that "MMPI-based scales for detecting faking are quite good at separating groups of subjects known or suspected of malingering from those completing the inventory honestly" (p. 594). In addition to the F scale, they examined the utility of the F minus K index (Gough, 1947), the Dissimulation scale (Ds; Gough, 1954), and Obvious minus Subtle scales (Wiener, 1948). Berry et al. found that the F scale was the strongest variable discriminating between groups of honest and malingering subjects, followed closely by the original Ds and $F - K$ indices. Much lower effect sizes were found for the revised Ds scale and the Obvious minus Subtle scales. Berry et al. concluded that the F scale, original Ds scale, and $F - K$ index are "currently the indices of choice for identifying malingering" (p. 594).

The original MMPI validity scales were modified and expanded when the MMPI was revised and the MMPI-2 created (Butcher et al., 1989). A parallel scale designed to complement the F scale, items of which appear only in the first half of the MMPI-2, was developed to detect deviant responses for the last half of the MMPI-2. Two scales were developed to identify inconsistency in responding, the Variable Response Inconsistency Scale (*VRIN*; Butcher et al., 1989), designed to detect inconsistency due to random responding, and the True Response Inconsistency scale (*TRIN*; Butcher et al., 1989), designed to detect inconsistent responding to items with similar content. Several studies have demonstrated that standard and new MMPI-2 validity scales are sensitive to malingering and random responding (Wetter et al., 1992; Wetter et al., 1993). Rogers, Bagby, and Chakraborty (1993) cautioned, however, that the MMPI-2 validity indices may be most effective in detecting naive malingerers, whereas persons knowledgeable about how to malinger a particular disorder may evade detection. Overall, the existing literature indicates that MMPI-2 validity indices, particularly the F scale, should be carefully examined when questions of malingering are at issue.

No validity indices parallel to the MMPI-2 validity scales have been developed for the Rorschach. Relatively little information has been paid to the possibility that exaggerated or defensive response sets could influence responses to the Rorschach, perhaps because of a belief that the Rorschach is impervious to conscious distortion. This belief appears to be based on the general assumption that the Rorschach taps unconscious psychological processes that, by definition, are not consciously controlled and therefore cannot be intentionally and deliberately manipulated. However, the results of empirical research show that this assumption is inaccurate. Exner (1991), for instance, pointedly dismissed the premise that the Rorschach stimuli are ambiguous (pp. 100–104) and that responses to the Rorschach are impervious to conscious control (pp. 111–116).

No firm conclusions have been reached regarding the effects malingering has on the Rorschach (Exner, 1991; Perry & Kinder, 1990). Ganellen et al. (1996) compared Rorschach protocols of two groups of subjects with a high incentive to malinger, persons accused of committing serious crimes waiting for trial. Subjects were assigned to honest and malingered groups on the basis of the scores they obtained on traditional MMPI validity scales. The Rorschach protocols of these two groups were compared to assess how successfully the malingerers could deliberately produce records that appeared psychotic on empirically derived Rorschach indices of psychosis. Despite an attempt to portray themselves as psychotic, subjects in the malingered group did not differ from honest responders on Rorschach variables of psychosis, including the $SCZI$, $X + \%$, $X- \%$, $Xu \%$, Populars, and Special scores. Although these results suggest that the malingering group was unable to deliberately produce Rorschach responses suggesting psychosis, Netter and Viglione (1994) found that subjects instructed to malinger schizophrenia who had been given information about the major symptoms and features of schizophrenia did produce a positive $SCZI$.

The results of these studies suggest the following: (a) The Rorschach is not efficient at detecting malingering; (b) subjects naive about a particular disorder are unlikely to be able to produce a Rorschach protocol consistent with that disorder, although (c) subjects knowledgeable about a disorder may be able to generate Rorschach responses consistent with that disorder.

Antisocial Personality Disorder.   Although not asked explicitly, one important question to consider is whether Mr. T's presentation is consistent with a diagnosis of antisocial personality disorder (APD). According to the *DSM-IV*, a diagnosis of antisocial personality disorder can be made only if there is a history of a conduct disorder with onset before the age of 15 followed by a history after age 15 of an attitude of callous disregard for and violation of the rights of others. For instance, individuals with antisocial personality disorder have histories of unlawful behavior, lying or conning others, impulsivity, irritability and aggression, irresponsibility, and a lack of remorse for their actions.

Although not developed specifically to match *DSM-IV* criteria for antisocial personality disorder, psychological test data can be useful in identifying persons who have many of the characteristics of this personality disorder. For instance, an elevation on MMPI-2 scale *4*, particularly a Spike 4 or a *49/94* profile, suggests a person is angry, impulsive, egocentric, emotionally shallow, nonconforming, irresponsible, resentful of authority figures, and interpersonally manipulative. This is particularly likely to be true if scale *4* is driven by conflicts with authority figures (*Pd2*), rather than dissatisfaction with family (*Pd1*). Similarly, an elevation on the MMPI-2 antisocial practices (ASP) content scale is associated with a history of behavioral problems and antisocial actions.

Many of the characteristics of the antisocial personality disorder described are also directly relevant to specific Rorschach variables. For instance, impulsivity may be manifested on Rorschach variables related to control (*D* score) and modulation of affect (*FC:CF* + *C*), whereas a lack of concern for the welfare of others may be apparent on Rorschach variables related to interpersonal relatedness, such as a lack of attachment (*T* = 0) or a view of others as part-objects existing to serve the needs of the antisocial individual rather than as real, separate people who have their own needs and desires (*H*<(*H*) + *Hd* + (*Hd*)).

These speculations concerning Rorschach data of antisocial personality disorder have been empirically examined in a series of studies of prison inmates (Gacono & Meloy, 1994). Gacono and Meloy presented Rorschach data for a sample of male inmates incarcerated in forensic hospitals and prisons meeting *DSM–III–R* criteria for Antisocial Personality Disorder. Consistent with predictions, this sample showed poor ability to modulate affect (*FC:CF* + *C* = 1:3 vs. the expected 2:1 ratio) with a higher than expected potential for uncontrolled emotional outbursts (*C* ≥ 1). Furthermore, the APD inmates view interpersonal relationships as lacking in mutuality (COP < 2), look at others as part-objects rather than whole-objects (*H:(H)* + *Hd* + *(Hd)* = 2.17:2.66 rather than 2:1), and more frequently than nonpatients approach others with mistrust and suspicion (*T* = 0). Unexpectedly, most of the APD inmates did not show *D* scores < 0, a marker of a chronic vulnerability to poor self-control and impulsivity. Gacono and Meloy suggested that the APD sample's criminal behavior may be related to a limited capacity to foresee future consequences (Lambda) and impaired reality testing and judgment (*X* + % < .70; *X* − %; *M* − > 0), rather than to chronic impulsivity.

MMPI-2 Data

Validity. The MMPI-2 validity scales show that Mr. T endorsed a moderate number of items related to unusual experiences associated with psychopathology (*F* = 79). The level of elevation on *F* is within the range

MMPI-2™
Minnesota Multiphasic Personality Inventory-2

Profile for Basic Scales

Minnesota Multiphasic Personality Inventory-2
Copyright © by THE REGENTS OF THE UNIVERSITY OF MINNESOTA
1942, 1943 (renewed 1970), 1989 This Profile Form 1989.
All rights reserved. Distributed exclusively by NATIONAL COMPUTER SYSTEMS, INC.
under license from The University of Minnesota.

"MMPI-2" and "Minnesota Multiphasic Personality Inventory-2" are trademarks owned by
The University of Minnesota. Printed in the United States of America.

Name _____ Mr. T. _____

Address _____

Occupation ____ Education __12__ Age __24__ Marital Status __Divorced__

Referred By _____

MMPI-2 Code _____

Scorer's Initials _____

Date Tested __/__/__

MALE

	L	F	K	Hs+.5K	D	Hy	Pd+.4K	Mf	Pa	Pt+1K	Sc+1K	Ma+.2K	Si
Raw Score	6	14	12	10	26	30	24	21	15	22	29	21	40
K to be Added				6			5			12	12	2	
Raw Score with K				16			29			34	41	23	

? Raw Score 0

Raw Score 2

Case 7 MMPI-2 Content and Supplementary Scales

	Raw Score	T Score
FB	18	115
True Response Inconsistency (TRIN)	12	72
Variable Response Inconsistency (VRIN)	12	76
Anxiety	23	68
Repression	17	54
MAC-R	23	53
Ego Strength (Es)	27	30
Dominance (Do)	12	35
Social Responsibility (Re)	16	40
Overcontrolled Hostility (O-H)	14	55
PTSD - Keane (PK)	15	62
PTSD - Schlenger (PS)	23	66
Addiction Potential (APS)	28	63
Addiction Admission (AAS)	6	65
Content Scales (Butcher et al., 1990)		
Anxiety (ANX)	15	72
Fears (FRS)	9	67
Obsessiveness (OBS)	5	50
Depression (DEP)	15	70
Health Concerns (HEA)	12	66
Bizarre Mentation (BIZ)	6	63
Anger (ANG)	5	48
Cynicism (CYN)	11	51
Antisocial Practices (ASP)	11	55
Type A (TPA)	4	41
Low Self-Esteem (LSE)	13	72
Social Discomfort (SOD)	15	65
Depression Subscales (Harris-Lingoes)		
Subjective Depression (D1)	14	69
Psychomotor Retardation (D2)	6	54
Physical Malfunctioning (D3)	5	67
Mental Dullness (D4)	5	62
Brooding (D5)	3	57
Hysteria Subscales (Harris-Lingoes)		
Denial of Social Anxiety (Hy1)	4	51
Need for Affection (Hy2)	5	43
Lassitude-Malaise (Hy3)	7	66
Somatic Complaints (Hy4)	7	72
Inhibition of Aggression (Hy5)	5	63

	Raw Score	T Score
Psychopathic Deviate Subscales (Harris-Lingoes)		
Familial Discord (Pd1)	3	51
Authority Problems (Pd2)	5	62
Social Imperturbability (Pd3)	6	64
Social Alienation (Pd4)	11	90
Self-Alienation (Pd5)	5	58
Paranoia Subscales (Harris-Lingoes)		
Persecutory Ideas (Pa1)	4	64
Poignancy (Pa2)	7	81
Naivete (Pa3)	3	41
Schizophrenia Subscales (Harris-Lingoes)		
Social Alienation (Sc1)	6	63
Emotional Alienation (Sc2)	3	59
Lack of Ego Mastery, Cognitive (Sc3)	6	77
Lack of Ego Mastery, Conative (Sc4)	5	65
Lack of Ego Mastery, Def. Inhib. (Sc5)	3	60
Bizarre Sensory Experiences (Sc6)	6	70
Hypomania Subscales (Harris-Lingoes)		
Amorality (Ma1)	2	50
Psychomotor Acceleration (Ma2)	6	53
Imperturbability (Ma3)	6	65
Ego Inflation (Ma4)	4	53
Social Introversion Subscales (Ben-Porath et al., 1989)		
Shyness/Self-Consciousness (Si1)	10	65
Social Avoidance (Si2)	7	67
Alienation -- Self and Others (Si3)	9	62

expected for patients who have psychological difficulties and provides no reason to suspect that Mr. T attempted to exaggerate, overreport, or fabricate problems. Thus, there were no signs of malingering. To the contrary, the elevation on *L* suggests that Mr. T tried to emphasize his virtues and minimize any flaws in a naive, unsophisticated manner. However, this interpretation of the *L* scale must be considered tentative given Mr. T's limited educational background and socioeconomic status.

Clinical Scales.   Mr. T's MMPI-2 profile is complicated with 6 clinical scales elevated over a *T*-score of 65. Of these, scale *3* and scale *8* are the two highest clinical scales. The profile thus interpreted as a *38/83* two-point code type. Because neither scale *4* nor Antisocial Practices (*ASP* = 55) are elevated, the MMPI-2 data provide no direct support for a diagnosis of an antisocial personality disorder.

The thinking and behavior of persons with a *38/83* codetype are often strange and peculiar. Mr. T is likely to experience difficulties in thinking, concentration, and memory that interfere with making even insignificant decisions. His ideas are likely to be unusual, unconventional, and illogical, and his speech may be marked by odd, loosely related connections among thoughts. This codetype is often associated with a psychotic disorder, most frequently schizophrenia, although this codetype is sometime produced by patients with a somatoform disorder. Some patients with this codetype have histories of brief, transient psychotic decompensations, such as what has been called an "hysterical psychotic episode" (Friedman et al., 1989; Trimboli & Kilgore, 1983).

The *38/83* code suggests Mr. T experiences considerable emotional turmoil, including anxiety, tension, and worry (*ANX* = 72). His outlook is sad, pessimistic, and hopeless (*DEP* = 70; *D1* = 69). Mr. T typically attempts to deny and repress problems that may cause him to respond in a vague or evasive manner when asked about difficulties and complaints. Emotional stress may be converted into physical symptoms for which no definite medical explanation is found, such as headaches, dizziness, musculoskeletal pain, numbness, weakness, blurred vision, or sleep disturbance (*HEA* = 66; *Hy4* = 72). These symptoms usually have an acute onset, occur suddenly, and subside without any specific medical treatment. He may also report feelings of unreality, such as depersonalization. These somatic symptoms do not bind his anxiety, but instead anxiety is temporarily displaced onto his physical problems that become a major focus of concern for a brief period of time before they are forgotten.

This profile suggests that Mr. T is rather immature and dependent and has an exaggerated need for attention and affection from others. However, he is shy and introverted and feels alienated, awkward, and socially anxious (scale *0* = 66; *SOD* = 65; *Pd4* = 90; *Si1* = 65; *Si2* = 67). He may keep a cautious distance from others because of fears about being rejected, embarrassed, or humiliated. When he does try to obtain affection from others, he does so in an awkward, childlike, immature manner that others might find strange and that can turn them off. It is likely that his unusual, unconventional thinking contributes to difficulties in communicating with others, both in terms of his ability to express himself to others and to understand what others say to him. This may cause considerable frustration and reinforce his tendency to withdraw from social involvement.

As noted previously, the *38/83* codetype is often associated with a psychotic decompensation. Greene (1991) noted that when a psychotic reaction occurs in a person with a *38/83* codetype, there is often a behavioral regression as well as infantile, narcissistic qualities. Trimboli and Kilgore (1983) and Friedman et al. (1989) also described a psychotic decompensation that involves behavioral regression and that may involve "brief, highly sexualized psychotic episodes, for which they have no memory later" (Friedman et al., 1989, p. 176).

Rorschach Data

Mr. T produced 20 Rorschach responses, which is within the expected range. The record appears valid for interpretation given the number of responses he produced, the amount of effort expended in responding ($Zf = 14$), and the absence of signs of defensiveness ($PER = 0$). The first positive key variable is the Schizophrenia Index ($SCZI = 4$). Although a positive *SCZI* indicates a strong likelihood the individual is schizophrenic or psychotic, false positives are most likely to occur when the *SCZI* is 4 as opposed to 5 or 6. Thus, interpretation of the positive *SCZI* should be handled with caution. Among Gacono and Meloy's sample of inmates with antisocial personality disorder, only 7% obtained a *SCZI* at this level.

When the *SCZI* is positive, the interpretive search strategy begins by examining the quality and effectiveness of the individual's thought processes. The *EB* indicates that Mr. T's characteristic problem-solving style is introversive ($EB = 6:2.5$). That is, he generally tries to minimize the extent to which feelings and intuition influence decisions and problem solving and instead relies on his thoughts and ideas. Mr. T's thinking is rigid and inflexible; it is quite difficult for him to alter an opinion once his mind is made up ($a:p = 9:2$). There were no signs of cognitive slippage or thought disorder that would suggest a current psychotic state ($Sum6 = 0$). One may question whether the absence of thought disorder can be explained by the current treatment with antipsychotic medication he is receiving. Although effective treatment with antipsychotic medication reduces psychotic symptoms, medication generally does not entirely eliminate all signs of thought disorder on the Rorschach.

Case 7   Rorschach Protocol

Card	Response	Inquiry
I	1. A bat. Flying in the air. Looking for s.t to eat.	E: (Rpts S's response) S: There. Whole big area. E: What reminded you of a bat? S: The way its wide. E: Flying in the air? S: Yeah.
	2. I d't k. E: Most p c more than 1 thing. S: I d.k. E: Take yr time. I'm sure y'll c s.t if u lk long enough. S: Like 2 p parachuting. (sighs) That's it.	E: (Rpts S's response) S: People there & there. Spreading & coming down. E: I'm not sure where y're lkg. S: There & there. E: People parachuting? S: Bec of the arms. E: Parachuting? S: Way they spread out when they're parachuting.
II	3. L.l s.o's head with a bloody lip.	E: (Rpts S's response) S: 2 eyes & mouth down here where its bleeding. E: Bleeding? S: There. It l.l blood. E: Blood? S: Bec its red.
	4. L.l 2 p holding hands.	E: (Rpts S's response) S: A hand, there & there. E: 2 people? S: Just the hands.
III	5. L.l 2 people holding hands. Dancing.	E: (Rpts S's response) S: 1 p here & here. They're holding hands. E: Dancing? S: Yeah. Way they're moving.
	6. L.l 2 horses. That's all I can get.	E: (Rpts S's response) S: There & there. E: Horses? S: I d.k. Just l.l horses. E: Show me. S: Way the head is. E: I'm not sure I c it. S: What do you mean? That's it. (sounds angry)

244

IV   7. L. a giant.   E: (Rpts S's response)
                                        S: Yeah. Here. The whole thing.
                                        E: Giant?
                                        S: Bec its r big. And wide.
                                        E: Big?
                                        S: I d.k! It j lks big!
                                        E: What abt the card makes it
                                        look big?
                                        S: The way it lks.
                                        E: I want to make sure I see it
                                        just like you do. Help me see
                                        the giant.
                                        S: The whole thing. 2 arms,
                                        legs, 2 feet.

      8. L.l a big person w big   E: (Rpts S's response)
      feet.   S: Yeah, bec here's the big feet.
                                        E: Big?
                                        S: Bec its r big.
                                        E: How does the card work to make
                                        it lk big?
                                        S: How does it what?
                                        E: What makes it l.l the person
                                        is big?
                                        S: It just lks big.

V   9. L.l a BF.   E: (Rpts S's response)
                                        S: The wings. And its little
                                        eyes. Feet.

      10. L.l an airplane.   E: (Rpts S's response)
      That's it.   S: Middle of it & 2 wings.

VI   11. L.l a jackhammer.   E: (Rpts S's response)
                                        S: There's the 2 handles of
                                        jackhammer & there's the
                                        jackhammer thing.
                                        E: Jackhammer thing?
                                        S: 2 handles & the bit.

      12. L.l s.o fell into a   E: (Rpts S's response)
      mud puddle. That's it.   S: Way it splashes.
                                        E: Splashes?
                                        S: Yeah.
                                        E: What l.l it splashes?
                                        S: Way its all spread out.
                                        E: Mud puddle?
                                        S: Bec its black, like the dirty
                                        water.
                                        E: U said u s.o fell.
                                        S: The way it is, 2 arms & feet.

245

VII 13. L.1 fried chicken.

E: (Rpts S's response)
S: Yeah, right here. L.1 a leg &
a thigh.
E: Fried?
S: Bec it l.1 the C of fried
chicken, the golden C. Way its
shaped.

14. L.1 a pair of people
parachuting. That's it.

E: (Rpts S's response)
S: Yeah, its spreading out.
There's the p there.
E: What gave that impression?
S: Way it spreads out. Feet.
E: Parachuting?
S: The way it spreads out.
E: U said its spreading out?
S: Its going in diff directions.

VIII 15. L.1 a little kid's C
book.

E: (Rpts S's response)
S: With all the diff C's all over
the place. That's it.

16. Then it l.1 2 big
A's, on the side. That's
it.

E: (Rpts S's response)
S: Right here & here.
E: A's?
S: Bec of that & that. Way
they're shaped.
E: Big?
S: Way they're walking, taking
big steps.

IX   17. L.1 a rib cage.

E: (Rpts S's response)
S: Here's ribs here & here.
E: I'm not sure I c it.
S: Bec the spine down the middle
& way it spreads out to the
sides.
E: Spreads out?
S: Way it goes in diff
directions. That's way out here,
that's way out here.

18. Like a car in an
accident. That's it.

E: (Rpts S's response)
S: Car here & pieces of car
flying all over the place.
E: What reminded u of that?
S: This l.1 a car here & diff
pieces of a car flying all over.

X   19. L.1 a whole bunch of
people gathering around a
picnic table, getting
ready to eat.

E: (Rpts S's response)
S: Here's a picnic table, here &
here & there's diff people
around.
E: Picnic table?

S: Way it lks.
E: Explain that.
S: Bec its long like a picnic
table.
E: People getting ready to eat.
S: Yeah. All around, these, diff
things. Getting ready to sit
down at table.

20. L.1 a whole bunch of
little kids, playing.
That's it.

E: (Rpts S's response)
S: Yeah. Here - all these diff
things, diff C's.
E: Little kids?
S: All diff little things, like
kids. 1 there, 1 there.

```
CASE07.R3==================== SEQUENCE OF SCORES =============================

CARD NO LOC  #  DETERMINANT(S)   (2) CONTENT(S)   POP Z  SPECIAL SCORES
======= ======  ================ === ==========  === =  ==============
  I  1 Wo   1  FMao                 A           P 1.0
     2 Do   2  Mao              2   H

 II  3 WS+  1  FC-                  Hd,Bl         4.5 MOR
     4 D+   4  Mpu              2   Hd            3.0

III  5 D+   1  Mao              2   H           P 3.0 COP
     6 Do   9  F-               2   A

 IV  7 Wo   1  Fo                   (H)         P 2.0
     8 Do   7  Fo                   H           P

  V  9 Wo'  1  Fo                   A           P 1.0
    10 Wo   1  Fu                   Sc            1.0

 VI 11 Wo   1  Fu                   Sc            2.5
    12 W+   1  ma.C'F-              Na,H          2.5

VII 13 Do   2  Fu                   Fd                  CP
    14 D+   1  Ma.mp-           2   H,Sc          1.0

VIII 15 Wv  1  C                    Art
    16 Do   1  FMao             2   A           P

 IX 17 Do   2  F-                   An
    18 W+   1  ma-                  Sc            5.5 MOR

  X 19 W+   1  Ma-                  H,Hh          5.5
    20 W+   1  Ma.FC-               H             5.5 COP


============================== SUMMARY OF APPROACH =============================

   I  :  W.D                        VI  :  W.W
  II  :  WS.D                      VII  :  D.D
 III  :  D.D                      VIII  :  W.D
  IV  :  W.D                        IX  :  D.W
   V  :  W.W                         X  :  W.W
```

248

```
CASE07.R3==================== STRUCTURAL SUMMARY ==============================

LOCATION                    DETERMINANTS              CONTENTS          S-CONSTELLATION
FEATURES              BLENDS              SINGLE                         NO..FV+VF+V+FD>2
                                                      H   = 6, 1         NO..Col-Shd Bl>0
Zf     = 13      m.C'F              M   = 4           (H) = 1, 0         YES..Ego<.31,>.44
ZSum   = 38.0    M.m                FM  = 2           Hd  = 2, 0         NO..MOR > 3
ZEst   = 41.5    M.FC               m   = 1           (Hd)= 0, 0         NO..Zd > +- 3.5
                                    FC  = 1           Hx  = 0, 0         NO..es > EA
W  = 11                             CF  = 0           A   = 4, 0         NO..CF+C > FC
  (Wv = 1)                          C   = 1           (A) = 0, 0         YES..X+% < .70
D  =  9                             Cn  = 0           Ad  = 0, 0         NO..S > 3
Dd =  0                             FC'= 0            (Ad)= 0, 0         NO..P < 3 or > 8
S  =  1                             C'F= 0            An  = 1, 0         NO..Pure H < 2
                                    C'  = 0           Art = 1, 0         NO..R < 17
   DQ                               FT  = 0           Ay  = 0, 0         2.....TOTAL
.........(FQ-)                      TF  = 0           Bl  = 0, 1
  +  =  8  ( 6)                     T   = 0           Bt  = 0, 0        SPECIAL SCORINGS
  o  = 11  ( 2)                     FV  = 0           Cg  = 0, 0                Lv1    Lv2
  v/+ =  0  ( 0)                    VF  = 0           Cl  = 0, 0        DV   = 0x1     0x2
  v  =  1  ( 0)                     V   = 0           Ex  = 0, 0        INC  = 0x2     0x4
                                    FY  = 0           Fd  = 1, 0        DR   = 0x3     0x6
                                    YF  = 0           Fi  = 0, 0        FAB  = 0x4     0x7
                                    Y   = 0           Ge  = 0, 0        ALOG = 0x5
       FORM QUALITY                 Fr  = 0           Hh  = 0, 1        CON  = 0x7
                                    rF  = 0           Ls  = 0, 0         Raw Sum6 =   0
       FQx  FQf  MQual  SQx         FD  = 0           Na  = 1, 0         Wgtd Sum6 =  0
  +  =   0    0     0     0         F   = 8           Sc  = 3, 1
  o  =   7    3     2     0                           Sx  = 0, 0        AB  = 0      CP  = 1
  u  =   4    3     1     0                           Xy  = 0, 0        AG  = 0      MOR = 2
  -  =   8    2     3     1                           Id  = 0, 0        CFB = 0      PER = 0
none =   1   --     0     0         (2) =  6                            COP = 2      PSV = 0

==================== RATIOS, PERCENTAGES, AND DERIVATIONS ====================

R = 20          L =  0.67              FC:CF+C = 2: 1     COP = 2    AG = 0
----------------------------------     Pure C  =    1     Food       = 1
EB = 6: 2.5  EA =  8.5  EBPer= 2.4     SumC':WSumC= 1:2.5 Isolate/R =0.10
eb = 5: 1    es =  6      D  =   0     Afr     =0.43      H:(H)Hd(Hd)= 7: 3
         Adj es =  4   Adj D =  +1     S       =   1      (HHd):(AAd)= 1: 0
----------------------------------     Blends:R= 3:20     H+A:Hd+Ad =12: 2
FM = 2  :  C'= 1  T = 0                CP      =   1
m  = 3  :  V = 0  Y = 0
                              P   = 6      Zf  =13        3r+(2)/R=0.30
a:p   =  9: 2  Sum6  =  0     X+% =0.35   Zd  = -3.5     Fr+rF  = 0
Ma:Mp =  5: 1  Lv2   =  0     F+% =0.38   W:D:Dd =11: 9: 0  FD  = 0
2AB+Art+Ay= 1  WSum6 =  0     X-% =0.40   W:M =11: 6     An+Xy  = 1
M-    =  3     Mnone =  0     S-% =0.13   DQ+ = 8        MOR    = 2
                             Xu% =0.20   DQv = 1

========================================================================
SCZI = 4*   DEPI = 2    CDI = 2    S-CON = 2    HVI = No   OBS = No
========================================================================
```

Mr. T responded to the obvious features of the test stimuli in a conventional fashion (Populars = 6), which suggests he understands conventional norms of social behavior. However, Mr. T's behavior may not conform to these rules because of difficulties with thinking, judgment, and reasoning, troubling findings for an individual who relies on his thought processes to size up a situation and formulate a plan of action to handle problems. His perceptions of events are markedly inaccurate and unrealistic, particularly in interpersonal contexts ($X + \% = .35$; $F + \% = .38$; $X - \% = .40$; $Xu\% = .20$; $M - = 3$). Significant difficulties with thinking exist that can interfere with sound, realistic decision making ($M - = 3$). In spite of his ability to act appropriately when expectations and standards of behavior are obvious ($P = 6$), these distortions and poor judgment contribute to a significant potential for inappropriate behavior.

The distortions in perception, thinking, and judgment described previously are related to the arbitrary way in which Mr. T characteristically approaches and analyzes events, rather than to a psychotic disorder. His "take" on a situation is based on a hasty, inefficient, and haphazard accounting of an event and a tendency to miss critical bits of information ($Zd = -3.5$). This inefficient approach to analyzing events causes him to misread the situation and to pay insufficient attention to relevant details. Most of his minus responses do not involve gross distortions of the card features, although he occasionally disregards specific stimulus features and instead responds in a global, impressionistic fashion (Responses 18, 19, and 20; $W > D + Dd$). He has limited ability to integrate and synthesize information and is likely to make errors when he tries to do so (6 minus responses with $DQ +$; 5 with W locations). Overall, these findings indicate a significant potential for Mr. T to make poor decisions, because he frequently does not notice important details and has difficulty integrating and accounting for relevant information in an accurate, realistic manner.

The search strategy continues by examining Mr. T's controls, the psychological resources he uses to cope with internal and external demands. The finding that the *Adj D* score is in the positive range suggests that Mr. T generally has sufficient resources to tolerate stress (*Adj D* = + 1). However, the high level of control suggested by a positive *Adj D* score is unexpected because EA, a measure of available psychological resources, is only in the average range (*EA* = 8.5 compared to the normative sample mean of 8.83). A review of the variables used to compute the *Adj D* score shows that the *Adj D* score is positive because of a low level of current emotional distress (*es* = 6), not because of greater than average ego strength. In spite of the average value of *es*, he appears to be currently anxious and worried (*m* = 3).

As noted previously, Mr. T's basic style is introversive, which indicates that feelings have less of an effect on his coping efforts than his thinking.

In most circumstances, he is able to control expressions of affect ($FC{:}CF +$ $C = 2{:}1$). However, a potential exists for lapses in self-control and for unrestrained and uninhibited discharges of emotion ($C = 1$). He tries to prevent losing control by avoiding or pulling back from affectively charged situations ($Afr = .43$).

An understanding of Mr. T's emotional state and control of affect must take into account the implications of the Color Projection response he produced ($CP = 1$), a rare response that occurs in only about 2% of the records of the normal population, 4% of inpatient depressives, and 1% of outpatients (Exner, 1993). Exner reported that the primary problems of patients who produced CP responses included psychosomatic symptoms, hysteroid approaches to dealing with affect, and depression. The therapists of these patients rated them as using denial as a defensive tactic significantly more often than other patients and as having problems modulating expression of emotions. The presence of the CP response suggests that Mr. T attempts to cope with emotional conflict and negative affect by refusing to acknowledge painful aspects of external reality, denying negative feelings, or substituting a false positive emotion for negative reactions, even if doing so means "bending reality." There were no indications of current sadness ($C' = 1$), self-criticism ($V = 0$), or anger ($S = 1$).

Mr. T's view of himself is negative, and he has a low estimate of self-worth (Egocentricity ratio $= .30$). He does not feel self-critical or guilty at present ($FV = 0$; $FD = 0$). Thus, there were no signs of regret or remorse for his actions. He has little capacity for introspection or self-reflection, which suggests he may be naive about himself ($FD = 0$). Review of the content of the two Morbid responses was notable for the rather dramatic response to Card IX (a car in an accident with pieces "flying all over the place"), which suggests a potential for a sudden, violent disintegration of his psychological organization.

Mr. T's approach to interpersonal relationships is characterized by marked conflicts and ambivalence about attachment ($T = 0$; Food $= 1$). In general, Mr. T does not perceive others as being reliable or trustworthy and so approaches relationships with caution and mistrust ($T = 0$). He is likely to be distant from most people and develops few relationships with others to whom he can turn to for emotional support, advice, and practical assistance when he experiences stress. At the same time, however, he has strong needs for attention, affection, and nurturance from others (Food $=$ 1). The strength of Mr. T's dependency needs is reinforced by the oral content of movement responses (Response 1 a bat searching for food; Response 19 people at a picnic getting ready to eat). Although he keeps a distance from most people, once he becomes attached to someone, he is likely to become quite dependent on him or her. It is interesting to note that the Food response occurred in combination with the CP response. One might speculate that this combination suggests he would react to a threat to his dependency needs by denying that problems exist, desperate attempts to convince himself everything will work out well, or by developing psycho-somatic symptoms.

Overall, in spite of the positive *SCZI*, these data are not consistent with schizophrenia given the absence of signs of cognitive slippage or thought disorder (*WSum6* = 0). Instead of suggesting a psychotic disorder, the *SCZI* is positive because of Mr. T's inaccurate perceptions of events and poor judgment.

Mr. T's protocol is not entirely consistent with Gacono and Meloy's (1994) description of Rorschach findings in antisocial personality disorder, as his affective modulation was generally adequate (*FC:CF* + *C* = 2:1); he viewed others as whole, real people (*H:(H)* + *Hd* + *(Hd)* = 7:3); and Lambda was within expected limits (.67). However, like Gacono and Meloy's sample, Mr. T did show signs of poor reality testing and judgment (*X* + % = .35: *X* − % = .40; *M* − = 3) and interpersonal detachment and distrust (*T* = 0).

Comment

The MMPI-2 and Rorschach match closely in several important respects. Both tests identify denial, repression, and somatization as Mr. T's primary defenses. Both describe him as reacting to stressful situations by converting emotional distress into somatic complaints that resemble a medical condition for which no physical cause can be found. This is consistent with the history of repeated presentations to physicians with symptoms suggestive of a physical disorder, such as epilepsy, a stroke, or a heart attack, although no explanation for these symptoms was found after thorough medical workups.

Both tests also converge in describing Mr. T as experiencing a conflict between strong, immature dependency needs and withdrawing from involvement with others because of considerable social discomfort. However, the MMPI-2 and Rorschach identify different sources for his interpersonal discomfort. The MMPI-2 emphasizes fears of being humiliated and embarrassed as the reason for this social discomfort, whereas the Rorschach portrays his discomfort as stemming from a basic mistrust of others.

Both the MMPI-2 and Rorschach raise significant concerns about whether Mr. T currently presents with a psychotic disorder. The *38/83* profile identifies his thinking as strange, peculiar, unconventional, and illogical, but leaves open the question of whether these characteristics indicate a psychotic disorder. Although similar concerns are raised by the Rorschach, the Rorschach protocol provides little evidence for a current psychotic disorder given the absence of responses involving cognitive slippage or overt thought disorder. Instead, the Rorschach suggests that the difficulties with thinking, inaccurate conclusions, and poor judgment are the result of his global, impressionistic approach to data; his tendency to scan the stimulus field hastily, inefficiently, and haphazardly; and his tendency to miss critical bits of information and cues about what has happened. However, the potential for him to generate inaccurate conclusions about situations and to display poor judgment are clearly reflected by both tests. Although no indications of a current psychotic disorder exist, both the MMPI-2 and Rorschach suggest a potential for a brief psychotic decompensation.

The MMPI-2 and Rorschach differ in their descriptions of Mr. T's emotional functioning. The MMPI-2 profile more clearly than the Rorschach suggests the presence of emotional turmoil, including anxiety, tension, and worry. Both tests also identify repression, denial, and somatization as primary defenses. The Rorschach augments these findings by identifying a vulnerability for lapses in self-control and for unrestrained, uninhibited, impulsive discharges of emotion.

MMPI-2–Rorschach Integration

Mr. T was able to read and understand test items and responded to them in a consistent and honest manner. The MMPI-2 validity scales gave no indications of an attempt to exaggerate, overreport, or fabricate problems and symptoms ($F = 80$). To the contrary, Mr. T may have tried to emphasize his virtues and minimize his flaws in a naive, unsophisticated manner ($L = 61$).

The pattern of Mr. T's responses suggest that his thinking and behavior are often strange and peculiar. He has difficulties in thinking, concentration, and memory that may interfere with making sound decisions, even decisions concerning insignificant matters (38/83). His ideas may be unusual, unconventional, and illogical. There were no signs of cognitive slippage or thought disorder suggestive of a current psychotic disorder ($WSum6 = 0$). Although there were no signs of a current psychotic disorder, a potential exists for a brief psychotic decompensation (38/83).

Although he is able to conform with social expectations when norms of acceptable conduct are clear and obvious ($P = 6$), there is a significant potential for Mr. T's actions to be impulsive and poorly thought out because his perceptions of events are markedly inaccurate and unrealistic ($X - \% = .40$; $Xu\% = .20$; $M - = 3$). This tendency to make errors in perception, thinking, and judgment is related to the arbitrary way in which Mr. T characteristically approaches and analyzes events, rather than to a psychotic disorder. His take on a situation is based on a hasty, inefficient, and haphazard accounting of an event and a tendency to miss critical bits of information ($Zd = -3.5$). He does not actively and systematically think through the best course of action and consider different options but instead typically acts following his first impressions or vague hunches. In other words, he pursues the first plan of action that "looks good" without considering possible flaws in this approach. His poor judgment, illogical thinking, and inaccurate perceptions of events are likely to be aggravated by use of alcohol.

Mr. T currently experiences considerable emotional turmoil, including anxiety, tension, and worry ($ANX = 72$; $m = 3$). His outlook is sad and pessimistic ($DEP = 70$; $D1 = 69$). Mr. T typically attempts to deny and repress problems and negative emotional reactions ($38/83$; $CP = 1$). He may refuse to acknowledge painful aspects of external reality, deny negative feelings, or substitute a false positive emotion for negative reactions, even to the extent of bending reality to avoid dealing with difficulties ($CP = 1$). One may speculate that Mr. T developed these defensive reactions to negative emotions as a result of his parents' refusal to acknowledge problems and their insistence that family members deny problems to others so as to avoid airing dirty laundry in public.

Mr. T relies on repression, denial, and somatization as primary defenses. Thus, emotional distress may be converted into physical symptoms for which no definite medical explanation is found, such as headaches, dizziness, chest pain, numbness, blurred vision, or sleep disturbance ($HEA = 66$; $Hy4 = 72$; $CP = 1$; $An + Xy = 1$). These symptoms are likely to have an acute onset, occur suddenly, and subside without any specific medical treatment. He may also report feelings of unreality, such as depersonalization. These somatic symptoms do not bind his anxiety, but instead anxiety is temporarily displaced onto his physical problems that become a major focus of concern for a brief period of time before they are forgotten.

Mr. T is rather immature and dependent and has an exaggerated need for attention and affection from others ($38/83$; Food $= 1$). However, he is shy and introverted, feels alienated from others, and is socially anxious and uncomfortable (scale $0 = 66$; $SOD = 65$; $Pd4 = 90$; $Si1 = 65$; $Si2 = 67$). Others might avoid interactions with Mr. T because his behavior is clumsy, awkward, childlike, and immature and because his unusual, unconventional thinking can cause difficulties in communicating with them. Mr. T experiences marked ambivalence about becoming involved with people because he does not perceive them as reliable or trustworthy ($T = 0$). He therefore often avoids others or approaches social interactions with caution and fearful mistrust to avoid being hurt, disappointed, rejected, embarrassed, or humiliated (scale $0 = 66$).

Although Mr. T keeps a distance from most people, if he does become attached to someone, he is likely to become quite dependent on that person and to have intense needs for him or her to provide affection and reassurance about his worth (Food = 1). He is particularly likely to have powerful emotional reactions and become disorganized should a relationship with a person upon whom he depends end or be threatened. This suggests he may have had difficulty separating from his family, because these strong dependency needs were gratified by family members and he had quite limited involement with others outside the family. The combination of vulnerability to intense emotional reactions to abandonment and the use of denial and somatization as defenses fits with the history of repeatedly developing physical symptoms for which no medical explanation was found following an actual or threatened loss of an important relationship, such as the death of Mr. T's grandfather, family conflict regarding his desire to live independently, and disruptions in relationships with women.

Mr. T's record indicates he has a negative view of himself and a low estimate of self-worth (Egocentricity ratio = .30). This is consistent with the school history of persistent problems with academic achievement, being teased and ridiculed by peers, and negative treatment by family members. He does not feel self-critical or guilty at present ($FV = 0$; $FD = 0$). Thus, there were no signs of regret or remorse for his actions. He does not appear to have much capacity for introspection or self-reflection, which suggests he may be naive about himself and is not psychologically minded ($FD = 0$).

The psychological characteristics described previously are relevant to an understanding of Mr. T's psychological state when he murdered the 68-year-old woman. Following the separation from his wife, Mr. T became intensely involved with and emotionally dependent on a new girlfriend. Their relationship changed when she was rebuked by her minister for her involvement with a married man. This led to quarrels with Mr. T about the rate at which his divorce was proceeding, reduced closeness and intimacy, and statements that she intended to end their relationship. Given his vulnerability to react intensely to actual or threatened abandonment, one can speculate that Mr. T experienced considerable emotional distress and turmoil when his girlfriend told him she could no longer be involved with him. This is the type of situation in which Mr. T is most likely to become psychologically disorganized.

Mr. T is likely to have felt an intense, desperate pressure to resolve his pending divorce when his girlfriend threatened to leave him. Consistent with his typical inefficient, haphazard approach to situations, he impulsively devised a poorly thought out, irrational plan to obtain the money needed to finalize his divorce by robbing the widow, a woman he thought had a substantial amount of money in her home. His judgment, reasoning, and logic were compromised by his emotional state and psychological disorganization, as well as by abuse of alcohol and cocaine the day of the murder. When it seemed clear that the robbery was being thwarted by the widow, Mr. T reacted with an explosive, uncontrolled emotional outburst. The combination of ineffectual defenses, poor judgment, faulty thinking, intense emotions, and intoxication resulted in a lapse of ego control, psychological disorganization, and behavioral regression. The irrational, uncontrolled, and bizarre circumstances of the murder suggest he suffered a brief, highly sexualized psychotic decompensation during the murder for which he later had no memory.

Diagnostic Impression

DSM-IV   Axis I   309.28 Adjustment disorder with mixed anxiety and
depressed mood
298.9   Psychotic disorder, not otherwise specified
300.11 Conversion disorder
305.00 Alcohol abuse

Axis II   301.22 Schizotypal personality disorder

TREATMENT RECOMMENDATIONS

This evaluation was conducted at the request of Mr. T's attorney to assess whether psychological problems exist that could be used as the foundation for a defense or for seeking mitigation of a guilty verdict, rather than for treatment planning. However, the results of this evaluation do have implications for psychological treatment and for effective management of Mr. T while he is incarcerated.

Any intervention with Mr. T must take into account his use of denial, repression, and somatization as primary defenses. Prison medical staff should be informed about Mr. T's tendency to develop physical symptoms when under stress. They can then be prepared to respond in a cautious, appropriate manner should he report physical symptoms without overreacting to these complaints.

Given his defensive structure, Mr. T has limited capacity for introspection and self-reflection and is likely to be quite naive and superficial in his understanding of himself (*FD* = 0). He has limited access to feelings and to identifying the motivations for his behavior. Thus, insight-oriented psychotherapy is unlikely to be an effective treatment modality with Mr. T. Instead, he would be most likely to benefit from a supportive approach.

Treatment with Mr. T must respect the conflict concerning involvement with others described previously. On the one hand, he has strong needs for support, reassurance, comfort, and affection from others but is reserved because he mistrusts others and is fearful, cautious, and apprehensive about becoming involved. Thus, any intervention should proceed slowly and should be primarily supportive in nature to help reduce his emotional distress and assist him in coping as effectively as possible with the stresses of being in jail and preparing for a trial, as well as in coping with the disruption of his relationship with his girlfriend. It is likely that any changes in his relationship with his girlfriend will have a more immediate and powerful effect on his emotional state than news about his criminal case.

Should Mr. T become involved with psychotherapy, his therapist may play an important role in assisting him to view situations more accurately and completely than he has in the past by helping him to stop, think over the different aspects of the situation, and consider the implications of different courses of action.

13

Case 8: Differential Diagnosis of Bipolar Disorder and ADHD

REASON FOR EVALUATION

Mr. A is a 49-year-old, married, White male who recently sought psychotherapy for depression. His therapist referred him for a psychological evaluation to assess the severity of his depression and whether any signs of a bipolar disorder exist. The possibility of a bipolar disorder was questioned because of a history of recurrent episodes of depression and because the patient described himself as restless, distractable, and unable to focus his thoughts that sometimes "dart from one thing to another." Mr. A wonders whether the restlessness and distractibility might be symptoms of attention deficit hyperactivity disorder (ADHD) that have persisted into adulthood. Finally, the therapist wondered whether Mr. A's difficulties suggest a personality disorder in addition to an affective disorder. In particular, the therapist questioned whether his presentation meets diagnostic criteria for a Narcissistic Personality Disorder.

BACKGROUND INFORMATION

During the clinical interview, Mr. A frequently stated he could not recall much of his childhood and commented his past seems like a blur to him. He is the second of three children. His father, a preacher in the rural South, was described by Mr. A as a failure and as "pathetic." Father was forced to leave his position when he was accused of making sexual advances to a woman in his congregation. This charge was never substantiated and some members of the community thought it was instigated by one of his father's rivals. Mr. A described his father as "the laughingstock of the town" because of these events. After stepping down from the church, he supported the family working as a mover for a moving company. Mr. A commented that much of his behavior during adolescence and after developed as a reaction to his father. For instance, he thinks he began smoking as a teenager after hearing his father remark with pride to a friend that his son did not smoke.

Mr. A described his mother as cold, unemotional, and judgmental. He recounted one incident when she became upset with him, made him kneel, prayed over him, and ordered the devil to leave her son's body. Mother never attempted an exorcism of Mr. A's brother or sister. He claimed he could not recall what prompted his mother's actions, but looking back on this incident, he sees mother as having been "pathetic." His sister has told Mr. A he was "forever challenging the folks in charge of you," a description that seemed to surprise him.

Mr. A graduated high school in the top 10% of his class. In spite of this, he always thought of himself as "lazy or stupid," as he was told by teachers he did not achieve up to his potential. When asked about behavior during grade school and junior high, he characterized himself as restless and fidgeting in class but tried to control himself, as he was a preacher's son and felt he "lived in a fishbowl." Mr. A recalled being bored during classes frequently, had difficulty concentrating, and was easily distracted by the actions of classmates or by noises and activity outside the classroom. He often shifted from one activity to another without completing what he had started. As a result, he often did not complete homework assignments or would do them in a sloppy, careless manner. He often forgot to take books or assignments to school.

Mr. A did not recall having difficulties in childhood peer relationships, such as having trouble waiting his turn during games or talking out of turn. He described himself as somewhat of a loner as a youngster. He reported a history of impulsively engaging in potentially dangerous behavior without considering the possible consequences of his actions. For instance, once he climbed over the fence of a prison farm to see whether he could sneak in and out of the prison grounds without being caught. He was indeed caught by a prison guard but does not recall whether he was punished. There is no history of stealing, lying, truancy, destruction of property, or fighting. He denied a history of physical or sexual abuse.

After graduating high school, Mr. A attended a community college for 2 years until he married. His first job was on an assembly line. He reported having difficulty tolerating the repetitive nature of this type of work, made frequent mistakes, and left after a short time. He remarked he probably would have been fired had he not left.

After leaving the factory, Mr. A began to work for a company in the transportation industry. He was promoted a number of times over 24 years and advanced from a file clerk to become a vice-president of public relations. He described his career as though he did not quite believe he ever deserved to be promoted. He reported having difficulty with concentration, focusing on tasks, and following through with things throughout his career. Mr. A commented that a number of people at work, including his supervisors, saw him as having many positive attributes, but he has never seen himself the same way. He explained that he succeeded not because of his own talents, but because he was able to quickly size up situations and delegate responsibility to others who "really did the dirty work. I didn't do the work. They did. I supervised 20 people who knew what they were doing. I never knew what I was doing." His job was eliminated 3 years prior to this evaluation when the company downsized.

Mr. A reported becoming depressed after his position was terminated. He felt sad, lacked energy and interest in events, spent excessive amounts of time in bed, and withdrew from the world. He stated he missed going to work every day and reacted strongly to being unemployed. He eventually sought treatment with a psychiatrist who diagnosed him as having a Major Depression and treated him with an antidepressant and insight-oriented psychotherapy. He ended therapy and discontinued the medication after the depression improved.

Mr. A received a generous termination package that allowed him to remain off work for 2 years without significant financial pressures. In the 9 months prior to this evaluation, he began to work as a sales associate for the company where his wife has worked for about 10 years. Although his wife is "terrific" at sales, "I do some business, not much. I don't really work at it. I'm not really satisfied." He considers himself a beginner in sales, finds it difficult to motivate himself to follow through on tasks, and expressed a desire to find a position comparable to his old position.

Mr. A described his current mood as anxious more than depressed. Sleep is good. He has gained over 30 pounds in the past 6 months. Energy has increased compared to the past but fluctuates. He described deriving little enjoyment from life. He acknowledged feeling critical of himself, although he believes this has been true throughout his life. He questions whether there is any point in continuing to attempt to find another job and has been comforted by the thought that his troubles would be over if he were dead. When asked about suicidality, he quickly denied any intent to harm himself and told the examiner repeatedly that he would never hurt himself. The examiner wondered if Mr. A was trying to reassure the examiner about this. Mr. A denied symptoms of mania at present or in the past. He recently resumed psychotherapy because of depression. He decided to see a new therapist, as he felt he had gotten as much as possible from the therapist with whom he had worked previously.

Mr. A denied a history of current or past alcohol or drug abuse. There is no family history of alcoholism. Family history of psychopathology is significant as father was depressed but never received treatment from a mental health professional. In addition, Mr. A's brother, a Viet Nam veteran, has been treated for a number of years for psychiatric difficulties. He did not know his brother's diagnosis, although he was aware his brother has been treated with Lithium.

DIAGNOSTIC CONSIDERATIONS

Adult Attention Deficit Hyperactivity Disorder.   Mr. A raised an important and difficult diagnostic question concerning ADHD in an adult. This question was rarely encountered in clinical practice until recently, in large part because of a widely held belief that ADHD naturally resolved after adolescence. The possibility that an adult has ADHD is taken more seriously, as it is now recognized that ADHD is not limited to childhood and adolescence, as was once thought, but can persist into adulthood (Barkley, 1990; Wender, 1995). The diagnosis of ADHD in adults is based primarily on data obtained from a careful history with particular emphasis on childhood history. Childhood history is of critical importance in making a diagnosis of ADHD in an adult, as the symptoms of ADHD must have been present in childhood; ADHD in adults cannot be diagnosed if the symptoms developed in adulthood. In addition, other psychiatric disorders must be carefully considered as symptoms of ADHD in adults, including difficulties with attention, distractibility, restlessness, failure to complete tasks, and impulsivity, may be symptoms of a Bipolar Disorder, anxiety disorder, depressive disorder, or personality disorder.

Neither the MMPI-2 nor the Rorschach addresses the presence of absence of ADHD in adults directly. However, these tests can provide useful information concerning the presence or absence of other psychiatric disorders, such as mania, depression, or anxiety. Of course, the presence of any of these disorders does not rule out ADHD in an adult as a psychological disorder may co-occur with ADHD.

Mr. A's history is notable for symptoms of ADHD in childhood including distractibility, restlessness, fidgeting, difficulty sustaining attention, not completing activities, forgetting things, difficulty following through on instructions, and impulsive behavior. He therefore meets *DSM–IV* criteria for ADHD in childhood. This condition appears to have persisted into adulthood as indicated by his description of difficulties working on an assembly line and continuing throughout his adult career. This does not rule out a current affective disorder or a personality disorder.

Bipolar Disorder.   A second issue involved in this evaluation is the possibility Mr. A presents with a bipolar disorder. Issues to be considered when a referral involves evaluation of the presence of absence of bipolar disorder were discussed in detail in Case 4.

Narcissistic Personality Disorder. According to the *DSM–IV* (1994), characteristics associated with a narcissistic personality disorder include grandiosity, beliefs of being special and unique, a sense of entitlement, excessive needs for praise and admiration, an exploitative approach to interpersonal relationships, a lack of empathy, and preoccupation with envy. Clinically, patients with a narcissistic personality disorder are also often particularly sensitive to criticism and react to criticism, real or implied, with shame and humiliation.

Neither the MMPI-2 nor the Rorschach has scales or clusters specifically related to a narcissistic personality disorder. However, several test variables are conceptually related to the clinical characteristics described previously. For instance, several Rorschach variables are related to issues of self-concept associated with a narcissistic personality disorder. Persons with a sense of entitlement and a grandiose, arrogant self-image often produce one or more Reflection responses. Some patients who are sensitive to criticism produce both an elevated Egocentricity Index and responses indicating a negative self-image ($MOR > 2$; $V > 1$; $FD > 2$). The interpersonal exploitativeness and lack of empathy often exhibited by patients with a narcissistic personality disorder might be associated with elevations on MMPI-2 scale *4* and scale *9* and with specific Rorschach variables ($Fr + rF > 0$; Egocentricity index $> .45$; $H < (H) + Hd + (Hd)$). The sparse literature on MMPI-2 and Rorschach protocols of patients with a narcissistic personality disorder, as well as for most other *DSM–IV* personality disorders, indicates a need for research.

MMPI-2 Data

Validity Scales. Mr. A admitted to personal difficulties and emotional distress in an honest, open, and consistent fashion. The *L, F,* and *K* scales indicate the clinical profile is valid. The *K* scale ($T = 37$) is lower than expected given Mr. A's socioeconomic status and suggests he has limited personal resources and a negative self-concept. The low *K* score also suggests he is currently going through a stressful time that taxes his coping resources.

Clinical Scales. The *20/02* codetype suggests Mr. A is a socially introverted man who feels shy, nervous, inhibited, and awkward in social gatherings ($SOD = 73$; $Hy1 = 34$; $Pd3 = 39$). He lacks self-confidence and frequently feels insecure, inadequate, and self-conscious ($LSE = 88$; $Ma4 = 30$; $Si1 = 68$). He finds it hard to talk with others he does not know well.

MMPI-2™
Minnesota Multiphasic Personality Inventory-2™

SR Hathaway and J C McKinley

Profile for Basic Scales

Name _____ Mr. A. _____

Address _____

Occupation _____ 12 _____ Age _____ 49 _____ Marital Status _____ Married _____ Date Tested _____ / _____ / _____

Education _____ 12 _____

Referred By _____

MMPI-2 Code _____

Scorer's Initials _____

MALE

	L	F	K	Hs+.5K 1	D 2	Hy 3	Pd+.4K 4	Mf 5	Pa 6	Pt+1K 7	Sc+1K 8	Ma+.2K 9	Si 0	
Raw Score	1	11	9	7	30	23	23	30	11	24	26	17	46	
K to be Added				5			4			9	9	2		
Raw Score with K			12	12			27			33	35	19		

? Raw Score _____ 0

Case 8 MMPI-2 Content and Supplementary Scales

	Raw Score	T Score
FB	11	87
True Response Inconsistency (TRIN)	9	50
Variable Response Inconsistency (VRIN)	4	46
Anxiety	28	75
Repression	17	54
MAC-R	19	44
Ego Strength (Es)	35	45
Dominance (Do)	15	45
Social Responsibility (Re)	15	37
Overcontrolled Hostility (O-H)	11	45
PTSD - Keane (PK)	21	72
PTSD - Schlenger (PS)	31	76
Addiction Potential (APS)	21	44
Addiction Admission (AAS)	4	56

Content Scales (Butcher et al., 1990)		
Anxiety (ANX)	14	70
Fears (FRS)	0	35
Obsessiveness (OBS)	5	50
Depression (DEP)	21	80
Health Concerns (HEA)	3	44
Bizarre Mentation (BIZ)	0	39
Anger (ANG)	7	53
Cynicism (CYN)	10	49
Antisocial Practices (ASP)	14	65
Type A (TPA)	9	50
Low Self-Esteem (LSE)	19	88
Social Discomfort (SOD)	18	73

Depression Subscales (Harris-Lingoes)		
Subjective Depression (D1)	17	77
Psychomotor Retardation (D2)	8	65
Physical Malfunctioning (D3)	4	59
Mental Dullness (D4)	8	77
Brooding (D5)	7	79

Hysteria Subscales (Harris-Lingoes)		
Denial of Social Anxiety (Hy1)	1	34
Need for Affection (Hy2)	4	40
Lassitude-Malaise (Hy3)	9	79
Somatic Complaints (Hy4)	3	52
Inhibition of Aggression (Hy5)	4	55

                                    Raw Score   T Score

Psychopathic Deviate Subscales (Harris-Lingoes)
       Familial Discord (Pd1)   2   51
       Authority Problems (Pd2)   7   73
       Social Imperturbability (Pd3)   2   39
       Social Alienation (Pd4)   5   56
       Self-Alienation (Pd5)   7   67

Paranoia Subscales (Harris-Lingoes)
       Persecutory Ideas (Pa1)   1   46
       Poignancy (Pa2)   4   62
       Naivete (Pa3)   5   51

Schizophrenia Subscales (Harris-Lingoes)
       Social Alienation (Sc1)   9   76
       Emotional Alienation (Sc2)   3   69
       Lack of Ego Mastery, Cognitive (Sc3) 4   66
       Lack of Ego Mastery, Conative (Sc4)   9   87
       Lack of Ego Mastery, Def. Inhib. (Sc5) 5   68
       Bizarre Sensory Experiences (Sc6)   2   51

Hypomania Subscales (Harris-Lingoes)
       Amorality (Ma1)   4   66
       Psychomotor Acceleration (Ma2)   6   53
       Imperturbability (Ma3)   3   47
       Ego Inflation (Ma4)   0   30

Social Introversion Subscales (Ben-Porath et al., 1989)
       Shyness/Self-Consciousness (Si1)   11   68
       Social Avoidance (Si2)   8   71
       Alienation -- Self and Others (Si3) 11   68

As a result, he avoids social interaction and, when this is not possible, escapes as soon as he can. Although he prefers to be alone rather than suffer through uncomfortable social encounters, he feels isolated and lonely (*Scl* = 76; *Si2* = 71).

Because of the longstanding difficulties in interpersonal relationships, poor social skills, and negative self-esteem described previously, Mr. A has often felt mildly depressed. The depression he experiences may be described as a chronic and characterologically deeply ingrained depression. Mr. A may have come to accept these frequent experiences of depression as an inevitable part of his life. At present, however, he feels more hopeless, pessimistic, and empty than usual; frequently questions his capabilities; and views himself in a critical, denigrating manner. He does not value his accomplishments and may dismiss praise or compliments given by others (*LSE* = 88; *Ma4* = 30). In addition, he tends to worry excessively and to ruminate about his situation in a self-critical fashion (scale *7* = 64; *A* = 75; *ANX* = 70).

The MMPI-2 data provide no support for a diagnosis of a Narcissistic Personality Disorder as none of the data suggested grandiosity or an egocentric, entitled approach to his personal relationships. As discussed previously, the *20/02* codetype suggests a deeply ingrained negative self-image and a tendency to avoid social interaction.

Rorschach Data

Although a number of key variables are positive on the Structural Summary (*D* < *Adj D*; *CDI* = 4; *DEPI* = 5), it is important to first note that the Suicide Constellation is positive (*S-CON* = 9). The *S-CON* is an empirically derived cluster of Rorschach variables that was developed in the following manner. Protocols of 59 subjects who committed suicide within 60 days after being administered the Rorschach were analyzed to identify variables that occurred in at least 30 of the records. After these variables were selected, the suicide completers were compared with three comparison groups (schizophrenics, inpatient depressives, and normals) to identify a cluster of variables that discriminated suicide completers from the comparison groups. These variables formed the *S-CON*. It was found that the suicide completers were identified most accurately with the lowest rate of false positives (identified as suicide completers when they were not) and false negatives (identified as nonsuicide completers when they were) if 8 or more of the 11 variables comprising the *S-CON* were positive (Exner & Wylie, 1977).

The *S-CON* was re-examined and cross-validated several years later with a new, larger sample of suicide completers (*N* = 101). One additional variable was added to the *S-CON* (*MOR* > 3), and a refinement to the

Case 8 Rorschach Protocol

Card Response	Inquiry
I 1. (Pt. sits with arms crossed.) Um...(sighs) Leaves. As they r pressed in a book. They d't use wax paper. They leach unevenly into the pages & a piece fell off. So its no longer recognizable, either by species or by color. What we have here is a badly pressed leaf.	E: (Rpts S's response) S: It was prob a maple leaf, bec of these points. The moisture of leaf, well, leaves dry from outside in. These (S) were pockets of moisture that have leached onto the paper bec they were moist. When leaf was removed it had adhered to the page of book. E: Badly pressed? S: Right. The idea is that you preserve the color and shape. E: Color? S: Absolutely not! Its gray! Leaves are not gray.
2. That's all. E: Most p see more than 1 thing on each card. S: Oh! This is a bat! That's been run over. He is flattened on the highway. In the southbound lane. Just kidding. (laughs)	E: (Rpts S's response) S: Yeah. Its the little hands here that bats have. Have these little graspers. E: Show me the bat. S: Wings and body here. E: Flattened? S: Its very 2-dimensional. There's no depth to it at all. Completely flat.
II 3. Its colorful...Ah, yes! These r the dancing bears at the Moscow Circus! Thy're wonderful. Brightly colored hats and shoes.	E: (Rpts S's response) S: These r bears dancing. Red hats & red shoes. E: Bears? S: I d.k. It just l.l. roughly the shape of dancing bears. L.l. a bear. 2 bears.
4. This is also a Stealth fighter. And its been discovered & the ack-ack is exploding around it as it tries to go home. Its heading south. (laughs)	E: (Rpts S's response) S: Yeah. This here ll the shape of the Stealth fighter. Swept wing look. Suppose to be for absorption of radar. Nonetheless, these r explosions in the night sky. E: Explosions?

S: This field of black was the night sky & the red was evocative of fire.

III 5. This is cooperative pot throwing. Its a new treatment offered by southern California mountain dwellers. For a mere $2 million on the weekend u can learn to make pots together. Here we have 2 p enjoying this effort, trying to make this come out symmetrical. Alth they appear well matched, 1 is a lot stronger than the other. Have trouble coordinating strength. Nevertheless, its all in the spirit of good fun & they will remember the exper fondly.

E: (Rpts S's response)
S: This is 1 p & this is the other p. This is the pot. They r, its a happy occasion. Trying to get this to be pot-like & symmetrical.
E: Happy?
S: Its not an athletic pose. Its not a pose of effort. Its a pose of good cheer. Wld like to see pot come out alright. Its doing it tog that's fun.

IV 6. Uhm...This is the smoke that comes out of a naragasett (sic) hogan on a brisk, fall evening. They're burning green wood bec the dry material thy've gathered has been loaded up for a trip south. Thy r willing to put up with this extra smoke bec they'd have to delay the trip in the morning to gather more dried material. This is hard. (lghs)

E: (Rpts S's response)
S: Their communal hearth. Hogan is the term.
E: Smoke?
S: Its in shades of grey & black. Just the way smoke lks at night.

V 7. Uhm...(sighs) This is a fossil. It has been laying in the British Museum for 150 years. Successive generations of scholars have looked at this & wondered what the hell it was. The present curator, d't remember if that is the right term, he has a theory abt what it may be & is taking it from the small dinosaur fossil tray & put it in the winged mammal tray to see if the scholars

E: (Rpts S's response)
S: Actually, I was looking at the toes down here of the beast. It reminds me of what fossilized digits l.l. I think I may have seen a fossil that looks much like this.
E: What part of the blot were u lkg at?
S: I see all of it. The whole structure l.l a fossil 2 me.
E: Fossil?
S: I have no idea. I d.k what evoked that.

will see what he did.
That's it.

VI 8. Oh, golly. These r
Indians way further west.
They have skinned a sea
otter & noticed the extra
flesh that grew, not flesh,
the fur that grew on this
otter, & have decided to
nail it to the side of
their, I d.k. the right
term, a ceremonial bldg in
hopes it will have some
totemic effect on some
bears that have been
maurauding their village.
Thy're really hopeful today
that finally a sign has
been sent to them in their
continuing effort to ward
off the bears.

E: (Rpts S's response)
S: Yeah. I thk it l.l a skin.
But then, this stuff up here
has to be explained in some
fashion, what it is. In the
absence of some natural expl,
its supernatural.
E: Skin?
S: I just put northwest Indians
and northwest fauna tog & came
up with it. It l.l a pelt.
E: Pelt?
S: It l.l a laid out pelt.
E: Nailed to the wall?
S: Bec its laid out so tightly.
Its been stretched.
E: Fur?
S: Here again I have no idea.
I was just warming to the
story.

VII 9. This is the footprint a
caribou makes in frozen
tundra. This may be
permafrost. Its the mushy
swamp material that is
perpetually cold. Now,
this is a grazing
footprint. The caribou r
not running here. Thy're
feeding on some
particularly tasty lichen
that have sprung up in the
spring.

E: (Rpts S's response)
S: This whole structure l.l a
footprint to me.
E: Footprint?
S: I have a sense that its
large. Its not, the hoof is
not cloven.
E: Grazing?
S: Its at rest. If it were
running I wld see less of it
and the depth of the front wld
be less than the back.

10. A very curious atoll.
We're lkg at it from a
bird's eye view. This
atoll was actually
photographed by Amelia
Earhart & caused quite a
sensation. Except when
they tried to find it again
it had disappeared once
again beneath the waves.
We know it existed though,
because of satellite
imagery. Its outline was
seen from abt 150 miles up
in abt 10 feet of water.

E: (Rpts S's response)
S: Cut from the whole cloth.
Just made up a story abt an
atoll gone for awhile & now
back.
E: Aerial photo?
S: Bec of the grainy aspect to
it and it is... atolls have a
way of being symmetrical.
E: Grainy?
S: Out of focus. Or its been
blown up past the capability of
the film.
E: Seen from 150 feet?
S: Again, made up a story abt
it. Covered over by the sea.

VIII 11. You have a lot of ethnography in yr pile of pictures. This happ to be a picture that was discovered when an archeologist thought to turn over the altar stone of the Tolteks. So much had been written abt the altar stone, so much curiousity abt the blood stains, whether H or A. One guy thght he wld turn it over. Actually only inter in seeing how the stone was based at first. Then he saw what he judged to be a coat of arms of the ruling family that built the pyramids. What was carved tended to emphasize sea creatures rather than terrestrial ones. This led the archeologist to begin a line of speculation that at 1 time there was a great sea covering this area & considerable legend abt them.

E: (Rpts S's response)
S: That's a coat of arms anyway.
E: Where were u looking?
S: These pink figures are evocative of a coat of arms. Some have lions rampant? These have sea A's rampant. These, the grey, maybe a stingray or other sea creature.
E: Blood stain?
S: No, didn't actually see that. The point of the story was that someone thght to look under the stone to see how it fit into its niche.

IX 12. Oh golly. OK! This is George Crapper, the inventor of the toilet, also invented the phony fireplace fire. It was produced with colored, these were foil streamers. Allowed to flap in the breeze created by the bellows. The youngest son in the family was allowed to blow the bellows. It was quite a privilege to make the fires crinkle & pop on Celtic holidays.

E: (Rpts S's response)
S: Just like the phony fireplaces I've seen. Have blowers & blow bits of colored foil. Supposed to 1.1 a fire & I guess it does.
E: Show me the fire.
S: This 1.1 someone attempted to make fire out of aluminum. Not fire itself, the look of fire. Its the sort of thing we put up with. The thing that's OK when its a holiday, when we have things that r highly representative, say like Father X-mas as an expr of the spirit of giving. Its a pale copy of the idea. But we have it bec its so much easier than doing the real thing. And I said Celts bec the holidays have alw struck me as partic strange.

271

X   13. Uhm...Ah!...This is a
    crystal! As a matter of
    fact, the first crystal
    that gave opthamologists
    the idea they cld grow
    eyeglasses. They cld grow
    crystals with the
    particular optic effect
    they wtd. Opened a whole
    branch of optical science.

E: (Rpts S's response)
S: Yes. I read a book 1 time
abt how crystals are done. Its
all I know abt crystals. The
structures are identified by
stains. And the stains used by
crystal growers to show
particular structures, these
are reds for the use of the
stain. I d't remember them.
E: Crystal?
S: No idea. The fact on all of
the cards, the R lookd exactly
like the L. That's always
troublesome. Casting abt for
things that have a perfect R &
L aspect to them.

14. I also may see...Naw.
Well, I'm going to say it
looks a lot like a stain I
had in a jacket one time.
Produced the most god-awful
thing. It had this look to
it. The mold & mildew done
its job.

E: (Rpts S's response)
S: Yeah! It wasn't quite this
colorful. It was an underarm
stain. I had worn this jacket
& stained it badly & noticed
this maybe a year later. The
pattern was like this.
E: What reminded you of the
stain?
S: I d.k. The satin was blue,
as I recall. Not the C at all.
It was the pattern.

```
CASE08.R3==================== SEQUENCE OF SCORES ==============================

CARD NO LOC  #  DETERMINANT(S)    (2) CONTENT(S)   POP Z  SPECIAL SCORES
======= ====== ================  === ==========    === =  ==============
   I  1 WSo  1  FC'+                  Bt               3.5 MOR
      2 Wo   1  Fo                    A             P 1.0 MOR,DV

  II  3 W+   1  FMa.CFo          2    A,Cg             5.5 COP
      4 WS+  1  ma.CF.C'u             Sc,Fi,Na         4.5 AG

 III  5 D+   1  Mao             2     H,Art         P 3.0 COP,DR

  IV  6 Wv   1  ma.YFu                Fi,Ay             DR

   V  7 Wo   1  F-                    An,Ay            1.0 DR,PER

  VI  8 W+   1  mpo                   Ad,Ay            2.5 DR,MOR

 VII  9 Wo   1  Fu                    Ad               2.5 DR
     10 Wo   1  FDo                   Ls,Art           2.5 DR

VIII 11 Wo   1  F+                    Art,Ay,A         4.5 DR

  IX 12 Wo   1  ma.FCu                Fi,Sc            5.5 DR2,PER

   X 13 Dv   9  F-                    Id                   PER,DR2
     14 Wv   1  F-                    Id                   PER,MOR

============================== SUMMARY OF APPROACH ==============================

     I : WS.W                        VI : W
    II : W.WS                       VII : W.W
   III : D                         VIII : W
    IV : W                           IX : W
     V : W                            X : D.W
```

273

```
LOCATION        DETERMINANTS              CONTENTS      S-CONSTELLATION
FEATURES      BLENDS      SINGLE                        NO..FV+VF+V+FD>2
                                      H   = 1, 0        YES..Col-Shd Bl>0
Zf    = 11    FM.CF       M   = 1     (H) = 0, 0        YES..Ego<.31,>.44
ZSum  = 36.0  m.CF.C'     FM  = 0     Hd  = 0, 0        YES..MOR > 3
ZEst  = 34.5  m.YF        m   = 1     (Hd)= 0, 0        NO...Zd > +- 3.5
              m.FC        FC  = 0     Hx  = 0, 0        YES..es > EA
W   = 12                  CF  = 0     A   = 2, 1        YES..CF+C > FC
  (Wv = 2)                C   = 0     (A) = 0, 0        YES..X+% < .70
D   = 2                   Cn  = 0     Ad  = 2, 0        NO..S > 3
Dd  = 0                   FC' = 1     (Ad)= 0, 0        YES..P < 3 or > 8
S   = 2                   C'F = 0     An  = 1, 0        YES..Pure H < 2
                          C'  = 0     Art = 1, 2        YES..R < 17
  DQ                      FT  = 0     Ay  = 0, 4         9.....TOTAL
........(FQ-)             TF  = 0     Bl  = 0, 0
  +  =  4  ( 0)           T   = 0     Bt  = 1, 0        SPECIAL SCORINGS
  o  =  7  ( 1)           FV  = 0     Cg  = 0, 1                 Lv1  Lv2
v/+  =  0  ( 0)           VF  = 0     Cl  = 0, 0        DV   =  1x1   0x2
  v  =  3  ( 2)           V   = 0     Ex  = 0, 0        INC  =  0x2   0x4
                          FY  = 0     Fd  = 0, 0        DR   =  7x3   2x6
                          YF  = 0     Fi  = 2, 1        FAB  =  0x4   0x7
                          Y   = 0     Ge  = 0, 0        ALOG =  0x5
      FORM QUALITY        Fr  = 0     Hh  = 0, 0        CON  =  0x7
                          rF  = 0     Ls  = 1, 0        Raw Sum6 =   10
     FQx  FQf MQual SQx   FD  = 1     Na  = 0, 1        Wgtd Sum6 =    34
  +  = 2    1   0    1    F   = 6     Sc  = 1, 1
  o  = 5    1   1    0                Sx  = 0, 0        AB  = 0     CP  = 0
  u  = 4    1   0    1                Xy  = 0, 0        AG  = 1     MOR = 4
  -  = 3    3   0    0                Id  = 2, 0        CFB = 0     PER = 4
none = 0   --   0    0    (2) =   2                     COP = 2     PSV = 0
```

```
==================== RATIOS, PERCENTAGES, AND DERIVATIONS =====================

R = 14        L =  0.75          FC:CF+C = 1: 2     COP = 2     AG = 1
-----------------------------    Pure C  =   0      Food       =   0
EB = 1: 2.5  EA =   3.5  EBPer= N/A  SumC':WSumC= 2:2.5  Isolate/R =0.29
eb = 5: 3    es =   8     D = -1  Afr    =0.40      H:(H)Hd(Hd)= 1: 0
          Adj es =   5  Adj D =  0   S      =   2      (HHd):(AAd)= 0: 0
-----------------------------    Blends:R= 4:14     H+A:Hd+Ad  = 4: 2
FM = 1  :  C'= 2   T = 0          CP      =  0
m  = 4  :  V = 0   Y = 1
                                 P  =  2       Zf  =11        3r+(2)/R=0.14
a:p    =  5: 1   Sum6  = 10   X+% =0.50       Zd   = +1.5    Fr+rF  = 0
Ma:Mp  =  1: 0   Lv2   =  2   F+% =0.33       W:D:Dd =12: 2: 0  FD   = 1
2AB+Art+Ay= 7    WSum6 = 34   X-% =0.21       W:M =12: 1     An+Xy  = 1
M-     =  0      Mnone =  0   S-% =0.00       DQ+ =  4       MOR    = 4
                             Xu% =0.29       DQv =  3

==============================================================================
SCZI = 2    DEPI = 5*   CDI = 4*   S-CON = 9*   HVI = No   OBS = No
==============================================================================
```

criteria for the Egocentricity Index was made. The group of suicide completers was again compared to groups of inpatient depressives, schizophrenics, and normals. The S-CON discriminated between the suicide and comparison groups with the lowest rate of false positives and false negatives with a cutoff of 8. Although a positive S-CON does not infallibly predict that an individual patient will engage in self-destructive behavior within 60 days after completing the Rorschach, it is an ominous sign that Mr. A's S-CON is positive. This indicates he has a significant number of the characteristics of subjects who do attempt suicide. This strongly suggests that his therapist be informed about the risk of a suicide attempt so that appropriate steps be taken to insure his safety.

The first positive key variable to consider after the S-CON indicates Mr. A is currently experiencing significant stress ($D < Adj\ D$), consistent with a history of having lost a high paying job with seniority, prestige, and responsibility in a company where he had worked for 24 years and uncertainty about his career. Although generally able to manage the demands in his life (D score $= 0$), he has limited psychological resources with which to cope with unpleasant situations and is likely to have a history of difficulties in functioning, particularly in interpersonal relationships ($Adj\ D = 0$; $CDI = 4$; $EA = 3.5$).

The lower than average EA, a measure of available psychological resources or ego strength, is quite significant as it indicates Mr. A is chronically vulnerable to becoming disorganized when stressful events occur. Although he can function adequately in structured situations with clearly defined expectations, he has difficulty responding effectively to changing situations, particularly when new situations are ambiguous and expectations are not well defined. The positive $DEPI$, to be discussed further later, indicates that this disorganization typically involves depression. At present, he feels overwhelmed and perceives himself as helpless and unable to constructively handle a situation that is objectively difficult, especially given his age and the economic climate ($m = 4$).

Mr. A has a longstanding, chronic vulnerability to feel depressed and to have marked fluctuations in mood as he reacts to the events of daily life ($DEPI = 5$; $CDI = 4$). That is, he is not a person who responds in a calm, evenhanded manner but instead responds to even relatively minor stresses with sharp shifts from feeling calm, optimistic, and self-confident to feeling down, discouraged, self-critical, and hopeless. He experiences emotions in a more intense way than is typical for most adults ($FC:CF+C = 1:2$), and his emotional reactions are frequently extreme, confusing, and upsetting (Color Shading Blends $= 1$). This can be disruptive in terms of his ability to function effectively.

Perhaps because of this, Mr. A tries to avoid being in situations that trigger emotional reactions ($Afr = .40$). He also tries to distance himself from feelings by emphasizing the rational, logical, and intellectual aspects of his reactions and attempting to deny the emotional side of his reactions (Intellectualization Index = 7). Doing so interferes with his ability to handle situations involving feelings in a realistic, direct manner. He is likely to function effectively when his defensive efforts keep emotions under control, such as in a work setting, but he may be overwhelmed by dysphoric emotional reactions in situations that elicit emotional responses, such as social interactions.

Mr. A's self-concept is extremely negative (Egocentricity Index = .14; MOR = 4). He sees himself as inadequate, incompetent, and worthless. His negative self-image is deeply ingrained and longstanding. He frequently thinks of himself in critical, disparaging terms and sees little that is good about himself, although he easily finds much about his actions, accomplishments, and personality to judge and castigate.

Mr. A is likely to have a history of difficulties in interpersonal relationships and may have poor social skills (CDI = 4). These difficulties may be due, in part, to the vulnerability to being overwhelmed by negative emotions described previously. In particular, social situations are likely to elicit self-criticism and feelings of incompetence and helplessness (Egocentricity Index = .14; MOR = 4; m = 4). Because of his insecurity, he is likely to respond quite defensively if he feels others are challenging or threatening his self-esteem by disagreeing with him or questioning his opinions and decisions (PER = 4). As a result, he has little interest in and avoids social encounters (T = 0; H content < 5). He is reserved and reveals personal information reluctantly and cautiously (T = 0). Others may perceive him as aloof, having little interest in participating in social activities, and hard to get to know.

Mr. A is able to use his innate intellectual abilities in a very effective manner. He makes a considerable effort to attend to and utilize available information when responding to problems (Zf = 11; $W:M$ = 12:1). The Zf score, although average, is actually more important than it appears at first glance because the number of responses he produced is lower than average (R = 14). Mr. A tends to be careful and even perfectionistic in his attempts to account for and use all of the facts when trying to solve problems ($FQ+$ = 2). Although he is typically careful and precise in how he organizes and thinks about information, he also has the ability to view situations in a creative way rather than being bound by an ordinary approach to situations (Populars = 2; $X+\%$ = .50; $Xu\%$ = .29; $X-\%$ = .21). His ability to integrate and use information in a careful, organized, yet creative manner has been an asset in his work and his ability to analyze problems, generate a strategy to deal with the problem, and delegate responsibility to carry out his plan. These abilities are of major importance in terms of understanding his success at work and his rise to a position of considerable responsibility.

The fact that Mr. A produced so few conventional responses (Populars = 2) and articulated his percepts in an unusual way ($Xu\% = .29$; $DR = 9$) in the absence of any history indicating difficulties with reality testing suggests he may be motivated to disregard what is expected in a situation and instead respond in an unconventional way. This does not necessarily mean he will act in an antisocial manner but suggests he places a premium on challenging the norms of social behavior.

As discussed previously, the Rorschach data are consistent with a chronic vulnerability to depression. There were no findings suggesting of a current manic episode.

There were no indications that his self-concept fluctuates from the polar opposite ego states characteristic of patients with a narcissistic personality disorder, such as from a grandiose to a depleted perception of self-worth. Furthermore, there were no indications of an exploitative approach to interpersonal relationships. Thus, the Rorschach offers no support for a diagnosis of a narcissistic personality disorder.

Comment

The data from the MMPI-2 and Rorschach match very closely in how they describe Mr. A's affective functioning, self-image, and interpersonal functioning. Both the MMPI-2 and Rorschach describe Mr. A as a man who has been chronically vulnerable to becoming depressed; who chronically feels self-critical, inadequate, incompetent, and inferior to others; and who is socially awkward, anxious, and withdrawn. Both tests also agree in describing him as having limited psychological resources with which to cope with stressful life events. Although the MMPI-2 and Rorschach converge in identifying these longstanding psychological and interpersonal difficulties, the Rorschach shows that Mr. A is struggling to avoid being overwhelmed by current life difficulties, whereas the MMPI-2 does not.

The Rorschach provides information concerning Mr. A's personality style and defensive operations not contained in the MMPI-2. His responses indicate he attempts to control emotional reactions by avoiding situations in which feelings are likely to be triggered and by the use of intellectualizing defenses. The Rorschach also highlighted a strength in Mr. A's ability to solve problems in a systematic and creative manner. In addition, responses to the Rorschach suggest a need to challenge and disregard the expected response in a situation, findings that are not apparent on the MMPI-2.

Both the MMPI-2 and Rorschach describe Mr. A as chronically vulnerability to becoming depressed. No evidence for a current manic episode was found on either test. Thus, his reports of difficulty concentrating, focusing thoughts, and maintaining attention cannot be explained by a manic episode.

These difficulties may either be residual symptoms of ADHD or a reflection of his rumination and preoccupation with emotionally troubling issues.

No support for a diagnosis of a narcissistic personality disorder was found on either the MMPI-2 or the Rorschach. There were no indications of a grandiose, arrogant self-image, entitlement, or interpersonal exploitation. It is possible that the therapist's concern about this diagnosis was elicited because of Mr. A's sensitivity to criticism and his defensiveness (PER = 4). In this case, the sensitivity to criticism appears to be due to chronic feelings of inadequacy and low self-esteem rather than to the shifts from a grandiose to a deflated self-image characteristic of patients with a narcissistic personality disorder.

MMPI-2-Rorschach Integration

Mr. A responded to the MMPI-2 in an honest, straightforward manner. He is currently experiencing significant depression superimposed on a chronic, longstanding depression that is deeply ingrained in his character (*20/02*; *CDI*). His vulnerability to reacting to even mildly stressful situations by feeling depressed, worried, and overwhelmed has resulted in periodic exacerbations of this chronic depression (*DEPI* = 5). His moods fluctuate a great deal, and he tends to respond to even relatively minor stresses with sharp shifts from feeling calm, optimistic, and self-confident to feeling down, discouraged, self-critical, and hopeless (*20/02*; *DEPI*; *CDI*; Color Shading Blend). There were no indications of a Bipolar Disorder in the data from the clinical interview or in his test responses. Thus, his reports of difficulty concentrating, focusing thoughts, and maintaining attention cannot be explained by a manic episode. These difficulties may be residual symptoms of ADHD and/or a reflection of his rumination and preoccupation with emotionally troubling issues.

One important feature of Mr. A's longstanding depression is very low self-esteem (*20/02*; *LSE* = 88; *Ma4* = 30; *Si1* = 68; Egocentricity Index = .14; *MOR* = 4). He has been persistently troubled by deeply ingrained feelings of inadequacy, self-doubt, and inferiority. He frequently thinks of himself in harshly critical, disparaging terms and sees little that is good about himself, although he easily finds much about his actions, accomplishments, and personality to judge and castigate. Given his negative self-image, he finds it quite difficult to identify his strengths and talents or to take credit for any achievements and successes. He generally minimizes, disregards, or rejects compliments and praise offered by others. One factor that may have contributed to these longstanding self-doubts is the ADHD that was not diagnosed in childhood but that undoubtedly led to his being told repeatedly that he was not performing up to his potential in school and that compromised his adult work performance. Another factor contributing to his negative self-image involves his view of his parents as pathetic and his father as a failure. Even though Mr. A consciously rejected his parents as role models and tried to distance himself from them, it is likely that the development of a positive self-image was hindered by these negative feelings about his parents.

Mr. A reported experiencing significant stress after losing a high paying job with seniority, prestige, and responsibility in a company where he had worked for 24 years. Currently, he is unsure about which career direction to pursue and is dissatisfied with his present job. Although generally able to manage the demands in his life, he has limited psychological resources with which to cope with unpleasant situations and is chronically vulnerable to becoming disorganized when stressful events occur (CDI = 4; EA = 3.5). At present, he feels worried, anxious, and overwhelmed and perceives himself as helpless and unable to constructively handle a situation that is objectively difficult, especially given his age and the economic climate (LSE = 88; $Ma4$ = 30; $Si1$ = 68; m = 4). It is likely that Mr. A dwells on the limitations and shortcomings he perceives himself as having. As a result, he passively withdraws, rather than actively attempting to use his personal strengths to achieve a positive outcome. His reaction of helpless panic is related to a negative self-image and fears he will be judged as lacking the qualifications to obtain another job. He may also worry that he will inevitably fail if he does secure a job at a level commensurate with his past position. One may speculate this reflects Mr. A's fear that he will ultimately prove to be the same "pathetic failure" as his father was.

Mr. A frequently feels uncomfortable, anxious, and awkward in social situations ($20/02$; SOD = 73; $Hy1$ = 34; $Pd3$ = 39; CDI = 4). This appears due in large part to feelings of inferiority and sensitivity to criticism and rejection. Interactions with others can elicit self-critical thoughts and feelings of being incompetent, inadequate, and helpless that trouble him and that he then ruminates about (Egocentricity Index = .14; MOR = 4; m = 4). Because of his insecurities, Mr. A is likely to respond quite defensively if he feels threaten by others (PER = 4). For example, he may react defensively if others disagree with him or question his opinions and decisions, as he interprets such interactions as a threat to his self-esteem.

To reduce the risk of feeling inadequate, inferior, and incompetent, Mr. A generally prefers to avoid social situations, particularly with people he does not know well, and leaves the situations in which he must participate as soon as possible. Because it is difficult for him to feel secure with others, he acts in a reserved, cautious manner; keeps others at a distance; and is careful about what he reveals to them (T = 0). Others may perceive him as aloof, having little interest in being with them, and hard to get to know (T = 0; H content = 1). Unfortunately, this contributes to his feeling lonely and unsupported by others, which can add to and deepen his chronic depression ($20/02$; Isolate Cluster $= .29$). His discomfort with others, reserved, detached demeanor, and tendency to react defensively may have an important influence on his success as a salesman, as well as his motivation to pursue this career.

Mr. A distances himself from affective reactions through the use of intellectualization, rationalization, and denial (Intellectualization Index $=$ 7). This defensive style may create an impression that he is not bothered by events, as he appears on the surface to react in a highly logical, reasonable manner. Beneath the surface, however, he continuously struggles to avoid being overwhelmed by depression, worries, and self-doubts. He may successfully deny and conceal feelings such that others are not aware of the depth of his emotional pain.

Mr. A's responses indicate he uses his intellectual abilities in a very effective and creative manner. He tends to be careful, precise, and accurate in his attempts to account for and use all of the facts when trying to solve problems ($Zf = 11$; $W:M = 12:1$; $DQ+ = 4$). He is also able to view situations in a creative way, rather than being bound by ordinary, conventional approaches to situations (Populars $= 2$; $Xu\% = .29$). His ability to integrate and use information in a careful, organized, yet creative manner has been an asset in his work and his ability to analyze problems, generate a strategy to deal with the problem, and delegate responsibility to carry out his plan.

Mr. A appears to be motivated to disregard what is expected in a situation and instead respond in an unconventional way (Populars $= 2$; $Xu\% = .29$; $DR = 9$). This does not suggest that he is likely to act in an antisocial manner but that he places a premium on challenging people's expectations about appropriate behavior. One may speculate that this style developed as a response to the pressures he experienced growing up as the son of a preacher, as well as pressures to conform to his parents' values. He reported having consciously rejected his parents' values and feels disdain for the conventional values espoused by them. The previous indicates that much of Mr. A's sense of identity developed in terms of a rejection of his parents' values and ideals and a need to prove he is different than them. For instance, he may take pleasure in and be proud of times when he "breaks the rules." One may speculate that Mr. A lacks a clear direction in life because he never developed a positive identity around which he organized his values, ideals, and aspirations (Egocentricity Index $= .14$).

Although he denied suicidal intent during the clinical interview, Mr. A's test protocol raised serious concerns about the potential for a suicide attempt, particularly if his condition worsens ($S\text{-}CON = 9$). Thus, careful attention should be given to his suicidal risk, particularly should he express increased depression or hopelessness.

Diagnostic Impression

DSM–IV   Axis I   300.40 Dysthymia
                       296.35 Major depression, recurrent, in partial
                              remission
                       314.01 Attention deficit hyperactivity disorder

            Axis II   301.82 Avoidant personality disorder

TREATMENT RECOMMENDATIONS

The results described previously suggest that Mr. A would benefit from a combination of medication and psychotherapy to reduce symptoms of depression, worry, and anxiety and improve his self-esteem. A trial of medication to treat residual symptoms of ADHD should also be considered. In terms of monitoring Mr. A's response to treatment, one must be careful to separate out improvement due to a reduction in emotional distress as distinct from decreased distractibility if symptoms of ADHD are treated with medications.

Mr. A's intellectual strengths and his current motivation to change are positive prognostic signs and suggest that he has the psychological strengths needed to benefit from individual psychotherapy. However, the results of the psychological evaluation suggest several potential obstacles to psychotherapy. First, Mr. A's tendency to distance from emotions and to rely on intellectualizing defenses may prevent others from recognizing the extent of his emotional distress and pain. The therapist should be sensitive to this issue and not accept at face value his reports about reactions to recent events or about his current mood.

Second, Mr. A tends to avoid contact with others, particularly when he is feeling down. Thus, there is the potential for him to retreat from his therapist at the time he needs help the most. As noted previously, he may benefit from psychotherapy if he develops enough trust in his therapist to persevere when he experiences emotional discomfort during the course of treatment.

Third, Mr. A appears quite sensitive to feeling inadequate, incompetent, or humiliated and reacts defensively when he feels criticized. Thus, he may resist exposing aspects of his inner life about which he feels vulnerable. The therapist should be alert to signs that Mr. A feels embarrassed or defensive and be prepared to talk about what triggered these reactions and how these situations impacted on his self-esteem. Doing so may assist Mr. A maintain feelings of self-worth more consistently.

The pattern of test results raise significant concerns about Mr. A's risk for attempting suicide in spite of his assurances to the contrary. His therapist should evaluate and monitor Mr. A's suicide potential so that his well-being is assured.

14

Case 9: Fitness to Return to Work and Past Promiscuous Sex

REASON FOR EVALUATION

Mr. K is a 43-year-old, married, Hispanic male who worked as a pharmacist until his license was revoked 3 years prior to this evaluation. A psychiatric evaluation was arranged by his attorney as part of an effort to have his license reinstated. The psychiatrist appointed to perform this evaluation requested this evaluation to help in assessing whether psychological problems exist that would prevent Mr. K from working effectively and without supervision as a pharmacist. Given a history of treatment for depression during the past 3 years, a specific question to be addressed concerns the presence and severity of a current depression.

BACKGROUND INFORMATION

The information presented here was obtained during a clinical interview and review of available records. During the interview, Mr. K repeatedly stressed his desire to have his pharmacist's license fully reinstated, so he can pursue his career without any limitations. He has wanted to be a pharmacist since the age of 13 when he began working in a local drugstore. After graduating high school, Mr. K attended college until he was forced to drop out of school for financial reasons when his father was hospitalized for treatment of a Bipolar Disorder. His father has been hospitalized numerous times since then. Mr. K returned to college, obtained a bachelor's degree in biology and then a degree in pharmacy. While in college, he worked part time at a drugstore.

Mr. K worked as a pharmacist at a local drug store for 3½ years until he had a falling out with his boss about his salary as well as about his part-time job as a sales representative for a home health care products company that sold merchandise to drugstores that competed with his employer. He was then hired as the Chief Pharmacist for a drugstore, which is part of a large regional chain. His responsibilities included hiring and supervising a staff of pharmacists, scheduling, overseeing inventory, and maintaining relationships with the clinics, doctor's offices, and insurance companies serviced by the store. Work performance was satisfactory during a 7-year period.

Mr. K's pharmacist's license was suspended 3 years prior to this evaluation subsequent to an investigation of his role in illegal distribution of controlled substances. He claims that he had no involvement in these activities and explained that the owners of the stores obtained these narcotic medications without his knowledge by filling phony prescriptions on his day off. He was disciplined because he was responsible for monitoring all supplies in the store. Mr. K told the examiner he was not aware of his employer's actions and emphatically insisted that he never profited from these transactions.

Concurrent with these work-related difficulties, Mr. K and his wife's relationship became more and more strained. They had been married 18 years, had two daughters ages 11 and 14, and had become increasingly distant. Their relationship worsened after Mr. K confessed that he had periodically been involved with prostitutes for a number of years. For instance, during his first job, he took a prostitute into the storage room of the drugstore and had sexual relations with her. The next day, the owner accused Mr. K of theft because merchandise was found missing during his shift. Mr. K made restitution for the missing merchandise, and the owner was appeased. He repeatedly told the examiner that he had not taken the merchandise, the prostitute had. He allowed that this episode may have been "dumb, really dumb of me" but commented that he was young at the time. He also reported having contact with prostitutes during a period of several weeks when he was moonlighting at a store in a different part of the city and worked the 11 p.m. to 7 a.m. shift. He carefully explained to the examiner that his sexual activity with the prostitutes only involved oral sex and stressed that he never had intercourse with them. Periodic contacts with prostitutes apparently continued until he made his confession to his wife.

Mr. K's wife was quite upset after hearing his confession and threatened to leave him. He reacted by becoming increasingly guilty and depressed. He was also worried, anxious, and fearful about the state's investigations of illegal medication distribution at the pharmacy, which began around this time. After a fight with his wife about his past sexual behavior, Mr. K ingested six Halcion pills, which he had taken from the pharmacy, and wrote a suicide note. When his wife found him unconscious and discovered the note, she immediately contacted their physician who arranged admission to the psychiatric unit of a hospital. Mr. K told the examiner he knew full well the amount of medication he had taken would not kill him but explained he had felt desperate at the time.

According to hospital records, at admission Mr. K presented as sad, agitated, speaking rapidly, expressing suicidal ideation, and having guilt of psychotic proportions manifested in somatic delusions that he had contracted AIDS as a result of promiscuous involvement with prostitutes. A complete medical work-up found no signs of physical illness. A series of tests for HIV repeated every 6 months for 2 years has been negative. He was initially treated with Xanax to reduce his anxiety and then with an antidepressant medication, Elavil, and an antipsychotic medication, Trilafon. During the 3-week hospitalization, his wife initiated divorce proceedings. At discharge, he was described as less depressed and no longer suicidal. Although the delusional intensity of these concerns had decreased, he was still obsessively preoccupied with fears and guilt about his sexual conduct; the psychiatrist described these concerns as "representing exaggerated worries instead of the psychotic proportions they had at the time of admission." His pharmacist's license was placed on probation because of his psychiatric condition. No psychological testing was obtained during this hospitalization.

Following discharge, Mr. K was seen in individual psychotherapy. Because he was displeased with treatment provided by the psychiatrist who had hospitalized him, he began treatment at a clinic with a psychiatrist for medication and a social worker for psychotherapy. He was initially described as sad, tearful, anxious, agitated, and talking in a rapid, pressured manner. The initial diagnostic impression was of an agitated depression. However, the psychiatrist questioned whether Mr. K's presentation also included a character disorder because of the history of lying, thefts, multiple contacts with prostitutes without concern for the consequences, and the absence of remorse for his past conduct. Specifically, the possibility of an antisocial personality disorder was considered. The medications started in the hospital were continued for about 2 months before Mr. K requested that all medications be discontinued. He has not been treated with medications since. He decided to terminate psychotherapy after about 6 months.

Several months after being discharged from the hospital, Mr. K became friendly with his ex-wife's best friend, who was also divorced. They eventually became involved, began living together after dating for 3 months, and married. They had been married for 2 years at the time of this evaluation. He described their relationship in very positive terms.

Mr. K tried to return to work as a pharmacist 3–4 months after the hospitalization but quit after 1 day because of difficulties concentrating. He then began working as a sales representative for a health care company. He commented that he was good at this. After investigating the charges against him, the state regulatory agency allowed Mr. K to work, but only under supervision. He told the examiner the decision to place him on probation occurred in part because of the history of treatment for a psychiatric disorder. At the time of this evaluation, he had been working as a pharmacist for 9 months. His job performance was satisfactory. He feels his probation is unfair and wants his license to be reinstated without restrictions so he has the opportunity to advance in his career. As he expressed his displeasure about the regulatory board's restrictions on his license, Mr. K stated strongly that he intends to fight them "even if it means spending my last dollar! I didn't do anything wrong!"

During the clinical interview, Mr. K denied experiencing any abnormalities in mood during the past 2 months. He described sleep and appetite as normal and denied having any current difficulties with concentration, self-esteem, or suicidal ideation. When asked about specific symptoms of depression, he described himself as very health conscious in his eating habits, having "terrific" concentration, and as "self-confident, but not grandiose. I have a high level of confidence and energy. But I'm very humble and don't have a chip on my shoulder." He did not acknowledge having past manic episodes. He denied a history of current or past alcohol or drug abuse. When asked about ongoing psychotherapy, he stated that he does not see any need for treatment because he can talk to his second wife.

Mr. K seemed extremely anxious and concerned about the evaluation. This was evident when he called the examiner several times after the testing session to correct answers he had missed on the WAIS-R. During the clinical interview, he spoke rapidly, and it was often difficult to follow his train of thought, in part because he gave overly detailed answers that made it difficult to grasp the point he was trying to make. Mr. K's mood was labile during the testing session, vacillating from anger to laughter. He made inappropriate disclosures about himself, such as spontaneously saying what his income was without being asked. He also made inappropriate jokes. For example, during administration of the intelligence tests, an item reminded him of a joke concerning Mickey Mouse's divorce from Minnie Mouse that ended with the punch line, "She's fucking Goofy!" at which he laughed uproariously and slapped the examiner's knee.

DIAGNOSTIC CONSIDERATIONS

The circumstances under which this evaluation was arranged should be kept in mind during this evaluation. Specifically, this evaluation was requested by Mr. K's attorney as part of an effort to have Mr. K's professional license reinstated without any limitations. As he was placed on probation in large part because of a history of psychiatric problems, Mr. K may have an incentive to try to show that he is well adjusted and that no psychological problems exist that would interfere with his professional performance or conduct.

The possibility that Mr. K may be motivated to portray himself in a favorable light should be carefully evaluated. It is understandable that subjects may attempt to create a positive impression by minimizing psychological difficulties when a psychological evaluation is administered in the context of assessing individuals' ability to work. This frequently occurs in the context of pre-employment screenings or fitness to return to work evaluations when subjects complete the MMPI in a manner that emphasizes their psychological health, moral integrity, self-control, and positive inter-personal relationships. Given job candidates' motivation to create a favor-able impression, it has been recommended that any signs of psychopa-thology revealed by a defensive job applicant be taken quite seriously (Butcher, 1979; Graham, 1993).

The MMPI validity scales were developed specifically to identify efforts to minimize emotional problems or to fake-good (Graham, 1993; Greene 1991). The ability of the MMPI to identify fake-good profiles has been less well established than identification of fake-good profiles, although a meta-analysis found significant differences between defensive and honest responders on standard and supplementary MMPI validity scales (Baer et al., 1992). In general, naive subjects attempting to fake-good produce an elevation on the Lic scale whereas more sophisticated subjects produce an elevation on the K scale with a relatively lower F scale score (Graham, Watts, & Timbrook, 1991; Grayson & Olinger, 1957; Grow, McVaugh, & Eno, 1980; Otto, Lang, Megargee, & Rosenblatt, 1988; Rappaport, 1958; Rice, Arnold, & Tate, 1983; Walters, White, & Greene, 1988; Woychyshyn, McElheran, & Romney, 1992). Gough (1950) proposed that the relationship of raw scores on the F and K scales could be used to identify fake-good protocols. If the difference between the two scales is in the negative direction (K greater than F), it can suggest an effort to fake-good. No firm cutoff for the $F-K$ index has been established, although some researchers have suggested that an $F-K$ index with a value less than -11 ($F-K < -11$) indicates a defensive response set (Grow et al., 1980; Hunt, 1948). However, because of a high degree of overlap between valid and fake-good profiles, the $F-K$ index has a high false positive rate, that is, it incorrectly identifies many valid protocols as invalid (Cofer et al., 1949; Exner, McDowell, Pabst, Strackman, & Kirkman, 1963; Grow et al., 1980; Hunt, 1948; McAnulty, Rappaport, & McAnulty, 1985). This is particularly true for subjects with higher socioeconomic status, as they would be expected to produce relatively high K scale scores even if they are not defensive.

Relatively few studies have examined whether defensive responses sets influence the results of the Rorschach. Some studies have reported that Rorschach protocols administered under standard as opposed to fake-good conditions do not differ (Carp & Shavzin, 1950; Fosberg, 1938, 1941), although Seamons et al. (1981) reported that the Rorschachs produced by inmates at a state prison differed when subjects were instructed to appear well adjusted as opposed to mentally ill. In the fake-good condition, subjects gave more popular responses and fewer unusual, deviant responses or responses with dramatic content.

A recent study examined whether subjects who responded to the MMPI in a defensive manner in the context of a fitness to return to work evaluation also produced defensive Rorschach protocols (Ganellen, 1994). Subjects were all commercial airlines pilots who were required to undergo an independent psychological evaluation after completing a treatment program for alcohol or substance abuse. Subjects knew the results of the psychological evaluation would be taken into account when a decision was made concerning whether to reinstate their pilots' license and allow them to return to work. Thus, subjects potentially had considerable incentive to attempt to create a favorable impression as their careers and livelihoods were at stake.

It was expected that a guarded, defensive response set would be manifested on the Rorschach by fewer than average responses, a constricted response style, and an attempt to appear conventional. It was also expected that no or few signs of difficulties would be produced on the Rorschach if subjects were successful in their efforts to create a favorable impression. Even though all subjects were quite defensive on the MMPI, they produced valid Rorschach protocols, indicating they experienced emotional distress, self-critical ideation, and difficulties in interpersonal relationships, problems denied during the clinical interview and on the MMPI. Ganellen (1994) suggested that it may be easier for subjects to successfully deny psychological difficulties on a self-report inventory, such as the MMPI, than on a projective test, such as the Rorschach, because of differences in the format of these tests. Because many of the MMPI items are face valid, an examinee who wishes to avoid appearing disturbed can consciously decide not to endorse MMPI items that contain pathological content. In contrast, the Rorschach offers few if any clues about how responses will be interpreted by the examiner. Therefore, it may be more difficult to deliberately skew responses on the Rorschach than on the MMPI.

MMPI-2 Data

Validity.   The MMPI-2 validity scale configuration suggests a deliberate, concerted, and naive effort to create the most favorable impression

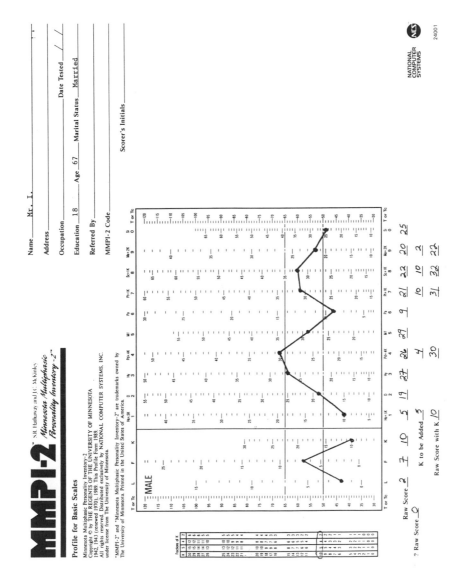

MMPI-2

S.R. Hathaway and J.C. McKinley

Minnesota Multiphasic
Personality Inventory-2™

Profile for Basic Scales

Minnesota Multiphasic Personality Inventory-2
Copyright © by THE REGENTS OF THE UNIVERSITY OF MINNESOTA
1942, 1943 (renewed 1970), 1989. This Profile Form 1989.
All rights reserved. Distributed exclusively by NATIONAL COMPUTER SYSTEMS, INC.
under license from The University of Minnesota.

"MMPI-2" and "Minnesota Multiphasic Personality Inventory-2" are trademarks owned by
The University of Minnesota. Printed in the United States of America.

MALE

Name __Mr. I.__

Address _____

Occupation _____ Date Tested __/__/__

Education __18__ Age __67__ Marital Status __Married__

Referred By _____

MMPI-2 Code _____

Scorer's Initials _____

289

Case 9 MMPI-2 Content and Supplementary Scales

	Raw Score	T Score
FB	1	46
True Response Inconsistency (TRIN)	9	50
Variable Response Inconsistency (VRIN)	4	46
Anxiety	2	39
Repression	15	50
MAC-R	21	48
Ego Strength (Es)	37	49
Dominance (Do)	16	48
Social Responsibility (Re)	27	68
Overcontrolled Hostility (O-H)	14	55
PTSD - Keane (PK)	1	38
PTSD - Schlenger (PS)	1	38
Addiction Potential (APS)	24	52
Addiction Admission (AAS)	2	46

Content Scales (Butcher et al., 1990)		
Anxiety (ANX)	3	45
Fears (FRS)	1	42
Obsessiveness (OBS)	5	50
Depression (DEP)	2	45
Health Concerns (HEA)	0	33
Bizarre Mentation (BIZ)	2	50
Anger (ANG)	5	48
Cynicism (CYN)	6	45
Antisocial Practices (ASP)	5	44
Type A (TPA)	9	50
Low Self-esteem (LSE)	4	52
Social Discomfort (SOD)	4	43

Depression Subscales (Harris-Lingoes)		
Subjective Depression (D1)	3	40
Psychomotor Retardation (D2)	6	54
Physical Malfunctioning (D3)	3	51
Mental Dullness (D4)	0	38
Brooding (D5)	0	40

Hysteria Subscales (Harris-Lingoes)		
Denial of Social Anxiety (Hy1)	4	51
Need for Affection (Hy2)	9	59
Lassitude-Malaise (Hy3)	0	38
Somatic Complaints (Hy4)	0	38
Inhibition of Aggression (Hy5)	5	63

```
                                              Raw Score  T Score

Psychopathic Deviate Subscales (Harris-Lingoes)
        Familial Discord (Pd1)                   0           38
        Authority Problems (Pd2)                 2           42
        Social Imperturbability (Pd3)            6           64
        Social Alienation (Pd4)                  3           45
        Self-Alienation (Pd5)                    4           53


Paranoia Subscales (Harris-Lingoes)
        Persecutory Ideas (Pa1)                  1           46
        Poignancy (Pa2)                          2           48
        Naivete (Pa3)                            7           60


Schizophrenia Subscales (Harris-Lingoes)
        Social Alienation (Sc1)                  0           48
        Emotional Alienation (Sc2)               1           50
        Lack of Ego Mastery, Cognitive (Sc3)     0           42
        Lack of Ego Mastery, Conative (Sc4)      1           43
        Lack of Ego Mastery, Def. Inhib. (Sc5)   0           40
        Bizarre Sensory Experiences (Sc6)        1           45


Hypomania Subscales (Harris-Lingoes)
        Amorality (Ma1)                          1           42
        Psychomotor Acceleration (Ma2)           3           39
        Imperturbability (Ma3)                   4           44
        Ego Inflation (Ma4)                      3           43


Social Introversion Subscales (Ben-Porath et al., 1989)
        Shyness/Self-Consciousness (Si1)         4           48
        Social Avoidance (Si2)                   3           49
        Alienation -- Self and Others (Si3)      4           47
```

possible by underreporting psychological problems and denying emotional troubles, personal difficulties, and any faults or flaws, even minor foibles to which most people would admit ($L = 70$; $K = 66$; $F - K = -22$). This is consistent with a fake-good response set motivated by Mr. K's desire to portray himself in the most favorable light possible. To do so, he responded to the MMPI-2 as though he were unusually virtuous, well-adjusted, and psychologically healthy. This suggests an extremely defensive approach to this evaluation. As a result, he is likely to present a rather biased picture of himself and his past behavior; to gloss over, minimize, and justify past difficulties; and to lack insight into the reasons for his behavior.

Clinical Scales. The effect of the defensive response set described previously is to lower scores on the MMPI-2 clinical scales. Consistent with this, no MMPI-2 clinical scale is elevated above a T-score of 65. In fact, the only scales above a T-score of 50 are scales *2* ($T = 52$) and *8* ($T = 51$). No reliable interpretation can be made based on these scores. Similarly, no reliable interpretation can be made from the elevations on the MMPI-2 content and supplementary scales. Graham (1993) suggested that no useful clinical information can be gleaned from a defensive MMPI-2 profile when all clinical scales are below a T-score of 60 because one cannot tell whether this reflects a well-adjusted person who is motivated to emphasize their positive adjustment as opposed to a poorly adjusted individual who is claiming to be well adjusted.

Rorschach Data

Mr. K's Rorschach protocol appears valid given the number of responses produced ($R = 27$) as well as the amount of psychological energy he expended as he responded to the test stimuli ($Zf = 20$; Blends $= 15$). His openness on the Rorschach is surprising given signs of a markedly defensive stance ($PER = 12$ vs. 1.02 *PER* responses for the normative sample). Before reviewing the key variables to determine the interpretive strategy to follow, the positive Suicide Constellation must be considered (S-$Con = 8$). As Mr. K has many of the psychological characteristics exhibited by a sample of patients who committed suicide within 60 days after completing the Rorschach, his risk for suicide must be considered carefully (see discussion of the *S-CON* in Case 8). This ominous possibility should be kept in mind while reviewing the rest of the protocol.

The first positive key variable is the Schizophrenia Index ($SCZI = 4$). As discussed in earlier cases, the *SCZI* is an actuarially based index for identifying patients with schizophrenia or other psychotic disorders that focuses primarily on distortions in thought processes and unrealistic, inaccurate perceptions. Although a positive score on the *SCZI* suggests a

Card	Response	Inquiry
I	1. L.1 2 dancers in a Broadway musical. In a Las Vegas show, fancy costume. That's it. E.b held up by dance partner, foot g here, step 1 this. Holding in uniformity.	E: (Rpts S's response) S: Here's the hands. Partner holding up. Costume out here. 2 men, so got to be 4 people. Arm here, 1 foot here. 1 here on hip of dance partner. E: Broadway musical? S: Bec of the costumes. Ruffles on the clothing. Not just a straight arm projecting out.
	2. Or ballerina against a pole, for a dance step.	E: (Rpts S's response) S: Because of the symmetry, bec of the position of the arms and feet. The leaps.
	3. I c a guy carrying, a strong arm guy carrying 2 X-mas tress. Y.k., 1 carrying 2 trees behind u. I remembered buying 1st X-mas tree right away.	E: (Rpts S's response) S: Turn it upside down. See back & shoulder blades. Dragging it. He's in the backdrop. What's the word? Draw s.t., sugg this is furthest part. Trees in forefront. E: I'm not sure where y're lkg. S: He's dragging trees, too heavy for him. Pretty strong, arms, legs. E: Strong? S: Muscular tissue, can see them. E: See them? S: Diff colorations. Can almost see the skeleton. Shading.
II	4. 2 clowns dancing. That's an easy one.	E: (Rpts S's response)' S: Yeah, here's hat, in the red. Here's the paint, ll a prank they did on stage. E: Paint? S: It ll red paint! What else – it _is_ red paint.

5. The, if I turn it around ...I'd rather not say what I see, but I'd ...No.
E: There are no right or wrong answers. Tell me e.t u see.
S: Well, u go to Catholic church. The image of Christ. Beard g this way. I'm not going to get penalized?
E: No. E.b sees diff things. No answers are the "right" one. Just tell me what the card l.l to u.
E: Well, I see Christ. He made the clouds closer in the sky. Made a clearing for s.t.

E: (Rpts S's response)
S: Here's the clouds. Then distance. Here's Christ, can see arms raising up. I'm sure u have Catholic friends. Can almost c the Turin, the shroud in white part. It lks as though Christ is appearing in the clouds.
E: Clouds?
S: Well, the - what's the terminology? Cumulus? Come on!
E: What l.l that?
S: Cumulus. Can c the structure. Like a darkening, abt to rain. The shading.
E: Shroud?
S: Darkness. Then a white space in betw. I know its not there.

6. I c s.o's fingerprints for an arrest record. Had an open record & blood spilled out fr a murder or rape or s.t.

E: (Rpts S's response)
S: Here.
E: What reminded u of that?
S: U know how...I went for one. Thght abt driving a cab in betw jobs. Y.k., roll thumbs. If have open cut it'll bleed.
E: U saw blood.
S: Its red, obv.
E: Print?
S: Way of smudging, see diff shading.

III 7. 2 jazz dancers playing the Bongo drum.

E: (Rpts S's response)
S: Right. Here's drums right · here. Here's high heel shoes & they're dancing.
E: Jazz dancers?
S: The outfits they're wearing.
E: Outfits?
S: Black leotards. P in Broadway shows d't usually wear black, short jackets & short hip huggers. I remember Lola Folana on TV, that's how I recognize it.

8. What else do I c...Y're g to thnk this is goofy. Breaking of a wishbone from a turkey. U k? Bone bending & this is blood fr turkey in the middle. Turkey not cooked. U k?

E: (Rpts S's response)
S: Here. How the turkey has beveled edge on e side? 4 places.
E: Show me where y're looking.
S: All this is part of it. Breaking.

<table>
<tr><td>

For children. How come
adults d't have happy
memories fr childhood? I
do. (Pt tells story)

</td><td>

E: Breaking?
S: Right. The wishbone.
E: Blood?
S: Its red! L.1 dripping, blood
or grease. Prob undercooked,
what's the word. Undercooked
blood or s.t.

</td></tr>
<tr><td>

IV   9. Uhm...I c a bird with
its wings spread. Ugly, l
a black owl. Really ugly.

</td><td>

E: (Rpts S's response)
S: Here's head, wings.
E: I'm not sure where y're lkg.
S: Not the whole thing. This is
the tree.
E: Owl?
S: Way the feathers are. Bushy
around the head, fluffy.
E: Fluffy?
S: Shading.
E: Ugly?
S: The C. Black is alw
associated w darkness & fear.

</td></tr>
<tr><td>

10. And...U ever see
aardvark cartoon, u k,
modern art stuff? U k, a
movie w a H character?
Blown up. Like mouse's
head or raccoon. L w H
characteristics. L if y're
on drugs, or a nightmare --
like the bogyman is going
to come & get u!

</td><td>

E: (Rpts S's response)
S: Here's face. L devil's
advocate. Can c horns coming
out. Frightening, wld be for a
child. 1/2 man, 1/2 beast.
E: Devil's advocate?
S: Watching too much TV. U k,
bec of cape of the Devil.
Horns, here & here.
E: Devil?
S: Horns & Prince of Darkness.
Dark features & smoke coming up
out of hell, I suppose.
E: Smoke?
S: Well, the shading. L.1 he's
coming out of shadows & smoke.

</td></tr>
<tr><td>

V   11. A Bf.

</td><td>

E: (Rpts S's response)
S: Cld be 1. If ever caught 1
as a child & he opened his
antlers &...what is it?
E: U said a BF.
S: Wings are spread out, far
out. L if u catch 1 & they're
nervous, spread their wings out.

</td></tr>
<tr><td>

12. And a bat.

</td><td>

E: (Rpts S's response)
S: The blackness again.
Darkness.
E: Where are u lkg?
S: Body is more mammalian than
insects. Wings of insect aren't

</td></tr>
</table>

l that at all. Believe me, I've seen bats in Wisconsin.

13. And a dancer, Jamaican w feathers on arm. Standing up, dancing. Ever see the commercial for the Bahamas? (sings) "Its better in Jamaica" etc. I watch too much TV.

E: (Rpts S's response)
S: Sure. This is the costume. Silhouette of hat or costume. Got feathers. Got fruit on hat, l in the commercials. I've been there. (tells story)
E: Feathers?
S: Bec they're ragged, edges there & there.

VI 14. It l.l...an X-ray of s.o's artery. What's that? An IVP? Dye is going down thr vein. Blood is squirting out in o vessels. C't believe I got that wrong.
E: Wrong?
S: A dumb mistake.

E: (Rpts S's response)
S: Sure. Can c where blood is going right there. There may be a break. Maybe a sign of cancer, like a blockage in the artery. I've seen enough X-rays.
E: Cancer or block?
S: The discoloration.
E: I'm not sure what u mean.
S: This l.l blood vessels & skin tissue. Coloration.

15. It l.l an insect, a caterpillar, crawling along the ground. Use the, what do they call them, night lens. L night crawlers. Ever gone fishing? Best time to get worms. Did u grow up in a small town?

E: (Rpts S's response)
S: Here's head of caterpillar. Ever see a mealworm? Crawling around. Been fishing w my uncle. Best times I ever had.
E: Where are u lkg?
S: Foliage, ground is wet. This is a night crawler. Lk for worms, for directions w feelers, l cats have whiskers.
E: Wet?
S: Just the coloration. L.l recently rained.
E: Night lens?
S: Well, bec wldn't be able to get picture w regular camera. Need special lens.

VII 16. Seahorses all around.. U k, seahorses...Under a microscope. Ever make yr own ant farm? Seahorses is what I c.

E: (Rpts S's response)
S: Here - l here, l here, l here, l here.
E: Seahorses?
S: Way contour is, structure.
E: Under microscope?
S: Bec u c't c w naked eye. C't see, l y can in aquarium, swimming around. Lkg at a close-up view of them, I guess.

17. I swear to God, Chicken McNuggets! (laughs) My daughter had some last night. (tells story)

E: (Rpts S's response)
S: All over. L battered chicken, gravy. L batter dripping on side of plate.
E: What gives it that impression?
S: I'm hungry! (laughs)
E: Help me c it.
S: I dk. The size. Actual size of what u get for $1.99. (laughs) "A little money for a lot of food." (as if an announcer)

18. It l.1 a basket full of shrimp, too. What else...

E: (Rpts S's response)
S: That's easy. Can actually c the dried shrimp in there. Elongation of fried batter.
E: Shrimp?
S: Again, close to lunch! Its erratic, not uniform as far as size of individual pieces.

19. It l.1 a pancake that got all torn up. U k, overlay, where pancake lays.

E: (Rpts S's response)
S: Right. Push it all tog & it l.1 scrapings from burnt part of pancake. People do that, leave burnt crusts.
E: Burnt?
S: Can c the darker parts. That's black, burnt. Called grizzle in Jewish.

VIII 20. That's more interesting, more colorful, anyway. L.1 Pirates of Carribbean. L going to Disneyworld. L.1 mast of old ship, but they did it up in Disneyland style.

E: (Rpts S's response)
S: Here's mast, 1st tier, bow, sails underneath. Great ride. Ever b there?
E: No, I haven't. U mentioned it was done in Disneyland style.
S: Colorful. V animated, but lks real, so-called "pull it off" to make it feel like living that time in history.

21. Whatever...It l.1 2 fish on open roasting rack on camping trip. They're pink, not done yet. Fire underneath them. L cooking trout. Blue supp to repr smoke. On roasting spigot. I must be getting hungry, thnkg abt lunch.

E: (Rpts S's response)
S: Here's the fish, 1 here & here. Can c head & gills. Got stick here. Got a new gimmick, put turkey on grill.
E: Fire?
S: There. The red repr fire, blue repr smoke.
E: U mentioned a roasting spigot.

S: Right. This thing jutting
out, l a hook. Not moving. On
a tower, can turn over the fire.

IX   22. What do I c? I c...   E: (Rpts S's response)
      tulips. Tulip bulbs. 4 on   S: Right. Here's the stem.
      top w 1 stem. Isn't that   E: Tulips?
      weird?   S: Pink. Purple. Just the way
                                     bulbs are. At Botanical Gardens
                                     last year I lkd at them.
                                     E: 1 stem?
                                     S: Yeah. 4 flowers on 1 stem.

      23. I c peppermint ice   E: (Rpts S's response)
      cream. Mixed in w lime   S: Here. Ice cream things.
      sherbet. What a mess.   Lime sherbet. And l.l its
                                     overflowing. Here's sugar cone.
                                     E: Peppermint?
                                     S: Its pink.
                                     E: U said its a mess.
                                     S: Bec it ll its dripping.

      24. What else - I c an   E: (Rpts S's response)
      electrician's fire. Here's   S: Right. Here's arc where
      the arc when, c a loose   there's a bad wire. Can see a
      wire that started a fire.   separation.
      How does that burn so   E: Fire?
      evenly? I k its j a   S: Yellow & red. See electrical
      picture. Orange smoke fr   fire, where spark flies, lks
      the chemicals burning.   white. (tells story)
      Burning. Blue shows   E: Chemical fire?
      chemical. Combination of   S: Bec chemicals wld burn diff
      paint, chemicals, &   C's.
      electrical fire. The cans
      of paint are all exploding.
      Shldn't be symmetrical.
      That's what I c.

X   25. This 1 is a little diff   E: (Rpts S's response)
      to decipher...L.l an   S: Fish. Here's coral part.
      aquarium & seeing diff   Here's algae, seahores.
      species of fish. L a coral   E: Coral?
      reef. Fish swimming. Blue   S: I've been over to Bahamas sev
      indicates fish, green   times.
      algae. Black indicates   E: What reminded u of that?
      some wood floating around.   S: Jagged edges.
      Can see where my childhood   E: Algae?
      memories are -- good times.   S: Just, u k, being around the
                                     pond. Algae are alw green.
                                     E: Wood?
                                     S: Its dark, diff than rest of
                                     picture.

298

26. What else do I c? I c
a bird sanctuary. A couple
of robins, a couple of
woodpeckers ·bouncing on the
wood. Some debris &
foliage.

E: (Rpts S's response)
S: Here's woodpeckers eating off
wood. Robins, 1, 2, 3, 4.
E: Robins?
S: I d't k. Maybe the
coloration. Ever seen a yellow
or brown robin? I have.

27. I c one really weird
thing. Captain Video
serials - d't k if y're old
enough. L.1 he's standing
there w helmet on, shooting
his gun off, smoking. Had
backpack, I remember that
now. P can actually fly
20-30 feet in air! Used to
be called jet-packs.
Ovaltine, Bosco. Remember
that?

E: (Rpts S's response)
S: (laughs) Yeah. Thinking of
when I was a kid. Here, arms
stretched out, 1 smoke coming
out of weapons.
E: Smoke?
S: Bec of darkness, blackness of
smoke.

```
CASE09.R3==================== SEQUENCE OF SCORES ==============================

CARD NO LOC  #  DETERMINANT(S)     (2) CONTENT(S)    POP Z  SPECIAL SCORES
======= ======  ===============    === ==========    === =  ===============
  I   1 W+   1  Ma+                 2  H,Cg           4.0    COP,DR
      2 W+   1  Mao                 2  H,Id           4.0
      3 W+   1  Ma.FD.FYu              H,Bt           4.0    DV

 II   4 W+   1  Ma.CFo              2  (H),Cg         4.5    COP
      5 DS+  3  Ma.FY.C'Fu             (H),Cl         4.5    DR2
      6 Do   2  CF.YF-                 Art,Bl                MOR,PER

III   7 D+   1  Ma.FC'o             2  H,Cg,Id      P 3.0    PER
      8 D+   1  mp.CFo                 An,Bl          4.0    MOR,DR2

 IV   9 W+   1  FMp.FT.FC'u            A,Bt           4.0    ALOG
     10 W+   1  FY.ma.FDu              (H),Fi,Cg      4.0    DR

  V  11 Wo   1  FMpo                   A            P 1.0    DV,PER,DR
     12 Wo   1  C'Fo                   A            P 1.0    PER
     13 W+   1  Mao                    H,Cg,Bt        2.5    DR2,PER

 VI  14 Wv   1  ma.YF-                 Xy,Bl                 PER,MOR
     15 W+   1  FMa.YF-                A,Na           2.5    PER,DR2

VII  16 Do   1  FD-                 2  A                     DR2
     17 Wv   1  Fo                     Fd                    DR
     18 Wv   1  Fu                     Fd
     19 Wv   1  FC'-                   Fd                    MOR,DR,DV

VIII 20 Wo   1  CFo                    Id             4.5    PER,DR2
     21 W+   1  CF-                    Fd,Fi          4.5    DV,DR

 IX  22 Do   9  FCu                    Bt                    PER,INC
     23 D/      ma.CF-                 Fd             2.5
     24 WS+  1  ma.CF.C'F-             Fi,Ex          5.5    DR2,AG

  X  25 W+   1  FMa.CF.mp.C'F+      2  A,Na           5.5    PER,DR
     26 D+  11  FMa.CFu             2  A,Bt           4.0    DR
     27 D+      Mp.C'F.ma-             (H),Sc,Fi      4.0    DR,PER


============================= SUMMARY OF APPROACH =============================

    I :   W.W.W                        VI :   W.W
   II :   W.DS.D                      VII :   D.W.W.W
  III :   D.D                        VIII :   W.W
   IV :   W.W                          IX :   D.D.WS
    V :   W.W.W                         X :   W.D.D
```

```
CASE09.R3==================== STRUCTURAL SUMMARY ================================

LOCATION              DETERMINANTS              CONTENTS       S-CONSTELLATION
FEATURES          BLENDS         SINGLE                       YES..FV+VF+V+FD>2
                                         H   = 5, 0           YES..Col-Shd Bl>0
Zf    = 20      M.FD.FY        M  = 3      (H) = 4, 0         YES..Ego<.31,>.44
ZSum  = 73.5    M.CF           FM = 1      Hd  = 0, 0         YES..MOR > 3
ZEst  = 66.5    M.FY.C'F       m  = 0      (Hd)= 0, 0         YES..Zd > +- 3.5
                CF.YF          FC = 1      Hx  = 0, 0         YES..es > EA
W    = 18       M.FC'          CF = 2      A   = 7, 0         YES..CF+C > FC
 (Wv = 4)       m.CF           C  = 0      (A) = 0, 0         YES..X+% < .70
D    = 9        FM.FT.FC'      Cn = 0      Ad  = 0, 0         NO..S > 3
Dd   = 0        FY.m.FD        FC'= 1      (Ad)= 0, 0         NO..P < 3 or > 8
S    = 2        m.YF           C'F= 1      An  = 1, 0         NO..Pure H < 2
                FM.YF          C'  = 0     Art = 1, 0         NO..R < 17
  DQ            m.CF           FT = 0      Ay  = 0, 0         8.....TOTAL
.........(FQ-)  m.CF.C'F       TF = 0      Bl  = 0, 3
 +  = 16  ( 4)  FM.CF.m.C'F    T  = 0      Bt  = 1, 4         SPECIAL SCORINGS
 o  =  6  ( 2)  FM.CF          FV = 0      Cg  = 0, 5                Lv1    Lv2
 v/+ = 1  ( 1)  M.C'F.m        VF = 0      Cl  = 0, 1         DV   =  4x1    0x2
 v  =  4  ( 2)                 V  = 0      Ex  = 0, 1         INC  =  1x2    0x4
                               FY = 0      Fd  = 5, 0         DR   =  9x3    7x6
                               YF = 0      Fi  = 1, 3         FAB  =  0x4    0x7
                               Y  = 0      Ge  = 0, 0         ALOG =  1x5
   FORM QUALITY                Fr = 0      Hh  = 0, 0         CON  =  0x7
                               rF = 0      Ls  = 0, 0         Raw Sum6  = 22
       FQx  FQf  MQual  SQx    FD = 1      Na  = 0, 2         Wgtd Sum6 = 80
 +  =   2    0     1     0     F  = 2      Sc  = 0, 1
 o  =   9    1     4     0                 Sx  = 0, 0         AB  = 0     CP  = 0
 u  =   7    1     2     1                 Xy  = 1, 0         AG  = 1     MOR = 4
 -  =   9    0     1     1                 Id  = 1, 2         CFB = 0     PER =11
 none=  0    --    0     0     (2) = 7                        COP = 2     PSV = 0

==================== RATIOS, PERCENTAGES, AND DERIVATIONS ====================

R = 27          L  =  0.08         FC:CF+C = 1: 9      COP = 2     AG = 1
-----------------------------------         Pure C  =   0       Food       = 5
EB = 8: 9.5  EA = 17.5   EBPer= N/A   SumC':WSumC= 8:9.5   Isolate/R  =0.41
eb =12:15    es = 27      D  =  -3     Afr    =0.42         H:(H)Hd(Hd)= 5: 4
         Adj es = 16     Adj D =   0   S      = 2           (HHd):(AAd)= 4: 0
-----------------------------------         Blends:R=15:27      H+A:Hd+Ad  =16: 0
FM = 5  :  C'= 8   T = 1               CP     = 0
m  = 7  :  V = 0   Y = 6
                               P   = 3       Zf   =20       3r+(2)/R=0.26
a:p   = 15: 5   Sum6  = 22     X+% =0.41     Zd   = +7.0    Fr+rF   = 0
Ma:Mp =  7: 1   Lv2   =  7     F+% =0.50     W:D:Dd =18: 9: 0  FD   = 3
2AB+Art+Ay= 1   WSum6 = 80     X-% =0.33     W:M  =18: 8     An+Xy   = 2
M-    =   1     Mnone =  0     S-% =0.11     DQ+  =16        MOR     = 4
                               Xu% =0.26     DQv  = 4

=============================================================================
SCZI = 4*    DEPI = 7*    CDI = 2    S-CON = 8*    HVI = No    OBS = No
=============================================================================
```

301

strong likelihood that the patient is schizophrenic, the risk of false positives (e.g., saying patients are schizophrenic when they are not) is highest when $SCZI = 4$. Thus, although the $SCZI$ is positive, considerable caution must be taken before one can conclude that Mr. K's Rorschach indicates he suffers from schizophrenia.

The search strategy begins by first examining Mr. K's thought processes and perceptual accuracy. Because he is an ambient, he is likely to be inefficient, indecisive, and inconsistent when he tries to solve problems and make decisions ($EA = 8:9.0$). He is hesitant and uncertain about making choices, doubts himself, and changes his mind frequently as he considers, reconsiders, and reconsiders again whether the choice he has made is the "right" choice. These tendencies create a vulnerability to making errors in judgment. He is particularly likely to show lapses in judgment and inefficient thought processes at this point because pessimistic worry, situational anxiety, and feelings of discouragement interfere with his ability to concentrate and sustain attention ($eb = 12:15$; $m = 7$; $MOR = 4$).

In addition, the likelihood of poorly thought-out action is quite high given the large number of responses Mr. K produced revealing a serious disturbance in thinking, disorganization, and flawed judgment and conceptualization ($WSum6 = 20$). A review of the responses containing the Special Scores suggests that most special scores were awarded because Mr. K included many irrelevant, extraneous, tangential ideas. For instance, Response 8 on Card III began with a description of a turkey wishbone being broken, but he then expressed a stream of details, such as memories from his childhood and odd, irrelevant comments (e.g., "How come adults don't have happy memories from childhood? I do."). Similarly, Response 13 on Card V is fairly common (a dancer in a costume) but was spoiled when he remarked that it reminded him of a commercial and then began singing the jingle from the commercial. It seemed in this instance, as well as when he told the examiner a joke about Mickey Mouse's divorce and slapped the examiner's knee after the punchline, that Mr. K could not restrain himself from saying what he was thinking, even though the response was quite inappropriate given the circumstances. These responses gave the impression of a pressure to talk, inappropriate jocularity, and a rapid flow of loosely related ideas expressed without self-restraint or concern about the social context. These are characteristics of a flight of ideas.

Mr. K's record contains only three Popular responses. The lower than expected number of Populars is particularly significant given the greater than average number of responses he produced ($R = 27$). This suggests Mr. K frequently perceives stimuli in an unusual, inaccurate, distorted manner, even stimuli that are relatively simple and about which most people agree ($X + \% = .33$; $Xu\% = .26$; $X - \% = .33$). In addition, his behavior is often unorthodox and reflects a disregard for social conventions and expectations. A review of the minus responses showed that minus responses occurred in no pattern. None was bizarre, although many were unusual because he included many irrelevant, unnecessary elements.

Mr. K becomes more involved with stimuli than do most people (L = .08). In general, a low Lambda can be produced either as a result of an overincorporative style or an excessive involvement with affect or ideation. Mr. K's record clearly shows both signs of intense affect and an overincorporative style. In fact, he expended an unusually large amount of energy trying to account for, explain, and integrate details in the stimulus field (Zd = +7.0; Zf = 20; $W > D+Dd$). Although this could reflect a careful, thorough, even precise style of thinking, Mr. K's responses are not particularly thoughtful or detailed. Instead, his responses reflect an expansive cognitive style, a flurry of thoughts, and rapid production of associations without concern for the logic, reasonableness, or appropriateness of the response. Although in some cases this spontaneous, rapid, and flexible style can be an asset, Mr. K's attempts to organize and integrate data are a liability because of how inaccurate, distorted, disorganized, and unfocused his thought processes are. In addition, his thought processes were less mature and sophisticated than expected, particularly given his level of education (DQv = 4; $DQv/+$ = 1).

In general, Mr. K appears to have adequate capacity for self-control and to cope with stressful events ($Adj\ D$ = 0; CDI = 2). A review of the variables making up the Adj D score reveals that his coping strengths are greater than average (EA = 17 vs. 8.87 for the normative sample). The finding that the $Adj\ D$ score, a measure of stress tolerance, is only zero is unexpected because EA, a measure of psychological resources, is so much higher than average. The lower than expected value of the $Adj\ D$ score may have occurred as the result of significantly higher than normal levels of stress. In spite of his protestations to the contrary during the clinical interview, the protocol shows that Mr. K's current level of distress is quite high (es = 27 vs. 8.20 for the normative sample). Although some of the distress may be related to concerns about this evaluation, these scores indicate that his distress is chronic rather than situational in nature ($Adj\ es$ = 16).

The positive Depression index ($DEPI$ = 7) strongly indicates that Mr. K's condition involves significant problems with affect. In general, Mr. K has quite intense emotional reactions and is not able to control or modulate emotions as much as most others do ($FC:CF+C$ = 2:8). He is likely to act in an impetuous, reckless manner, as he responds to feelings and impulses without considering the possible consequences of his behavior. He tries to avoid becoming emotionally aroused, perhaps to avoid such a loss of control (Afr = .42). The quality of his responses and the emphasis on cheerful, upbeat, positive images (e.g., Card I dancers in a Broadway musical; Card II two clowns dancing; Card III two jazz dancers playing bongo drums; Card V a Jamaican dancer) suggests that he may attempt to avoid negative affect through hypomanic defenses.

In spite of these efforts to contain his feelings, Mr. K is currently overwhelmed by very strong emotional reactions including intense feelings of sadness, anxiety, worry, helplessness, and powerlessness ($C = 8$; $m = 7$; $Y = 6$). His current affective state is quite painful and confusing (Color Shading Blends = 3). The presence of two Shading-Shading Blends (e.g., $M.FY.CF$) is very uncommon and signals that Mr. K's current emotional state includes intensely painful and negative affective reactions that disrupt his psychological functioning, dominate his emotional experience, and intrude on his thinking. The disruptive effects on his thinking are shown by the considerably greater than expected number of blends produced, which indicates that affect provokes overly complex psychological functioning (Blends:R = 15:27 as opposed to the expected 7:27). A review of the blends shows that the blends are much more complex than is typical (Blends with 3 determinants = 6 and Blends with 4 determinants = 1). The number and complexity of the blends produced by Mr. K indicates that affective factors generate inordinately complex psychological functioning. These findings suggest that much of the difficulty in thinking described previously ($WSum6 = 77$; $DR = 15$; $X+\% = .41$; $X-\% = .33$) is related to the disruptive and disorganizing effects of painful emotions on Mr. K's thought processes.

Mr. K's self-image is quite negative, and he feels inadequate and inferior to others (Egocentricity Index = .26). His self-image includes feelings of being damaged, vulnerable, and hurt ($MOR = 4$). Although Mr. K adamantly denied any wrongdoing during the clinical interview, he may question or even blame himself for his current troubles ($FD = 3$). In addition, Mr. K appears to have greater than expected concern about his bodily integrity, which suggests he is worried about his health ($An + Xy = 2$; the combination of MOR and responses related to bodily functioning, e.g., Response 6 blood from fingerprints; Response 8 blood from a turkey wishbone; Response 14 an X-ray of cancer).

Mr. K's responses are quite unusual for the number of food responses he produced (Food = 5). Normatively it is expected that individuals will produce no food responses (median Food responses = 0). The unusually large number of food responses suggests Mr. K has intense dependency needs; that is, he needs much more attention, comfort, nurturance, and support from others than most other adults. Consistent with these strong dependency needs, he has greater than average interest in others (Human Content = 9). Although able to form attachments to others ($T = 1$), Mr. K presently feels lonely, isolated, and unsupported by others (Isolation index = .41). Although almost all people who have a positive Isolation

Index also perceive interpersonal interactions as lacking in mutuality, Mr. K does not ($COP = 2$). This suggests he chronically feels lonely as a function of his inordinately high dependency needs ($Fd = 5$), as it may be difficult for him to feel satisfied with the amount of attention he does receive. In addition, establishing and maintaining relationships with others may be difficult because of problems communicating with them ($WSum6 = 21$), labile emotionality ($FC:CF+C = 2:8$), and a tendency to react to others in a defensive, argumentative fashion because of his deep sense of insecurity ($PER = 12$; Egocentricity Index $= .26$).

Comment

In this case, the MMPI-2 and Rorschach provide different information about Mr. K. As is often the case when an evaluation is requested to assess an individual's capacity to work, Mr. K's MMPI-2 was quite defensive and showed a deliberate denial of psychopathology. In contrast, the Rorschach showed significant psychological problems including an affective disturbance, disorganized thought processes, flight of ideas, extreme interpersonal dependency, and preoccupation with bodily integrity. Thus, although Mr. K asserted that he was psychologically healthy and untroubled by any emotional or personal concerns during the clinical interview and on the MMPI-2, the Rorschach data strongly suggests otherwise.

As pointed out by Ganellen (1994), it may be more difficult to deliberately skew responses on the Rorschach than on the MMPI-2 because of differences in the format of the two tests. An individual who wishes to avoid admitting psychological difficulties may be able to do so on the MMPI-2, as many items are face valid. In contrast, the Rorschach provides little guidance about how to either conceal or create the impression of psychopathology.

MMPI-2–Rorschach Integration

Mr. K responded to this evaluation with a naive effort to portray himself in the most favorable light possible. He attempted to create a positive impression by deliberately denying and underreporting psychological problems, emotional troubles, and personal difficulties, even minor foibles to which most people would admit ($L = 70$; $K = 66$; $F-K = -22$; $PER = 12$). To do so, he responded as though he were unusually virtuous, well adjusted, and psychologically healthy. As a result, he is likely to present a rather biased picture of himself and his past behavior; to gloss over, minimize, and justify past difficulties; and to lack insight into the reasons for his behavior.

In spite of his protestations to the contrary during the clinical interview, responses to the Rorschach show that Mr. K's current level of emotional distress is quite high ($es = 27$ vs. 8.20 for the normative sample). Although some of his distress may be related to situational concerns about this evaluation, his test responses indicate he has been chronically distressed (*Adj es* = 16).

Mr. K's current condition involves a significant affective disturbance (*DEPI* = 7; *S-CON* = 8). In general, Mr. K has quite intense emotional reactions and does not have the capacity to control or modulate feelings as much as most others do (*FC:CF+C* = 2:8). As a result of his limited control over feelings and impulses, he frequently acts in an impetuous, rash, reckless manner without considering the possible consequences of his behavior. He tries to avoid becoming emotionally aroused, perhaps to avoid loss of self-control (*Afr* = .42). His emphasis on cheerful, upbeat, positive images suggests that he attempts to avoid negative affect through the use of hypomanic defenses, such as denial, disavowal, and involvement in constant activity to distract from and avoid dysphoric affect.

In spite of these efforts to contain his feelings, Mr. K appears to be overwhelmed by intense sadness, anxiety, worry, helplessness, and powerlessness (*C′* = 8; *m* = 7; *Y* = 6). His current affective state is quite painful and confusing. These powerful, negative feelings disrupt his psychological functioning, dominate his emotional experience, and intrude on his thinking (Color Shading Blends = 3; Shading Shading Blends = 2). These affective reactions also provoke overly complex psychological functioning that interfere with his thought processes (Blends:R = 15:27; Blends with 3 determinants = 6 and Blends with 4 determinants = 1).

Mr. K's responses revealed a serious disturbance in thinking, cognitive disorganization, and flawed judgment and conceptualization (*WSum6* = 20). His responses were remarkable for the large number of irrelevant, tangential comments and ideas expressed without any self-consciousness or concern about the effect his behavior had on the examiner, particularly given the circumstances of this evaluation and his attempts to create a positive impression (*L* = 70; *K* = 66; *F−K* = −22). His responses were characterized by a pressure to talk, inappropriate jocularity, and a rapid flow of loosely related ideas expressed without self-restraint or concern about the social context. These are characteristics of a flight of ideas. He perceived stimuli in an unusual, inaccurate, distorted manner, even stimuli that are relatively simple and about which most people agree (*P* = 3; *X+%* = .33; *Xu%* = .26; *X−%* = .33). As a result, his behavior is often unorthodox and reflects a disregard for social conventions and expectations. It appeared that much of this difficulty in thinking is secondary to the disruptive and disorganizing effects painful emotions have on Mr. K's thought processes.

In general, Mr. K is inefficient, indecisive, and inconsistent when he tries to solve problems and make decisions (EA = 8:9.0). He is hesitant and uncertain about making choices, doubts himself, and changes his mind frequently as he considers, reconsiders, and reconsiders again whether the choice he has made is the "right" choice. These tendencies create a vulnerability to making errors in judgment. He is particularly likely to show lapses in judgment and inefficient thought processes at this point because pessimistic worry, situational anxiety, and feelings of discouragement interfere with his ability to concentrate and sustain attention (eb = 12:15; m = 7; MOR = 4).

Mr. K's self-image is quite negative, and he perceives himself as inadequate and inferior to others (Egocentricity Index = .26). He views himself as damaged, vulnerable, and hurt (MOR = 4). Although Mr. K adamantly presented himself as innocent of any wrongdoing during the clinical interview, he appears concerned about his responsibility for his problems (FD = 3). In addition, Mr. K has greater than expected concern about his bodily integrity ($An+Xy$ = 2). This finding is particularly relevant given the history of somatic delusions involving the conviction he had contracted AIDS as a result of contact with prostitutes and suggests he continues to be preoccupied with worries about his health in spite of medical evidence to the contrary.

Mr. K has intense dependency needs, that is, he needs much more attention, comfort, nurturance and support from others than most other adults and feels insecure, worthless, and inadequate if he does not get this attention (Food = 5; Human Content = 9). He feels lonely, isolated, and unsupported by others (Isolation Index = .41), perhaps because his inordinately high dependency needs make it difficult to be satisfied with the amount of interest others show. However, establishing and maintaining relationships with others may be difficult because of problems communicating with them ($WSum6$ = 21), labile emotionality ($FC:CF+C$ = 2:8), and a tendency to react to others in a defensive, argumentative fashion because of a deep sense of insecurity (PER = 12; Egocentricity Index = .26). One may speculate that his contacts with prostitutes may have been motivated by his chronic loneliness and desire for involvement with someone who treated him as desirable, attractive, and special, even if only for a brief time and only for money.

The available history, Mr. K's behavior during the clinical interview and evaluation, and the test data show that Mr. K presents with clinically significant depression, rapid, pressured speech, inappropriate jocularity, flight of ideas, affective instability, and excessive involvement in goal directed and pleasurable activities. Although some of these characteristics were thought of as part of an agitated depression in the past, these are also clinical features of a bipolar disorder. In particular, the presence of significant thought disorganization and flight of ideas secondary to affective disturbance, inappropriate jocularity, and hypomanic defenses are strongly suggestive of a bipolar disorder. Because no history of past manic episodes was reported, his presentation is most consistent with a bipolar II disorder in which there has been at least one episode of major depression and one or more hypomanic episodes. There was no evidence that his lapses in judgment and problems with behavior reflect the presence of an antisocial personality disorder. The possibility that Mr. K's behavioral problems, such as involvement with prostitutes, occurred during a hypomanic episode should be considered.

Diagnostic Impression

DSM–IV   Axis I   296.89 Bipolar II disorder, most recent episode mixed; moderate severity

Axis II   799.9   Deferred

TREATMENT RECOMMENDATIONS

Although Mr. K claimed to be emotionally healthy and free of symptoms of psychopathology, the results of this evaluation clearly show significant psychological difficulties exist. Specifically, Mr. K is troubled by affective problems including intense sadness, worry, helplessness, powerlessness, and preoccupation with health-related issues. The extent to which this painful affective state disrupts psychological functioning, intrudes on his thinking and causes cognitive disorganization, errors in judgment, and flight of ideas is worrisome, as a pharmacist's job requires careful attention to detail. For instance, a potential for causing harm or even death exists if careless errors are made when dispensing medications. Mr. K's apparent lack of awareness and/or lack of concern about his inappropriate behavior and disregard of social conventions is also a concern. These results suggest that (a) Mr. K would benefit from treatment and (b) any decisions about his professional status should be postponed until treatment has gotten underway and his psychological status has improved.

Mr. K should be evaluated by a psychiatrist regarding medication treatment of the bipolar disorder. Collateral information should be obtained regarding past manic or hypomanic episodes, particularly because Mr. K's self-report of psychological difficulties is not likely to be complete. Psychotherapy is also recommended to assist Mr. K in realistically assessing decisions about his career and his readiness to assume additional professional responsibilities. The psychotherapist may help him develop better self-control and anticipate the effects of his behavior, so that he does not show poor judgment and jeopardize his career or current marital relationship. Psychotherapy may also help Mr. K address difficulties in his interpersonal relationships including ways in which his strong dependency needs are manifested and the effects his behavior has on others. Finally, treatment may assist him in dealing with any concerns about his health and the guilt about past sexual indiscretions these somatic concerns represent.

It is possible that Mr. K may be as defensive with a treating psychiatrist as he was during this evaluation, particularly because future decisions about his career will be based in part on his compliance with and response to this treatment. Every effort should be made by the mental health professionals to attempt to establish and foster a therapeutic alliance by educating Mr. K about the nature of his condition, the expected response of a bipolar disorder to treatment with medication and psychotherapy, and the role of the treating professionals.

The professionals treating Mr. K should be aware of his intense dependency needs and alert to how these needs influence his reactions to therapy and his feelings about the therapeutic relationship. For instance, it is possible that during the course of psychotherapy, Mr. K may become overly dependent on the therapist and make a considerable effort to please the therapist at the expense of his own autonomy.

15 Case 10: Reactions to Health Problems

REASON FOR EVALUATION

Mr. I is a 67-year-old, married, White male referred for a psychological evaluation by his internist to assess his level of depression and psychological adjustment following recent medical problems.

BACKGROUND INFORMATION

About 6 months prior to this evaluation, Mr. I had a series of serious cardiovascular problems that were treated with angioplasty and the insertion of a pacemaker. Complications developed several days after cardiac surgery, and he was rushed back to the hospital for an emergency medical intervention to control an accumulation of fluid in his chest. His condition was touch and go for several hours. He has vivid recollections of overhearing doctors and nurses talking in grave tones of voice about the possibility of his death while he was in the cardiac intensive care unit. He thinks repeatedly about a comment his doctor made the next morning, after his condition was stabilized, when the doctor referred to him as "knocking on death's door" the night before. He described this as a "horrendous" experience and stated, "I don't think I will ever recover from such a graphic reminder of my mortality."

Mr. I reported being preoccupied with thoughts about his death since this episode. He no longer thinks about or plans for the future and instead questions how long he will be alive. He denied changes in sleep, appetite, or energy. He is able to concentrate but reported that it requires a great effort on his part to do so. Prior to his illness, he felt he could handle any difficulty he faced but now doubts his competence to do so. He denied suicidal ideation or intent.

While discussing his reactions to his medical problems, Mr. I mentioned that there has been friction in his marital relationship for many years. He described feeling unhappy and dissatisfied with his marriage but commented that he feels stuck with his wife. He does not recall when they last had sexual relations. This pattern of sexual activity existed for several years prior to the onset of his cardiovascular problems and has not been affected by his medical condition.

Mr. I reported becoming increasingly irritable with his wife and recently has nearly acted violently towards her. When asked what triggers these reactions, he described becoming intensely angry since the surgery when his wife has appeared overly concerned about his physical condition and health or when she questions a decision he has made. He acknowledged that similar angry outbursts occurred in the past. When these fights erupted, he generally stormed out of the house before he lost control of himself, although there have been several occasions in the past when he and his wife slapped and pushed each other. He admitted that his wife was injured during one fight but insisted this was an accident. She was injured when she threw a dish at him, and he responded by throwing a glass bowl at her, which shattered. A shard of glass cut her arm and caused a deep gash that required stitches.

After graduating from college, Mr. I earned a masters degree in political science and then began working for the federal government in the early 1960s. He described himself as a "Kennedy era liberal" who was strongly committed to enforcing policies intended to insure civil rights. He worked for the federal government until he retired, received a number of promotions, and was awarded several commendations for the quality of his work. He described having warm relationships with colleagues and coworkers and has maintained contact with many of them since he retired.

Since retiring about 7 years ago, Mr. I has worked several part-time or volunteer jobs to keep active. Most recently he has worked part time at a community service center developing relationships with community organizations and institutions. He was recruited for this position because of his reputation in the community and because of the relationships he has with these organizations, many of which were developed while he worked for the government. He commented that the community service center is poorly managed and believes he could do a better job as indicated by his comment that, "This is a text book example of how not to manage."

As Mr. I described himself, he commented spontaneously that friends and coworkers see him very differently than he sees himself. He believes friends would describe him as a leader, a friendly, witty, confident man who gets things done. He recounted a number of incidents to support this. For instance, during his recent illness, he got calls, cards, and visits from a large number of people expressing genuine concern, some of whom he has only recently met. However, he stated that others are not aware of an internal "silent debate" that constantly occurs when he has to make a decision, even a minor decision, such as which shirt he was going to wear to our meeting. It is a struggle for him to reach a conclusion he is satisfied with, as he ruminates about his choices and goes back and forth between the alternatives. Mr. I questions why he wastes his time doing this but cannot stop himself. He also commented that he perceives himself as often acting in a rigid, robotic manner without emotions or feeling. He acknowledged that this internal debate has existed for many years and sought psychotherapy because of it and because of depression while in his 20s. Although therapy helped, he continued to ruminate about making decisions throughout his adult life.

Mr. I denied alcohol or substance abuse. There is no history of arrests or other legal difficulties.

DIAGNOSTIC CONSIDERATIONS

The preoccupation with death, pessimistic view of the future, decreased interest in events, difficulties with concentration, and loss of self-confidence Mr. I experiences are consistent with a current depression. Test data supporting a diagnosis of depression would include elevations on MMPI-2 scales *2* and *DEP* and a positive Rorschach *DEPI* and/or *CDI*.

During the clinical interview, Mr. I also disclosed struggles over maintaining control of anger, difficulties making decisions, rumination, and detachment from feelings. The anger may be one manifestation of an episode of depression, as the mood of many depressed patients is not only sad, but also often angry and irritable. Irritability and anger are also associated with other Axis I disorders, including a bipolar disorder, and a number of Axis II disorders, including antisocial personality disorder, paranoid personality disorder, narcissistic personality disorder, borderline personality disorder, and obsessive–compulsive personality disorder. The difficulties related to making decisions and repetitive thinking about alternatives are suggestive of an obsessive personality style, although this could also be associated with self-doubts, low self-esteem, or other factors. Thus, Mr. I's personality structure, defenses, and control over expression of anger must be explored, as well as the nature of his anger and the situations in which anger is most likely to be elicited.

MMPI-2 Data

Validity.   Mr. I responded to the MMPI-2 items in an honest, open manner. He cooperated with test administration and frankly acknowledged symptoms and personal difficulties. The K score ($T = 39$) is quite low, particularly for his level of education, which suggests he is dissatisfied, overly critical of himself, and readily admits to emotional distress.

Clinical Scales.   The MMPI-2 profile is unexpected given Mr. I's presenting complaints of being discouraged, hopeless, lacking in self-confidence, and worried about his physical condition. One would expect that his pessimistic, discouraged attitude would be reflected by elevations on scales *2* ($T = 52$) and *7* ($T = 59$), but this was not the case. In addition, one might also have predicted that concerns about his health might have resulted in elevations on scales *1* ($T = 42$) or Health Concerns ($HEA = 48$).

The only clinical scale over 65 is scale *4* ($T = 67$). A spike 4 profile could suggest that Mr. I is a rebellious, impulsive man with poor frustration tolerance who is likely to get into scrapes with authority figures. This elevation is unexpected, in part because of Mr. I's age; typically scores on Scale 4 decrease with age (Colligan, Osborne, Swenson, & Offord, 1989; Swenson et al., 1973). Duckworth and Anderson (1995) suggested that an elevation on scale *4* for an older person, particularly if over 65, is more likely to reflect longstanding self-centered behavior, social alienation, apathy, and lack of involvement than antisocial behavior.

Before concluding that Mr. I has many characteristics associated with an antisocial personality disorder, the supplementary and content scales should be examined, particularly given the absence of a history of antisocial behavior. The Antisocial Practices content scale (ASP) was in the average range ($T = 53$), whereas the Family Problems content scale was elevated ($FAM = 82$). Among the Harris–Lingoes *Pd* subscales, Familial Discord ($Pd1 = 84$) and Social Alienation ($Pd4 = 67$) were elevated, whereas Authority Problems ($Pd2 = 42$) and Social Imperturbability ($Pd3 = 52$) were not. Thus, the mild elevation on scale *4* appears to be due not to antisocial characteristics as much as to a perception of his home environment as unpleasant and antagonistic, lacking in love, understanding, and support, and as having a considerable amount of friction and tension.

Rather than view the MMPI-2 profile as a spike 4 profile, it can be interpreted as a *34/43* profile, even though scale *3* with a *T*-score of 64 is not clinically elevated. Persons with a *34/43* codetype typically have difficulty with control over anger and have not developed socially appropriate ways to express anger constructively. The *34/43* codetype suggests his difficulties are related to deep, chronic feelings of resentment and hostility toward family members whom he feels do not understand him and do not pay enough attention to him. He is likely to be egocentric, demanding of

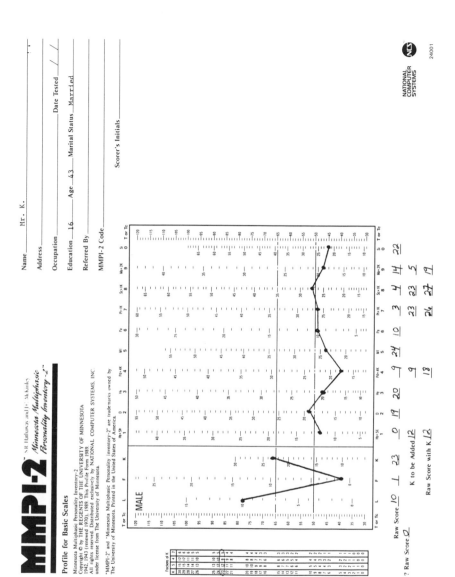

315

Case 10 MMPI-2 Content and Supplementary Scales

	Raw Score	T Score
FB	6	67
True Response Inconsistency (TRIN)	10	57
Variable Response Inconsistency (VRIN)	4	46
Anxiety	20	60
Repression	13	45
MAC-R	17	39
Ego Strength (Es)	31	36
Dominance (Do)	18	55
Social Responsibility (Re)	22	55
Overcontrolled Hostility (O-H)	12	48
PTSD - Keane (PK)	16	63
PTSD - Schlenger (PS)	23	66
Addiction Potential (APS)	26	57
Addiction Admission (AAS)	1	41
Content Scales (Butcher et al., 1990)		
Anxiety (ANX)	14	70
Fears (FRS)	2	45
Obsessiveness (OBS)	10	66
Depression (DEP)	14	68
Health Concerns (HEA)	4	48
Bizarre Mentation (BIZ)	1	46
Anger (ANG)	9	59
Cynicism (CYN)	14	56
Antisocial Practices (ASP)	10	53
Type A (TPA)	14	68
Low Self-Esteem (LSE)	9	62
Social Discomfort (SOD)	2	39
Depression Subscales (Harris-Lingoes)		
Subjective Depression (D1)	11	64
Psychomotor Retardation (D2)	2	32
Physical Malfunctioning (D3)	3	51
Mental Dullness (D4)	6	67
Brooding (D5)	5	68
Hysteria Subscales (Harris-Lingoes)		
Denial of Social Anxiety (Hy1)	5	56
Need for Affection (Hy2)	6	47
Lassitude-Malaise (Hy3)	6	66
Somatic Complaints (Hy4)	4	57
Inhibition of Aggression (Hy5)	3	48

Psychopathic Deviate Subscales (Harris-Lingoes)
    Familial Discord (Pd1)   7   84
    Authority Problems (Pd2)   2   42
    Social Imperturbability (Pd3)   4   52
    Social Alienation (Pd4)   7   67
    Self-Alienation (Pd5)   6   63

Paranoia Subscales (Harris-Lingoes)
    Persecutory Ideas (Pa1)   3   58
    Poignancy (Pa2)   1   41
    Naivete (Pa3)   4   46

Schizophrenia Subscales (Harris-Lingoes)
    Social Alienation (Sc1)   6   64
    Emotional Alienation (Sc2)   2   59
    Lack of Ego Mastery, Cognitive (Sc3)   4   66
    Lack of Ego Mastery, Conative (Sc4)   5   65
    Lack of Ego Mastery, Def. Inhib. (Sc5)   2   54
    Bizarre Sensory Experiences (Sc6)   1   46

Hypomania Subscales (Harris-Lingoes)
    Amorality (Ma1)   2   50
    Psychomotor Acceleration (Ma2)   6   53
    Imperturbability (Ma3)   5   59
    Ego Inflation (Ma4)   4   56

Social Introversion Subscales (Ben-Porath et al., 1989)
    Shyness/Self-Consciousness (Si1)   2   42
    Social Avoidance (Si2)   1   41
    Alienation -- Self and Others (Si3)   10   65

attention, and very sensitive to rejection. He is most likely to flare up in a volatile, angry manner when he feels he has been criticized, misunderstood, or ignored.

The MMPI literature and clinical lore suggests that the relative elevations of scales *3* and *4* are important signs of whether the individual has control over anger or if anger is expressed more impulsively. Anger is more likely to be inhibited and expressed indirectly when scale *3* is higher than scale *4*, whereas anger is more likely to be expressed directly when scale *4* is greater than scale *3*. Mr. I's 43 codetype suggests he is emotionally overcontrolled much of the time and generally acts in a socially appropriate manner. However, his behavior is punctuated by hostile, aggressive outbursts that may occur in a cyclical pattern. The hostile outbursts may occur because anger has built up gradually over time, as he accumulates a reservoir of incidents about which he felt resentful and then blows up out of proportion to the situation that ostensibly triggered his reaction. These outbursts may be a surprise to others. This latter interpretation is consistent with the history reported by Mr. I of fights with his wife during which he lost control of his temper and was physically aggressive. Although other people may see his angry behavior as a problem, Mr. I is not likely to agree. Instead, he typically denies having problems and attributes blame to others. As a result, it may be extremely difficult to change this pattern of behavior.

Although the MMPI-2 clinical scales do not suggest his mood is dysphoric, the content scales do ($ANX = 70$; $DEP = 68$). These scores indicate he is worried, anxious, and sad; feels life is a strain; doubts that things will get better, and questions whether life is futile. In addition, his score on the Obsessiveness Scale ($OBS = 66$) suggests he ruminates, frets, and worries a great deal, even about minor, trivial matters; has difficulty making decisions; and is bothered by intrusive, upsetting thoughts. In addition, he may engage in repetitive, compulsive behavior.

As discussed in chapters 4 and 5, discrepancies among findings from related MMPI-2 scales are to be expected routinely in clinical practice. In this case, a discrepancy exists between scale *2* and *DEP* and between scale *7* and *ANX* and *OBS*. Greene (1991) and Graham (1993) pointed out that the empirical correlates of MMPI-2 content scales have not been firmly established and suggested that caution be used when findings based on the content scales do not agree with findings based on the clinical scales, which have a much stronger, well-established empirical foundation. Thus, content scale scores suggesting he is unhappy, worried, and ruminative should be viewed as tentative unless other data support these conclusions.

Rorschach Data

The search strategy for Mr. I's Rorschach protocol begins with findings suggestive of situational distress (D score $<$ Adjusted D). Mr. I's scores

Card	Response	Inquiry
I	1. An exotic BF.	E: (Rpts S's response) S: That's not it. E: The 1st thing u said u saw was an exotic BF. S: Oh, yes. Right. The 2 drawings on the side 1.1 gigantic, gauzy wings that BFs have, with the black veins. Not veins, the connecting ribs. And the little tiny feelers. Not feelers, antennas. E: Gauzy? S: Bec you can see, they're translucent. E: Translucent? S: Lighter in some parts than other parts. E: You said the wings looked gigantic. S: Well, when you lk at the whole thing, it seems to be over 1/2, occupies over 1/2 the space. Lkd at the middle as body & 2 side things larger than body.
	2. You can c more than 1 thing in them? E: Most p see more than 1 thing. S: At 1st blush an exotic BF. On the other hand, 2 figures both 1.1 women. Some kind of statues. Like winged figures sort of holding onto e.o. Arms flying out. In the middle is another figure sort of holding them.	E: (Rpts S's response) S: Yes. 2 arms flying out. This is where they're holding e.o. In the center is another figure holding them together in a unified fashion. If you can differentiate between the light & dark parts, here r the legs & torso & arms of middle figure & the winged figures r holding onto the arm. P: Light & dark parts? S: Here, in the center, 1.1 some kind of clothing & the body inside the light.
II	3. (Pt lghs) At 1st blush, these 1.1 2 elephants. Thy're sort of meeting with their	E: (Rpts S's response) S: Yeah. Then I changed my mind. E: The 1st thing you saw was 2 elephants.

trunks. L.1 thy're
fighting over s.t. The
red splotch l.1 blood.
As strange as it is,
seems like baby
elephants. D't have
tusks. M.b not
elephants, pygmy A's
fighting over s.t.

4. On the other hand, it
cld be sort of like a
dance. Clapping of the
hands. I d.k. what the
red spots mean. Have no
idea of how to fit that
into what I see.

III 5. Well, these r 2 male
figures. They're doffing
their hats to e.o & in
betw is a red bow. I
haven't the foggiest idea
what it means, but its a
red bow.

6. Maybe, that stuff in
the background of the 2
men doffing their
hats...Uhm...I d.k., but
it l.1 dead cats. Not
dead. L.1 some kind of
decoration.

S: These 2 things extending, l.1
tusks. That made it l.1
elephants.
E: Fighting?
S: Bec of the red splotches.
Then I saw didn't have tusks, so
how can they make e.o. bleed?

E: (Rpts S's response)
S: That's right.
E: Show me where you were lkg.
S: Well, its like (Pt claps
hands) 2 dancers coming tog & hit
hands & back away & come
together. Like folk dancers.
Again, I c't make out what the
red blotches are.

E: (Rpts S's response)
S: Right. Here's 1 male figure &
the other. This is their hats
down here, like old-fashioned top
hats or bowler hats. The way p
used to greet e.o., I gather.
E: Top hats?
S: Well, 1st thought it cld be
beaver hats bec thy're round.
Round & furry.
E: Furry?
S: Well, its not, its a regular
outline of the hats. If beaver,
wld be more irregular. Fur c't
be completely, can look straggly.
E: Then u mentioned a red bow.
S: Cldn't figure it out. Cldn't
tell if part of a backgr or a
woman walking away with an old
fashioned dress & bow in the
back. Or a woman walking towards
them w bow in the front.

E: (Rpts S's response)
S: I said dead cats, then I
changed my mind. But at 1st
thght dead cats being hurled out
of the window.
E: Show me that.
P: See the tail & they look
lifeless. The heads r still.
Cats r pretty lively.
E: Decoration?
P: No. D't see that.

IV	7. Oh, s.t. like an ogre out of a child's story, sitting on his throne. Awaiting his retinue. He's sort of immobile. His feet r huge & enormous. His body is chunky. His arms r very weak. So, I guess he's dependent on his retinue. L.l an ogre from a children's story. I d't think he has much of a brain, has a very small head.	E: (Rpts S's response) S: That's right! The whole thing is an ogre. This is the throne he's sitting on. E: You mentioned his feet are huge. S: Well, these r the shoes, the wider part r shoes or boots. Relative to the body they l enormous, much closer to you than body. That's the pants the shoes fit into. E: And he has a small head. S: Yes. This is his head here. Sits on top of this ruff or collar. Can just see the little nose & head.
V	8. This is a BF. A beautiful BF. Huge BF! Prob in Africa or some exotic, tropical place. And its flying and...I guess some bird of prey will see this BF & destroy her. Or some predator.	E: (Rpts S's response) S: Yes. That's right. E: Exotic? S: Here's the wings, spread, & antenna, body. Sort of a mottled thing, the dark & light. Its the biggest BF I've ever seen! From Africa, bec I gather BFs r bigger in tropical climates, bigger there than in a northern climate, such as here.
VI	9. A combination of things. This is a bear skin.	E: (Rpts S's response) S: It is flat, legs of bear, or the skin of him. It looked tawny l a bear skin. Like a brown bear. It L.l it had been split here. Like a bear skin in position by a hearth. E: Tawny? S: The diff shadings. E: Split? S: Here. Its darker in the center, lighter there. It reminds me of a picture I've seen.
	10. Somehow, it l.l a rocket taking off! (laughs) Yeah. That's what it is, its the burst of flame from a rocket taking off into space. Once again, engaging in some fruitless mission NASA is engaged in.	E: (Rpts S's response) S: That's right. Here's the spaceship. All of this, the bearskin becomes the flame billowing out from it. This is the nose of the spaceship. E: You mentioned the red flame in back.

There, its taking off
with a roar. This is the
red flame in back, taking
off.

VII   11. Cld see many things.
These cld be clouds.

S: Well, this l.1 the red, the
dark l.1 a dark red, the flame &
e.t.

E: (Rpts S's response)
S: Yes. The W thing. The W
thing lkd gauzy, fleecy like
clouds do. Gauzy bec of the
shading.
E: Peaceful & calming?
S: No violent activity. Its sort
of, at most sort of floating. At
the least, sort of static.

12. There's 2 women's
faces, facing e.o. with
hair in an upsweep. It
l.1 fleecy, soft clouds,
if y're lying on peaceful
green grass, lkg up, or a
meadow & you can make
whatever you wt out of
the clouds. Somehow it
appears very peaceful &
calming.

E: (Rpts S's response)
S: Here's 1 and here's 1. Facing
e.o.
E: Hair?
S: This is hair in an upsweep.

VIII   13. (Shakes head) Damned
if I know!...Well. This
is a...a decorative piece
of some sort. On e side
is a bear. In the middle
its sort of an Indian
work. I supp, not
knowing symbols Indians
know, it tells the story
of a partic indiv. His
symbol is the bear, which
I underst Indians have.
Tells the story of his
tribe. Its v colorful.
Its a saga of some sort.

E: (Rpts S's response)
S: That's right. On e side is 2
bears. And my association was
Indian, Native American, let's be
politically correct, are always
described in terms of being close
to nature, knowing how to live
with nature. They adopt A
symbols. Then I thght, what has
to be in the middle, the bears
symbolize a man or a tribe. And
in middle is the saga of the
indiv or tribe. I c't make out
what that story wld be. Its like
hieroglyphics, except Indian
style.

IX   14. Part of an abstract
drawing or painting. By
an artist that uses,
almost water Cs. The
different Cs are
reflecting diff moods.
Like the greenish hue or
aqua is one of forbidding
or foreboding. The
orange is showing hope.

E: (Rpts S's response)
S: Yes. The green was
forebidding or foreboding.
Orange was of, I guess I
associated it with a sunrise.
Assoc sun with hope. Maybe
that's the story of life - the
struggle betw 2 opposite poles.

322

Its on top of the foreboding, s.t. y look forward to. The bottom is the red, red blood, I guess, of people having those feelings.

X   15. It l.1 sea life. Crabs, shrimp, & lobster, all at the bottom of the sea. Living out their lifespan. What do you call, what's on the bottom that everything eats? There are kelp & crab. These maybe fishermen's hooks at top and 2, undistinguished something, sea urchins are the bait. It l.1 a colorful display of sea life, that a scuba diver may see.

E: (Rpts S's response)
S: That's right. Here are the crab & shrimp. This l.1 a lobster. I have never seen 1, but I'm not great on lobster. For some reason the word kelp sprang to mind. Maybe using kelp to catch lobsters. I know in reality they use pots to catch lobster, but this has nothing to do with reality. Here are some, l.1 plankton other sealife feeds on. It l.1 a graphic scene of sealife, even with the interference of man!

```
CASE10.R3==================== SEQUENCE OF SCORES ============================

CARD NO LOC  #  DETERMINANT(S)    (2) CONTENT(S)   POP Z  SPECIAL SCORES
======= ======  ================  === ==========   === =  ===============
  I   1 Wo   1  FV.FC'+               A            P 1.0
      2 W+   1  Ma.FYo            2   (H),H,Cg       4.0  COP

 II   3 D+   1  FMa.CFo           2   A,Bl         P 3.0  AG,MOR,DR
      4 W+   1  Mao              2   H              4.5  COP

III   5 D+   1  Ma.CF+            2   H,Cg         P 4.0  DR
      6 Do   2  mao               2   A                  MOR,AG

 IV   7 W+   1  Mp.FD+                (H),Hh       P 4.0

  V   8 Wo   1  FMa.FY+               A            P 1.0

 VI   9 Do   1  FYo                   Ad           P      MOR,PER
     10 W+   1  ma.YF+                Sc,Fi          2.5  CP

VII  11 WS/  1  mp.C'F.YFo            Cl             4.0
     12 Do   1  Fo                2   Hd           P

VIII 13 W+   1  FCo               2   Art,A,Ay     P 4.5  AB

 IX  14 W/   1  C                     Art,Bl              AB

  X  15 W+   1  FCo               2   A            P 5.5  DR,FAB


============================= SUMMARY OF APPROACH ============================

     I  :  W.W                      VI  :  D.W
    II  :  D.W                     VII  :  WS.D
   III  :  D.D                    VIII  :  W
    IV  :  W                       IX  :  W
     V  :  W                        X  :  W
```

324

```
CASE10.R3===================== STRUCTURAL SUMMARY ===============================

LOCATION              DETERMINANTS              CONTENTS        S-CONSTELLATION
FEATURES         BLENDS          SINGLE                         NO..FV+VF+V+FD>2
                                              H   = 2, 1        NO..Col-Shd Bl>0
Zf    = 11     FV.FC'         M   = 1        (H) = 2, 0        YES..Ego<.31,>.44
ZSum  = 38.0   M.FY           FM  = 0        Hd  = 1, 0        NO..MOR > 3
ZEst  = 34.5   FM.CF          m   = 1        (Hd)= 0, 0        NO..Zd > +- 3.5
               M.CF           FC  = 2        Hx  = 0, 0        YES..es > EA
W  = 10        M.FD           CF  = 0        A   = 5, 1        YES..CF+C > FC
 (Wv = 0)      FM.FY          C   = 1        (A) = 0, 0        NO..X+% < .70
D  =  5        m.YF           Cn  = 0        Ad  = 1, 0        NO..S > 3
Dd =  0        m.C'F.YF       FC'= 0        (Ad)= 0, 0        YES..P < 3 or > 8
S  =  1                       C'F= 0        An  = 0, 0        NO..Pure H < 2
                              C'  = 0        Art = 2, 0        YES..R < 17
  DQ                          FT  = 0        Ay  = 0, 1        5.....TOTAL
.........(FQ-)                TF  = 0        Bl  = 0, 2
  +  = 8  ( 0)               T   = 0        Bt  = 0, 0        SPECIAL SCORINGS
  o  = 5  ( 0)               FV  = 0        Cg  = 0, 2                Lv1    Lv2
 v/+ = 2  ( 0)               VF  = 0        Cl  = 1, 0        DV  =   0x1    0x2
  v  = 0  ( 0)               V   = 0        Ex  = 0, 0        INC =   0x2    0x4
                             FY  = 1        Fd  = 0, 0        DR  =   3x3    0x6
                             YF  = 0        Fi  = 0, 1        FAB =   1x4    0x7
                             Y   = 0        Ge  = 0, 0        ALOG =  0x5
     FORM QUALITY            Fr  = 0        Hh  = 0, 1        CON  =  0x7
                             rF  = 0        Ls  = 0, 0        Raw Sum6 =    4
       FQx  FQf  MQual  SQx  FD  = 0        Na  = 0, 0        Wgtd Sum6 =  13
  +  =  5    0     2     0    F   = 1        Sc  = 1, 0
  o  =  9    1     2     1                   Sx  = 0, 0        AB  = 2      CP  = 1
  u  =  0    0     0     0                   Xy  = 0, 0        AG  = 2      MOR = 3
  -  =  0    0     0     0                   Id  = 0, 0        CFB = 0      PER = 1
 none=  1    --    0     0         (2) =  8                    COP = 2      PSV = 0

==================== RATIOS, PERCENTAGES, AND DERIVATIONS =====================

R = 15         L  =  0.07            FC:CF+C = 2: 3      COP = 2     AG = 2
-----------------------------------  Pure C  =    1      Food        = 0
EB = 4: 4.5  EA  =  8.5   EBPer= N/A  SumC':WSumC= 2:4.5  Isolate/R  =0.13
eb = 5: 8    es  = 13        D =  -1  Afr     =0.25      H:(H)Hd(Hd)= 3: 3
          Adj es =  7    Adj D =   0  S       =  1       (HHd):(AAd)= 2: 0
-----------------------------------  Blends:R= 8:15      H+A:Hd+Ad  =11: 2
FM = 2  :  C'= 2   T = 0              CP      =  1
m  = 3  :  V = 1   Y = 5
                              P   = 9      Zf   =11       3r+(2)/R=0.53
a:p   = 7: 2   Sum6  =  4    X+% =0.93     Zd   = +3.5    Fr+rF   = 0
Ma:Mp = 3: 1   Lv2   =  0    F+% =1.00     W:D:Dd =10: 5: 0  FD    = 1
2AB+Art+Ay= 7  WSum6 = 13    X-% =0.00     W:M  =10: 4     An+Xy   = 0
M-    = 0      Mnone =  0    S-% =0.00     DQ+  = 8        MOR     = 3
                             Xu% =0.00     DQv  = 0

==============================================================================
  SCZI = 1    DEPI = 5*    CDI = 1    S-CON = 5    HVI = No    OBS =YES
==============================================================================
```

indicate that in general he possesses adequate ego strength to handle stress ($Adj\ D = 0$; $CDI < 4$; $EA = 8.5$). At present, however, he is experiencing considerable situational stress that is impacting on his psychological equilibrium (D Score $= -1$; $es = 13$) and affects both thoughts and feelings ($m = 3$; $Y = 5$). This results in intense anxiety, worry, rumination, and helplessness, most likely as a reaction to his recent medical problems. He is also troubled by self-critical and self-denigrating reactions ($V = 1$).

The next step in the interpretive process is directed by the positive Obsessive Style Index (OBS). The OBS is an empirically derived index that identifies individuals who are perfectionistic, overly preoccupied with details, indecisive, and have trouble expressing their feelings (Exner, 1991). The OBS was developed by comparing a group of 146 outpatients with obsessive–compulsive disorder or compulsive personality disorders against other groups of psychiatric patients (i.e., depressive, schizophrenic, or character disorder groups). The results of discriminant function analyses found that the combination of six Rorschach variables discriminated between the obsessive and comparison groups. The OBS is rarely positive in the adult nonpatient sample or in groups of psychiatric patients other than obsessives; in other words, there is a low false positive rate. For instance, only 2% of the normative sample obtained a positive OBS. Thus, the positive OBS score obtained by Mr. I is noteworthy and suggests he has many or all of the characteristics described previously.

Several variables show that Mr. I has a marked tendency towards perfectionism (OBS; $FQx + = 5$; $X + \% = .93$; Populars $= 9$). He carefully, thoroughly, and methodically attends to information and tries to determine relationships among stimuli ($W > D + Dd$; $DQ + = 8$, $Zd = +3.5$). He is an overincorporator ($Zd = +3.5$), an enduring trait that has been shown empirically to be related to a cautious, conscientious, precise style of responding to data and solving problems. These characteristics may certainly be strengths in some instances, such as at a job that involves careful attention to detail or when he is faced with solving an unfamiliar, technically demanding problem. These characteristics can also be weaknesses if he becomes overly cautious, ruminative, and unable to see the "big picture" because of a preoccupation with trivial details. Because he is so attuned to details, he may be unable to distinguish between what is essential and what is insignificant.

The low Lambda score ($L = .07$) indicates that Mr. I can become excessively involved with thoughts and feelings and may be unable to stop thinking about subjects that bother him. This may be manifested by intrusive thoughts about upsetting matters, such as fearful rumination about his recent medical difficulties. His inability to stop thinking about a topic may disrupt his ability to attend to and concentrate on other matters ($m = 3$). This can also interfere with his ability to make a decision, as he weighs his choices repeatedly. Given his perfectionistic tendencies, he may have difficulty finalizing a decision because of a fear of making a mistake.

Once Mr. I develops an idea or formulates an opinion about a subject, he is likely to stick to that position inflexibly ($a{:}p$ = 7:2). He does not consider seriously the opinions others present if they differ from his own and instead defends his own position in a dogmatic, opinionated manner. Thus, it is hard to alter his opinions and attitudes. This may contribute to difficulties in interpersonal relationships.

In general, Mr I is quite uncomfortable with emotions, fears he will not be able to control his reactions, and attempts to protect himself against a loss of control by restricting his involvement with affect (Afr = .25). It is quite important to note that he produced one Color Projection response. The Color Projection response occurs very infrequently in both clinical and nonclinical samples. For instance, less than 2% of the normative sample produced one or more CP responses. Thus, the presence of this unusual response is quite significant. The CP response suggests Mr. I characteristically denies unpleasant, negative reactions in a rigid, inflexible manner to the extent that he will insist he is not upset in the least even though his actions obviously indicate that he is. He may also disregard or ignore negative aspects of a situation. His attempt to deny having a negative reaction may take the form of substituting a false positive emotion for a negative one, such as through the use of reaction formation.

Mr. I's defensive efforts to restrain affective reactions also include the use of intellectualization, rationalization, and isolation of affect (Intellectualization Index = 7). This suggests he would prefer to react to situations with logic, intellect, and rationality rather than with feelings. His determined efforts to maintain control over emotions may explain why he sees himself as "robotic" and as functioning without emotion or feeling.

A review of the content of Mr. I's responses suggests the defenses described previously may be particularly focused upon control of aggressive feelings and impulses. For instance, on Card II, Response 3, he initially described 2 elephants fighting over something who have drawn blood but then negates the aggressive action by stating, "Then I saw they didn't have tusks, so how can they make each other bleed?" On Card VI, Response 8, he described a beautiful, exotic butterfly flying and commented that "some bird of prey will see this BF and destroy her. Or some predator." The bulk of the response revolves around descriptions of the exotic insect and the tropical region it is from while not referring again to the aggressive aspect of his percept. On Card VIII, Response 11, he emphasizes the peaceful quality of a cloud formation and, when asked to describe the peaceful impression, he replied, there's "no violent activity." These responses suggest he uses intellectualizing defenses to distance himself from hostile impulses that he struggles to control. When these defenses function effectively, aggression is likely to be expressed in a controlled, intellectualized manner that he can justify. For instance, hostility may be channeled into a critical comment that he perceives as being an objective, constructive comment that was intended to be helpful, although the recipient of the criticism may feel otherwise.

Although Mr. I attempts to restrict expression of emotions and appear reasonable, rational, and logical, there is a potential for him to react with uncontrolled outbursts of emotion ($FC:CF + C = 2:3$; $C = 1$). The presence of a pure C response (Card IX, Response 14) indicates there are times when emotions are experienced intensely and behavior is unrestrained. This pure C response also involves a perception of abstract art that again suggests that he attempts to control emotions with intellectualized defenses, although these defenses are not effective in every situation. As discussed previously, much of his defensive activity is directed at controlling hostile reactions. Thus, there is a potential for him to react with a fit of anger during which he acts in an impulsive manner without thinking or caring about the effects of his words or actions.

Another reason Mr. I tries to keep his emotional reactions under control and to contain how emotionally stimulated he becomes is that he is vulnerable to experiencing episodes of negative, depressive affect ($DEPI = 5$). These episodes may be of brief duration, but his emotional equilibrium can be significantly disrupted, and he can become psychologically disorganized during these episodes. Such a state was apparently precipitated by his recent medical problems that he reacted to with significant levels of anxiety, helplessness, self-criticism, and pessimism ($m = 3$; $Y = 5$; $V = 1$; $MOR = 3$). Thus, he feels discouraged, worried, negative, and gloomy about the future and about himself. As noted previously, he is prone to ruminate about these upsetting matters.

In general, Mr. I has a positive self-image, believes in himself, and is confident about his abilities (Egocentricity Index = .53). At present, however, he questions his capabilities, sees himself as damaged and vulnerable, and experiences uncharacteristic self-critical thoughts (Vista = 1; $MOR = 3$). These upsetting thoughts are most likely a reaction to his recent medical problems that have caused him to feel vulnerable and defenseless. Two of the MOR responses are common (on Card II 2 animals fighting and on Card VI a bearskin rug), but the third is quite idiosyncratic (on Card III 2 dead, lifeless cats being hurled out of a window). This responses may reflect considerable anxiety about being treated in a heartless, cruel manner if he becomes ill.

Somewhat surprisingly given Mr. I's description of easily developing warm relationships with colleagues and coworkers, his responses suggest he tends to be quite reserved with and perhaps detached from others ($T = 0$). He anticipates interpersonal interactions will have both cooperative and aggressive aspects ($COP = 2$; $AG = 2$). A review of the content of M responses involving pairs was notable for his description of two men "doffing their hats to each other" on Card III. This unusual phrase suggests that his interpersonal behavior has a formal, if not stiff quality. The combination of this formal quality and the high number of Popular responses ($P = 9$) suggests he emphasizes acting in a proper, correct, and conventional manner and may be quite critical and disapproving of behavior that does not match his standards.

Comment

The MMPI-2 clinical scales and Rorschach findings provide quite different, although complementary views of Mr. I's psychological state. The *34/43* codetype emphasizes Mr. I's struggle over containing anger and his potential for repeated, episodic, uncontrolled outbursts. Rorschach findings also show his attempts to restrict and control expressions of feelings, particularly anger. The Rorschach complements MMPI-2 findings by describing in considerable depth the ways in which he distances from emotional experience, namely through the use of intellectualization, rationalization, isolation of affect, and denial.

Although the MMPI-2 clinical scales provide no indication of current emotional distress, the MMPI-2 content scales and Rorschach do identify signs of intense worry, sadness, and anxious rumination. As noted in chapter 5, in general one should have greater confidence in findings from the clinical scales than the content scales, unless findings suggested by the content scales are supported by other data. In this instance, the Rorschach data confirms the hypotheses suggested by the content scales. Thus, if only MMPI-2 data were available, the clinician might not emphasize the results of the content scales as much as one can in this case when the concordance between Rorschach findings and MMPI-2 content scales so clearly reveal Mr. I's emotional turmoil, worries, and fears.

The Rorschach provides very strong evidence for obsessive personality characteristics, including perfectionism; excessive attention to detail; a careful, precise approach to tasks; and a formal if not stiff quality to his presentation. These characteristics are not at all apparent in the MMPI-2 clinical scale configuration, although the *OBS* content scale does suggest this.

The Rorschach provides information about Mr. I's self-image and self-esteem not suggested by the MMPI-2. Finally, the Rorschach identifies several potential sources of difficulty in interpersonal relationships not seen on the MMPI-2, including rigid, inflexible attitudes and an emotionally detached approach to interactions. The *34/43* codetype suggests that he is most likely to become angry when he feels ignored, slighted, or "short-changed" by others who do not understand him, findings that are not suggested by the Rorschach.

MMPI-2–Rorschach Integration

Mr. I responded to the MMPI-2 and the Rorschach in an open, honest manner. Mr. I is currently experiencing considerable situational distress apparently precipitated by recent serious medical problems, including a nearly fatal complication of cardiac surgery (*ANX; DEP; D* score $<$ *Adj D; D* score $= -1$; *es*). He has responded to these recent, frightening events with significant levels of sadness, anxiety, worry, and pessimism and with feelings of helplessness and discouragement (*m* $= 3$; *Y* $= 5$; *V* $= 1$; *MOR* $= 3$). He questions whether life is futile, doubts that things will get better, and fears that his condition will worsen and he will die.

This current episode is not unique in Mr. I's experience, as he has a longstanding vulnerability to becoming depressed and anxious (*DEPI* $= 5$). Although these episodes may be of brief duration, during such episodes his emotional equilibrium can be significantly disrupted, he can become psychologically disorganized, and he is prone to ruminate about matters that worry and upset him. These tendencies are currently manifested by intrusive, fearful thoughts about his health and the prospect of his death (MMPI-2 *OBS* $= 66$; *Lambda* $= .07$). The repetitive, intrusive nature of these thoughts can interfere with his ability to productively attend to and concentrate on other, unrelated matters (*m* $= 3$).

In general, Mr. I has a positive self-image, believes in himself, and is confident about his abilities (Egocentricity Index $= .53$). At present, however, he questions his capabilities, sees himself as damaged and vulnerable, and is troubled by self-critical thoughts, reactions that are out of character (Vista $= 1$; *MOR* $= 3$). These upsetting thoughts are most likely a reaction to his recent medical problems that have caused him to feel vulnerable and defenseless.

In general, Mr. I is quite uncomfortable with emotions, fears he will not be able to control his reactions, and attempts to protect himself from a loss of control by restricting his involvement with affect (*Afr* $= .25$; Color Projection $= 1$). He would prefer to react to situations in a calm, dispassionate, logical manner rather than with feelings (Intellectualization Index $= 7$). He attempts to restrict expression of emotions and appear reasonable, rational, and logical to the extent that he may be emotionally overcontrolled (*34/43* codetype; *Afr* $= .25$; Intellectualization Index $= 7$). This may result in his feeling as though he were living a mechanical, "robotic" existence with a limited range of affective experience.

Mr. I's responses suggest his efforts to control emotions are particularly focused on suppression and inhibition of angry, aggressive feelings and impulses. When his defenses function effectively, anger is likely to be expressed in a controlled, intellectualized manner. For instance, hostility may be channeled into a critical comment that he can justify as an attempt to be helpful and constructive, although others may experience these comments as harsh, disparaging, and judgmental. When his defenses and self-control fail, however, there is a potential for his behavior, which is generally restrained and socially appropriate, to be punctuated by outbursts of hostility and explosive anger. At these times, emotions are experienced intensely and behavior is unchecked ($FC:CF + C = 2:3; C = 1$). His reactions may be out of proportion to the event that ostensibly triggered his outburst, and the intensity of his reactions are likely to take others by surprise. This is consistent with the history reported by Mr. I of recurrent fights with his wife during which he has lost control of his temper and became physically aggressive.

The MMPI-2 suggests that Mr. I's difficulties with anger are related to deep, chronic feelings of resentment and hostility towards family members whom he feels do not understand him and do not pay enough attention to him (43 codetype; $FAM = 82$; $Pd1 = 84$). He can be quite egocentric and demanding of attention. He is most likely to flare up in a volatile, angry manner when he feels criticized, misunderstood, slighted, or ignored.

Mr. I's responses are consistent with obsessive personality characteristics (MMPI-2 $OBS = 66$; positive OBS). In general, he is a careful, cautious, conscientious, and methodical man with a marked tendency towards perfectionism ($FQ + = 5$; $X + \% = .93$: Populars $= 9$). These characteristics may be areas of strength when careful attention to detail or a precise, thorough approach to solving a technically demanding problem is required. These characteristics can also be weaknesses, however, if he becomes overly cautious, ruminative, and preoccupied with details. Given his perfectionistic tendencies, he has difficulty making decisions because of a fear of making a mistake and may fret, worry, and ruminate about which of several alternatives is the best and the possible consequences if he chooses one over the other.

In his interpersonal relationships, Mr. I tends to be reserved, and others may perceive him as aloof, cold, and detached ($T = 0$; $Afr = .25$). He is likely to approach social interactions in a formal, if not stiff quality. He may emphasize acting in a proper, correct, and conventional manner and be quite critical and disapproving of behavior that does not meet his standards (Populars $= 9$). He may encounter difficulty in interpersonal relationships as a result of a tendency to act in an opinionated, dogmatic manner such that he ignores and rejects the views of others and instead doggedly and inflexibly defends his own position ($a:p = 7:2$). Others may experience his perfectionistic, inflexible style as quite demanding or controlling.

Diagnostic Impression

DSM–III–R   Axis I   296.32 Major depression, recurrent, moderate severity

Axis II   301.40 Obsessive–compulsive personality disorder

TREATMENT RECOMMENDATIONS

The results described previously suggest that Mr. I would benefit from individual psychotherapy to assist him in putting into perspective his pessimistic worries and fears regarding his medical condition and his mortality and to decrease self-critical thinking. The therapist should be aware of Mr. I's tendency to ruminate about unpleasant matters in a repetitive, nonproductive fashion. Rather than allow him to go over the same ground repeatedly using an unstructured approach to therapy, Mr. I may respond best to attempts to interrupt the cycle of pessimistic rumination and to identify, examine, and correct distortions in thinking that contribute to his emotional distress.

One of the dangers of therapy involves the potential for Mr. I to be detached from and to fend off feelings by discussing his concerns in an overly logical, intellectualized manner with little genuine vitality. Of course, the therapist must be respectful of these defenses, particularly given Mr. I's age, and not attempt to push him too quickly to be more expressive. The danger of doing so is Mr. I might perceive the therapist as demanding, controlling, and judgmental.

Although Mr. I may be most interested in reducing his distress about his medical condition and mortality, therapy may also be of benefit if he were helped to develop more constructive ways to manage anger and to avoid explosive outbursts. Doing so may require a commitment to longer term treatment than is required only to reduce his current reactions to his medical condition. If he agrees to continue psychotherapy, the therapist should be particularly alert to talk about instances when Mr. I reacted angrily to the therapist. One should expect Mr. I will deny or minimize any reactions of irritation or frustration in these situations. However, talking about these reactions and his defenses against being angry with a therapist who is accepting, noncritical, and who does not retaliate may help him recognize and ultimately express anger in a more controlled and less destructive manner.

References

Acklin, M. W. (1993). Integrating the Rorschach and the MMPI in clinical assessment: Conceptual and methodological issues. *Journal of Personality Assessment, 60,* 125–131.

Allison, J., Blatt, S. J., & Zimet, C. N. (1988). *The interpretation of psychological tests.* New York: Hemisphere.

American Psychiatric Association. (1994). *Diagnostic and statistical manual of mental disorders* (4th ed.). Washington, DC: Author.

Anastasi, A. (1988). *Psychological testing* (6th ed.). New York: Macmillan.

Andreasen, N. C., & Olsen, S. (1982). Negative v positive schizophrenia: Definition and validation. *Archives of General Psychiatry, 39,* 789–794.

Archer, R. P. (1987). *Using the MMPI with adolescents.* Hillsdale, NJ: Lawrence Erlbaum Associates.

Archer, R. P., & Gordon, R. A. (1988). MMPI and Rorschach indices of schizophrenic and depressive disorders among adolescent inpatients. *Journal of Personality Assessment, 52,* 276–287.

Archer, R. P., Gordon, R. A., Giannetti, R. A., & Singles, J. M. (1988). MMPI scale correlates for adolescent inpatients. *Journal of Personality Assessment, 52,* 707–721.

Archer, R. A., & Krishnamurthy, R. (1993a). Combining the Rorschach and the MMPI in the assessment of adolescents. *Journal of Personality Assessment, 60,* 132–140.

Archer, R. A., & Krishnamurthy, R. (1993b). A review of MMPI and Rorschach interrelationships in adult samples. *Journal of Personality Assessment, 61,* 277–293.

Archer, R. P., Maruish, M., Imhof, E. A., & Piotrowksi, C. (1991). Psychological test usage with adolescent clients: 1990 survey findings. *Professional Psychology: Research and Practice, 22,* 247–252.

Arieti, S. (1974). *Interpretation of schizophrenia.* New York: Basic Books.

Arkes, H. R. (1981). Impediments to accurate clinical judgment and possible ways to minimize their impact. *Journal of Consulting and Clinical Psychology, 49,* 323–330.

Arkes, H. R., & Harkness, A. R. (1980). Effect of making a diagnosis on subsequent recognition of symptoms. *Journal of Experimental Psychology: Human Learning and Memory, 6,* 586–575.

Aronow, E., Reznikoff, M., & Moreland, K. L. (1995). The Rorschach: Projective technique or psychometric test? *Journal of Personality Assessment, 64,* 213–228.

Atkinson, L. (1986). The comparative validities of the Rorschach and MMPI: A meta-analysis. *Canadian Psychology, 27,* 238–247.

Atkinson, L., Quarrington, B., Alp, I. E., & Cyr, J. J. (1986). Rorschach validity: An empirical approach to the literature. *Journal of Clinical Psychology, 42,* 360–362.

Baer, R. A., Wetter, M. W., & Berry, D. T. R. (1992). Detection of underreporting of psychopathology on the MMPI: A meta-analysis. *Clinical Psychology Review, 12,* 509–526.

Ball, J. D., Archer, R. P., Gordon, R. A., & French, J. (1991). Rorschach depression indices with children and adolescents: Concurrent validity findings. *Journal of Personality Assessment, 57,* 465–476.

Barkley, R. A. (1990). *Attention-deficit hyperactivity disorder: A handbook for diagnosis and treatment.* New York: Guilford.

Barley, W. D., Dorr, D., & Reid, V. (1985). The Rorschach Comprehensive System Egocentricity Index in psychiatric inpatients. *Journal of Personality Assessment, 49,* 137–140.

Barron, F. (1953). An ego strength scale which predicts response to psychotherapy. *Journal of Consulting Psychology, 17,* 327–333.

Beck, S. J., Beck, A. C., Levitt, E. E., & Molish, H. B. (1961). *Rorschach's test: Vol. I. Basic processes* (3rd ed.). New York: Grune & Stratton.

Ben-Porath, Y. S., & Butcher, J. N., & Graham, J. R. (1991). Contribution of the MMPI-2 content scales to the differential diagnosis of schizophrenia and major depression. *Psychological Assessment, 3,* 634–640.

Berry, D. T., Baer, R. A., & Harris, M. J. (1991). Detection of malingering on the MMPI: A meta-analysis. *Clinical Psychology Review, 11,* 585–598.

Bleuler, E. (1950). *Dementia praecox or the group of schizophrenias.* New York: International Universities Press.

Bornstein, R. F., Bowers, K. S., & Robinson, K. J. (1995). Differential relationships of objective and projective dependency scores to self-reports of interpersonal life events in college student subjects. *Journal of Personality Assessment, 65,* 255–269.

Brehmer, B. (1980). In one word: Not from experience. *Acta Psychologica, 45,* 223–241.

Brems, C., & Johnson, M. E. (1990). Further explorations of the egocentricity index in an inpatient psychiatric sample. *Journal of Clinical Psychology, 46,* 675–679.

Brinkman, D. C., Overholser, J. C., & Klier, D. (1994). Emotional distress in adolescent psychiatric patients: Direct and indirect measures. *Journal of Personality Assessment, 62,* 472–484.

Butcher, J. N. (1979). Use of the MMPI in personnel selection. In J. N. Butcher (Ed.), *New developments in the use of the MMPI* (pp. 165–201). Minneapolis: University of Minnesota Press.

Butcher, J. N. (1985). Interpreting defensive profiles. In J. N. Butcher & J. R. Graham (Eds.), *Clinical applications of the MMPI* (No. 3, pp. 5–7). Minneapolis: University of Minnesota Department of Professional Development and Conference Services, Continuing Education and Extension.

Butcher, J. N., Dahlstrom, W., Graham, J., Tellegen, A., & Kaemmer, B. (1989). *Minnesota Multiphasic Personality Inventory-2 (MMPI-2): Manual for administration and scoring.* Minneapolis: University of Minnesota Press.

Butcher, J. N., Graham, J. R., & Ben-Porath, Y. S. (1995). Methodological problems and issues in MMPI, MMPI-2, and MMPI-A research. *Psychological Assessment, 7,* 320–329.

Butcher, J. N., Graham, J. R., Williams, C. L., & Ben-Porath, Y. S. (1989). *Development and use of the MMPI-2 content scales.* Minneapolis: University of Minnesota Press.

Butcher, J. N., & Rouse, S. V. (in press). Personality: Individual differences and clinical assessment. *Annual Review of Psychology.*

Butcher, J. N., & Williams, C. L. (1992). *MMPI-2/MMPI-A: Essentials of interpretation.* Minneapolis: University of Minnesota Press.

Butcher, J. N., Williams, C. L., Graham, J. R., Archer, R. P., Tellegen, A., Ben-Porath, Y. S., & Kaemmer, B. (1992). *Minnesota Multiphasic Personality Inventory-Adolescent (MMPI-A): Manual for administration and scoring.* Minneapolis: University of Minnesota Press.

Campbell, D. T., & Fiske, D. W. (1959). Convergent and discriminant validation by the multitrait-multimethod matrix. *Psychological Bulletin, 56,* 81–105.

Caputo-Sacco, L., & Lewis, R. J. (1991). MMPI correlates of Exner's egocentricity index in an adolescent psychiatric population. *Journal of Personality Assessment, 56,* 29–34.

Carp, A. L., & Shavzin, A. R. (1950). The susceptibility to falsification of the Rorschach psychodiagnostic technique. *Journal of Consulting Psychology, 14,* 230–233.

Clark, J. H. (1948). Some MMPI correlates of color responses in the Group Rorschach. *Journal of Consulting Psychology, 12,* 384–386.

Cofer, C. N., Chance, J., & Judsin, A. J. A. (1949). Study of malingering on the MMPI. *Journal of Psychology, 27,* 491–499.

Colligan, R. C., Osborne, D., Swenson, W. M., & Offord, K. P. (1989). *The MMPI: A contemporary normative study of adults* (2nd ed.). Odessa, FL: Psychological Assessment Resources.

Crow, T. J. (1985). The two-syndrome concept: Origins and current status. *Schizophrenia Bulletin, 11,* 471–486.

Dana, R. Y., & Bolton, B. (1982). Interrelationships between Rorschach and MMPI scores for female college students. *Psychological Reports, 51,* 1281–1282.

Donders, J., & Kirsch, N. (1991). Nature and implications of selective impairment on the Booklet Category Test and the Wisconsin Card Sorting Test. *The Clinical Neuropsychologist, 5,* 78–82.

Duckworth, J. C., & Anderson, W. P. (1995). *MMPI & MMPI-2: Interpretation manual for counselors and clinicians* (4th ed.). Bristol: Taylor & Francis.

Duckworth, J. C., & Barley, W. D. (1988). Within-normal-limits profiles. In R. L. Greene (Ed.), *The MMPI: Use with specific populations* (pp. 278–315). Philadelphia: Grune & Stratton.

Einhorn, H. J. (1986). Accepting error to make less error. *Journal of Personality Assessment, 50,* 387–395.

Exner, J. E. (1969). *The Rorschach systems.* New York: Grune & Stratton.

Exner, J. E. (1986). *The Rorschach: A comprehensive system. Vol. 1: Basic foundations* (2nd ed.). New York: Wiley.

Exner, J. E. (1988). Problems with brief Rorschach protocols. *Journal of Personality Assessment, 52,* 640–647.

Exner, J. E. (1991). *The Rorschach comprehensive system. Vol. 2: Current treatment and advanced interpretations* (2nd ed.). New York: Wiley.

Exner, J. E. (1993). *The Rorschach: A comprehensive system. Volume 1: Basic foundations* (3rd ed.). New York: Wiley.

Exner, J. E., McDowell, E., Pabst, J., Strackman, W., & Kirkman, L. (1963). On the detection of willful falsification on the MMPI. *Journal of Consulting Psychology, 27,* 91–94.

Exner, J. E., & Wylie, J. (1977). Some Rorschach data concerning suicide. *Journal of Personality Assessment, 41,* 339–348.

Finch, A. J., Imm, P. S., & Belter, R. W. (1990). Brief Rorschach records with children and adolescents. *Journal of Personality Assessment, 55,* 640–646.

Finn, S. E., Hartman, M., Leon, G. R., & Lawson, L. (1986). Eating disorders and sexual abuse: Lack of confirmation for a clinical hypothesis. *International Journal of Eating Disorders, 5,* 1051–1060.

Finn, S. E., & Kamphius, J. H. (1995). What a clinician needs to know about base rates. In J. N. Butcher (Ed.), *Clinical personality assessment* (pp. 224–235). New York: Oxford University Press.

Fischoff, B. (1975). Hindsight ≠ foresight: The effect of outcome knowledge on judgment under uncertainty. *Journal of Experimental Psychology: Human Perception and Performance, 1,* 288–299.

Fosberg, I. A. (1938). Rorschach reactions under varied instructions. *Rorschach Research Exchange, 3,* 12–30.

Fosberg, I. A. (1941). An experimental study of the reliability of the Rorschach psychodiagnostic technique. *Rorschach Research Exchange, 5,* 72–84.

Frank, L. K. (1939). Projective methods for the study of personality. *Journal of Psychology, 8,* 389–413.

Friedman, A. F., Webb, J. T., & Lewak, R. (1989). *Psychological assessment with the MMPI.* Hillsdale, NJ: Lawrence Erlbaum Associates.

Frueh, C. B., & Kinder, B. N. (1994). The susceptibility of the Rorschach Inkblot Test to malingering of combat-related PTSD. *Journal of Personality Assessment, 62,* 280–298.

Gacono, C. B., & Meloy, J. R. (1994). *The Rorschach assessment of aggressive and psychopathic personalities.* Hillsdale, NJ: Lawrence Erlbaum Associates.

Ganellen, R. J. (1994). Attempting to conceal psychological disturbance: MMPI defensive response sets and the Rorschach. *Journal of Personality Assessment, 63,* 423–437.

Ganellen, R. J. (1995). *Response sets, repression, and the Rorschach.* Unpublished manuscript.

Ganellen, R. J., Wasyliw, O. E., Haywood, T. W., & Grossman, L. S. (1996). Can psychosis be faked on the Rorschach?: An empirical study. *Journal of Personality Assessment, 66* 65–80.

Garb, H. N. (1984). Clinical judgment, clinical training, and professional experience. *Psychological Bulletin, 105,* 387–396.

Gauron, E. F., & Dickinson, J. K. (1969). The influence of seeing the patient first on diagnostic decision making in psychiatry. *American Journal of Psychiatry, 126,* 199–205.

Gilberstadt, H., & Duker, J. A. (1965). *A handbook for clinical and actuarial MMPI interpretation.* Philadelphia: Saunders.

Goodwin, F. K., & Jamison, K. R. (1990). *Manic-depressive illness.* New York: Oxford.

Gottesman, I. I., & Prescott, C. A. (1989). Abuses of the MacAndrew MMPI alcoholism scale: A critical review. *Clinical Psychology Review, 9,* 223–242.

Gough, H. (1947). Simulated patterns on the MMPI. *Journal of Abnormal and Social Psychology, 42,* 215–225.

Gough, H. G. (1950). The F minus K dissimulation index for the MMPI. *Journal of Consulting Psychology, 14,* 408–413.

Gough, H. (1954). Some common misconceptions about neuroticism. *Journal of Consulting Psychology, 18,* 287–292.

Graham, J. R. (1984). Interpreting normal range profiles. In J. N. Butcher & J. R. Graham (Eds.), *Clinical applications of the MMPI* (No. 17, pp. 40–41). Minneapolis: University of Minnesota Department of Professional Development and Conference Services, Continuing Education and Extension.

Graham, J. R. (1987). *The MMPI: A practical guide* (2nd ed.). New York: Oxford.

Graham, J. R. (1993). *The MMPI-2: Assessing personality and psychopathology* (2nd ed.). New York: Oxford University Press.

Graham, J. R., Watts, D., & Timbrook, R. E. (1991). Detecting fake-good and fake-bad MMPI-2 profiles. *Journal of Personality Assessment, 57,* 264–277.

Grayson, H. M., & Olinger, L. B. (1957). Simulation of "normalcy" by psychiatric patients on the MMPI. *Journal of Consulting Psychology, 21,* 73–77.

Greene, R. (1991). *The MMPI/MMPI-2: An interpretive manual.* Boston: Allyn & Bacon.

Grow, R., McVaugh, W., & Eno, T. D. (1980). Faking and the MMPI. *Journal of Clinical Psychology, 36,* 910–917.

Harrow, M., Grossman, L. S., Silverstein, M. L., & Meltzer, H. Y. (1982). Thought pathology in manic and schizophrenic patients: Its occurence at hospital admission and seven weeks later. *Archives of General Psychiatry, 39,* 665–671.

Harrow, M., & Quinlan, D. (1977). Is disordered thinking unique to schizophrenia? *Archives of General Psychiatry, 34,* 15–21.

Hawkins, S. A., & Hastie, R. (1990). Hindsight: Biased judgments of past events after the outcomes are known. *Psychological Bulletin, 107,* 311–327.

Heaton, R. K. (1981). *A manual for the Wisconsin Card Sorting Test.* Odessa, FL: Psychological Assessment Resources Inc.

Hegarty, J. D., Baldessarini, R. J., Tohen, M., Waternaux, C., & Oepen, G. (1994). One hundred years of schizophrenia: A meta-analysis of the outcome literature. *American Journal of Psychiatry, 151,* 1409–1416.

Hogarth, R. M. (1987). *Judgment and choice: The psychology of decision* (2nd ed.). Chichester, England: Wiley.

Holt, R. R. (1968). Editor's Foreword. In Rapaport, Gill, & Schafer, *Diagnostic psychological testing* (pp. 1–43). New York: International Universities Press.

Holt, R. R. (1986). Clinical and statistical prediction: A retrospective and would-be integrative perspective. *Journal of Personality Assessment, 50,* 376–386.

Hunt, H. F. (1948). The effect of deliberate deception on MMPI performance. *Journal of Consulting Psychology, 12,* 396–402.

Jensen, A. R. (1958). Personality. *Annual Review of Psychology, 9,* 395–422.

Jensen, A. R. (1965). A review of the Rorschach. In O. K. Buros (Ed.), *Sixth mental measurements yearbook* (pp. 501–509). Highland Park, NJ: Gryphon.

Kahneman, D., & Tversky, A. (1973). On the psychology of prediction. *Psychological Review, 80,* 237–251.

Kendall, P. C., & Norton-Ford, J. D. (1982). *Clinical psychology.* New York: Wiley.

Kinder, B. N. (1992). The problems of R in clinical settings and in research: Suggestions for the future. *Journal of Personality Assessment, 58,* 252–259.

Kleiger, J. H. (1992). A conceptual critique of the EA:es comparison in the Comprehensive Rorschach System. *Psychological Assessment, 4,* 288–296.

Kleinmuntz, B. (1990). Why we still use our heads instead of formulas: Toward an integrative approach. *Psychological Bulletin, 107,* 296–310.

Klopfer, B., & Kelley, D. M. (1942). *The Rorschach technique.* Tarrytown-on-Hudson, New York: World.

Lachar, D. (1974). *The MMPI: Clinical assessment and automated interpretation.* Los Angeles: Western Psychological Services.

Lerner, P. M. (1991). *Psychoanalytic theory and the Rorschach.* Hillsdale, NJ: Analytic Press.

Lipovsky, J., Finch, A. J., & Belter, R. (1989). Assessment of depression in adolescents: Objective and projective measures. *Journal of Personality Assessment, 53,* 449–458.

Lubin, B., Larsen, R. M., & Matarazzo, J. D. (1984). Patterns of psychological test usage in the United States: 1935–1982. *American Psychologist, 39,* 451–454.

Lubin, B., Larsen, R. M., Matarazzo, J. D. & Seever, M. (1985). Psychological test usage patterns in five professional settings. *American Psychologist, 40,* 857–861.

MacAndrew, C. (1965). The differentiation of male alcoholic patients from nonalcoholic psychiatric patients by means of the MMPI. *Quarterly Journal of Studies on Alcohol, 28,* 43–51.

Masling, J. M., Rabie, L., & Blondheim, S. H. (1967). Obesity, level of aspiration, and Rorschach and TAT measures of oral dependence. *Journal of Consulting Psychology, 31,* 233–239.

Mayerhoff, D. I., Loebel, A. D., Alvir, J. M. M., Szymanski, S. R., Geisler, S. H.,

Borenstein, M., & Lieberman, J. A. (1994). The deficit state in first-episode schizophrenia. *American Journal of Psychiatry, 151,* 1417–1422.

McAnulty, D. P., Rappaport, N. B., & McAnulty, R. D. (1985). An aposteriori investigation of standard MMPI validity scales. *Psychological Reports, 57,* 95–98.

McClelland, D. C., Koestner, R., & Weinberger, J. (1989). How do self-attributed and implicit motives differ? *Psychological Review, 96,* 690–702.

Meehl, P. E. (1954). *Clinical versus statistical prediction: A theoretical analysis and a review of the evidence.* Minneapolis: University of Minnesota Press.

Meehl, P. E. (1956). Wanted—a good cookbook. *American Psychologist, 11,* 263–272.

Meehl, P. E. (1967) What can the clinician do well? In D. N. Jackson & S. Messick (Eds.), *Problems in human assessment* (pp. 594–599). New York: McGraw-Hill.

Meehl, P. E. (1973). *Psychodiagnosis: Selected papers.* Minneapolis: University of Minnesota Press.

Meehl, P. E. (1986). Causes and effects of my disturbing little book. *Journal of Personality Assessment, 50,* 370–375.

Meehl, P. E., & Hathaway, S. R. (1946). The *K* factor as a suppressor variable in the MMPI. *Journal of Applied Psychology, 30,* 525–564.

Meyer, G. (1994). *On the integration of personality assessment methods: The Rorschach and MMPI-2.* Paper presented at the 29th Annual Symposium on Recent Developments in the Use of the MMPI/MMPI-2/MMPI-A, Minneapolis, MN.

Millon, T. (1969). *Modern psychopathology.* Philadelphia: Saunders.

Mullins, L. S., & Kopelman, R. E. (1988). Toward an assessment of the construct validity of four measures of narcissism. *Journal of Personality Assessment, 52,* 610–625.

Netter, B. E.C., & Viglione, D. J. (1994). An empirical study of malingering schizophrenia on the Rorschach. *Journal of Personality Assessment, 62,* 45–57.

Nichols, D. S. (1988). Mood disorders. In R. L. Greene (Ed.), *The MMPI: Use with specific populations* (pp. 74–129). Philadelphia: Grune & Stratton.

Otto, R. K., Lang, A. R., Megargee, E. I., & Rosenblatt, A. I. (1988). Ability of alcoholics to escape detection by the MMPI. *Journal of Consulting and Clinical Psychology, 56,* 452–457.

Parker, K. C. H. (1983). A meta-analysis of the reliability and validity of the Rorschach. *Journal of Personality Assessment, 42,* 227–231.

Parker, K. C. H., Hanson, R. K., & Hunsley, J. (1988). MMPI, Rorschach, and WAIS: A meta-analytic comparison of reliability, stability, and validity. *Psychological Bulletin, 103,* 367–373.

Paulhaus, D. L. (1986). Self-deception and impression management in test responses. In A. Angleitner & J. S. Wiggins (Eds.), *Personality assessment via questionnaires: Current issues in theory and measurement* (pp. 143–165). Berlin: Springer-Verlag.

Pendleton, M. G., & Heaton, R. K. (1982). A comparison of the Wisconsin Card Sorting Test and the Category Test. *Journal of Clinical Psychology, 38,* 392–396.

Perrine, K. (1993). Differential aspects of conceptual processing in the Category Test and Wisconsin Card Sorting Test. *Journal of Clinical and Experimental Neuropsychology, 15,* 461–473.

Perry, C. G., & Kinder, B. N. (1990). The susceptibility of the Rorschach to malingering: A critical review. *Journal of Personality Assessment, 54,* 47–57.

Perry, C. G., & Kinder, B. N. (1992). Susceptibility of the Rorschach to malingering: A schizophrenia analogue. In C. D. Spielberger & J. Butcher (Eds.), *Advances in Personality Assessment* (Vol. 9, pp. 127–140). Hillsdale, NJ: Lawrence Erlbaum Associates, Inc.

Peterson, R. A. (1978). Review. In O. K. Buros (Ed.), *The eighth mental measurements yearbook* (pp. 1042–1045). Highland Park, NJ: Gryphon.

Phillips, K. A., (1991). Body Dysmorphic Disorder: The distress of imagined ugliness. *American Journal of Psychiatry, 148,* 1138–1149.

Piotrowski, C., Sherry, D., & Keller, J. W. (1985). Psychodiagnostic test usage: A survey for the Society of Personality Assessment. *Journal of Personality Assessment, 49*, 155–119.

Piotrowski, Z. A. (1957). *Perceptanalysis.* New York: Macmillan.

Pogue-Geile, M. F., & Harrow, M. (1985). Negative symptoms in schizophrenia: Their longitudinal course and prognostic significance. *Schizophrenia Bulletin, 11*, 427–439.

Rapaport, D., Gill, M., & Schafer, R. (1945) *Diagnostic psychological testing.* Chicago: Year Book Medical Publishers.

Rappaport, G. M. (1958). "Ideal self" instructions, MMPI profile changes, and the prediction of clinical improvement. *Journal of Consulting Psychology, 27*, 459–463.

Reitan, R. M., & Wolfson, D. (1985). *The Halstead-Reitan Neuropsychological Test Battery.* Tucson, AZ: Neuropsychology Press.

Rice, M. E., Arnold, L. S., & Tate, D. L. (1983). Faking good and bad adjustment on the MMPI and overcontrolled-hostility in maximum security psychiatric patients. *Canadian Journal of Behavioral Sciences, 15*, 45–51.

Rogers, R. (Ed.). (1988). *Clinical assessment of malingering and deception.* New York: Guilford.

Rogers, R., Bagby, R. M., & Chakraborty, D. (1993). Feigning schizophrenic disorders on the MMPI-2: Detection of coached simulators. *Journal of Personality Assessment, 60*, 215–226.

Rorschach, H. (1942). *Psychodiagnostics* (5th ed.; P. Lemkau & B. Kroonenberg, Trans.). Berne, Switzerland: Verlag Hans Huber. (Original work published 1921)

Rosen, A. (1954). Detection of suicidal patients: An example of some limitations in the prediction of infrequent events. *Journal of Consulting Psychology, 18*, 397–403.

Ross, L., Lepper, M. R., Strack, F., & Steinmetz, J. (1977). Social explanation and social expectation: Effects of real and hypothetical explanations on subjective likelihood. *Journal of Personality and Social Psychology, 35*, 817–829.

Sarbin, T. R. (1986). Prediction and clinical inference: Forty years later. *Journal of Personality Assessment, 50*, 362–369.

Sawyer, J. (1966). Measurement and prediction, clinical and statistical. *Psychological Bulletin, 66*, 178–200.

Schafer, R. (1954). *Psychoanalytic interpretation in Rorschach testing.* New York: Grune & Stratton.

Schretlen, D. (1988). The use of psychological tests to identify malingered symptoms of mental disorders. *Clinical Psychology Review, 8*, 451–476.

Seamons, D. T., Howell, R. J., Carlisle, A. L., & Roe, A. V. (1981). Rorschach simulation of mental illness and normality by psychotic and non-psychotic normal offenders. *Journal of Personality Assessment, 45*, 130–135.

Serkownek, K. (1975). *Subscales for scales 5 and 0 of the Minnesota Multiphasic Personality Inventory.* Unpublished materials.

Shapiro, J. P., Leifer, M., Martone, M. W., & Kassem, L. (1990). Multimethod assessment of depression in sexually abused girls. *Journal of Personality Assessment, 55*, 234–248.

Shedler, J., Mayman, M., & Manis, M. (1993). The illusion of mental health. *American Psychologist, 48*, 1117–1131.

Simon, M. J. (1989). Comparison of the Rorschach Comprehensive System's Isolation Index and MMPI Social Introversion score. *Psychological Reports, 65*, 499–502.

Singer, H. K, & Brabender, V. (1993). The use of the Rorschach to differentiate unipolar and bipolar disorders. *Journal of Personality Assessment, 60*, 333–345.

Smith, M. L., & Glass, G. V. (1977). Meta-analysis of psychotherapy outcome studies. *American Psychologist, 32*, 752–760.

Sugarman, A. (1991). Where's the beef? Putting personality back into personality assessment. *Journal of Personality Assessment, 56*, 130–144.

Swenson, W. M., Pearson, J. S., & Osborne, D. (1973). *An MMPI sourcebook: Basic item, scale, and pattern data on 50,000 medical patients.* Minneapolis: University of Minnesota Press.

Trimboli, F., & Kilgore, R. (1983). A psychodynamic approach to MMPI interpretation. *Journal of Personality Assessment, 47,* 614–626.

Tversky & Kahneman (1978). Judgment under uncertainty: Heuristics and biases. *Science, 185,* 1124–1131.

Walters, G. D., & Greene, R. L. (1988). Differentiating between schizophrenic and manic inpatients by means of the MMPI. *Journal of Personality Assessment, 52,* 91–95.

Walters, G. D., White, T. W., & Greene, R. L. (1988). Use of the MMPI to identify malingering and exaggeration of psychiatric symptomatology in male prison inmates. *Journal of Consulting and Clinical Psychology, 56,* 111–117.

Watkins, C. E. (1991). What have surveys taught us about the teaching and practice of psychological assessment? *Journal of Personality Assessment, 56,* 426–437.

Watkins, C. E., Campbell, V. L., Nieberding, R., & Hallmark, R. (1995). Contemporary practice of psychological assessment by clinical psychologists. *Professional Psychological Research and Practice, 26,* 54–60.

Wechsler, D. (1981). *WAIS-R manual: Wechsler Adult Intelligence Scale — Revised.* San Antonio, TX: Psychological Corporation.

Wechsler, D. (1991). *Manual for the Wechsler Intelligence Scale for Children — Third Edition.* San Antonio, TX: Psychological Corporation.

Weed, N. C., Butcher, J. N., McKenna, T., & Ben-Porath, Y. S. (1992). New measures for assessing alcohol and drug abuse with the MMPI-2: The APS and AAS. *Journal of Personality Assessment, 58,* 389–404.

Weiner, I. B. (1991). Editor's note: Interscore agreement in Rorschach research. *Journal of Personality Assessment, 56,* 1.

Weiner, I. B. (1995a). Methodological considerations in Rorschach research. *Psychological Assessment, 7,* 330–337.

Weiner, I. B. (1995b). Psychometric issues in forensic application of the MMPI-2. In Y. Ben-Porath, J. Graham, G. C. N. Hall, & M. Zaragoza (Eds.), *Forensic applications of the MMPI-2* (pp. 48–81). Newbury Park, CA: Sage.

Welsh, G. S. (1956). Factor dimensions in A and R. In G. S. Welsh & W. G. Dahlstrom (Eds.), *Basic readings on the MMPI in psychology and medicine* (pp. 264–281). Minneapolis: University of Minnesota Press.

Wender, P. H. (1995). *Attention-deficit hyperactivity disorder in adults.* New York: Oxford.

Wetter, M. W., Baer, R. A., Berry, D. T. R., Robison, L. H., & Sumpter, J. (1993). MMPI-2 profiles of motivated fakers given specific symptom information: A comparison to matched patients. *Psychological Assessment, 5,* 317–323.

Wetter, M. W., Baer, R. A., Berry, D. T. R., Smith, G. T., & Larsen, L. H. (1992). Sensitivity of MMPI-2 validity scales to random responding and malingering. *Psychological Assessment, 4,* 369–374.

Wetzler, S., & Marlowe, D. B. (1993). The diagnosis and assessment of depression, mania, and psychosis by self-report. *Journal of Personality Assessment, 60,* 1–31.

Wiener, D. (1948). Subtle and obvious keys for the MMPI. *Journal of Consulting Psychology, 12* 164–170.

Wiggins, J. S. (1973). *Personality and prediction: Principles of personality assessment.* Reading, MA: Addison-Wesley.

Winter, W. D., & Salcines, R. A. (1958). The validity of the Objective Rorschach and the MMPI. *Journal of Consulting Psychology, 22,* 199–202.

Winters, K. C., Newmark, C. S., Lumry, A. E., Leach, K., & Weintraub, A. (1985). MMPI codetypes characteristic of DSM–III schizophrenics, depressives, and bipolars. *Journal of Clinical Psychology, 41,* 382–386.

Woychyshyn, C. A., McElheran, W. G., & Romney, D. M. (1992). MMPI validity measures:

A comparative study of original with alternative indices. *Journal of Personality Assessment, 58,* 138–148.

Ziskin, J., & Faust, D. (1988). *Coping with psychiatric and psychological testimony* (4th ed.). Marina del Rey, CA: Law and Psychology Press.

Zubin, J., Eron, L. D., & Schumer, F. (1965). *An experimental approach to projective techniques.* New York: Wiley.

Author Index

Subject Index